MW00635776

JESUS CHRIST, THE SON OF GOD

VOLUME 4

VOLUME 4

JESUS CHRIST, THE SON OF GOD

THE WITNESS OF THE GOSPELS

STEVEN R. MCMURRAY

Acknowledgments

I am profoundly grateful for the encouragement of my sweet wife, Lorna. She has made invaluable suggestions regarding some of the more difficult concepts that are discussed in this volume. Her insight cannot be overstated, and her support has been unwavering.

I am likewise grateful for the wonderful and insightful help of this book's editor. She is a marvelous editor and contributed much toward the writing and publication of this book. I am so grateful for her help and encouragement. Rather than only addressing punctuation and grammar, which she did very well, she also made my rather complex sentences simpler without altering the meaning. She moved sentences and paragraphs when needed, provided insights and challenged certain statements and points of doctrine, and suggested how to make each chapter more accurate and flow better. She has wonderful knowledge of the gospel and contributed that knowledge to this volume. She also gave a woman's perspective when needed, was always easy to work with, and was always very encouraging and supportive. I could not have had a better editor.

I am also grateful for the invaluable assistance of Christina Crosland for carefully checking each footnote against each quoted or referenced passage of scripture and making corrections when necessary. Given the number of footnotes, this task was daunting and somewhat tedious, yet she was always willing to help to make this book worthy of its title. She also typeset this volume and designed the cover, just as she has for each of the previous volumes in this series. She took my concept for the cover and created a cover that I think is striking and portrays the message of Christ and His glorious return. She too has been marvelous to work with.

I also thank Rebecca Timmons, who has laboriously proofread this volume, and Abbey Huch, who skillfully created the index. I very much appreciate their help and encouragement. Also, I offer thanks to all others who encouraged me to complete this volume and publish this book and the others in this series.

Table of Contents

Jesus Speaks to His Mother and John (John 19:25–27)

Darkness Covers the Land from the Sixth Hour to the Ninth Hour (Matt. 27:45; Mark 15:33; Luke 23:44–45)

Jesus Speaks to His Father (Matt. 27:46; Mark 15:34–35)

Jesus Says He Thirsts (Matt. 27:48; Mark 15:36; John 19:28–29)

Jesus Releases His Spirit and Says His Work Is Finished (Matt. 27:50; Mark 15:37; Luke 23:46; John 19:30)

The Veil of the Temple Is Torn, and the Earth Shakes (Matt. 27:51; Mark 15:38; Luke 23:45)

A Centurion Testifies That Jesus Is the Son of God (Matt. 27:54–56; Mark 15:39–41; Luke 23:47–49)

A Soldier Pierces Jesus's Side (John 19:31–37)

Jesus Is Buried (Matt. 27:57–61; Mark 15:42–47; Luke 23:50–56; John 19:38–42)

The Tomb Is Sealed (Matt. 27:62–66)

Jesus Is the Son of God and Died for All People

Jesus Has the Keys of Resurrection

Jesus Prophesied That He Would Rise on the Third Day

The Stone Is Rolled Away (Matt. 28:2–4)

Women Come to the Tomb and See Angels and the Stone Rolled Away (Matt. 28:1, 5–7; Mark 16:1–7; JST Mark 16:1–7; Luke 24:1–8; John 20:1)

The Women Leave to Tell the Apostles That Jesus Is No Longer in the Tomb (Matt. 28:8; Mark 16:8; Luke 24:9–10; John 20:2)

The Chief Priests Bribe the Soldiers to Lie (Matt. 28:11–15)

Peter and John Run to the Sepulchre (John 20:3–10)

Jesus Appears to Mary Magdalene (Mark 16:9; John 20:11–18)

Jesus Appears to the Other Women (Matt. 28:9–10)

The Women Tell the Apostles and Others That Jesus Is No Longer in the Tomb (Mark 16:10–11; Luke 24:10–11)

Jesus Appears to Peter and to Two Disciples, and the Disciples Report to the Apostles (Mark 16:12–13; Luke 24:13–35)

Jesus Appears to Ten of the Apostles and Other Disciples (Mark 16:14; Luke 24:36–43; John 20:19–20)

Jesus Explains Scriptures That Refer to Him (Luke 24:44–48)

Jesus Gives the Apostles the Holy Ghost and the Authority to Forgive Sins on Behalf of the Church (Luke 24:49; John 20:21–23)

Others Who Had Died Arose from Their Graves (Matt. 27:52–53)

Jesus's Resurrection Testifies That He Is the Son of God

Jesus Appears to Thomas and the Other Apostles (John 20:24–29)

Jesus Gives the Apostles Additional Signs (John 20:30)

Jesus Appears to His Apostles at the Sea of Galilee (John 21:1–8)

Chapter 49

THE TRIUMPHAL ENTRY INTO JERUSALEM

(Sunday)

In the early spring, Jesus left Bethany on a Sunday morning and made His way to Jerusalem. He knew what He must do and what He would face in Jerusalem during the final days of His mortality. He also knew that His Father would be with Him and that He would be able to endure all that would come. As Jesus, speaking as Jehovah, had told Isaiah centuries earlier: "The Lord God will help me; therefore shall I not be confounded: therefore have I set my face like a flint, and I know that I shall not be ashamed."[1]

On this last Sunday of Jesus's mortal life, He rode triumphantly into Jerusalem on the back of a colt while people waved palm branches, laid clothing before Him, and shouted "Hosanna." The honor and homage that the people gave to Jesus was not welcomed by the Pharisees, who asked Jesus to put a stop to this public display, and Jesus rebuked them. As Jesus neared Jerusalem, He wept because of the hardness of the Jews' hearts and the destruction that would come to Jerusalem. Upon entering the city, Jesus went to the temple courtyard, where He would have seen people preparing for the Passover, as well as the corruption created by the greedy money changers plying their lucrative trade.

---

1. Isa. 50:7; see also Isa. 53.

Jesus's Disciples Obtain a Colt (Matt. 21:1–7; Mark 11:1–7; Luke 19:29–35; John 12:14–16)

As Jesus and His disciples[2] walked on the road between Bethany and Jerusalem,[3] they approached the village of Bethphage,[4] located about a mile from both Bethany and Jerusalem. Jesus gave two of His disciples instructions to go into the village. The following is Mark's account:

> **Mark 11:1–7.** And when they came nigh to Jerusalem, unto Bethphage and Bethany, at the mount of Olives, he sendeth forth two of his disciples, and saith unto them, Go your way into the village over against you: and as soon as ye be entered into it, ye shall find a colt tied, whereon never man sat; loose him, and bring him. And if any man say unto you, Why do ye this? say ye that the Lord hath need of him; and straightway he will send him hither. And they went their way, and found the colt tied by the door without in a place where two ways met; and they loose him. And certain of them that stood there said unto them, What do ye, loosing the colt? And they said unto them even as Jesus had commanded: and they let them go. And they brought the colt to Jesus, and cast their garments on him; and he sat upon him.

Mark's account is more detailed than the accounts in the other Gospels, and some scholars have therefore assumed that Peter, who was the principal source of information for Mark's Gospel, was one of the two disciples whom Jesus sent.[5] Whoever the two disciples were, Jesus told them that they would

---

2.   Presumably, *disciples* here includes all the Apostles. It is unknown whether some of Jesus's other disciples initially were with the Apostles; however, it is presumed that other disciples joined Jesus as He rode triumphantly into Jerusalem (see Matt. 21:8; Mark 1:8; Luke 19:36; John 17–18).

3.   Other Jews were also making their way to Jerusalem along this road to complete their purification before the Passover began. The times of day Jesus departed Bethany and then Bethphage are unknown. It could not have taken too long to travel the approximately two miles from Bethany to Jerusalem.

4.   *Bethphage* (beth'fuh-jee) is a Hebrew word meaning "house of unripe figs" (*HarperCollins Bible Dictionary*, s.v. "Bethphage").

5.   See Edersheim, *Life and Times of Jesus the Messiah*, p. 726; Farrar, *Life of Christ*, p. 475.

find a colt and were to bring it to Him.[6] If anyone asked why the disciples were taking the colt, they were to state that Jesus needed it, and then the owners would immediately consent.

The two disciples went into the village and found the colt tied by the door of a building, presumably a house near where two paths or small roads met. After the disciples untied the colt, the owners asked what the disciples were doing. They explained that they were doing what Jesus had directed them to do, and the owners let the disciples take the colt. The disciples brought the colt to Jesus and laid their outer clothing on the colt, and Jesus sat on the colt's back.

Matthew explained that the events that had just occurred were a fulfillment of prophecy:

> **Matthew 21:4–5.** All this was done, that it might be fulfilled which was spoken by the prophet, saying, Tell ye the daughter of Sion, Behold, thy King cometh unto thee, meek, and sitting upon an ass, and a colt the foal of an ass.

The prophet whom Matthew referred to was Zechariah, who prophesied: "Rejoice greatly, O daughter of Zion; shout, O daughter of Jerusalem: behold, thy King cometh unto thee: he is just, and having salvation; lowly, and riding upon an ass, and upon a colt the foal of an ass."[7] The colt[8] Jesus sat on had never before been ridden, symbolizing, among other things, its purity to bear the sinless Messiah. Further, riding on the colt signified that Jesus came to Jerusalem humbly, a fact that was further confirmed as He suffered the agony of atoning in Gethsemane and death on the Roman cross on Golgotha.

---

6.   According to Matthew's account, Jesus told the two disciples that they would find a colt and its mother (see Matt. 21:2). Joseph Smith's inspired translation of this verse does not include the reference to the mother. This omission makes the verse consistent with the records in the other three Gospels. Matthew wrote his Gospel for the Jews and therefore used Old Testament prophecy to testify of Christ. Matthew may have wanted to make his account about the disciples finding a colt align more closely with the prophecy in Zechariah 9:9.

7.   Zech. 9:9.

8.   In the Bible, horses are a symbol of power and pride and are associated with war (see *HarperCollins Bible Dictionary*, s.v. "horse"; Dummelow, *Bible Commentary*, p. 693). In contrast, asses are a symbol of peace and humility (see Dummelow, *Bible Commentary*, p. 693) and Jewish royalty (see Talmage, *Jesus the Christ*, p. 482).

Isaiah had earlier prophesied, "Behold, the Lord hath proclaimed unto the end of the world, Say ye to the daughter of Zion, Behold, thy salvation cometh; behold, his reward is with him, and his work before him."[9] Therefore, although Jesus came humbly, He also came triumphantly to Jerusalem (Zion), and He would there finish His earthly mission and thereby bring salvation to the world. Afterward, He would receive glory at the right hand of God.[10] His intent in coming to Jerusalem was not to overthrow the Roman government or the Jewish hierarchy, yet He came as "King of kings and Lord of lords."[11]

John made it clear that Jesus's disciples did not immediately recognize that Zechariah's prophecy was being fulfilled:

John 12:16. These things understood not his disciples at the first: but when Jesus was glorified, then remembered they that these things were written of him, and that they had done these things unto him.

Likely through the Holy Ghost's inspiration, after Jesus was resurrected His disciples remembered the prophecies and understood that they were fulfilled. One can only imagine what His disciples must have felt as they recognized that the events that had occurred on the road to Jerusalem were foreseen and recorded by a prophet of old.

People Lay Their Garments and Branches before Jesus (Matt. 21:8–9; Mark 11:8; Luke 19:36; John 12:12–13)

After the two disciples placed clothing on the colt, they and many others who were traveling on the road to Jerusalem spread clothing and tree branches on the road and waved palm branches. Matthew and John recorded the following:

Matthew 21:8. And a very great multitude spread their garments in the way; others cut down branches from the trees, and strawed them in the way.

John 12:12–13. On the next day much people that were come to the feast, when they heard that Jesus was coming to Jerusalem, took branches of palm trees, and went forth to meet him.

---

9.   Isa. 62:11.
10.   See Acts 1:9–10; 7:55–56.
11.   Rev. 19:16.

Spreading clothes and palm branches on the road and waving branches in the air were extraordinary tokens of honor and respect, such as were given to kings and great conquerors.[12] By showing honor and respect to Jesus in this way, each person was also making an individual commitment to Him, although this honor and commitment may have been somewhat fleeting in some of those present.

Palm branches were also symbolically significant in other ways. Branches were sometimes used as tokens of victory and peace[13] and were also a symbol of joy and celebration.[14] Additionally, palm trees were a symbol of holiness: they were carved onto the walls and doors of Solomon's temple,[15] and Ezekiel saw in a vision that palm trees would appear on the temple to be built in Jerusalem in the latter days.[16]

Palm branches are also mentioned in scriptures referring to Jesus's Second Coming. For example, the book of Revelation recounts John's vision of "a great multitude, which no man could number, of all nations, and kindreds, and people, and tongues, [who] stood before the throne, and before the Lamb, clothed with white robes, and palms in their hands; and cried with a loud voice, saying, Salvation to our God which sitteth upon the throne, and unto the Lamb."[17] As another example, the Kirtland Temple's dedicatory prayer, which Joseph Smith received by revelation, contains a petition to God that His people be spiritually prepared when Christ returns, "that our garments may be pure, that we may be clothed upon with robes of righteousness, with palms in our hands."[18] The palms referenced in the book of Revelation and in the dedicatory prayer may be literal, or they may be symbolic. When Christ returns, perhaps some will figuratively wave palm branches and shout "Hosanna" as a way of giving holy thanks, praise, and honor to Him.

Palm has an additional possible symbolic meaning. The Hebrew word for *palm* is *kaph*, meaning "palm of hand or sole of foot."[19] When Christ was

---

12.   See Dummelow, *Bible Commentary*, p. 693; see also 2 Kgs. 9:13.
13.   See Smith, *Bible Dictionary*, s.v. "palm."
14.   See Edersheim, *Life and Times of Jesus the Messiah*, p. 734.
15.   See 1 Kgs. 6:29, 32, 35; 7:36.
16.   See Ezek. 40:22, 26, 31, 34, 37; 41:18–20, 25–26.
17.   Rev. 7:9–10.
18.   D&C 109:76.
19.   Young, *Analytical Concordance*, s.v. "palm."

crucified, nails were driven through the palms of His hands and wrists and through His feet by Roman soldiers. Centuries earlier, the Lord had declared, "Behold, I have graven thee upon the palms of my hands."[20] After Christ's death and Resurrection, He and His Apostles testified that the nail marks in the palms of His hands and in His feet were a witness that He indeed had risen from the dead and was the divine Son of God.[21] *Palm*, therefore, may also indirectly symbolize Christ's marvelous sacrifice for each person.

Multitudes Shout Hosanna (Matt. 21:9; Mark 11:9–10; Luke 19:37–38; John 12:12–13, 17–18)

As Jesus, His disciples, and others continued toward Jerusalem for the Passover, many in the multitude expressed thanks to God. Some may have felt gratitude in part because of remembering that Jesus had restored Lazarus to life[22] and had performed other miracles. The Gospel writers used somewhat different language to describe the thanks and praise the multitude expressed:

Matthew 21:9. And the multitudes that went before, and that followed, cried, saying, Hosanna to the Son of David: Blessed is he that cometh in the name of the Lord; Hosanna in the highest.

Mark 11:9–10. And they that went before [Jesus], and they that followed, cried, saying, Hosanna; Blessed is he that cometh in the name of the Lord: Blessed be the kingdom of our father David, that cometh in the name of the Lord: Hosanna in the highest.

Luke 19:37–38. And when he was come nigh, even now at the descent of the mount of Olives, the whole multitude of the disciples began to rejoice and praise God with a loud voice for all the mighty works that they had seen; saying, Blessed be the King that cometh in the name of the Lord: peace in heaven, and glory in the highest.

John 12:13. Hosanna: Blessed is the King of Israel that cometh in the name of the Lord.

---

20.   Isa. 49:16.
21.   See Luke 24:36–40; John 20:24–28; 3 Ne. 11:14–17.
22.   See John 12:17–18.

Those in the multitude used the word *hosanna*, which is a Hebrew exclamation meaning "save, I pray."[23] Some in the multitude may have remembered Psalm 118:25: "Save now, I beseech thee, O Lord: O Lord, I beseech thee, send now prosperity." This psalm was recited once daily during the first six days of the Festival of Tabernacles and was recited seven times on the seventh day; each time the psalm was recited, the people waved branches. By the time of Jesus's mortal ministry, *hosanna* had become associated with hope in the coming of the Messiah.[24] And now it was being cried by those in the multitude on the road to Jerusalem. At the Lord's Second Coming, all who believe in Him will likewise shout, "Hosanna."

Pharisees Ask Jesus to Rebuke His Disciples (Luke 19:39–40)

As Jesus approached Jerusalem, some of the Pharisees among the multitude demanded that Jesus rebuke His disciples for expressing their joy. Jesus responded by telling the Pharisees that if His disciples were to stop their rejoicing, stones would cry out. Jesus was presumably referring to stones that could be seen nearby. In making this statement, He implicitly witnessed that He was the Son of God, with power over all the earth, and that even His physical creations recognized His divinity. Stunned by Jesus's bold rebuke, the Pharisees presumably recognized the futility of trying to stop the multitude from giving praise, seeing that the "world is gone after him."[25] Of this incident, Luke wrote the following:

> **Luke 19:39–40.** And some of the Pharisees from among the multitude said unto him, Master, rebuke thy disciples. And he answered and said unto them, I tell you that, if these should hold their peace, the stones would immediately cry out.

Just as Pharisees wanted people in the multitude to stop their praise of God, some people in the latter days may demand that believers remain quiet or may belittle believers' faith and ostracize them. But these critics will not have power to quiet the believers. Although there has not been a prophet in

---

23. *HarperCollins Bible Dictionary*, s.v. "hosanna"; Young, *Analytical Concordance*, s.v. "hosanna."

24. See *HarperCollins Bible Dictionary*, s.v. "hosanna."

25. John 12:19.

Jerusalem since the original Apostles died, the very stones of that city still cause many to remember Jesus and where He walked.

Jesus Weeps over Jerusalem (Luke 19:41–44)

As Jesus came around the southwest slope of the Mount of Olives, He saw Jerusalem in all its splendor, including its buildings and the temple's spire, which perhaps glistened in the sunlight. Upon seeing the holy city, Jesus lamented and wept over Jerusalem. The following is Luke's record:

> **Luke 19:41–44.** And when he was come near, he beheld the city, and wept over it, saying, If thou hadst known, even thou, at least in this thy day, the things which belong unto thy peace! but now they are hid from thine eyes. For the days shall come upon thee, that thine enemies shall cast a trench about thee, and compass thee round, and keep thee in on every side, and shall lay thee even with the ground, and thy children within thee; and they shall not leave in thee one stone upon another; because thou knewest not the time of thy visitation.

Jesus wept because of the hardness of the hearts of the people and their rejection of Him as the Son of God, the Holy Messiah. He knew that many would continue to reject Him, leading to His Crucifixion. He likely sorrowed because most of the ruling Sanhedrin were greedy and prideful and had given their hearts to Satan rather than to God. He also lamented that because the Jews would not believe and repent, Jerusalem would eventually be destroyed by the Romans; not one stone of the temple would be left on another.[26]

He may have also wept because of what Jewish leaders would do to Him in a few days. He likely also wept because of the deep remorse that many would feel as they realized they had brought about the Crucifixion of the Savior of the world.[27]

---

26. Less than forty years after Jesus was crucified, Titus led Roman forces in a siege of Jerusalem, destroying its temple and other buildings and killing many people.

27. The Gospels contain one other account of Jesus crying: when He heard that Lazarus had died. Jesus's tears came not only because of Lazarus's death but also because of the sadness and loss that Mary and Martha felt (see John 11:20–36). Upon restoring Lazarus's life, Jesus may have wept again, this time in gratitude that His friend lived once again and that this miracle would be a witness to all people that Jesus was the Son of God.

People Ask Who Jesus Is (Matt. 21:10–11)

As Jesus entered Jerusalem, many in the multitude continued to praise God and wave branches at Jesus. As a result, many others came into the streets and climbed onto housetops to see Jesus. Some of these individuals had not previously heard of Jesus and wanted to know the reason for the celebration. The following is Matthew's record:

> **Matthew 21:10–11.** And when he was come into Jerusalem, all the city was moved, saying, Who is this? And the multitude said, This is Jesus the prophet of Nazareth of Galilee.

Those asking who He was were likely not from Jerusalem but, rather, had traveled to the city for the Passover. In response to this question, others declared, "This is Jesus the prophet of Nazareth of Galilee." This response may have come from Galilean Jews who were proud that Jesus was one of their own. Those who made the declaration considered Jesus to be a prophet who performed great miracles, but they apparently failed to fully believe or comprehend that He was the Son of God, who had come to bring them salvation.

Jesus's triumphal entry into the city apparently did not concern the Romans. Talmage suggested, "The Romans saw nothing to fear, perhaps much to smile at, in the spectacle of a King mounted upon an ass, and attended by subjects, who, though numerous, brandished no weapons but waved instead palm branches and myrtle sprigs."[28]

Jesus Enters the Temple (Mark 11:11)

After Jesus entered the city, He went into the temple courts. Mark recorded the following:

> **Mark 11:11.** And Jesus entered into Jerusalem, and into the temple: and when he had looked round about upon all things, and now the eventide was come, he went out unto Bethany with the twelve.

At the temple, Jesus surely saw the sacrifices that were being offered in remembrance of Israel's deliverance from Egyptian bondage and in

---

28. Talmage, *Jesus the Christ*, p. 482.

symbolism of the great and last sacrifice that He would soon make for the world. He would have seen numerous people completing their purification before the Passover began. He would have seen people who were sincere in their offerings and desired to be better, and He must have been moved as He witnessed these people's devotion. It is interesting that many others offered sacrifices in similitude of the man who stood among them but that they either failed to comprehend who He was or they simply disbelieved.

He would have seen those who, for their own gain, sold doves, pigeons, and lambs inside and outside the temple courts. He also would have seen those who made a profit by exchanging the currency of people from various areas for temple coins. The greedy and corrupt were defiling His house and the house of His Father.

Jesus was likely moved with compassion and also saddened by what He saw. In the evening, He and His disciples left the city and returned the two miles to Bethany. They presumably went to the home of Martha, Mary, and Lazarus but may have gone to the home of Simon, whom Jesus had healed of leprosy. Or perhaps Jesus and His disciples simply found a quiet place to rest near Bethany, wanting an opportunity to ponder what tomorrow would bring.

Chapter 50

THE BARREN FIG TREE AND THE SECOND CLEANSING OF THE TEMPLE

(Monday)

On Monday, the day following Jesus's triumphal entry into Jerusalem, He and His Apostles again traveled to Jerusalem, having stayed in or near Bethany the prior night. On their way back to Jerusalem, they saw a barren fig tree and Jesus cursed it as a way to instruct His Apostles about hypocrisy and the need to bring forth fruit. When Jesus entered Jerusalem on Monday, He went to the temple, cleansed it of corruption, and castigated the chief priests and scribes for their wickedness and disbelief. The events discussed in this chapter were certainly ones that the Jewish leaders would not forget, nor would the other people who witnessed Jesus's majesty and authority.

Jesus Curses a Barren Fig Tree (Matt. 21:18–19; Mark 11:12–14)

On Monday morning of the week of the Passover, Jesus and His Apostles again walked from Bethany or the surrounding area to Jerusalem. There is no record regarding whether, on this second occasion, people waved palm branches or shouted, "Hosanna." It is likely that Jesus and the Apostles were traveling early in the morning and that few other travelers were on the road.[1] As the group traveled, Jesus was hungry and presumably looked for food to eat. He spotted a fig tree, and as He approached it, He saw that it had leaves but no figs.[2] Jesus took this opportunity to teach His Apostles an important lesson. Of this incident, Mark wrote the following:

> **Mark 11:12–14.** And on the morrow, when they were come from Bethany, he was hungry: and seeing a fig tree afar off having leaves, he came, if haply he might find any thing thereon: and when he came to it, he found nothing but leaves; for the time of figs was not yet. And Jesus answered and said unto it, No man eat fruit of thee hereafter for ever. And his disciples heard it.

There were presumably many fig trees around Bethphage, for the name of this small village, located on the Mount of Olives between Bethany and Jerusalem, means "house of unripe figs."[3] Fig trees beside the road were common property, and anyone could eat their fruit.[4] Fig trees in Judea generally began to develop fruit before leaves, and when the trees had fully leafed out, the figs were beginning to ripen. Jesus was passing by the fig tree in early spring, before fig trees generally produced fruit; nevertheless, the fig tree Jesus saw had leaves. When the group came to this fig tree, they likely expected to find new fruit on the tree since it had leaves or to find fruit left over from the previous fall and winter, since sometimes fruit from the previous year remained in the spring.[5] But the tree had only leaves, meaning it would not produce fruit that year and likely had not produced fruit the prior year. Finding no figs on the tree, Jesus cursed it, saying: "No man eat

---

1.   The conjecture that Jesus's group was traveling early in the morning is based on the fact that Jesus was hungry when He saw the barren fig tree (see Mark 11:12). If the group had stayed the night at the house of Simon or of Martha, Mary, and Lazarus, the group may have left before the morning meal. If the group stayed the night in the open, they may not have had access to food.

2.   Farrar stated, "A few dates or figs, a piece of black bread, a draught of water, are sufficient at any time . . . [for] a simple meal" (Farrar, *Life of Christ*, p. 487).

3.   *HarperCollins Bible Dictionary*, s.v. "Bethphage."

4.   See Geikie, *Life and Words of Christ*, vol. 2, p. 378.

5.   Edersheim, *Life and Times of Jesus the Messiah*, p. 732; Farrar, *Life of Christ*, p. 487.

fruit of thee hereafter for ever." The next day, Jesus would use this fig tree, which by then had withered, to further instruct His Apostles.[6]

Jesus Cleanses the Temple a Second Time (Matt. 21:12–13; Mark 11:15–17; Luke 19:45–46)

After Jesus and His Apostles made their way past the barren fig tree Monday morning, they continued down from the Mount of Olives, traveled across the Kidron Valley, and went up the road to Jerusalem. Upon their arrival in the city, Jesus made His way to the temple. As He climbed the steps leading to the temple, He presumably saw many other people also coming to the temple. He likely also saw people buy sacrificial animals for an exorbitant price, He likely smelled the stench of the animals, and He likely heard the bleating of sheep and lowering of cattle. He probably also saw the greed of those who sold sacrificial offerings and saw the corruption of those who earned a profit by exchanging money, especially foreign currency, for temple coins. In addition to seeing these individuals' tables, benches, and chairs, Jesus likely heard loud bartering and the clank of money being dropped into receptacles and saw bartered goods being collected. Additionally, He likely saw the poor being figuratively ground down by the weight of excessive costs and becoming angry and discouraged because of the hypocrisy these individuals faced when trying to worship. Jesus knew what He must do. The following is Mark's record:

> **Mark 11:15–17.** And they come to Jerusalem: and Jesus went into the temple, and began to cast out them that sold and bought in the temple, and overthrew the tables of the moneychangers, and the seats of them that sold doves; and would not suffer that any man should carry any vessel through the temple. And he taught, saying unto them, Is it not written, My house shall be called of all nations the house of prayer? but ye have made it a den of thieves.

Jesus had cleansed the temple once before, while He was in Jerusalem for the Passover three years earlier. On both occasions, His indignation had surfaced because of the greed, corruption, and hypocrisy He observed in the

---

6.   On Tuesday morning, Jesus and the Apostles saw that the fig tree had withered to its roots, and Jesus used the withered fig tree as an object lesson for further teaching the Apostles. For more information, see chapter 51 in this volume.

temple. The first time He cleansed the temple, He made a whip[7] and drove out all who sold animals and exchanged money for temple coins. The second time He cleansed the temple, there is no record of Him using a whip. The record indicates He authoritatively commanded that all who bought and sold in the temple should leave and He overturned their tables and chairs. There is no record that anyone challenged His actions or declaration. Perhaps their consciences were stung by what they had done and by the purity of the one who had cleansed the temple after they had turned it into, according to Jesus, "a den of thieves."

During Jesus's first cleansing of the temple, He told those who sold and who exchanged money that they should "make not my Father's house an house of merchandise."[8] In so doing, He had implicitly declared that He was the Son of God. The Jews then asked for a sign that would verify His authority, and He responded by referring symbolically to His Resurrection.[9] During the second cleansing, Jesus referred to the temple as "my house" rather than to His Father's house. His Resurrection would occur the following Sunday morning, providing a grand sign that He was the Messiah and that the temple was indeed His house.

Because the temple was Jesus's house, He had every right to drive the unworthy from it. It is important to note that when cleansing the temple, Jesus drove out those who were avaricious and who took advantage of those who came to worship. Jesus did not cast out those who came to make holy offerings to the Lord. Similarly, latter-day temples are for individuals who are found worthy and who desire to worship the Lord and to serve others.

In driving out those who sold animals and exchanged money, Jesus was interrupting the commerce of the leaders of the Jews, including the temple priests and the Sanhedrin, thereby stopping them from earning a profit and defiling the temple. According to Dummelow, "the bulk of the enormous profits went to increase the wealth of Annas, his family, and adherents."[10] Jesus knew full well that stopping their commerce would anger them to the point that they would demand that His life be taken. That consequence was

---

7.   See John 2:15.
8.   John 2:16.
9.   See John 2:18–22.
10.   Dummelow, *Bible Commentary*, p. 694.

part of the divine plan of the Father, for His Only Begotten Son must "be lifted up upon the cross" and suffer and die so that He could bring all humankind unto Him and so that they could "be judged of their works, whether they be good or whether they be evil."[11]

Jesus not only drove out the moneychangers and those who sold animals but also directed that no one should "carry any vessel"—such as baskets or household utensils[12]—through the temple. Jesus needed to give this instruction because many people had begun to view the temple as a public thoroughfare rather than as the sacred house of God. Because Jesus cleansed the temple this second time, the temple was again holy and undefiled, just as Jesus's life was pure and sinless.

One reason the temple needed to be cleansed is that it was designed to be a place for people to pray. According to Matthew's account, Jesus said: "It is written, My house shall be called the house of prayer."[13] Mark's account includes an extra detail, explaining that Jesus stated that the temple should be a place of prayer for all nations. This teaching was not new. Centuries earlier, Isaiah had written: "Even them will I bring to my holy mountain, and make them joyful in my house of prayer: their burnt offerings and their sacrifices shall be accepted upon mine altar; for mine house shall be called an house of prayer for all people."[14] Perhaps some of those who heard Jesus's words and saw what Jesus had done remembered what Isaiah had written.

In the latter days, Jesus has also taught that the temple is a house of prayer. For example, when He revealed the words that Joseph Smith should say in the dedicatory prayer for the Kirtland Temple, He included the phrase that the temple was to be a "house of prayer . . . a house of God."[15] Likewise, Jesus revealed that the dedicatory prayer should include the phrase "all people who shall enter upon the threshold of the Lord's house may feel thy power, and feel constrained to acknowledge that thou has sanctified it, and that it is thy house, a place of holiness."[16]

---

11.   See 3 Ne. 27:14–15.
12.   See Dummelow, *Bible Commentary*, p. 730; Geikie, *Life and Words of Christ*, vol. 2, p. 42.
13.   Matt. 21:13.
14.   Isa. 56:7.
15.   D&C 109:8.
16.   D&C 109:13.

Jesus's cleansing of the temple is also symbolic of His ability to cleanse people through His atoning sacrifice. The idea of a temple symbolizing people was highlighted by Paul: "Know ye not that ye are the temple of god, and the Spirit of God dwelleth in you? If any man defile the temple of God, him shall God destroy; for the temple of God is holy, which temple ye are."[17] In the Book of Mormon, the prophet Alma said: "There can no man be saved except his garments are washed white; yea, his garments must be purified until they are cleansed from all stain, through the blood of him of whom it has been spoken by our fathers, who should come to redeem his people from their sins."[18]

Jesus Heals in the Temple (Matt. 21:14)

After Jesus cleansed the temple, many people came to Him to be healed. The following is Matthew's account:

Matthew 21:14. And the blind and the lame came to him in the temple; and he healed them.

One might wish for a more detailed account of the miracles Jesus performed at the temple. These miracles were presumably seen by the Sanhedrin and chief priests and may have also been seen by representatives of Rome, who attempted to oversee all that transpired during this festival season. Whether or not the Jewish leaders witnessed the miracles, the hearts of these leaders were hardened, perhaps including because they could not perform such miracles themselves. To the wicked, the miracles that occurred at the temple were a stumbling block.

Jesus Castigates the Chief Priests and Scribes (Matt. 21:15–16)

While Jesus was in the temple, children also recognized His divinity and cried out, "Hosanna to the Son of David." The following is Matthew's account:

Matthew 21:15–16. And when the chief priests and scribes saw the wonderful things that he did, and the children crying in the temple, and saying, Hosanna

17.   1 Cor. 3:16–17.
18.   Alma 5:21; see also 1 Ne. 12:10–11; Alma 5:27; 13:11; 34:36; 3 Ne. 27:19; Ether 12:37; 13:10; Rev. 7:13–14.

to the Son of David; they were sore displeased, and said unto him, Hearest thou what these say? And Jesus saith unto them, Yea; have ye never read, Out of the mouth of babes and sucklings thou hast perfected praise?

Farrar stated that the children may have been "boys employed in the musical services of the Temple, and if so the priestly party would be still more enraged."[19] The purity of the children's testimony likely cut deeply into the hearts of the chief priests and scribes, and they were "sore displeased."[20] Satan was certainly at the heart of their displeasure.

The chief priests and scribes wanted Jesus to quiet the children, presumably using the excuse that the noise interrupted the reverence that was supposed to prevail in the temple. The real intent was to stop the children from witnessing of Jesus while other people were present. Jesus responded to the chief priests and scribes by asking a question rather than directly rebuking them: "Yea; have ye never read, Out of the mouth of babes and sucklings thou hast perfected praise?"[21] The chief priests and scribes had no answer, and they continued conspiring to cause Jesus's death.

Chief Priests and Scribes Seek to Destroy Jesus (Mark 11:18; Luke 19:47–48)

While Jesus was in the temple, He also taught those who would listen:

Luke 19:47–48. And he taught daily in the temple. But the chief priests and the scribes and the chief of the people sought to destroy him, and could not find what they might do: for all the people were very attentive to hear him.

During the Passover, the temple would have been thronged by people from all areas of Israel and from neighboring countries. Many of these individuals may have heard Jesus teach. Unfortunately, none of His discourses during this time have been preserved. Presumably, He taught of His gospel, the characteristics that people should develop, and the way that people should live. He may have also taught about His coming death and Resurrection.

Jesus's teachings in the temple angered the Jewish leaders, just as had His triumphal entry into Jerusalem, His cleansing of the temple, His miracles,

19. Farrar, *Life of Christ*, p. 483.
20. Matt. 21:15.
21. See Ps. 8:2.

and the faith that many people had in Him. Consequently, the Jewish leaders once again conspired to destroy Jesus.[22] They did not take Him immediately, for they did not know how to take Him openly in the daytime, especially at the temple; doing so might upset all the people who supported Him and who were astonished by His miracles and gospel message.

When evening came, Jesus departed the temple and the city. He may have left from the gate facing east, taken the path down to the Kidron brook, and then ascended the Mount of Olives by way of the pass on the road, either to lodge on the side of the mount or to return to Bethany for the night.[23]

---

22.   All the events occurring during Jesus's entry into and time in Jerusalem were likely observed by Pilate personally or by his representatives. Pilate could not have been innocent in the Crucifixion of this good and holy man, the Son of God.

23.   See Matt. 21:17; Mark 11:19; Luke 21:37.

Chapter 51

A DAY OF WARNING

(Tuesday)

On Tuesday morning, Jesus and His Apostles[1] left the area of Bethany and traveled to Jerusalem. This day was filled with Jesus teaching, both on the road and in the temple, about a variety of topics, including hypocrisy, responsibility, faith, prayer, and repentance. Jesus's instruction was a warning to His Apostles, Jewish leaders, and others present and was also an invitation for the learned Jews to repent. This day was the last time during Jesus's mortality that He stood in the temple courts and taught the people there. This day was also the last time that Jesus instructed the chief priests, scribes, Pharisees, and Sadducees. Additionally, this day was the last time that Jesus called all who would hear Him in mortality to repent and follow Him.[2]

The Cursed Fig Tree Withers (Matt. 21:20; Mark 11:20–21)

As Jesus and His Apostles traveled on the road to Jerusalem Tuesday morning, they saw the fig tree that Jesus had cursed the morning before. Peter commented that the fig tree had dried up in a single day and was presumably dead. Mark's record states the following:

---

1.   The Gospel accounts are unclear regarding who Jesus was with on Tuesday morning while journeying from Bethany. Matthew 21:20 uses the word *disciples*, and Mark 11 uses the pronouns *they*, *their*, and *them*. The Gospels often use the word *disciples* to refer to the Apostles, and based on the lesson Jesus taught about the withered fig tree, it is assumed that only the Apostles were with Jesus that morning.

2.   See Edersheim, *Life and Teachings of Jesus the Messiah*, p. 736.

Mark 11:20–21. And in the morning, as they passed by, they saw the fig tree dried up from the roots. And Peter calling to remembrance saith unto him, Master, behold, the fig tree which thou cursedst is withered away.

The cursing and withering of the fig tree was in effect a parable for the Apostles to learn from. Jesus, the Master Teacher and the Creator of the earth, knew before He had seen the tree the prior day that the tree was barren of fruit. Just as He had been hungry, the Apostles had likely been hungry and had anticipated satiating their hunger when they saw the tree in full leaf. Now, Jesus used the withered fig tree to teach the Apostles about hypocrisy, their responsibilities, and His divine authority.

In the New Testament, almost all things point to and teach of Christ and His divinity as the Only Begotten Son of God. For about three years, Christ had walked with His Apostles and taught them His gospel. They had heard Him give the Sermon on the Mount, in which He taught what people must be like to inherit the kingdom of heaven. The Apostles had seen Him heal the sick and infirm and raise three people from death to life. The Apostles had heard Him forgive sins and miraculously feed five thousand and then four thousand people. Three of the Apostles had seen Him transfigured and had heard the voice of Heavenly Father declare that Jesus was the divine Son. The Apostles had seen His power over the wind and waves of the sea as He said, "Peace, be still."[3] Now the Apostles had seen His divine power over nature in another way: the fig tree withered at only Christ's word. Each of Christ's miracles was an individual witness of Him; collectively, they were an irrefutable witness. This incident manifested not only Christ's divinity but also His humanity, for He hungered.

Jesus did not curse the fig tree because it lacked fruit but because the presence of leaves deceptively suggested it would. The lesson was about hypocrisy—leaves but no fruit. The Jews were the children of Abraham and therefore part of the covenant people of the Lord. They had been given the gospel and had leaves, but they looked solely to their dead law. Many would not accept Jesus as the Messiah, despite all His miracles and His teachings. Jewish leaders had polluted the temple with their greed. They pretended to be keepers of the law, but they sought Jesus's life in order to maintain their own

---

3.   Mark 4:39.

wealth, position, and power. They were ignoring the sixth commandment of the very law they were supposed to uphold: "Thou shalt not kill."[4]

The Jewish nation, and in particular the chief priests and scribes, had become withered, just as had the fig tree, both the roots and branches. In a more individual sense, what happened to the fig tree symbolizes that the wicked, having lost faith, lose the authority of the priesthood and thereby risk losing the binding ties of their roots (their ancestors) and their future fruit (their posterity).

Just as this fig tree needed to bear fruit to fulfill its existence, the Apostles (who had figurative leaves because of being chosen and ordained) needed to bear fruit after Jesus's death in order to fulfill their calling and ordination. The Apostles would have differing degrees of success, for people in some nations would be more receptive to the gospel than people in other nations would be. Moreover, the Apostles' spiritual roots needed to run deep and have the solid foundation resulting from a testimony of Christ, for the Apostles would endure a variety of tribulations, with most of the Apostles even being martyred. To establish deep roots, the Apostles would need the spiritual nutrients that come through the Atonement, just as the branches and leaves of a tree need vital nutrients available from the tree's roots. Further, the Apostles needed the assistance of the Light of the World, just as trees need sunlight in order to flourish and fulfill their purpose.

As Jesus and His Apostles walked to Jerusalem on Monday and Tuesday, the incidents regarding the fig tree may have reminded the Apostles of Jesus's authority over all creations on the earth, an authority He had received from His Father before the Creation.[5] On the third day of the Creation, under the direction of Heavenly Father,[6] Jesus had commanded: "Let the earth bring forth . . . the fruit tree yielding fruit after his kind, whose seed is in itself, upon the earth: and it was so."[7] The barren fig tree had failed to fulfill the measure of its creation and was now the subject of Jesus's judgment. This occurrence gave the Apostles the opportunity to learn and to teach others that there would be a day of reckoning and judgment.

---

4.   See Ex. 20:13.
5.   See John 5:22.
6.   See Moses 1:32.
7.   Gen. 1:11; see also Gen. 1:12; Moses 2:11–12; Abr. 4:11–12.

Pronouncing a curse upon this barren fig tree was a warning—a warning to the Apostles and to all who would subsequently learn about this occurrence that they needed to fulfill their responsibilities and to do so without hypocrisy. The Apostles had seen another example of this lesson the day before, when Jesus had driven greedy, hypocritical individuals from the temple.

Just as Jesus had pronounced judgment on the barren fig tree, judgment was implicitly pronounced upon the Jews at Jerusalem after they crucified Christ. The Jews not only withered spiritually but also suffered at the hands of the Romans about forty years later when Jerusalem was besieged and destroyed. So great was the destruction that not one stone of the temple was left upon another. The Jews who were not killed were without their city, and some were scattered over much of the then-known world.

Today, people generally do not see leafy but fruitless fig trees along the roadside, but people do see many individuals who put on an appearance of righteousness but lack a testimony of Christ. People may wonder why some who are wicked prosper while some who are righteous have challenges. A message from the incident with the fig tree is that there will come a day of reckoning and judgment for both the wicked and the righteous, with each receiving the reward they are entitled to.

Jesus had previously taught about the judgment of the righteous and the wicked. He gave the parable of the wheat and the tares to indicate that before His Second Coming, the righteous will be gathered and kept safe, whereas the wicked will be gathered and punished.[8] Similarly, Jesus used the parable of the gospel net to indicate that "at the end of the world" the wicked will be separated from the just and cast into a "furnace of fire: there shall be wailing and gnashing of teeth."[9] As the prophet Nephi explained, "For the time speedily cometh that the Lord God shall cause a great division among the people, and the wicked will he destroy; and he will spare his people, yea, even if it so be that he must destroy the wicked by fire."[10] Just as the barren fig tree was a warning to the Apostles of God's judgment, it is also a warning to all people today.

---

8.   See Matt. 13:24–30; D&C 86:1–7.
9.   Matt. 13:49–50.
10.   2 Ne. 30:10.

As Malachi prophesied, "The day cometh, that shall burn as an oven; and all the proud, yea, and all that do wickedly, shall be stubble: and the day that cometh shall burn them up, saith the Lord of hosts, that it shall leave them neither root nor branch."[11] Like the barren fig tree, Malachi's prophecy is also a warning of the Lord's judgment yet to come. But it is more. At the day of judgment, the wicked will be left with "neither root nor branch," similar to the fig tree drying up from the roots, with the branches withering.

However, unlike with the fig tree, individuals can become fruitful again through repentance and Christ's Atonement. Christ's teaching can cause people to recognize the error of their ways and to believe in Him, and through His atoning sacrifice they can be forgiven.

Christ's atoning sacrifice and the resulting opportunity for people to repent and be forgiven extend into the spirit world. As the Apostle Peter expressed, "Christ also hath once suffered for sins, the just for the unjust, that he might bring us to God, being put to death in the flesh, but quickened by the Spirit: by which also he went and preached unto the spirits in prison. . . . For for this cause was the gospel preached also to them that are dead, that they might be judged according to men in the flesh, but live according to God in the spirit."[12]

Jesus Teaches about Faith, Prayer, and Forgiveness (Matt. 21:20–22; Mark 11:22–26)

After Peter observed that the fig tree had withered, Jesus used this opportunity to once again teach His Apostles about faith, prayer, and forgiveness. The following is Mark's account:

Mark 11:22–26. And Jesus answering saith unto them, Have faith in God. For verily I say unto you, That whosoever shall say unto this mountain, Be thou removed, and be thou cast into the sea; and shall not doubt in his heart, but shall believe that those things which he saith shall come to pass; he shall have whatsoever he saith. Therefore I say unto you, What things soever ye desire, when ye pray, believe that ye receive them, and ye shall have them. And when ye stand praying, forgive, if ye have ought against any: that your Father also

11.   Mal. 4:1; see also 3 Ne. 25:1; Smith, *History of the Church*, vol. 1, p. 37.
12.   1 Pet. 3:18–19; 4:6.

which is in heaven may forgive you your trespasses. But if ye do not forgive, neither will your Father which is in heaven forgive your trespasses.

Jesus spoke of faith sufficient to move mountains (and to cause fig trees to become withered). This type of faith springs from deep within, even the roots. The Apostles would need strong faith to sustain them through the great trials resulting from Jesus's Crucifixion, including His separation from them while He was in the borrowed tomb and then His final Ascension into heaven, after which they would be tasked with taking the gospel to the world. Jesus taught that faith was a prerequisite of performing miracles. Jesus also taught that His Apostles needed to express their faith in prayer by asking for what they desired and to learn of God's will and act under His authority. Interestingly, Jesus also linked faith to forgiving others. The ability to forgive derives from humility, and humility is the opposite of pride. Humility brings about love for and forgiveness of others, as well as increases faith. Jesus further emphasized the importance of forgiving others by stating that people need to forgive in order to be forgiven by God.

Jesus Enters the Temple Courts, and His Authority Is Challenged (Matt. 21:23–27; Mark 11:27–33; Luke 20:1–8)

Upon entering Jerusalem,[13] Jesus made His way to the temple, where He would soon be confronted by various groups of Jews. Sometimes, to really understand the scriptures, one needs to visualize the setting and imagine the emotions of those present. Imagining and pondering the setting, who was present, whom Jesus was speaking to, and what was transpiring may be helpful in understanding Jesus's last Tuesday in mortality as He reached the temple in Jerusalem and taught in the temple courts.[14]

Perhaps the sky was clear or obscured by clouds as Jesus and His disciples approached the temple. They arrived in early spring, and the temperature likely was not hot. One can only wonder what Jesus thought as He ascended

---

13.   Edersheim placed this event and the remaining events discussed in this chapter as occurring on Wednesday (see Edersheim, *Life and Times of Jesus the Messiah*, p. 736).

14.   Joseph Smith provided additional guidance about understanding the scriptures: "I have a key by which I understand the scriptures. I enquire, what was the question which drew out the answer, or caused Jesus to utter the parable?" (Smith, *History of the Church*, vol. 5, p. 261.)

the pale yellow-tan limestone steps to the temple. Perhaps He looked at the Mount of Olives and pondered that it would be the location of His final Ascension into heaven. He may have turned to the east and seen the Kidron Valley and Gethsemane, causing Him to think about what would shortly transpire. Perhaps He looked at the houses in the portion of Jerusalem He could see and mourned for the people who lived there.[15]

He may have heard the bleating of sheep and goats that were being readied for the Passover sacrifice, and He may have smelled their odors. It is likely that He looked at others who were in the temple courts, likely including not only the Apostles and other disciples but also many people from Jerusalem, Palestine, and surrounding nations—people who were going to complete ritual purification in preparation for the Passover. With a few exceptions, He was almost always with and teaching people. He surely wanted all people to believe in Him and to return to the presence of Heavenly Father, yet Jesus knew that many would reject Him.

Presumably, He knew that He would be confronted by Jewish leaders who would attempt to trap Him into doing something for which they could justify seeking His life and convincing Pilate to put Him to death. Jesus likely stood majestically yet humbly before the people. He may have stood before them with grace and love for everyone as well as with confidence, for He knew who He was and what His earthly mission. He spoke with pointed words but likely also conveyed mercy, for He wanted all to believe in Him and repent. Through His words and actions, He also was an unwavering witness of His divinity and of His Father.

As Jesus walked in the temple courts, a delegation of chief priests,[16] scribes, and elders, with apparent animosity and arrogance, confronted Him in the presence of the multitude that had come to see and hear Him. The following is Mark's account:

Mark 11:27–33. And they come again to Jerusalem: and as he was walking in the temple, there come to him the chief priests, and the scribes, and the elders, and say unto him, By what authority doest thou these things? and

15. See Matt. 23:37–39; Luke 13:34.
16. "The chief priests described in the NT were the officiating high priests and the former high priests" (Smith, *Bible Dictionary*, s.v. "priest"). The chief priests referred to may have been members of the Sanhedrin (see *HarperCollins Bible Dictionary*, s.v. "council, the").

who gave thee this authority to do these things? And Jesus answered and said unto them, I will also ask of you one question, and answer me, and I will tell you by what authority I do these things. The baptism of John, was it from heaven, or of men? answer me. And they reasoned with themselves, saying, If we shall say, From heaven; he will say, Why then did ye not believe him? But if we shall say, Of men; they feared the people: for all men counted John, that he was a prophet indeed. And they answered and said unto Jesus, We cannot tell. And Jesus answering saith unto them, Neither do I tell you by what authority I do these things.

The Jewish leaders had undoubtedly engaged in considerable discussion about the events of the previous two days, including Jesus being hailed as the Jews' king as He rode into the city. Notwithstanding the Jewish leaders' commitment to kill Jesus, they feared that taking Him publicly in the daytime would lead to an uprising among His followers. So, they had decided to attempt to discredit Jesus in the eyes of the people.

Presumably, the Jews who confronted Jesus were sent by the Sanhedrin[17] to inquire about Jesus's authority to cleanse the temple and thereby disrupt temple commerce, to publicly teach in the temple courts and elsewhere in Israel,[18] and to perform miracles. The delegation of Jewish leaders likely assumed that the people recognized that the priests had responsibility for the physical structure of the temple and for the theocratic system, rights, sacrifices, and purifications that occurred in the temple, which Jesus had cleansed without the leaders' authorization. These leaders, and those who sent them, likely also assumed that most Jews believed that doctrine should be taught only by authorized rabbis so that people would not be taught incorrect information.

These leaders had certainly heard about Jesus restoring Lazarus to life[19] and likely had heard about Jesus giving sight to the blind in Jericho.[20] Further,

---

17.   See Dummelow, *Bible Commentary*, p. 695.

18.   Authorized rabbis were ordained under the regulations of the Sanhedrin. A potential rabbi had to undergo a period of studying and being taught by others, sitting before the Sanhedrin, delivering a discourse, singing designated hymns, and reciting certain poems. The presence of at least three ordained individuals was required at the ordination of a new rabbi. Rabbis who were to go abroad were given "letters of orders," certifying their ordination and authority to teach. (See Edersheim, *Life and Times of Jesus the Messiah*, p. 737.)

19.   See John 11:47–53; Talmage, *Jesus the Christ*, p. 495.

20.   See Mark 10:46–52; John 11:47.

in just the few days since Jesus had returned to Jerusalem, He had healed the sick and given sight to the blind in the temple.[21] Because the Sanhedrin had not authorized Jesus to preach or heal, in asking Jesus about His authority to do these things, the Jewish delegation might have been insinuating that Jesus was acting under the authority of Beelzebub.[22] They likely hoped they could trick Jesus into declaring that His Father was the source of His authority, indicating that Jesus was the Son of God—a declaration that the delegation would consider blasphemy. All these things likely caused the delegation to confront Jesus in the temple courts.

Jesus was more intelligent and wiser than all of the Jewish leaders combined. Rather than directly answering them, Jesus posed a question to them, as He often did when Jewish leaders tried to trap Him. Jesus asked the group to tell Him whether John the Baptist was authorized by God or by men. Rather than immediately responding to Jesus's question, the leaders "reasoned with themselves," perhaps stepping aside to discuss the matter with each other.

They reasoned that if they said John was authorized by God, then Jesus would ask why they did not believe John when he called all to repent and be baptized. If the leaders said John was not authorized by God but by men, then the common people would be upset and possibly rebel because many of them believed that John was a prophet sent by God and had authority to teach even though he was not a temple priest or an accredited rabbi. The Jewish leaders recognized that they were trapped, so they responded that they could not give Jesus an answer. Jesus then said that He would not tell the leaders where His authority came from.

Jesus had turned the tables: rather than the Jews discrediting Jesus, they were the ones who were humiliated, outwitted, and discredited, particularly in the eyes of the people, for how could they not know the source of John's authority?

It is somewhat ironic that the Jewish leaders asked about Jesus's authority, since Caiaphas (the high priest) and his recent predecessors had not been

---

21. See Matt. 21:14.
22. See Edersheim, *Life and Times of Jesus the Messiah*, p. 738.

called of God by His authorized prophet, as was Aaron,[23] but had been appointed by the authority of Rome.

These Jews rejected Jesus's declarations that the temple was His Father's house and Jesus's house.[24] It was obvious that Jesus was declaring that He was the Son of God. The divine authority that resulted from being God's Son superseded all the authority that the chief priests, scribes, and elders claimed.

Jesus Gives the Parable of the Two Sons (Matt. 21:28–32)

Jesus continued to respond to the chief priests, scribes, and elders by giving three parables, partly as a warning and partly as an invitation to repent. The first was a parable about a man with two sons:

> Matthew 21:28–32. But what think ye? A certain man had two sons; and he came to the first, and said, Son, go work to day in my vineyard. He answered and said, I will not: but afterward he repented, and went. And he came to the second, and said likewise. And he answered and said, I go, sir: and went not. Whether of them twain did the will of his father? They say unto him, The first. Jesus saith unto them, Verily I say unto you, That the publicans and the harlots go into the kingdom of God before you. For John came unto you in the way of righteousness, and ye believed him not: but the publicans and the harlots believed him: and ye, when ye had seen it, repented not afterward, that ye might believe him.

Jesus began this parable with a thought-provoking question: "But what think ye?" Because the chief priests, scribes, and elders were some of the most educated Jewish leaders, they may have thought that Jesus was deferring to them by asking their opinion. They were likely more than willing to impart of their wisdom and knowledge to Jesus and others who were listening.

If these Jewish leaders did indeed think Jesus wanted their opinion, they were quickly disappointed, for after Jesus asked the question, He began to give the brief but pointed parable of the father and his two sons. In the parable, the man represents God, who desires to show His love to all people, including the Jews. The two sons in the parable represent different classes of Jews. The father gave both sons an equal opportunity to work in the vineyard, which

---

23.   See Heb. 5:1, 4–6; Ex. 28:1–4; Lev. 8–9.
24.   See John 2:16; Matt. 21:13; Luke 19:46.

represents the Jewish nation. The parable does not state that the opportunity differed based on the sons' ages, education, capabilities, or experiences. The first son initially declined to work but then repented and labored in the vineyard. The second said he would work but did not follow through.

After finishing the parable, Jesus masterfully asked the delegation of Jewish elite which of the two sons did their father's will. These leaders were likely eager to present their opinion, in part because their opinion undoubtedly coincided with the opinion of the other people who were listening: the first son had done his father's will. Jesus responded to the leaders' answer by stating that the publicans and harlots would enter the kingdom of God before the Jewish leaders did.

Jesus then explained why, and in doing so He answered the question He had posed earlier regarding John's authority. Jesus unequivocally stated that John came to the Jewish nation "in the way of righteousness"—that is, his authority was from God—and the publicans and harlots believed John, but the Jewish leaders did not. Jesus told the Jewish leaders, in effect, that the publicans (whom the leaders viewed as unrighteous) and the harlots believed, repented, were baptized, and changed their lives forever. The Jewish leaders had heard John's teachings, had seen him baptize, and had witnessed the change wrought upon even sinners who believed John's words, but the Jewish leaders had not believed or repented.

Through the Jewish leaders' response to Jesus's question, they were condemned before God, themselves, and the other people listening to Jesus. Unlike those who had recognized their unrighteousness, these leaders had refused to humble themselves, repent, and accept baptism at the hand of John in the Jordan River. As Joseph Smith's translation states, "For he that believed not John concerning me, cannot believe me, except he first repent. And except ye repent, the preaching of John shall condemn you in the day of judgment."[25]

However, there was still hope for these Jewish leaders. When Jesus told them that the publicans and harlots would "go into the kingdom of God before you," He left open the possibility that these leaders could change their lives, accept Jesus, repent, be forgiven, and inherit the kingdom of heaven.

---

25.   JST Matt. 21:33–34.

There is an additional important lesson from this parable, a lesson that relates to Christ's Atonement. Most Jews considered the publicans, who collected Roman taxes, to be sinners. Of course, Jews also considered harlots to be sinners, having committed one of the most serious of sins. Nevertheless, even publicans and harlots could believe, repent, be forgiven, and inherit the kingdom of heaven—all because of Christ's Atonement. And so could the Jews listening to His parables.

Jesus Gives the Parable of the Wicked Husbandmen (Matt. 21:33–46; Mark 12:1–12; Luke 20:9–19)

Jesus then gave the parable of the wicked husbandmen. Jesus was likely addressing all who heard—both the Jewish leaders and all others in the temple courts—for the parable's message is applicable to all people.

Matthew's account of the parable is presented here. The account has been divided into parts for ease of discussion. The account begins as follows:

> **Matthew 21:33.** Hear another parable: There was a certain householder, which planted a vineyard, and hedged it round about, and digged a winepress in it, and built a tower, and let it out to husbandmen, and went into a far country.

In this parable, in one sense the householder is God;[26] in another sense, the householder is His Son, acting under God's direction as the Jehovah[27] of the Old Testament. The vineyard that Jehovah planted was Israel, in that He delivered the Israelites from bondage and "planted" them in the promised land—the land of Canaan. The metaphor of a vineyard is found in various places in the Old Testament. For example, Psalm 80:8 states: "Thou hast brought a vine out of Egypt: thou hast cast out the heathen, and planted it."[28] Isaiah 5:2–7 states: "And he fenced it [the vineyard], and gathered out

---

26. A householder is "the head of a household" (*Merriam-Webster*, s.v. "householder"). Because God is the Father of all people, all are members of His household (see vol. 1, pp. 4–6, in this series).

27. Joseph Smith's translation suggests that the householder—the lord of the vineyard—is Christ: ". . . when the Lord should descend out of heaven to reign in his vineyard, which is the earth and the inhabitants thereof" (JST Matt. 21:56; see also vol. 1, pp. 22–23 and 42–45, in this series).

28. See also Ps. 80:9–11.

the stones thereof, and planted it with the choicest vine, and built a tower in the midst of it, and also made a winepress therein: and he looked that it should bring forth grapes, and it brought forth wild grapes. . . . For the vineyard of the Lord of hosts is the house of Israel, and the men of Judah his pleasant plant." Additionally, Jeremiah 2:21 states: "Yet I had planted thee a noble vine, wholly a right seed: how then art thou turned into the degenerate plant of a strange vine unto me?" The metaphor of a vineyard and a vine would have been well-known to the Jewish leaders confronting Jesus, as well as to other people who were listening to Jesus teach in the temple courts.

In the parable and in Isaiah 5, the hedge or fence represents the law that Jehovah gave to Moses on Mount Sinai.[29] The purpose of the law was to keep Jehovah's people—Israel—distinct from the idolatrous nations so that the Israelites would not become idolatrous too.[30]

The winepress[31] may represent the altar of sacrifice in the temple.[32] Of course, sacrificing an animal on a temple altar symbolizes Christ's sacrifice of His blood for all people. The imagery of a winepress has also been used in describing God's displeasure with the wicked. For example, in the book of Revelation, the Apostle John recounted a vision in which an "angel thrust in his sickle into the earth, and gathered the vine of the earth, and cast it into the great winepress of the wrath of God."[33] Similarly, Isaiah quoted the Lord as saying: "I have trodden the winepress alone; and of the people there was none with me: for I will tread them in mine anger, and trample them in my fury; and their blood shall be sprinkled upon my garments, and I will stain all my raiment."[34] Christ also referenced a wine press in a revelation He gave to Joseph Smith: "I have trodden the winepress alone, and have brought judgment upon all people; and none were with me; and I have trampled them

---

29. See Dummelow, *Bible Commentary*, p. 695.

30. See Trench, *Notes on the Parables*, p. 69.

31. In ancient times, a winepress was often made by digging a large hole in the dirt, lining the hole with masonry, and placing the harvested grapes in the hole.

32. See Dummelow, *Bible Commentary*, p. 695.

33. Rev. 14:19.

34. Isa. 63:3.

in my fury, and I did tread upon them in mine anger, and their blood have I sprinkled upon my garments, and stained all my raiment."[35]

Dummelow suggested that the tower represents the temple[36] and is a place in which the watchmen can overlook the vineyard. In a spiritual sense, the tower is a place of revelation in which those who have responsibility for the vineyard can see the world, what is to come, and the cunning devices the devil uses in attempts to destroy the vineyard and its fruit.

Watchmen give warnings from the Lord in order to protect the vineyard. As the Lord told Ezekiel, "Son of man, I have made thee a watchman unto the house of Israel: therefore hear the word at my mouth, and give them warning from me."[37] Likewise, the Lord told Joseph Smith, "And behold, the watchman upon the tower would have seen the enemy while he was yet afar off; and then ye could have made ready and kept the enemy from breaking down the hedge thereof, and saved my vineyard from the hands of the destroyer."[38] Watchmen must be vigilant and not fall asleep.[39] The Jewish elite were supposed to be watchmen on the tower, but they had fallen asleep. They had failed to listen to the Lord's warning, did not warn the people about those who were enemies and destroyers of righteousness, and had become enemies of righteousness themselves.

The husbandmen represent the priests and Levites, who were to be in charge of the vineyard.[40] They were given priesthood responsibility and political authority,[41] and the Lord had directed that the Levites should be His.[42] In the parable, the householder put the husbandmen in charge of the vineyard and then "went into a far country." Likewise, after the Lord had visited the Israelites in a cloud by day and a pillar of fire by night and had spoken on Mount Sinai,[43] He was no longer visible in a way that all the people could personally see Him.

---

35. D&C 133:50–51; see also 133:48–49.
36. See Dummelow, *Bible Commentary*, p. 695.
37. Ezek. 3:17.
38. D&C 101:54; see also 101:45, 53.
39. See D&C 101:53; Isa. 21:11.
40. See Trench, *Notes on the Parables*, p. 70.
41. See Ex. 28–29; Lev. 8.
42. See Num. 3:41–45, 8:14.
43. See Ex. 13:31; 19:9–17.

Matthew's account continues:

Matthew 21:34–36. And when the time of the fruit drew near, he sent his servants to the husbandmen, that they might receive the fruits of it. And the husbandmen took his servants, and beat one, and killed another, and stoned another. Again, he sent other servants more than the first: and they did unto them likewise.

The servants symbolize prophets, who receive God's word and then convey it to the people. In the parable, the servants were beaten and even killed by the husbandmen. Likewise, certain Old Testament prophets were persecuted and even killed. For example, tradition indicates that Isaiah was sawn asunder with a wooden saw by order of King Manasseh,[44] and Jeremiah was imprisoned, put in a miry dungeon, and carried to Egypt, where tradition indicates he was stoned to death.[45] In Paul's letter to the Hebrews, he recounts the persecution of the prophets: "And others had trial of cruel mockings and scourgings, yea, moreover of bonds and imprisonment: they were stoned, they were sawn asunder, were tempted, were slain with the sword: they wandered about in sheepskins and goatskins; being destitute, afflicted, tormented; (of whom the world was not worthy:) they wandered in deserts, and in mountains, and in dens and caves of the earth."[46] The delegation of Jewish leaders listening to Jesus's parable surely knew of the cruel treatment that the prophets of old received and would have understood the meaning of servants in this parable. Further, in Jesus's day, Herod Antipas imprisoned John the Baptist and had him beheaded.[47]

Matthew 21:37–39. But last of all he sent unto them his son, saying, They will reverence my son. But when the husbandmen saw the son, they said among themselves, This is the heir; come, let us kill him, and let us seize on his inheritance. And they caught him, and cast him out of the vineyard, and slew him.

---

44.   See Smith, *Bible Dictionary*, s.v. "Isaiah"; Trench, *Notes on the Parables*, p. 71.

45.   See Smith, *Bible Dictionary*, s.v. "Jeremiah"; Trench, *Notes on the Parables*, p. 71.

46.   Heb. 11:36–38. Malachi and Nehemiah are the last prophets whose records are included in the Old Testament. No additional revelation was recorded until the angel of the Lord appeared to Zacharias in the temple in Jerusalem to declare the coming birth of John the Baptist.

47.   See Matt. 14:6–12; Mark 6:21–28; Luke 7; Luke 9:9; Josephus, *Antiquities*, 18.5.2.

The son represents Christ, who voluntarily came to the earth under the direction of His Father,[48] "for God so loved the world, that he gave his only begotten Son."[49] By the time Christ gave this parable, the Sanhedrin had already conspired to kill Him so that they could preserve their wealth and their religious and political positions. The Jewish leaders would enact their plan in just three days. After atoning in the Garden of Gethsemane, Jesus would be taken, illegally tried, and found guilty by the Sanhedrin and would then be killed on the cross. In this way, He would be cast out of the Jewish nation (the vineyard).

Having finished the parable, Jesus posed a question:

Matthew 21:40–41. When the lord therefore of the vineyard cometh, what will he do unto those husbandmen? They say unto him, He will miserably destroy those wicked men, and will let out his vineyard unto other husbandmen, which shall render him the fruits in their seasons.

Jesus asked the Jewish leaders what the householder would do to the husbandmen who had killed his son. According to Matthew's account, the Jewish leaders responded that he would destroy the men and select others to oversee his vineyard. In giving this response, the Jewish leaders were condemning themselves. In contrast to Matthew's account, Mark's and Luke's accounts suggest that Jesus was the one who said that the husbandmen would be destroyed.[50] Luke's account indicates that the chief priests and Pharisees said in response, "God forbid."[51]

Jesus then upbraided them by asking them about a particular scripture:

Matthew 21:42. Jesus saith unto them, Did ye never read in the scriptures, The stone which the builders rejected, the same is become the head of the corner: this is the Lord's doing, and it is marvellous in our eyes?

The scripture Jesus quoted was Psalm 118:22–23. Psalm 118 is part of what is known as the Hallel (comprising Psalms 113–118), a Messianic prayer of praise and thanksgiving that Jews sang as part of the Passover meal, an

---

48. See Moses 4:2; Mosiah 15:7.
49. John 3:16.
50. See Mark 12:9; Luke 20:15–16.
51. Luke 20:16.

event that would occur two days after Jesus gave the parable.[52] The Jews may have recognized that Jesus was referencing Himself as the stone that the Jewish leaders had rejected. He was the "head of the corner"—that is, the chief cornerstone.[53] In architecture, the chief cornerstone is a stone that is placed at or near the base of two walls in a way that connects them and prevents them from falling down; this stone is generally laid during a formal ceremony.[54] Dummelow suggested that the two walls represent the Jews and the Gentiles and that through faith in Jesus they can be united.[55] The unification resulting from faith will be marvelous to those who experience it. Another possible interpretation is that Jesus is the chief cornerstone of the Church, enabling it to have a firm, complete foundation.[56]

Jesus then brought the entire parable to a point by condemning the Jewish nation:

> **Matthew 21:43–44.** Therefore say I unto you, The kingdom of God shall be taken from you, and given to a nation bringing forth the fruits thereof. And whosoever shall fall on this stone shall be broken: but on whomsoever it shall fall, it will grind him to powder.

Jesus was prophesying that God's kingdom would be taken from the Jews and would be given to another nation. This prophecy was fulfilled when Jerusalem was destroyed by the Romans in AD 70 and when the gospel was restored in the United States in 1830. Jesus also said that whoever fell on the cornerstone or whoever the cornerstone fell on would be broken or ground to powder. Although not part of the parable, the first verse in the psalm Jesus quoted gives hope that people can repent and be saved: "O give thanks unto the Lord; for he is good: because his mercy endureth for ever."[57]

A possible reason Jesus left the imagery of the vineyard is that He needed to include a further central part of his message: regardless of the Jews' hatred for Him, which would ultimately result in His death, the purpose of

---

52. See *HarperCollins Bible Dictionary*, s.v. "Hallel."
53. See Eph. 2:20.
54. See *Merriam-Webster*, s.v. "cornerstone."
55. See Dummelow, *Bible Commentary*, p. 696.
56. See Matt. 7:24–27.
57. Ps. 118:1; see also v. 29.

God would not be defeated and Jesus would remain the heir of God and the chief cornerstone of the Church. Jesus was the promised Messiah and would triumph over evil, including the Jews' wicked plot to kill Him.

Matthew's account continues:

Matthew 21:45–46. And when the chief priests and Pharisees had heard his parables, they perceived that he spake of them. But when they sought to lay hands on him, they feared the multitude, because they took him for a prophet.[58]

The Jewish leaders knew that Jesus was speaking about them, and they likely felt humiliated and angry as they stood condemned before people who revered Jesus as a great prophet. These leaders wanted to take Jesus but did not do so because of the multitude that had gathered in the temple courts to hear Jesus.

Jesus Gives the Parable of the Marriage of the King's Son (Matt. 22:1–14)

Jesus then gave the parable of the marriage of the king's son.[59] This parable was the last parable that Jesus gave publicly during His mortal ministry.[60] As with the discussion of the parable of the wicked husbandmen, this parable will be divided into parts for ease of discussion. The parable starts as follows:

Matthew 22:1–2. And Jesus answered and spake unto them again by parables, and said, The kingdom of heaven is like unto a certain king, which made a marriage for his son.

In this parable, as with many others Jesus gave, He started by stating that "the kingdom of heaven is like . . ." Presumably, Jesus wanted all who heard this parable to focus on the eternal and heavenly aspects of what they were about to hear and to carefully and honestly examine their own hearts to

---

58.   See note 1 at the end of this chapter for language added by Joseph Smith in his inspired translation of the Bible.

59.   See note 2 at the end of this chapter for a discussion of similarities between this parable and the parable of the great feast.

60.   Jesus gave two parables to His Apostles after He gave this parable and before He was crucified.

determine where they stood in relation to the kingdom of heaven. That is, what did they believe, what did they think of Jesus, and what would they do after hearing His words in the temple?

The king in this parable symbolizes God the Father. The marriage represents Jesus Christ, the Son of God, coming to His covenant people during His mortal ministry. Alternatively, the marriage may represent Christ's Second Coming, with His mortal ministry among the Jews considered to be the marriage engagement and associated festivities.[61]

Matthew 22:3. And sent forth his servants to call them that were bidden to the wedding: and they would not come.

The words *were bidden* suggest that invitations were extended and accepted prior to the date of the wedding. Symbolically, the words may refer to individuals chosen in the premortal world to be the Lord's covenant people, with Old Testament prophets acting as servants who reminded the Lord's people throughout the generations of the invitation they had received. The Jews at the time of Christ had the records of these prophets and were also bidden by John the Baptist and by Christ.

Matthew 22:4. Again, he sent forth other servants, saying, Tell them which are bidden, Behold, I have prepared my dinner: my oxen and my fatlings are killed, and all things are ready: come unto the marriage.

The "other servants" may refer to the Twelve Apostles and the Seventy, all of whom Jesus called, ordained, and sent forth to teach that the wedding feast was ready and to invite all to attend. Following Jesus's death, the Apostles (including Paul) and other disciples (including Stephen, Barnabus, and Silas) declared to those they taught that Christ was the Son of God and had atoned for the sins of all people so they could be forgiven if they would repent. The fact that multiple servants were sent and at multiple times demonstrates that God is merciful and gives ample opportunity for each person to repent and come unto Him. They are invited, not coerced, to attend.

Matthew 22:5. But they made light of it, and went their ways, one to his farm, another to his merchandise.

---

61. See Trench, *Notes on the Parables,* p. 76.

Those invited to the wedding feast ignored the invitation, presumably because their focus was on themselves, what they wanted to do, their work, and their material possessions. Of course, an invitation from a king was more important than an invitation from someone else, and ignoring the invitation was the height of disrespect. It is reasonable to assume that long before the servants' reminders, some of the people invited to the feast had decided not to attend the wedding feast. Symbolically, they had decided to ignore the invitation to attend God's feast and had focused on themselves and their interests instead, just as do so many people today.

Matthew 22:6. And the remnant took his servants, and entreated them spitefully, and slew them.

In the parable, the word *remnant* implies that time had passed. The Apostles were present when Jesus gave this parable, and they may have pondered what they would be called upon in the future to suffer in the name of Christ. In the decades following Jesus's death, Jews, Romans, and others persecuted and put to death the Apostles and some other Christians. According to scripture or tradition, Stephen was stoned outside of Jerusalem;[62] Peter was crucified upside down in Rome; Andrew was scourged and then tied to a cross in western Greece; James was beheaded in or around Jerusalem; Philip was scourged, thrown into prison, and crucified in Egypt; Bartholomew was beaten, crucified or skinned alive, and then beheaded, possibly in India; Thomas was speared to death, possibly in Edessa, Persia, or India; Matthew was stabbed in the back, possibly in Ethiopia; James was beaten, stoned, and then clubbed to death in Jerusalem; Thaddaeus, Judas, or Jude may have been crucified in Turkey or Greece; and Simon the Zealot was crucified in England.[63] Many other members of the early Church who preached, ministered, and served were also persecuted, and many suffered horrible deaths.[64] As an example, tradition indicates that Nero "had some

62. See Acts 7:54–60.

63. See Smith, *Bible Dictionary*, and *HarperCollins Bible Dictionary*, s.v. names of those martyred; see also Foxe, *Book of Martyrs*, pp. 4–7; *Church News*, January 13, 2019, pp. 14–15. The traditions regarding the martyrdom of the Apostles may not be accurate in all respects; nevertheless, it is almost certain that all the Apostles suffered for witnessing of Christ and that many sealed their witnesses with their blood.

64. See Foxe, *Book of Martyrs*, pp. 3–50.

[Christians] sewed up in the skins of wild beasts, and then worried by dogs till they expired; and others dressed in shirts made stiff with wax, fixed to axle-trees, and set on fire in his garden. . . . He ordered that the city of Rome should be set on fire."[65]

Matthew 22:7. But when the king heard thereof, he was wroth: and he sent forth his armies, and destroyed those murderers, and burned up their city.

Just like the murderers in the parable were killed and the city was burned, wicked Jews were killed and their city—Jerusalem—was destroyed when Roman armies attacked the city a few decades after Christ's mortal ministry ended. In this parable, Christ was teaching that those who disregard God's commandments, refuse to believe in Him, and harm His servants will ultimately face a day of reckoning.

Matthew 22:8–10. Then saith he to his servants, The wedding is ready, but they which were bidden were not worthy. Go ye therefore into the highways, and as many as ye shall find, bid to the marriage. So those servants went out into the highways, and gathered together all as many as they found, both bad and good: and the wedding was furnished with guests.

In this parable, Jesus was warning the Jews of the consequences of their wicked ways—the Jews were symbolically declining to attend the marriage of the king's son even though they were the covenant people of the Lord. Aware of the invited individuals' refusal to attend, the king told his servants to go to the highways, meaning the Gentiles, and gather all who would come. Both bad and good in the highways were invited, implying that all people will have the opportunity to be invited to learn about the gospel, repent, and come unto Christ.

Matthew 22:11–13. And when the king came in to see the guests, he saw there a man which had not on a wedding garment: And he saith unto him, Friend, how camest thou in hither not having a wedding garment? And he was speechless. Then said the king to the servants, Bind him hand and foot, and take him away, and cast him into outer darkness; there shall be weeping and gnashing of teeth.

---

65. Foxe, *Book of Martyrs*, pp. 7–8.

Jesus next introduced the importance of wearing clothing that is proper for a wedding feast. Because many people were invited to the wedding feast without time to prepare, it is assumed that the king's servants would ensure that all who entered the room where the feast was being held were wearing clothes fit for a royal occasion. Presumably, the servants would freely offer proper clothing to anyone who needed it, just as Christ would freely give His life in order to atone for people's sins.

To understand the symbolic importance of wearing proper wedding clothing, it can be helpful to consider Revelation 19:7–9: "Let us be glad and rejoice, and give honour to him: for the marriage of the Lamb is come, and his wife hath made herself ready. And to her was granted that she should be arrayed in fine linen, clean and white: for the fine linen is the righteousness of saints."[66]

Apparently, one guest made his way into the feast without wearing appropriate clothing.[67] The king noticed and commanded that the man be cast out because he was not worthy to partake of the wedding feast. Likewise, the Lord will examine every person and will not allow the unworthy to enter the celestial kingdom. As Jacob in the Book of Mormon taught, "The keeper of the gate is the Holy One of Israel; and he employeth no servant there; and there is none other way save it be by the gate; for he cannot be deceived, for the Lord God is his name."[68]

All who heard this parable and considered its implications would have recognized that neither God nor Christ can be deceived. God knows all His children and sees all. No one can sneak into His presence. The same is true of Christ. This parable may have caused some who heard it to examine their lives and judge whether they were "arrayed in fine linen, clean and white,"[69] and therefore were sufficiently righteous to stand in the presence of God without condemnation.

---

66.   Rev. 19:7–9.

67.   Christ offered a somewhat similar metaphor when He stated, "Verily, verily, I say unto you, He that entereth not by the door into the sheepfold, but climbeth up some other way, the same is a thief and a robber" (John 10:1).

68.   2 Ne. 9:41.

69.   Rev. 19:8.

The man who was not wearing proper clothing at the wedding feast was speechless when confronted by the king and did not offer any excuse for his attire (symbolizing his character). The man knew he was not worthy to be in the king's presence and was condemned not only by the king but also by himself. Similarly, an individual who has lived unrighteously will find it pointless to offer an excuse to God or Christ in the day of judgment. As with the man in this parable, who was bound securely by the king's servants (likely symbolizing angels[70]) and cast out, unrepentant individuals will be cast into outer darkness, where they will be shut out from the light of God and Christ. These individuals will weep and gnash their teeth, for they will then know with certainty what they could have received if they had only repented. As Trench wrote, "A time arrives when every man will discover that he needs another covering for his soul. Woe unto him who, like this guest, only discovers it when it is too late to provide himself with such!"[71]

Matthew 22:14. For many are called, but few are chosen.

Christ concluded the parable with a final warning: "For many are called, but few are chosen." Even though the Jews were part of the covenant people of the Lord, they would lose all their promised blessings if they failed to repent. They had been called to attend the royal wedding feast, and whether to attend was up to them. The Lord explained in a revelation to Joseph Smith why few are chosen: "Behold, there are many called, but few are chosen. And why are they not chosen? Because their hearts are set so much upon the things of this world, and aspire to the honors of men, that they do not learn this one lesson—that the rights of the priesthood are inseparably connected with the powers of heaven, and that the powers of heaven cannot be controlled nor handled only upon the principles of righteousness."[72]

In giving these three parables, Jesus was giving a divine warning that a day of reckoning would surely come and that the gospel would be taken from the Jews and given to the Gentiles, who, if they repented, would be able to

---

70. See Edersheim, *Life and Times of Jesus the Messiah*, p. 771.

71. Trench, *Notes on the Parables*, p. 82; see also the parable of the ten virgins (Matt. 25:1–13).

72. D&C 121:34–36.

enter heaven. The parables are an invitation and impetus for all people to search their souls, repent, embrace the gospel, and follow Christ.

Notes to Chapter 51

1. Addition to the parable of the wicked husbandmen. In Joseph Smith's translation of Matthew 21, he added the following after verse 46:

> And now his disciples came to him, and Jesus said unto them, Marvel ye at the words of the parable which I spake unto them? Verily, I say unto you, I am the stone, and those wicked ones reject me. I am the head of the corner. These Jews shall fall upon me, and shall be broken. And the kingdom of God shall be taken from them, and shall be given to a nation bringing forth the fruits thereof; (meaning the Gentiles.) Wherefore, on whomsoever this stone shall fall, it shall grind him to powder. And when the Lord therefore of the vineyard cometh, he will destroy those miserable, wicked men, and will let again his vineyard unto other husbandmen, even in the last days, who shall render him the fruits in their seasons. And then understood they the parable which he spake unto them, that the Gentiles should be destroyed also, when the Lord should descend out of heaven to reign in his vineyard, which is the earth and the inhabitants thereof.[73]

2. Similarities between the parable of the marriage of the king's son and the parable of the great feast. The parable of the marriage of the king's son has some similarities to the parable of the great feast.[74] Both parables include a feast that some of those invited did not attend, leading to invitations being extended to those outside of the city. Although both parables were directed to the Jewish elite, Jesus gave the parable of the marriage of the king's son in the temple courts, whereas He gave the parable of the great feast in a Pharisee's house in Perea. In the parable of the marriage of the king's son, the feast was

---

73. JST Matt. 21:50–56.
74. See Luke 14:16–24 and chapter 43 in volume 2 of this series. The parable of the marriage of the king's son also has similarities to the parable of the ten virgins in Matthew 25 and to the marriage of the Lamb referred to in Revelation 19.

held by a king; in the parable of the great feast, the feast was held by a "certain man,"[75] who was presumably wealthy. The king may symbolize God or Christ; the certain man may symbolize one of the Lord's prophets. The reason for the feast in the first parable is the marriage of the king's son, whereas the reason for the feast in the second parable is not specified. In the parable of the marriage of the king's son, those initially invited did not attend because they took the invitation lightly; those initially invited in the parable of the great feast gave somewhat reasonable excuses. Further, in the parable of the marriage of the king's son, the consequence of not attending was destruction, whereas in the parable of the great feast, the consequence of not attending was exclusion from the feast. Perhaps one reason that the consequence was much more severe in the parable of the marriage of the king's son is that by the time Jesus gave this parable, opposition had reached its climax, with members of the Sanhedrin now seeking Jesus's life.

---

75.   Luke 14:16.

Chapter 52

THE JEWS' FURTHER QUESTIONING OF JESUS

(Tuesday)

As the Tuesday before Jesus's last Passover progressed, He continued to teach in the temple courts. The delegation of Pharisees, chief priests, and elders had been humiliated in front of the people and had returned to report to the Sanhedrin. The Pharisees determined to send a second group, consisting of Pharisees and Herodians, to trap Jesus. They challenged Jesus by asking Him about paying tribute money. After this second group failed to achieve its objective, a third group—comprising Sadducees—was sent to inquire of Jesus concerning the resurrection. This third group also failed, and then a scribe asked Jesus about which of the commandments is most important. He too failed to trap Jesus into giving a reason for the Jewish leaders to condemn Him to death. Jesus then challenged a group of Pharisees by asking, "What think ye of Christ?"[1] These events are explored in this chapter.

Pharisees and Herodians Ask Jesus about Paying Tribute to Caesar (Matt. 22:15–22; Mark 12:13–17; Luke 20:20–26)

After Jesus gave the parable of the two sons and the parable of the wicked husbandmen, the Jewish leaders who heard the parables were angry and sought to take Jesus's life.[2] In counsel, the Pharisees devised a new

---

1. See Matt. 22:42.
2. See Matt. 21:45; Mark 12:12; Mark 20:19.

plan to trap Jesus with His own words, presumably to provide a reason to condemn Jesus before the Sanhedrin and Pilate. The following is Matthew's account of Jesus being confronted by Pharisees and Herodians:

> **Matthew 22:15–22.** Then went the Pharisees, and took counsel how they might entangle him in his talk. And they sent out unto him their disciples with the Herodians, saying, Master, we know that thou art true, and teachest the way of God in truth, neither carest thou for any man: for thou regardest not the person of men. Tell us therefore, What thinkest thou? Is it lawful to give tribute unto Caesar, or not? But Jesus perceived their wickedness, and said, Why tempt ye me, ye hypocrites? Shew me the tribute money. And they brought unto him a penny. And he saith unto them, Whose is this image and superscription? They say unto him, Caesar's. Then saith he unto them, Render therefore unto Caesar the things which are Caesar's; and unto God the things that are God's. When they had heard these words, they marvelled, and left him, and went their way.

To implement the plan to ensnare Jesus, the Pharisees conspired with the Herodians, who were a Jewish political faction that wanted the posterity of Herod the Great to maintain control of all the Jewish nation. Since brothers Herod Antipas and Herod Philip held their positions as tetrarchs at the pleasure of the Roman government, of necessity the Herodians also sought the favor of Rome, a practice that brought the Herodians in opposition with the Pharisees and Sadducees in Jerusalem. Despite this generally adversarial relationship, the Pharisees and Herodians conspired together to seek Jesus's life.

The Pharisees and Herodians sent a delegation of men who "feigned themselves just men"[3] seeking Jesus's wisdom; their intent was to "catch him in his words,"[4] that "they might deliver him unto the power and authority of the governor," Pilate.[5]

This delegation craftily began by referring to Jesus as *Master*, presumably with the hope that He would believe they were sincere. They pretended to desire to better understand how to act. Matthew's and Mark's accounts state that the men told Jesus, "We know that thou are true," that is, that He taught the truth. Similarly, Luke's account states that the men said, "We know that

---

3.   Luke 20:20.
4.   Mark 12:13.
5.   Luke 20:20.

thou sayest and teachest rightly . . . [and] teachest the way of God truly."[6] The men then stated they knew that Jesus did not teach to gain favor with people but that He taught "the way of God in truth," without regard to the consequences. These men were correct, but their intent was wicked.

This delegation of Pharisees and Herodians then asked a question that they presumably considered was impossible to answer without giving offense to the multitude: "Is it lawful to give tribute unto Caesar, or not?" All Jews recognized the necessity of paying the Roman-levied taxes, and those who asked Jesus the question thought that however He answered, they would win. If Jesus answered that it was lawful to pay tribute to Caesar, He would be considered disloyal in the eyes of the people, who hated Rome for occupying their nation and imposing a tax, and certainly could not be the Messiah, though many had honored Him as such when He had triumphantly entered Jerusalem just two days before. If He answered that it was not lawful to give tribute to Caesar, He could be taken before Pilate, the Roman governor, and condemned for sedition. The delegation thought their trap had been expertly set. The Atonement was just days away, and Satan was making a desperate attempt to thwart Heavenly Father's plan through prompting the Pharisees and Herodians to ask questions for an evil purpose. The Pharisees likely paid particular attention to whether Jesus's response contradicted in any way the Mosaic law as interpreted by the rabbis, and the Herodians likely paid particular attention to whether Jesus's response indicated any disloyalty to the Roman sovereign.

Jesus perceived their wickedness, hypocrisy, and craftiness[7] and asked, "Why tempt ye me, ye hypocrites?" Imagine their thoughts as they realized that Jesus knew of their devious plot and as Jesus called them hypocrites, possibly in front of other people. They were hypocrites for feigning to desire wisdom from Jesus but in reality seeking His life. They were hypocrites because they pretended to believe that He taught the principles of God but in reality ignored Jesus's goodness, holiness, and mercy, which were evident in His many miracles and His teachings.

---

6.   Luke 20:21.
7.   See Matt 22:18; Mark 12:15; Luke 20:23.

One can only wonder what effect Jesus's words had on the Pharisees' and Herodians' hearts and minds. Perhaps they became more enraged and hardened in their opinion of Him. Perhaps they dismissed Him as one having no authority or wisdom. In contrast, perhaps some of them seriously considered their hearts and motivations, repented, and came to believe in the one they had sought to condemn before the people. Jesus surely hoped for the latter.

Jesus then said, "Shew me the tribute money." They brought Him a penny, or Roman denarius, which was the typical wage for a day's labor.[8] Perhaps holding the coin so that all could see it, He then asked about the image and text on the coin. The Pharisees' and Herodians' answer, of course, was that Caesar's image and name were on the coin. Jesus's response to this answer has become the basis of the proper relationship between church and state: "Render therefore unto Caesar the things which are Caesar's; and unto God the things that are God's."[9]

Jesus's response presents a foundational principle of religious freedom in that His instruction to "render . . . unto God the things that are God's" indicates that the state is not higher than God and has no moral authority to prohibit religion or religious practices or to prefer a particular religion. Similarly, no church has the right to use the state's authority to contend against any other religion.[10] In addition, Jesus's answer neither backed the nationalists, who wanted to be rid of Roman authority, nor supported the Roman government. His answer also affirmed that His kingdom is not of this world. No wonder, then, that the Pharisees and Herodians marveled at Christ's words, held their peace, and left.

Jesus's wise response can help people understand the need to balance work and life with one's commitment to God, Christ, and service in the Church. By any standard, Jesus's reply was masterful, thwarting the tactic these Jews used in an attempt to validly claim that Jesus sought for an earthly kingdom or that He was an enemy to Rome.

The Roman denarius was used in commerce throughout the Roman world, providing a regular reminder of Caesar and his authority. Just as the

---

8.   See Edersheim, *Life and Times of Jesus the Messiah*, p. 762.

9.   See note 1 at the end of this chapter for a discussion of obedience to secular authority.

10.   See Dummelow, *Bible Commentary*, p. 697.

coin bore the image of Caesar, each member of the human family bears the image of God, for "God created man in his own image, in the image of God created he him; male and female created he them."[11] This knowledge can help people recognize the divine spark of creation within them and also understand their ultimate potential. Sometimes, the image of God that people bear becomes somewhat tarnished through neglect, sin, or a focus on the things of the world. The tarnish can be removed through effort, making the holy image of God shine brightly once again.

Sadducees Ask Jesus about Marriage after the Resurrection (Matt. 22:23–33; Mark 12:18–27; Luke 20:27–40)

Shortly after the delegation of Pharisees and Herodians left, a group of Sadducees came to Jesus. They presented Him with a complex scenario and then asked His opinion on the matter. The following is Luke's account:

Luke 20:27–40. Then came to him certain of the Sadducees, which deny that there is any resurrection; and they asked him, Saying, Master, Moses wrote unto us, If any man's brother die, having a wife, and he die without children, that his brother should take his wife, and raise up seed unto his brother. There were therefore seven brethren: and the first took a wife, and died without children. And the second took her to wife, and he died childless. And the third took her; and in like manner the seven also: and they left no children, and died. Last of all the woman died also. Therefore in the resurrection whose wife of them is she? for seven had her to wife. And Jesus answering said unto them, The children of this world marry, and are given in marriage: but they which shall be accounted worthy to obtain that world, and the resurrection from the dead, neither marry, nor are given in marriage: neither can they die any more: for they are equal unto the angels; and are the children of God, being the children of the resurrection. Now that the dead are raised, even Moses shewed at the bush, when he calleth the Lord the God of Abraham, and the God of Isaac, and the God of Jacob. For he is not a God of the dead, but of the living: for all live unto him. Then certain of the scribes answering said, Master, thou hast well said. And after that they durst not ask him any question at all.

---

11.   Gen. 1:27.

The Sadducees, unlike the Pharisees, believed that there was no resurrection. Whereas the Pharisees argued that the Old Testament referred to the reality of the resurrection, the Sadducees contended that the scripture references that the Pharisees used as justification of the resurrection were oblique or just highly poetic language of the prophets.[12] Moreover, rabbis had debated questions concerning the resurrection to the point that the resurrection had almost lost any spiritual significance. These questions included whether deceased people would rise wearing the clothes in which they had died; whether people who were buried naked would rise wearing clothes; and whether resurrected people would look exactly as they had during mortality and would have the same physical limitations, such as lameness, blindness, or deafness.[13] These Pharisaic debates rose to the level of absurdity, buttressing the Sadducees' view that the Pharisees' belief in the resurrection was illogical. Of course, Satan was at the heart of the Sadducees' belief; Christ was less than a week away from making possible the resurrection of all humankind, and Satan wanted those who would not be personal witnesses of Christ's Resurrection to doubt its actuality.

The Sadducees' question extended Moses's instruction regarding marriage to the improbable circumstance of seven brothers in succession marrying a woman and then dying. After presenting the scenario, the Sadducees asked Jesus which brother would be the woman's husband in the resurrection. This complex question presupposed that the Jews' present law would be in force in heaven and presented the resurrection in a ridiculous manner; the purpose was to buttress the Sadducees' opinion that there was no resurrection and to thereby discredit the Pharisees' view.[14] The question was presented to Jesus even though the requirement that a brother marry a deceased brother's wife was no longer common practice among the Jews. Further, the Sadducees believed that Moses's direction applied only to a betrothed woman, not to a woman who had already married.[15]

---

12.   See Edersheim, *Life and Times of Jesus the Messiah*, p. 748.
13.   See Edersheim, *Life and Times of Jesus the Messiah*, p. 749.
14.   See Dummelow, *Bible Commentary*, p. 698.
15.   See Edersheim, *Life and Times of Jesus the Messiah*, p. 750.

In asking the question, the Sadducees presumably hoped that Jesus would reject the idea of a resurrection or would give such a complicated or absurd answer that He would be ridiculed by those listening in the temple.

In responding, Jesus refuted the Sadducees' view that there would be no resurrection. Jesus said that those who die will be resurrected and will not die again. Jesus then bolstered this statement by citing Moses's experience with the burning bush, when he referred to the Lord as the God of Abraham, Isaac, and Jacob. Jesus then said, "For he is not a God of the dead, but of the living: for all live unto him."[16] As Mark recorded, Jesus next said, "He is not the God of the dead, but the God of the living: ye therefore do greatly err."[17] Jesus had frustrated the Sadducees' attempt to trap Him in front of others in the temple courts, many of whom presumably were Pharisees or sympathetic to their views.

Jesus also pointed out an erroneous assumption regarding the resurrection: that marriages among those unworthy of exaltation would be performed in heaven. Jesus repeatedly used the word *they* when referring to those who would not marry in the resurrection. Jesus was referring to, as Paul stated, those who "know not God, and that obey not the gospel of our Lord Jesus Christ."[18] These individuals are wicked, rebellious, or ambivalent toward God and live after the manner of the world. They reject the witness of the Holy Spirit that Jesus is the Christ, the Son of God.[19] These individuals will not have the sacred privilege of entering into marriage in heaven.

This principle was in a revelation that Joseph Smith received concerning marriage. In this revelation, recorded in Doctrine and Covenants 132:15–17, the Lord taught the following:

> Therefore, if a man marry him a wife in the world, and he marry her not by me nor by my word, and he covenant with her so long as he is in the world and she with him, their covenant and marriage are not of force when they are dead, and when they are out of the world; therefore, they are not bound

---

16. See also Ex. 3:6.

17. Mark 12:27. Joseph Smith's revision states, "He is not therefore the God of the dead, but the God of the living; for he raiseth them up out of their graves. Ye therefore do greatly err" (JST Mark 12:32).

18. 2 Thes. 1:8; see also McConkie, *Mortal Messiah*, vol. 3, p. 379.

19. See D&C 76:71–90.

by any law when they are out of the world. Therefore, when they are out of the world they neither marry nor are given in marriage; but are appointed angels in heaven, which angels are ministering servants, to minister for those who are worthy of a far more, and an exceeding, and an eternal weight of glory. For these angels did not abide my law; therefore, they cannot be enlarged, but remain separately and singly, without exaltation, in their saved condition, to all eternity; and from henceforth are not gods, but are angels of God forever and ever.[20]

The Lord has clarified in the latter days that for marriages to be recognized in heaven, a husband and wife must be sealed by priesthood authority and keep their covenants; today, marriage sealings occur in the holy temples of The Church of Jesus Christ of Latter-day Saints.[21] Because the Jews during Jesus's mortal ministry did not have the sealing authority, their mortal marriages are not binding in heaven. For these marriages to be binding, the spouses need to be sealed via proxy in temples, but these Jews, now in the postmortal world, will probably reject a proxy sealing because they chose to not repent and accept the gospel during mortality.[22]

Jesus had just taught eternal truths, including the divine relationship between God and humankind, and many of those who heard were likely edified by Jesus's words. Some of the scribes present recognized Jesus's learning and wisdom and publicly called Him *Master* and stated, "Thou hast well said." Those who heard Jesus speak were astonished by the doctrine He taught.[23] In five days, Jesus would provide proof of the resurrection by being resurrected Himself following His Crucifixion.

A Scribe Asks about the Great Commandment (Matt. 22:34–40; Mark 12:28–34)

Upon hearing that Jesus had silenced the Sadducees, the Pharisees gathered together, presumably to decide what now should be done.[24] One of

---

20. D&C 132:15–17; see also vv. 7–14.
21. See D&C 132:19. In similar manner, children can be sealed to their parents so that family members throughout all generations will be bound together in the eternities (see D&C 128:18).
22. See Alma 34:34–35; Hel. 13:38.
23. See Matt. 22:33.
24. See Matt. 22:34.

the Pharisees came to Jesus and asked Him a question to tempt or test Him. This Pharisee was a scribe or a lawyer[25] and presumably was an expert in and teacher of the law. The following is Mark's account:

> **Mark 12:28–34.** And one of the scribes came, and having heard them reasoning together, and perceiving that he had answered them well, asked him, Which is the first commandment of all? And Jesus answered him, The first of all the commandments is, Hear, O Israel; The Lord our God is one Lord: And thou shalt love the Lord thy God with all thy heart, and with all thy soul, and with all thy mind, and with all thy strength: this is the first commandment. And the second is like, namely this, Thou shalt love thy neighbour as thyself. There is none other commandment greater than these. And the scribe said unto him, Well, Master, thou hast said the truth: for there is one God; and there is none other but he: And to love him with all the heart, and with all the understanding, and with all the soul, and with all the strength, and to love his neighbour as himself, is more than all whole burnt offerings and sacrifices. And when Jesus saw that he answered discreetly, he said unto him, Thou art not far from the kingdom of God. And no man after that durst ask him any question.

Mark's account states that the scribe asked, "Which is the first commandment of all?" Matthew's account presents the question as "Master, which is the great commandment in the law?"[26] Jesus's response is as applicable today as it was to the scribe and anyone else listening to Jesus speak: "Hear, O Israel; The Lord our God is one Lord." Jesus's response is similar to and flows from the first of the Ten Commandments given to Moses: "Thou shalt have no other Gods before me."[27] As one of Jesus's concluding statements before His death, He made it absolutely clear here in the temple courts that there was only one eternal God. The Jews believed as much, whereas the Romans and Greeks believed in many gods. Since the Passover was in a few days, some who were present may have come from Greece and found Jesus's teaching particularly insightful.

---

25. See Matt. 22:35. "The 'lawyers' Jesus engages in conversations are essentially Bible Scholars" (*HarperCollins Bible Dictionary*, s.v. "lawyer").
26. Matt. 22:36.
27. See Ex. 20:3.

Jesus continued by stating, "And thou shalt love the Lord thy God with all thy heart, and with all thy soul, and with all thy mind, and with all thy strength: this is the first commandment." All those listening would have instantly recognized that Jesus was repeating what Moses had taught the ancient Israelites in the wilderness: that loving the Lord meant keeping His teachings and commandments in their hearts,[28] that they needed to teach Jesus's commandments to their children, and that they needed to talk of the commandments regularly.[29] The Israelites had further been directed to write the commandments on scrolls and "bind them for a sign upon thine hand, and they shall be as frontlets between thine eyes,"[30] to make fringes on the borders of their garments,[31] and to write the commandments "upon the posts of thy house, and on thy gates."[32]

Completely loving God requires having faith in Him, in His Son, and in the plan of salvation. Completely loving God includes understanding that He is the father of all people and that they therefore have divine potential. Completely loving God also requires keeping His commandments, not simply because they are commandments but because obeying the commandments will enable people to be drawn to the divine within, overcome the world, and become like Him.[33] Of course, completely loving God also involves loving others.

Again quoting from the Old Testament, Jesus then taught of the second great commandment: "Thou shalt love thy neighbour as thyself."[34] Jesus had previously taught this principle when He was questioned by a lawyer. At that time, He elaborated on this teaching by giving the parable of the good Samaritan,[35] clarifying that everyone is a neighbor, and explaining that people should not let the press of the world keep them from helping others in need. Jesus would soon repeat this principle to His Apostles, telling them

---

28.   See Deut. 6:6.
29.   See Deut. 6:7.
30.   Deut. 6:8; see also note 2 at the end of this chapter.
31.   See Num. 15:38–39; Deut. 22:12; see also note 3 at the end of this chapter.
32.   Deut. 6:9.
33.   See Matt. 5:48.
34.   Lev. 19:18.
35.   See Luke 10:25–28. Some people have proposed that Luke 10:25–28 and Mark 12:28–34 are accounts of the same incident (see Dummelow, *Bible Commentary*, p. 698); however, others (including the author of this volume) believe the accounts describe different events.

to "love one another, as I have loved you."[36] Of course, He demonstrated this perfect love through His Atonement and Crucifixion. As the Apostle John later wrote, "Beloved, let us love one another: for love is of God; and every one that loveth is born of God, and knoweth God."[37]

After Jesus responded to the scribe, the scribe stated he recognized that Jesus spoke the truth and that honoring and living these two grand commandments is worth "more than all whole burnt offerings and sacrifices." Jesus then replied, "Thou art not far from the kingdom of God." One can only imagine the scribe's thoughts upon hearing Jesus's reply. The scribe may have pondered the words even more after Jesus's Crucifixion and Resurrection.

Jesus Asks the Pharisees, "What Think Ye of Christ?" (Matt. 22:41–46; Mark 12:35–37; Luke 20:41–44)

When Jesus rode triumphantly into Jerusalem to shouts of "Hosanna" and then cleansed the temple,[38] it was as if He had figuratively disturbed a hornet's nest, and the leaders of the Jews had again conspired to sting—that is, kill—Him. On Tuesday in the temple courts, Jesus had silenced the chief priests, elders, Pharisees, Herodians, Sadducees, and scribes, who represented the major bodies of Judaism, and He likely did so in the hearing of others. Now Jesus became the inquisitor. The following is Matthew's account:

> **Matthew 22:41–46.** While the Pharisees were gathered together, Jesus asked them, saying, What think ye of Christ? whose son is he? They say unto him, The Son of David. He saith unto them, How then doth David in spirit call him Lord, saying, The Lord said unto my Lord, Sit thou on my right hand, till I make thine enemies thy footstool? If David then call him Lord, how is he his son? And no man was able to answer him a word, neither durst any man from that day forth ask him any more questions.

Jesus directed two questions to the Pharisees, who undoubtedly were not the only ones present with Jesus in the temple courts. The questions were "What think ye of Christ?" and "Whose son is he?" *Christ* is the Greek word for the Hebrew word *Messiah* and is not a name but a title meaning

---

36. John 13:34.
37. 1 John 4:7; see also 1 Ne. 8:10–12; 11:21–23, 25.
38. See Matt. 21:9–11; Mark 11:15–17.

"anointed one."[39] By using the present tense in the second question, Jesus was implying that Christ was on the earth at that time. The Pharisees chose to answer the second question only, saying that Christ was the son of David. They were not willing to say that Christ was the Son of God, and they did not respond or object to Jesus's implication that Christ was among the Jews at that time.

The Pharisees' response that Christ was the son—that is, descendant—of David[40] expressed a belief held by all Jews and acknowledged that the title referred to the Messiah.[41] For this reason, Jesus's genealogy is traced back to David in the Gospels of Matthew and Luke.[42] In reply to the Pharisees' statement, Jesus asked why David called Christ the name Lord, and then Jesus quoted from Psalm 110:1, which is attributed to David: "The Lord said unto my Lord . . ." In using the word *Lord* the second time, David was referring to the Jehovah of the Old Testament—that is, Jesus. In other words, David stated that God said to Christ, "Sit thou on my right hand, till I make thine enemies thy footstool." In other words, God was saying that He would constantly be with Christ until Satan and his emissaries of evil had been vanquished.

Jesus then asked the Pharisees how David could refer to Christ as the Lord if Christ was also a descendent of David. The Pharisees could not or would not provide an answer. Jesus had already answered the question by citing Psalm 110:1, affirming that He was indeed the divine Son of God, not just any descendant of David.

The Pharisees' silence regarding this question and the first question Jesus posed ("What think ye of Christ?") was presumably witnessed by others in the temple. Everyone must have noticed the lack of response.

In answering the questions of the Herodians, Pharisees, Sadducees, and scribes in the temple courts this day, Jesus had taught about the need to receive authority from God to act in His behalf and about how to serve

---

39. See *HarperCollins Bible Dictionary*, s.v. "Christ" and "Jesus Christ"; Young, *Analytical Concordance*, s.v. "Christ" and "Messiah"; Talmage, *Jesus the Christ*, p. 34.

40. By implication, the Pharisees were acknowledging that Christ either had been or was with them in mortality because Jesus's question was in the present tense and they responded without contesting the tense.

41. See Clarke, *Commentary, Matthew–Revelation*, vol. 5, p. 216; John 7:42.

42. See Matt. 1:1–17; Luke 3:23–38.

diligently and be clothed in righteousness when engaged in God's work. Jesus had warned of a day of judgment, and He had taught about the importance of rendering to God the things that are God's and to not be distracted by the world. Jesus had taught of the resurrection and of the truth that God rules in the heavens and over all things and people. Jesus had also taught about the importance of loving God and others above all else, and in so doing, Jesus had borne a powerful witness of God. Last of all, Jesus had borne witness of Himself as the Christ, the divine Son of God, and had taught that when His earthly mission was complete, He would sit on the right hand of God. Jesus's message and witness to the Jews that Tuesday in the temple was complete and had been given to help those listening to engage in deep self-introspection, ideally leading to repentance and faith in who He was.

Jesus had silenced the various delegations of Jews, and the fact that they were sent is evidence of the Jewish leaders' evil motives. As Jesus asked the Pharisees, "What think ye of Christ," the answer was clear though not admitted: He is the Son of God. Jesus spent the remainder of the day in the temple courts with His disciples and others.

Notes to Chapter 52

1. Obedience to secular authority. Talmage stated the following:

Governments are instituted of God, sometimes by His direct interposition, sometimes by His permission. When the Jews had been brought into subjection by Nebuchadnezzar, king of Babylon, the Lord commanded through the prophet Jeremiah (27:4–8) that the people render obedience to their conqueror, whom He called his servant; for verily the Lord had used the pagan king to chastise the recreant and unfaithful children of the covenant. The obedience so enjoined included the payment of taxes and extended to complete submission. After the death of Christ the apostles taught obedience to the powers that be, which powers, Paul declared "are ordained of god." See Rom. 13:1–7; Titus 3:1; 1 Tim. 2:1–3; see also 1 Pet. 2:13, 14. Through the medium of modern revelation, the Lord has required of His people in the present dispensation, obedience to and loyal support of the duly established and existing governments in all lands. See D&C 58:21–22; 98:4–6; and Section 134 throughout. The restored Church proclaims as an essential part of its belief and practice: "We believe in being subject to kings, presidents, rulers, and magistrates, in obeying, honoring, and sustaining the law."[43]

2. Phylacteries. According to the *HarperCollins Bible Dictionary*, "the Jews wore phylacteries upon their foreheads and left arm containing the law. . . . Phylacteries included two small black boxes containing passages from scripture written on parchment which [were] normally fastened by black straps to the upper left arm and above the forehead. The laws governing the wearing of phylacteries were derived . . . from four Biblical passages (Deut. 6:8; 11:18; Ex. 13:9, 16)." The phylacteries contained four small strips of parchment made from animal skin, on which was inscribed part of the following scriptures: Exodus 13:2–10, Exodus 11–17, Deuteronomy 6:4–9, and Deuteronomy 11:13–21. Each strip of parchment was placed in a separate compartment of a small leather box. A strip of leather "held the box in place on the forehead between the eyes." Additionally, the four scriptures were inscribed on a piece of parchment, the parchment was placed in a small box, and the box was tied to the inside of a person's left inside arm. "Apparently, the Pharisees wore the arm phylactery above the elbow two fist widths from the shoulder-blade, while the Sadducees fastened it to the palm of the hand. Phylacteries were generally worn only at prayer time, but some of the Pharisees displayed them throughout the day. Phylacteries were only worn by males after the age of thirteen. Women, slaves and minors were exempt."[44]

3. Fringes and borders. Numbers 15:37–40 sets forth the Lord's instructions regarding fringes and borders on garments:

And the Lord spake unto Moses, saying, Speak unto the children of Israel, and bid them that they make them fringes in the borders of their garments throughout their generations, and that they put upon the fringe of the borders a ribband of blue: And it shall be unto you for a fringe, that ye may look upon it, and remember all the commandments of the Lord, and

43. Talmage, *Jesus the Christ*, p. 524n2.
44. *HarperCollins Bible Dictionary*, s.v. "phylacteries"; see also *Jewish Encyclopedia*, s.v. "phylacteries ('tefilin')"; Talmage, *Jesus the Christ*, p. 524n5.

do them; and that ye seek not after your own heart and your own eyes, after which ye use to go a whoring: that ye may remember, and do all my commandments, and be holy unto your God.

As recorded in Deuteronomy 22:12, the Lord prescribed that these fringes should be "upon the four quarters of thy vesture, wherewith thou coverest thyself." These fringes and the blue-ribbon border were to remind the Israelites to keep the commandments, not seek their own desires, and be holy. The Pharisees hypocritically enlarged the borders to make them more visible to other people, with the intent that more people would view the Pharisees as pious even though the Pharisees failed to remember the very purpose of these borders and fringes and failed to keep the commandments.

Chapter 53

JESUS'S FINAL HOURS AT THE TEMPLE

(Tuesday)

There were now only a few hours remaining in Jesus's public ministry. With this precious time, He further addressed His disciples and others in the multitude regarding what they should learn from the actions of the scribes, Pharisees, and other leaders of the Jewish nation.[1] He warned against pride and hypocrisy, and He reemphasized the importance of humility in daily life and in service in His kingdom.[2] Jesus lamented over Jerusalem, testified of Himself and of the Father, and was deeply impressed by a widow who donated two mites—all she had. Jesus then gave a final, sorrowful warning to the scribes and Pharisees.[3]

Jesus Warns against the Actions of the Scribes and Pharisees (Matt. 23:1–12; Mark 12:38–40; Luke 20:45–47)

The Gospel of Matthew contains the lengthiest and most complete account of Christ's instructions to His disciples and others in the multitude regarding the actions of the scribes and Pharisees, some of whom may have been present:

Matthew 23:1–7. Then spake Jesus to the multitude, and to his disciples, saying, The scribes and the Pharisees sit in Moses' seat: all therefore

---

1. See Matt. 23:1–7.
2. See Matt. 23:8–12.
3. See Matt. 23:13–36.

whatsoever they bid you observe, that observe and do; but do not ye after their works: for they say, and do not. For they bind heavy burdens and grievous to be borne, and lay them on men's shoulders; but they themselves will not move them with one of their fingers. But all their works they do for to be seen of men: they make broad their phylacteries, and enlarge the borders of their garments, and love the uppermost rooms at feasts, and the chief seats in the synagogues, and greetings in the markets, and to be called of men, Rabbi, Rabbi.

Jesus did not encourage His disciples to seek political authority, nor did Jesus want to create an insurrection to overthrow the Jewish rulers and cause chaos in the nation. His kingdom was a heavenly kingdom, and His desire was to teach about spiritual matters, including living righteously and serving selflessly. Here, Jesus was teaching that the Jews should obey the laws of the country in which they lived or in which they would teach and testify. In Israel, the ecclesiastical leaders of the Jews were in effect their political leaders as well, subject to the Roman government.

Regarding Jesus's statement that the scribes and Pharisees sat "in Moses' seat," Dummelow provided the following insight: "The scribes (who were ordained with the laying-on of hands) claimed to have received their authority through an unbroken succession from Moses. The 'sitting' refers to the judicial power and the authority to teach, which all scribes or rabbis possessed, and which was centered in the Great Sanhedrin. In rabbinical writings one who succeeds a rabbi at the head of his school is described as 'sitting on his seat,' because the rabbis taught sitting on a raised seat."[4]

Jesus's teaching about obeying the scribes' and Pharisees' instructions is similar to the statement in the twelfth article of faith: "We believe in being subject to kings, presidents, rulers, and magistrates, in obeying, honoring, and sustaining the law." The eleventh article of faith clarifies that even while obeying the laws of the land, "we claim the privilege of worshiping Almighty God according to the dictates of our own conscience, and allow all men the same privilege, let them worship how, where, or what they may."

Though Jesus encouraged the Jews to obey the scribes' and Pharisees' laws, the people were not to follow the example of the scribes and

---

4.   Dummelow, *Bible Commentary*, p. 699.

Pharisees. The scribes and Pharisees had studied the law extensively but failed to grasp its spirit and how to appropriately apply the law of Moses in their lives. They failed to comprehend that the law was not the end in and of itself but was a means of helping them live righteously and thereby draw closer to God. Thus, the scribes and Pharisees placed their oral interpretations of the law and their traditions above the law. These leaders believed and taught that once a rabbinical rule had been pronounced, it needed to be observed. As a result, burdens upon burdens were heaped on the people, to the point that the burdens became intolerable.[5] In addition, the differing beliefs of the Sadducees and Pharisees and of the rival schools of Hillel and Shammai prompted a spirit of contention, further driving out the true meaning of religion in the lives of the people.[6]

Focused on wrangling over the meaning of the law,[7] the scribes, Pharisees, and others who sat "in Moses' seat" failed to give aid to those in need. These leaders desired to publicize their supposed righteousness by increasing the size of their phylacteries and the width of the borders on their clothes[8] rather than to understand what true religion really is. As James stated, "Pure religion and undefiled before God and the Father is this, To visit the fatherless and widows in their affliction, and to keep himself unspotted from the world."[9] The scribes and Pharisees utterly failed to practice this principle.

Continuing to call attention to the hypocrisy of the scribes and Pharisees, Jesus said that they "love the uppermost rooms at feasts, and the chief seats in the synagogues, and greetings in the markets, and to be called of men, Rabbi, Rabbi." Jesus had similarly rebuked the Pharisees when He dined with them in the home of an unnamed Pharisee in Perea.[10] One of the Pharisees' sins was pride. They engaged in outward displays of piety through strictly

---

5.   See Edersheim, *Life and Times of Jesus the Messiah*, pp. 754–755.

6.   See Edersheim, *Life and Times of Jesus the Messiah*, p. 755.

7.   Edersheim observed, "Conceive, for example, two schools in controversy whether it was lawful to kill a louse on the Sabbath" (Edersheim, *Life and Times of Jesus the Messiah*, p. 755n29).

8.   See notes 2 and 3 in chapter 52 of this volume.

9.   James 1:27.

10.   See Luke 11:43; see also chapter 41 in volume 2 of this series for a discussion of Jesus's rebuke of the Pharisees in Perea.

and almost ridiculously adhering to the numerous and tedious rabbinical rules. The Pharisees had become blind to the spirit of the law.

According to Farrar, most Pharisees also had inappropriate motivations:

> There is the "Shechemite" Pharisee, who obeys the law from self-interest; the Tumbling Pharisee (*nikfi*), who is so humble that he is always stumbling because he will not lift his feet from the ground; the Bleeding Pharisee (*kinai*), who is always hurting himself against walls, because he is so modest as to be unable to walk about with his eyes open lest he should see a woman; the Mortar Pharisee (*medorkia*), who covers his eyes as with mortar for the same reason; the *Tell-me-another-duty-and-I-will-do-it* Pharisee—several of whom occur in our Lord's ministry; and the *Timid* Pharisee, who is actuated by motives of fear alone. The seventh class only is the class of "Pharisees from love," who obey God because they love Him from the heart.[11]

Pride can be the downfall of people, institutions, governments, and nations. Pride was ultimately the reason that Satan was cast out of heaven and became the devil. Pride caused the downfall of the Nephite nation in the Book of Mormon.[12] Pride is at the heart of almost all sin. Pride destroys faith and inhibits repentance. Pride gradually binds people with chains that are difficult to break. Pride is characterized by questions such as the following: What can I do to demonstrate to others that I am important? What can I do to show others that I am obedient? What accolades can I receive? In contrast, those who are humble ask questions such as the following: What would God have me do with my life? How can I unselfishly help and give to others? The scribes and Pharisees resembled some members of the Church in the Americas during Alma the Younger's day. Alma 4:12 states that there was "great inequality among the people, some lifting themselves up with their pride, despising others, turning their backs upon the needy and the naked and those who were hungry, and those who were athirst, and those who were sick and afflicted."[13]

The opposite of pride is humility, which Christ characterized His entire life and which He taught the importance of. For example, humility is one of the core principles He taught about in the Sermon on the Mount. Humility

11. Farrar, *Life of Christ*, p. 512.
12. See Moro. 8:27.
13. Alma 4:12.

was an important principle for the Apostles to understand, particularly as they proselytized after Christ's death.

There is also an important lesson to learn from Jesus's statement that the scribes and Pharisees loved "to be called of men, Rabbi, Rabbi." *Rabbi* is a title meaning "my master," "my great one," and "my teacher."[14] In Jesus's day, rabbis were filled with vanity and the desire to be called the greatest. When greeted, they were to be called *rabbi*, and failure to do so resulted in a heavy punishment. The most aged rabbis were honored by being given the upper seats at feasts. The rabbis were so arrogant that if a rabbi cursed someone and that person suffered for a cause unrelated to the rabbi's curse, then the rabbi and his followers believed that the suffering resulted from the rabbi's curse.[15] The rabbis had removed the spirit of religion, reducing it to an intellectual display.[16]

Jesus then explained the following:

Matthew 23:8–12. But be not ye called Rabbi: for one is your Master, even Christ; and all ye are brethren. And call no man your father upon the earth: for one is your Father, which is in heaven. Neither be ye called masters: for one is your Master, even Christ. But he that is greatest among you shall be your servant. And whosoever shall exalt himself shall be abased; and he that shall humble himself shall be exalted.

Jesus instructed His disciples that they should not desire to be called rabbis. Jesus's disciples were not to be anyone's master; they were to be His servants, ministering to others. Jesus also made it clear that His disciples should not be called *rabbi* or *master* because He was the only Master and His disciples were to serve Him by serving others; His disciples were not to be constantly served by or elevated in station by others. Similarly, neither His disciples nor any other mortals were to be called *father*, because God is the only Father and He is the only person whom people should bow before and pray to. The essence of Jesus's instruction is that His disciples should be meek, humble, and lowly in heart[17] rather than seek to be exalted above others.

---

14. *HarperCollins Bible Dictionary*, s.v. "rabbi." In the Hebrew Bible, *rab* means "chief" or "officer" (*HarperCollins Bible Dictionary*, s.v. "rabbi").

15. See Edersheim, *Life and Times of Jesus the Messiah*, p. 755.

16. See Edersheim, *Life and Times of Jesus the Messiah*, p. 755.

17. See Matt. 11:29.

Jesus Presents the Scribes and Pharisees with Eight "Woes" (Matt. 23:13–36; Mark 12:40; Luke 20:47)

Jesus next spoke to the scribes and Pharisees, declaring eight "woes" and repeatedly calling the scribes and Pharisees *hypocrites*; doing so must have angered them even more. The word *woe* is an interjection "used to express grief, regret, or distress."[18] There is no doubt that Jesus was sharply rebuking the scribes and Pharisees. He was giving them one last warning that if they failed to repent, justice would claim what was due. Jesus's grief came from whom the scribes and Pharisees had become and because He was not sent "into the world to condemn the world; but that the world through him might be saved."[19] With His divine discernment, He knew, however, that their fate was sealed, for they would not repent in this world or in the next.

The following is the first woe:

> **Matthew 23:13.** But woe unto you, scribes and Pharisees, hypocrites! for ye shut up the kingdom of heaven against men: for ye neither go in yourselves, neither suffer ye them that are entering to go in.

The scribes and Pharisees "shut up the kingdom of heaven" to themselves and to others by opposing Christ, influencing others to not follow Christ, and excommunicating or threatening to excommunicate those who did believe. As Edersheim stated, "They stood with their back to the door of the Kingdom, and prevented the entrance of others."[20] One reason the scribes and Pharisees opposed Christ is that they feared that their ecclesiastical positions would be diminished if many people followed Him. Therefore, these Jewish leaders attributed Christ's miracles to an association with Beelzebub, and they publicly condemned Him for such things as healing on the Sabbath. They also claimed that because Christ had not been taught by Jewish leaders in Jerusalem, He could not possess the degree of knowledge that, in their view, was necessary to be the Son of God.

The scribes' and Pharisees' standards for righteousness and piety were their learning and strict observance of the law as explained and amplified by

---

18.   *Merriam-Webster*, s.v. "woe," accessed August 4, 2022, https://www.merriam -webster.com/dictionary/woe.

19.   John 3:17.

20.   Edersheim, *Life and Times of Jesus the Messiah*, p. 757.

the rabbis. The many requirements and burdens added to the law perverted the spirit of the law and caused the common people to be confused and misled, thereby serving as another way that the scribes and Pharisees were a barrier to others entering the kingdom of heaven.

Jesus then pronounced the second woe:

> **Matthew 23:14.** Woe unto you, scribes and Pharisees, hypocrites! for ye devour widows' houses, and for a pretence make long prayer: therefore ye shall receive the greater damnation.

Certain leaders of the Jews amassed wealth through levying temple taxes, selling animals to be sacrificed in the temple, and making a profit when people exchanged money for temple coins. These leaders even exacted money from widows. The leaders' avarice was a public scandal. They offered long prayers for a pretense of piety instead of because they desired to humbly petition God for themselves and others, especially those in need. For these actions, Jesus declared that they would receive damnation.

Moving to the third woe, Jesus stated the following:

> **Matthew 23:15.** Woe unto you, scribes and Pharisees, hypocrites! for ye compass sea and land to make one proselyte, and when he is made, ye make him twofold more the child of hell than yourselves.

The Jews were isolationists who wanted to keep their nation untainted from foreigners and their gods, as illustrated frequently in the Old Testament. For example, the Lord commanded the ancient Israelites to "utterly destroy . . . the Hittites, and the Amorites, the Canaanites, and the Perizzites, the Hivites and the Jebusites . . . that they teach you not to do after all their abominations, which they have done unto their gods."[21] The Lord also commanded the ancient Israelites to not intermarry with those people or the Girgashites, "for they will turn away thy son from following me, that they may serve other gods."[22] In Christ's day, the Pharisees sought to persuade people, especially those from other nations who moved to Palestine, to become Pharisees and to associate with one of its schools of thought instead of the other school of thought. The Pharisees focused more on increasing the number of members in their religious party than on bringing people

---

21.   Deut. 20:17–18.
22.   Deut. 7:4; see also vv. 5–6 and 13.

to God and teaching them of righteousness, faith, and service to those in need. Those who became Pharisees, adopting the same beliefs, were likewise condemned by the Lord.

Jesus next gave the fourth woe:

Matthew 23:16–22. Woe unto you, ye blind guides, which say, Whosoever shall swear by the temple, it is nothing; but whosoever shall swear by the gold of the temple, he is a debtor! Ye fools and blind: for whether is greater, the gold, or the temple that sanctifieth the gold? And, Whosoever shall swear by the altar, it is nothing; but whosoever sweareth by the gift that is upon it, he is guilty. Ye fools and blind: for whether is greater, the gift, or the altar that sanctifieth the gift? Whoso therefore shall swear by the altar, sweareth by it, and by all things thereon. And whoso shall swear by the temple, sweareth by it, and by him that dwelleth therein. And he that shall swear by heaven, sweareth by the throne of God, and by him that sitteth thereon.

The scribes and Pharisees were blind to the truth and to their own sins. Therefore, these individuals were not fit to lead. Jesus also condemned the inconsistent and hypocritical rules of the Pharisees and the Sanhedrin concerning oaths.[23] These rules demonstrated the lax morals of the time, in that these rules provided an approved means of breaking an oath. Jesus gave two examples of how an oath could be broken, and He contrasted these methods with methods that were not acceptable, thereby pointing out the inconsistency and hypocrisy of the rules. In the first example, Jesus referred to the rabbis' teaching that if a person swore an oath referencing the temple, to give assurance that the oath would be binding, the person could obtain an indulgence, meaning that the oath could be broken or not enforced. In contrast, if a person swore by the gold of the temple, the oath could not be broken and must be enforced. In the second example, Jesus referred to the

---

23.   In the Sermon on the Mount, Christ taught that people should not make oaths, in contrast to the practice in Old Testament times (see Matt. 5:33–37; see also *HarperCollins Bible Dictionary*, s.v. "oath"). Not making worldly oaths was important to understand because Christ implicitly taught that "one day there will come a time when a man's word will be as good as his oath" (Dummelow, *Bible Commentary*, p. 642; see also McConkie, *Mortal Messiah*, vol. 2, p. 140). Today, oaths are common in certain judicial proceedings; similarly, vows are common in certain marriage ceremonies, and covenants involve binding agreements and are associated with certain ordinances in The Church of Jesus Christ of Latter-day Saints and in other religions.

fact that if a person swore an oath referencing the altar, to give assurance that the oath would be binding, the oath could be broken, but if a person swore by gold or another offering placed on the altar as a donation, the obligation could not be broken and must be enforced. These distinctions had no basis in the law; rather, they were developed to provide a way to be dishonest when it suited the one making the oath.

Morality had been replaced by hypocrisy. The scribes and Pharisees placed greater emphasis on the gold of the temple than on the house of the Lord. The scribes' and Pharisees' greed was evident, and they had missed the mark—they were blind and could not recognize Jesus, who stood in the temple courts, as the Son of God.

Moreover, the temple altar represented Christ's Atonement, during which He shed His blood for the sins of humankind. Therefore, the rabbis' decision to allow an oath sworn by the temple or altar to be broken may have been influenced by Satan as a subtle way to downplay the importance of God and Christ and Their commitment to all of God's children—a commitment that was evident in Christ's soon-to-come Atonement.

Jesus then declared the fifth woe:

Matthew 23:23–24. Woe unto you, scribes and Pharisees, hypocrites! for ye pay tithe of mint and anise and cummin, and have omitted the weightier matters of the law, judgment, mercy, and faith: these ought ye to have done, and not to leave the other undone. Ye blind guides, which strain at a gnat, and swallow a camel.

The Israelites had long observed the law of tithing. For example, Genesis 14:20 describes Abraham paying "tithes of all" to Melchizedek, the great high priest and king of Salem.[24] The Lord reaffirmed the principle of tithing in Moses's time when He directed that one-tenth of the land, the food it produced, and flocks of animals should be tithed and "holy unto the Lord."[25] The rabbis in Jesus's day had extended the law of the tithe to

---

24. See also Gen. 14:18–19.
25. Lev. 27:32; see also Lev. 27:30–31. In Moses's day, tithes were used, in part, to support the Levites, who did not have an inheritance in Canaan (see Num. 18:26). The Levites were to offer a heave offering unto the Lord as a way to express thanks to Him for the tithing they received (see Num. 18:24, 28; see also Edersheim, *Life and Times of Jesus the Messiah*, p. 101; Clarke, *Commentary*, vol. 1, p. 604).

include the smallest items, including herbs, such as mint, anise, and cumin, and the seeds, leaves, and stalks of certain plants.[26]

The Pharisees had fastidiously observed not only the law of tithing but also the rabbinical gloss put on the law. In doing so, they had ignored the more important aspects of the law, such as love, mercy, faith, and service to others, especially to those in need. The Pharisees scrupulously avoided insignificant breaches of the law while continually breaking its great commandments. Jesus then gave a rebuke: "Ye blind guides, which strain at a gnat, and swallow a camel." In most Bible translations, the word *at* in "straining at a gnat" is replaced with *out*, as in straining out a gnat from wine or water that a person is about to drink. Dummelow noted that gnats were considered by the rabbis to be unclean.[27] Pharisees would carefully strain their wine and drinking water through a cloth to avoid swallowing any gnats. Pharisees would, however, figuratively swallow a camel, which was one of the largest of the unclean animals. Perhaps the Pharisees' greatest sin was that they overlooked the sixth commandment—"Thou shalt not kill"[28]—as they plotted to take Jesus's life.

Jesus next gave the sixth woe:

> **Matthew 23:25–26.** Woe unto you, scribes and Pharisees, hypocrites! for ye make clean the outside of the cup and of the platter, but within they are full of extortion and excess. Thou blind Pharisee, cleanse first that which is within the cup and platter, that the outside of them may be clean also.

The Pharisees scrupulously cleaned cups, plates, and eating utensils, not just so that they were clean from disease but also so that the Pharisees would be ceremonially clean. Jesus called the scribes and Pharisees hypocrites for carefully washing the outside but ignoring what was inside, which included greed, excess, and extortion. The Pharisees loved money and luxury, including costly robes and luxurious homes, and became rich by taking advantage of people who worshiped at the temple. The Pharisees should have instead focused on supplying the poor with basic needs.

---

26. See Edersheim, *Life and Times of Jesus the Messiah*, p. 758.
27. Dummelow, *Bible Commentary*, p. 700.
28. Ex. 20:13.

Jesus then pronounced the seventh woe, which is one of the most poignant:

Matthew 23:27–28. Woe unto you, scribes and Pharisees, hypocrites! for ye are like unto whited sepulchres, which indeed appear beautiful outward, but are within full of dead men's bones, and of all uncleanness. Even so ye also outwardly appear righteous unto men, but within ye are full of hypocrisy and iniquity.

Likening the scribes and Pharisee to dead men's rotting bones and flesh must have caused revulsion and great anger in the scribes and Pharisees present, particularly because rabbis had pronounced that even the slightest contact with a corpse, its burial clothes, a funeral bier, or a grave caused personal defilement, which only ceremonial washing and sacrificial offerings could remove. Because of this teaching, the Jews put lime wash on sepulchers each fifteenth day of Adar (February/March)[29] to make the sepulchers stand out so that people, especially travelers, would not touch the sepulchers unawares and thereby be made unclean.[30]

However, no amount of whitening on the outside could prevent or cleanse decay within. Similarly, no amount of piety on the outside could prevent or cleanse the corruption within the Pharisees.[31] They were full of hypocrisy, corruption, and iniquity.

Jesus then gave the eighth woe:[32]

Matthew 23:29–33. Woe unto you, scribes and Pharisees, hypocrites! because ye build the tombs of the prophets, and garnish the sepulchres of the

29. *HarperCollins Bible Dictionary*, s.v. "calendar."
30. Dummelow, *Bible Commentary*, p. 700.
31. In Luke 11:44, Jesus compared the Pharisees to unmarked sepulchers. In Matthew 23:29–33, Jesus's likening of Pharisees to whited sepulchers emphasizes the Pharisees' hypocrisy.
32. The eight woes are somewhat similar to parts of the vision that the Apostle John saw and recorded in chapters 2 and 3 of the book of Revelation. He saw that the "angel" (i.e., bishop) in Ephesus and those in his congregation had "left thy first love"—that is, their zeal for the gospel. John saw the Jews in Smyrna blaspheme, the Church members in Pergamos uphold the doctrine of Balaam, and Jezebel in Thyatira seduce people "to commit fornication, and to eat things sacrificed unto idols" (Rev. 2:20). John also saw the Lord's servants in Sardis perform dead works, Jews in Philadelphia worship in "the synagogue of Satan" (Rev. 3:9), and the members in Laodicea demonstrate lukewarm faith. What John saw is also symbolic of the world today. One can learn much from Jesus's castigation of the scribes and Pharisees, along with the challenges that John saw.

righteous, and say, If we had been in the days of our fathers, we would not have been partakers with them in the blood of the prophets. Wherefore ye be witnesses unto yourselves, that ye are the children of them which killed the prophets. Fill ye up then the measure of your fathers. Ye serpents, ye generation of vipers, how can ye escape the damnation of hell?

People in many nations honor their esteemed dead. They build beautiful tombs and erect elegant headstones, garnishing them with plants, wreaths, and flowers. To honor those who have gone before is noble and uplifting. Jesus condemned the scribes and Pharisees for stating that they, unlike their ancestors, would not have taken the lives of prophets. Jesus stated that the scribes and Pharisees were of the same character as their ancestors who killed prophets. These scribes and Pharisees were witnesses against themselves, for they had already plotted to take Jesus's life. He then told them, "Fill ye up then the measure of your fathers." In other words, Jesus was saying, "Do as your fathers have done, by putting me to death." He would be voluntarily giving up His life, but they would be condemned for killing Him, just as they had condemned those who killed the prophets of old. He then referred to them as serpents and a "generation of vipers." Not only can serpents cause illness and possibly even death through their venom, but they are also symbolic of Satan, as he appeared as a serpent in the Garden of Eden when tempting Adam and Eve. These scribes and Pharisees soon would do Satan's bidding in taking Jesus's life. Evil and venom had filled their hearts.

Jesus then extended the idea in the eighth woe by stating that the scribes and Pharisees would persecute and take the lives of some of those who were righteous:

Matthew 23:34–36. Wherefore, behold, I send unto you prophets, and wise men, and scribes: and some of them ye shall kill and crucify; and some of them shall ye scourge in your synagogues, and persecute them from city to city: that upon you may come all the righteous blood shed upon the earth, from the blood of righteous Abel unto the blood of Zacharias son of Barachias, whom ye slew between the temple and the altar. Verily I say unto you, All these things shall come upon this generation.

Imagine the thoughts of the Apostles and other disciples as they heard Jesus say that some of them would be persecuted and even killed. Jesus then said that the blood of all righteous people from Abel to Zacharias[33] would serve as a witness of the scribes' and Pharisees' wickedness. The day of judgment would come.

Jesus's final teachings to the multitude in the temple on the last Tuesday of His life centered on the sins related to pride and hypocrisy. These teachings are worth serious consideration, as are Jesus's other teachings, because the sins of pride and hypocrisy are prevalent today throughout the world. As has been repeatedly mentioned, pride is at the heart of most sins, and hypocrisy deals with sin buried beneath outward appearances of righteousness. Jesus's castigation of the scribes and Pharisees may lead people to self-reflect and ask questions such as the following: Do I act differently when no one else is around? Am I a different person at work or in business than at home or at church? Am I honest? Do I take advantage of others? Am I greedy? Do I really love my neighbor? Am I willing to forgive? Hypocrisy and its attendant sins drive away the Spirit of the Lord and put people at risk of becoming "whited sepulchers."

Jesus Laments over Jerusalem (Matt. 23:37–39)

From the temple mount, Jesus could see the temple, its courts, and the multitude of people at the temple in preparation for the Passover. He could also see a large portion of Jerusalem. To the east, He could see Gethsemane below, and to the west He could see Golgotha. With deep sorrow, Jesus presumably looked out from the temple and pondered the fate of the city and, more importantly, its people—His people. People He had taught and left His witness with. People who would be born in upcoming years and would witness Jerusalem's destruction. With the deepest anguish of soul, He declared the following, perhaps in the hearing of others:

> **Matthew 23:37–39.** O Jerusalem, Jerusalem, thou that killest the prophets, and stonest them which are sent unto thee, how often would I have gathered thy children together, even as a hen gathereth her chickens under her wings, and ye would not! Behold, your house is left unto you desolate. For I say

---

33.   See chapter 41 note 1 in volume 3 of this series for a discussion of which Zacharias Jesus was speaking about.

unto you, Ye shall not see me henceforth, till ye shall say, Blessed is he that cometh in the name of the Lord.

Even though Jews had killed ancient prophets and now conspired to cause Jesus's death, He wished with infinite love and mercy to spread His protective wings over the people. But most had chosen to reject Him. The temple, which He had previously declared to be His and His Father's house, He now declared to be the Jews' house and stated that it would be left desolate. In fewer than forty years, the Roman eagle would spread its wings over Jerusalem, causing its total destruction and slaying or taking captive approximately two million Jews.

Jesus's anguished statement is expanded in Joseph Smith's translation of verse 39: "For I say unto you, that ye shall not see me henceforth and know that I am he of whom it is written by the prophets, until ye shall say: Blessed is he who cometh in the name of the Lord, in the clouds of heaven, and all the holy angels with him. Then understood his disciples that he should come again on the earth, after that he was glorified and crowned on the right hand of God."[34]

Jesus will not publicly come to the Jews again until the time of His glorious Second Coming, when His feet will be upon the Mount of Olives as it cleaves in two.[35] At that day, "one shall say unto him, What are these wounds in thine hands? Then he shall answer, Those with which I was wounded in the house of my friends."[36]

Even though the Apostles would see Jesus die on the cross and spend forty days with Him after His Resurrection,[37] they will not fully comprehend who He is and the fulness of his glory until He returns to earth in the "clouds of heaven"[38] and is "crowned on the right hand of God." All the righteous on earth and in heaven will then say, "Blessed is he that cometh in the name of the Lord."[39]

---

34. JST Matt. 1:1.
35. See Zech. 14:2–4.
36. Zech. 13:6.
37. See Acts 1:3.
38. Matt. 24:30.
39. This prophecy was the impetus for the Apostles' inquiry in Matthew 24 about the future of the temple and Christ's return to the earth.

Greeks Seek Jesus, He Testifies of Himself, and God Speaks from Heaven (John 12:20–36)

Some of the people who came to Jerusalem for the Feast of the Passover were from Greece. These Greeks likely had heard of Jesus's miracles and teachings and desired to see Jesus. Presumably out of respect and possibly not wanting to interrupt Jesus, they asked Philip for an introduction. They must have recognized Philip as one of Jesus's closest followers, and they likely saw the awe and respect Philip had for Jesus. Philip sought out his close associate Andrew to discuss whether to trouble Jesus with an introduction. They decided to approach Jesus on behalf of the Greeks, and though the record is silent as to whether Jesus met with the Greeks, presumably He graciously did. They may have been with Him when He declared that "the hour is come, that the Son of man should be glorified."[40]

The following is John's account:

John 12:20–36. And there were certain Greeks among them that came up to worship at the feast: the same came therefore to Philip, which was of Bethsaida of Galilee, and desired him, saying, Sir, we would see Jesus. Philip cometh and telleth Andrew: and again Andrew and Philip tell Jesus. And Jesus answered them, saying, The hour is come, that the Son of man should be glorified. Verily, verily, I say unto you, Except a corn of wheat fall into the ground and die, it abideth alone: but if it die, it bringeth forth much fruit. He that loveth his life shall lose it; and he that hateth his life in this world shall keep it unto life eternal. If any man serve me, let him follow me; and where I am, there shall also my servant be: if any man serve me, him will my Father honour. Now is my soul troubled; and what shall I say? Father, save me from this hour: but for this cause came I unto this hour. Father, glorify thy name. Then came there a voice from heaven, saying, I have both glorified it, and will glorify it again. The people therefore, that stood by, and heard it, said that it thundered: others said, An angel spake to him. Jesus answered and said, This voice came not because of me, but for your sakes. Now is the judgment of this world: now shall the prince of this world be cast out. And I, if I be lifted up from the earth, will draw all men unto me. This he said, signifying what death he should die. The people answered him, We have

---

40. John 12:23.

heard out of the law that Christ abideth for ever: and how sayest thou, The
Son of man must be lifted up? who is this Son of man? Then Jesus said unto
them, Yet a little while is the light with you. Walk while ye have the light,
lest darkness come upon you: for he that walketh in darkness knoweth not
whither he goeth. While ye have light, believe in the light, that ye may be the
children of light.[41]

Jesus presented a metaphor involving farming, presumably to help those
listening to understand, ponder, and remember what He was teaching. In
speaking about a grain of wheat, Jesus was essentially stating that if a farmer
eats all the wheat rather than planting some, the farmer will never reap a
harvest. The seeds must be sacrificed to bring forth a bounty. Those who
heard Jesus speak at this time might have for the rest of their lives thought
of Jesus whenever they saw a wheat seed or a field of wheat. And they would
certainly come to understand more fully the deeper meaning of Jesus's words
when they saw Him die just three days later, when they heard that He was
buried in a borrowed tomb, and when they learned that He rose from the
tomb the following Sunday.

Jesus then emphasized His teaching by stating, "He that loveth his life
shall lose it; and he that hateth his life in this world shall keep it unto life
eternal." In other words, those who selfishly focus on themselves will lose
their opportunity to receive eternal life, and those who are willing to sacrifice
even their own lives for the sake of God's kingdom will inherit eternal life.
This teaching was particularly applicable to the Apostles, who would be
severely persecuted following Jesus's death. He then explained that if people
believed in Him as the Light of the World and followed and served Him,
their Father in Heaven would honor them.

Next, Jesus stated that His soul was troubled. Presumably, He was thinking
about what He still needed to do as part of His mortal mission, particularly
atoning in Gethsemane and on the cross for the sins of humankind and then

---

41.   It is uncertain when the Greeks approached Philip. Some scholars believe that the
Greeks asked for an introduction on the Sunday that Jesus triumphantly entered Jerusalem,
whereas other scholars believe that the Greeks asked the next day (see Farrar, *Life of Christ*,
p. 483; Talmage, *Jesus the Christ*, p. 482). In this volume, the account is placed toward the
end of Tuesday—the last time Jesus taught publicly—because at this time Jesus beseeched
His Father to save Him "from this hour" (John 12:27) and the voice of His Father was heard
glorifying Jesus.

being resurrected, enabling all people to live again. Jesus raised His voice to His Father and pled, presumably in the hearing of those present, "Save me from this hour," but then He added He knew that what was to occur in "this hour" was the principal reason He had come to the earth. Then He said, "Father, glorify thy name." Even though Jesus would soon suffer beyond that of any other mortal, He desired to glorify the name of His Father. Jesus was not seeking glory for Himself, as Satan had in the premortal world. The glory was always to be the Father's. Jesus's words at this time were a great demonstration of His humility and His determination to fulfill the commitment He had made in the premortal realms.

After Jesus finished praying to His Father, "then came there a voice from heaven, saying, I have both glorified it, and will glorify it again." In essence, Heavenly Father was saying He had complete confidence that Christ would valiantly complete His earthly mission. Hearing these words must have given Christ great comfort.

The scriptures speak of two other times that the voice of God was heard during Christ's life: (1) at His baptism, in the presence of John the Baptist, and (2) at His transfiguration, in the presence of Peter, James, and John.[42] Those who were present with Christ could serve as additional witnesses of God. This third time, some of those who heard God's voice thought it sounded like thunder; others thought an angel had spoken. Of course, Christ—and presumably some others—knew that the voice was God's. Christ then explained that God had spoken not only for Christ but for them. How marvelous to hear God witness of His Son. Hearing the voice of God likely strengthened the testimonies of the Apostles and other disciples, further preparing them for what was to come. Perhaps, this witness in some way helped pave the way for the ministry of Paul, who saw the risen Christ and heard His voice while traveling to Damascus.[43]

Jesus then declared that Satan, the "prince of this world,"[44] would ultimately be cast out of this world. The book of Revelation states that

---

42. See Matt. 3:17; Mark 1:11; Matt. 17:5; Mark 9:7. There were likely additional times that God spoke from heaven during Jesus's ministry, such as during His youth, during His forty-day fast following His baptism, and during other times when He prayed alone.

43. See Acts 9:1–7.

44. See also 2 Cor. 4:4.

when Jesus institutes His millennial reign, He will bind Satan, cast him into a bottomless pit, and set a seal upon him. After a thousand years, Satan will be loosed to once again tempt humankind and then will be cast into a lake of fire and brimstone, there to reside forever.[45] Ultimately, good will triumph over evil. This principle is profoundly important for all people to understand.

Next, Christ explained that He would "be lifted up"—a reference to the manner of His death—and would thereby draw all people unto Him.[46] Those present asked who the Son of Man was. They apparently understood that the promised Messiah would reign forever but did not understand that His glory would result from His overcoming the world and that He would reign forever as the resurrected Lord.

Rather than answering the question directly, Jesus told those with Him to walk in His light while He remained on earth and then to continue to walk in that light so that darkness would not overcome them. Jesus was teaching that all people need to believe in Him as the Light of the World so that they can become "children of light."

The People React to Jesus's Teachings (John 12:37–43)

The Gospel of John then states that even though Jesus had performed great miracles, many refused to believe in Him, whereas others believed but would not admit that they did:

> **John 12:37–43.** But though he had done so many miracles before them, yet they believed not on him: That the saying of Esaias the prophet might be fulfilled, which he spake, Lord, who hath believed our report? and to whom hath the arm of the Lord been revealed? Therefore they could not believe, because that Esaias said again, He hath blinded their eyes, and hardened their heart; that they should not see with their eyes, nor understand with their heart, and be converted, and I should heal them. These things said Esaias, when he saw his glory, and spake of him. Nevertheless among the chief rulers also many believed on him; but because of the Pharisees they did not confess him, lest they should be put out of the synagogue: for they loved the praise of men more than the praise of God.

---

45.   See Rev. 20:1–3, 7–10.
46.   See also 3 Ne. 27:13–16.

The name Esaias refers to Isaiah, who had asked in Old Testament times: "Who hath believed our report? And to whom is the arm of the Lord revealed?"[47] John continued by referring to more of Isaiah's words: "Make the heart of this people fat, and make their ears heavy, and shut their eyes; lest they see with their eyes, and hear with their ears, and understand with their heart, and convert, and be healed."[48] Isaiah foresaw that many during Jesus's mortal ministry would refuse to believe in Him because they could not spiritually hear, see, or understand.

In contrast, some of the chief rulers, such as Nicodemus, did believe but chose not to openly confess their belief, because "they loved the praise of men more than the praise of God." Similarly, many people today refuse to believe, and some believers do not openly admit they believe because they do not want to face the scorn of unbelievers.

Jesus Declares That Those Who Believe in Him Will Believe in His Father (John 12:44–50)

The Gospel of John then returns to what Jesus was teaching the people:

John 12:44–50. Jesus cried and said, He that believeth on me, believeth not on me, but on him that sent me. And he that seeth me seeth him that sent me. I am come a light into the world, that whosoever believeth on me should not abide in darkness. And if any man hear my words, and believe not, I judge him not: for I came not to judge the world, but to save the world. He that rejecteth me, and receiveth not my words, hath one that judgeth him: the word that I have spoken, the same shall judge him in the last day. For I have not spoken of myself; but the Father which sent me, he gave me a commandment, what I should say, and what I should speak. And I know that his commandment is life everlasting: whatsoever I speak therefore, even as the Father said unto me, so I speak.

Jesus exclaimed that those who believed in Him would also believe in God, who had sent Jesus, and that He was in the image of His Father. Jesus then affirmed that He was the Light of the World and that those who believe in Him would not be comfortable in the spiritual darkness that Satan creates.

---

47. Isa. 53:1.
48. Isa. 6:10.

Jesus then stated, as He had done before, that He was sent to the world to save it, not to judge or condemn it.[49] This salvation came through Jesus's Atonement, death, and Resurrection.

Jesus also taught that all people will be judged according to whether they follow His teachings, which came from God. Jesus then testified that following the commandments of God leads to everlasting life. Jesus then reaffirmed that His gospel message is of the Father. What marvelous truths Jesus declared! With some of His final words, He gave His witness of the Father and of willingness to do the Father's will.

The Widow Donates Two Mites (Mark 12:41–44; Luke 21:1–4)

Jesus now moved to the temple's easternmost court, known as the Court of the Women, which contained the temple treasury, where donations were made. While there, Jesus saw a widow make a most significant monetary sacrifice:

Mark 12:41–44. And Jesus sat over against the treasury, and beheld how the people cast money into the treasury: and many that were rich cast in much. And there came a certain poor widow, and she threw in two mites, which make a farthing. And he called unto him his disciples, and saith unto them, Verily I say unto you, That this poor widow hath cast more in, than all they which have cast into the treasury: for all they did cast in of their abundance; but she of her want did cast in all that she had, even all her living.

While Jesus was in the Court of the Women, He must have been filled with sorrow because the Pharisees, Sadducees, and scribes had rejected Him and had attempted to trap Him in some violation of the law, such as committing blasphemy. Malice, pride, and hypocrisy had filled their hearts. Presumably, it was now in the afternoon, and Jesus was likely exhausted because of all that had already occurred in the temple courts this day. He likely sought a moment of peace while in the Court of the Women.

The temple treasury in the Court of the Women contained thirteen chests, each of which had receptacles that were shaped like trumpets.[50] Eleven of the chests were for voluntary offerings of money, and two were for the half-shekel temple tax. Each of the voluntary-offering chests was for

49. See also John 3:17.
50. See Edersheim, *Life and Times of Jesus the Messiah*, p. 741.

a different category of offerings. One of the chests was for donations to use in purchasing turtledoves for burnt and sin offerings. Another chest was for donating funds to purchase pigeons to be used as an offering, and another chest was for contributions for the wood used in temple offerings. Other chests were for donating money for incense, the temple ministry, trespass offerings, the offering of the Nazarite, offerings of cleansed lepers, and other voluntary offerings. There was also a chest called the "chamber of the silent," in which people secretly deposited money for educating children of the poor.[51]

While in the Court of the Women, Jesus saw people deposit money in the chests. Some of these people were rich and likely dressed in fine robes. They may have ostentatiously dropped large numbers of gold and silver coins into the chests, desiring all other people in the court to see the donations being made and to hear the clink of the money as it was deposited into the chests. Jesus also saw a poor widow deposit, perhaps timidly, into one of the chests her tiny contribution of two mites—the minimum amount lawful to donate. Mites, also called prutahs or leptons, were bronze coins and were the currency with the smallest value.[52] A mite is equivalent to less than one cent in US money today.[53]

This widow may have shrunk with the shame of her poverty as she donated such a trivial amount while the rich were depositing much greater amounts. If the rich saw her donation, they may have even ridiculed her for giving so little.

Jesus had spent much of the day responding to and rebuking the hypocritical Pharisees, and here was a poor widow who had given all she had. He called His disciples to Him to teach a sweet lesson—a lesson that His disciples would likely never forget. He told them, "This poor widow hath cast more in, than all they which have cast into the treasury: for all they did cast in of their abundance; but she of her want did cast in all that she had,

---

51. See Edersheim, *Life and Times of Jesus the Messiah*, p. 741; see also Dummelow, *Bible Commentary*, p. 731.

52. See Edersheim, *Life and Times of Jesus the Messiah*, p. 741; Farrar, *Life of Christ*, p. 515; Talmage, *Jesus the Christ*, p. 522. Two mites amounted to approximately a farthing (see Smith, *Bible Dictionary*, s.v. "farthing").

53. See Smith, *Bible Dictionary*, s.v. "mite."

even all her living." As St. Ambrose stated, "One coin out of a little is better than a treasure out of much; for it is not considered how much is given, but how much remains behind."[54] Additionally, Paul told the Corinthian Saints, "For if there be first a willing mind, it is accepted according to that a man hath, and not according to that he hath not."[55] The widow's name is not mentioned, nor is anything known about her family or where she lived; further, she did not have a high station in life. Nevertheless, the story of her simple but significant act has been told through the centuries and is an example to all people.

Heavenly Father and Jesus Christ are aware of each person, including his or her financial situation, weaknesses and strengths, and thoughts and desires. Though people are not equal in terms of wealth and abilities, all people have an equal opportunity to develop a Christlike character. This impoverished woman gave all she had. Her great sacrifice and deep devotion will be eternally rewarded. Although this widow's donation was modest, in a spiritual sense it was the largest of gifts donated in the temple treasury and represented her consecration and devotion to the Lord. Her sacrifice was presumably recorded in heaven and engraved on her heart. This scene was a fitting end to Christ's time in the temple courts this last Tuesday of His life. What a sweet and joyful experience it must have been for the Savior of the world to witness this woman's humble gift.

Sometime after seeing the widow make her generous donation, Jesus left the temple for the last time in His mortality. His public ministry was now at a solemn end.[56]

---

54.   As qtd. in Farrar, *Life of Christ*, p. 515.
55.   2 Cor. 8:12.
56.   See John 12:36.

Chapter 54

JESUS'S PROPHECY OF COMING TRIBULATIONS

(Tuesday)

It was now Tuesday afternoon, and Jesus and His Apostles were ready to depart from the temple. Jesus's declaration that "your house is left unto you desolate"[1] apparently led His Apostles to ask Him two questions: one about the coming destruction of Jerusalem and the other about His Second Coming. This chapter explores Jesus's response to the first question.[2]

Jesus Foretells the Destruction of the Temple (Matt. 23:38; 24:1–2; Mark 13:1–2; Luke 21:5–6; JS—M 1:2–3)

After departing the temple, Jesus and His Apostles headed to the Mount of Olives.[3] Apparently contemplating Jesus's recent words about the temple, the Apostles discussed with Him this imposing building—with its massive stones, impressive walls, great doors, and beautiful colonnades[4]—and its future:[5]

Mark 13:1–2. And as he went out of the temple, one of his disciples saith unto him, Master, see what manner of stones and what buildings

---

1.   Matt. 23:38.
2.   Chapters 55 and 56 of this volume explore Jesus's response to the second question.
3.   See Matt. 24:3.
4.   See note 1 at the end of this chapter for Farrar's description of the temple.
5.   In a revelation to Joseph Smith, the Lord recounted His response to His Apostles as follows: "And now ye behold this temple which is in Jerusalem, which ye call the house of God, and your enemies say that this house shall never fall. . . . And this temple which ye now see shall be thrown down that there shall not be left one stone upon another." (D&C 45:18, 20.)

are here! And Jesus answering said unto him, Seest thou these great buildings? There shall not be left one stone upon another, that shall not be thrown down.

Luke 21:5–6. And as some spake of the temple, how it was adorned with goodly stoanes and gifts, he said, As for these things which ye behold, the days will come, in the which there shall not be left one stone upon another, that shall not be thrown down.

Jesus and the Apostles had spent most of the last two and possibly three days at the temple, and the Apostles seemed to be focusing on the temple's magnificent structure, not on its purpose as the house of the Lord or on those who humbly worshipped and gave offerings there.

In response to the Apostles' praise of the structure, Jesus gave them a dire prophecy concerning the future of this great building. The temple had been known as His and His Father's house but had been reduced to the house of the Jews, for its sacredness had been defiled by the avarice of some of the temple priests, scribes, Pharisees, Sanhedrin, the high priest, and his family and would be further defiled by the wickedness of the common people.[6] Jesus's statement that the temple would be destroyed raised further questions in the minds of the Apostles, which they asked Jesus after arriving at the Mount of Olives.

Jesus Prophesies concerning the Destruction of Jerusalem (Matt. 24:3–22; Mark 13:3–22; Luke 21:7–24; JS—M 1:4–22)

Jesus may have walked ahead of the Apostles as they ascended the Mount of Olives. Perhaps He looked for a secluded place where Jerusalem, including the temple, was in view. After finding a place to stop, Jesus sat down, presumably to rest, absorb the scene of the city He loved, and contemplate the people there preparing for the Passover and what was to occur on Thursday and Friday and then on Sunday morning.

---

6. See note 2 at the end of this chapter for a synopsis of the events leading up to and during the destruction of Jerusalem.

Apostles[7] came to Jesus and asked Him two questions:

Matthew 24:3. And as he sat upon the mount of Olives, the disciples came unto him privately, saying, Tell us, when shall these things be? and what shall be the sign of thy coming, and of the end of the world?

When Jesus responded to His Apostles' question about the timing of the destruction of Jerusalem and the temple, rather than telling the Apostles the date, He told them about signs they should look for. The implication was that some time would elapse before the destruction occurred and that at least some of the Apostles might be alive to see some of the signs spoken of.

Jesus Warns about Being Deceived by False Christs (Matt. 24:4–5; Mark 13:5–6; Luke 21:8; JS—M 1:5–6)

All three synoptic Gospel writers recorded the first sign Jesus gave: that there would be false Christs:

Luke 21:8. And he said, Take heed that ye be not deceived: for many shall come in my name, saying, I am Christ; and the time draweth near: go ye not therefore after them.

In conjunction with this sign, Jesus warned His Apostles to beware of false Christs, who would claim that the glorious Second Coming drew near. There is little scriptural evidence of such false Christs; however, there were those, especially among the Zealots,[8] who claimed they could save the city and the temple or set in motion things that the Zealots thought would force the Messiah to come and deliver them. Jesus had already told His Apostles that the temple would be destroyed and that the time of Jerusalem's destruction drew near, so they were not to be deceived either by false claims that the city would be delivered or by false predictions concerning the Messiah's coming. Jesus's first and paramount counsel to His Apostles was to "go ye not therefore after them"—that is, do not believe or follow false Christs.

---

7.   Mark 13:3 specifies that Peter, James, John, and Andrew came to Christ, whereas the other accounts, including the Joseph Smith translation of Mark 13:3, indicate that the "disciples" (i.e., Apostles) came to Jesus. Perhaps Peter, James, John, and Andrew were followed by the other Apostles.

8.   See note 2 at the end of this chapter.

Nor were the Apostles to follow the emperors of Rome who claimed to be the embodiment of deity. Rome, with all its power and might, would destroy the city and the temple but could not give anyone eternal life.

Jesus presumably wanted the Apostles to understand that the destruction of Jerusalem and the temple would come relatively shortly and was not a sign of His glorious Second Coming.

Jesus Warns about Persecution (Matt. 24:9–10; Mark 13:9; Luke 21:12–19; JS—M 1:7–8)

Jesus then gave His Apostles the second sign: that they would face serious persecution as they went forth as His representatives. Luke's account is as follows:

> **Luke 21:12–19.** But before all these, they shall lay their hands on you, and persecute you, delivering you up to the synagogues, and into prisons, being brought before kings and rulers for my name's sake. And it shall turn to you for a testimony. Settle it therefore in your hearts, not to meditate before what ye shall answer: For I will give you a mouth and wisdom, which all your adversaries shall not be able to gainsay nor resist. And ye shall be betrayed both by parents, and brethren, and kinsfolks, and friends; and some of you shall they cause to be put to death. And ye shall be hated of all men for my name's sake. But there shall not an hair of your head perish. In your patience possess ye your souls.

Jesus's statement that the Apostles would be delivered "up to the synagogues" indicates that other Jews would be among those who persecuted the Apostles. Jesus also told the Apostles that they would be cast into prison and "brought before kings and rulers"—that is, the Apostles would also suffer persecution at the hands of Rome. Amid this persecution, the Apostles' testimonies would increase, for the Holy Ghost would give them the words they needed to say, thereby confounding their enemies.

The Romans' persecution, particularly under Nero, of Christians is well documented.[9] For example, Nero had some Christians "sewed up in the skins of wild beasts, and then worried by dogs till they expired; and others dressed in shirts made stiff with wax, fixed to axles-trees, and set on fire in

---

9.   Fox, *Book of Martyrs*, pp. 7–8.

his garden."[10] Some historians believe that Nero was the arsonist who caused the great fire in Rome and that he blamed Christians.[11]

Clarke stated the following regarding examples of the persecution of Christians:

> We need go no farther than the Acts of the Apostles for the completion of these particulars. Some were delivered to councils, as Peter and John, Acts iv.5. Some were brought before rulers and kings, as Paul before Gallio, chap. Xviii.12, before Felix, xxiv., before Festus and Agrippa, xxv. Some had utterance and wisdom which their adversaries were not able to resist: so Stephen, chap. Vi.10, and Paul, who made even Felix himself tremble, chap 22iv.25. Some were imprisoned, as Peter and John, chapt.1v.3. Some were beaten, as Paul and Silas, chap. Xvi23. Some were put to death, as Stephen, chap. Vii.59, and James the brother of John, chap. Xii.2. But if we look beyond the book of Acts of the Apostles, to the bloody persecutions under Nero, we shall find these predictions still more amply fulfilled: in these, numberless Christians fell, beside those two champions of the faith, Peter and Paul.[12]

Next, Jesus told the Apostles that they would be betrayed by family members and friends. Perhaps this statement cut deeper than the thought of being imprisoned did, for not only would they be betrayed but their betrayers would be family or friends who had either lost their testimonies or rejected the Apostles' witness of Christ. Further, some of the betrayers would even cause the Apostles to be killed.[13] History confirms the truth of Jesus's prophecy.

It is human nature to want to be liked and respected, but Jesus then told His Apostles that they would be hated by all people because the Apostles were emissaries of the gospel. By teaching of coming persecution, Jesus was implicitly teaching about the foundational principles of faith, obedience, sacrifice, consecration, and endurance to the end.

After prophesying of the severe challenges the Apostles would face, Jesus gave marvelous assurance that God was mindful of them, for not even a hair of their heads would ultimately be lost. In other words, though death would come, they would be resurrected with perfect bodies. As the prophet

---

10. Fox, *Book of Martyrs*, pp. 7–8.
11. See Fox, *Book of Martyrs*, p. 9.
12. Clarke, *Commentary*, vol. 5, p. 228.
13. See chapter 51 of this volume for a discussion about Apostles who were martyred.

Alma in the Book of Mormon taught, "The soul shall be restored to the body, and the body to the soul; yea, and every limb and joint shall be restored to its body; yea, even a hair of the head shall not be lost; but all things shall be restored to their proper and perfect frame."[14]

Jesus Warns about False Prophets (Matt. 24:11; JST Mark 13:12; JS—M 1:9)

Christ then gave the third sign: false prophets:

Matthew 24:11. And many false prophets shall rise, and shall deceive many.

Regarding false prophets prior to the destruction of Jerusalem, Josephus wrote that "there came out of Egypt about this time to Jerusalem, one that said he was a prophet, and advised the multitude of the common people to go along with him to the mount of Olives, as it was called, which lay over against the city, and at the distance of five furlongs. He said further, that he would shew them from hence, how, at his command, the walls of Jerusalem would fall down; and he promised them that he would procure them an entrance into the city through those walls, when they were fallen down."[15]

Josephus further recorded that "a false prophet was the occasion of these people's destruction, who had made a public proclamation in the city that very day, that God commanded them to get up upon the temple, and that there they should receive miraculous signs of their deliverance. Now, there was then a great number of false prophets suborned by the tyrants to impose upon the people . . . that they should wait for deliverance from God."[16]

Jesus Teaches That the Love of Many Will Wax Cold (Matt. 24:12; JST Mark 13:13; JS—M 1:10)

The following is the fourth sign Jesus told His Apostles about:

Matthew 24:12. And because iniquity shall abound, the love of many shall wax cold.

Jesus's statement indicates that the destruction of Jerusalem was not to occur solely because of Rome but also because of iniquity among the Jews.[17]

---

14. Alma 40:23.
15. Josephus, *Antiquities*, 20.8.6.
16. Josephus, *Wars*, 6.5.2.
17. Note 2 at the end of this chapter describes the iniquity and strife among the Jews.

Love that has waxed cold may involve various things. Certainly, a lack of love for God brings about spiritual coldness, as can a lack of love for others. A lack of love for God and others leads to characteristics and actions such as those Paul discussed in his letter to the Romans: "Being filled with all unrighteousness, fornication, wickedness, covetousness, maliciousness; full of envy, murder, debate, deceit, malignity; whisperers, backbiters, haters of God, despiteful, proud, boasters, inventors of evil things, disobedient to parents, without understanding, covenantbreakers, without natural affection, implacable, unmerciful: who knowing the judgment of God, that they which commit such things are worthy of death, not only do the same, but have pleasure in them that do them."[18]

Jesus Prophesies about Wars, Natural Disasters, and Other Troubles (Matt. 24:6–8; Mark 13:7–8; Luke 21:9–11)

Jesus then identified the fifth sign:

Mark 13:7–8. And when ye shall hear of wars and rumours of wars, be ye not troubled: for such things must needs be; but the end shall not be yet. For nation shall rise against nation, and kingdom against kingdom: and there shall be earthquakes in divers places, and there shall be famines and troubles: these are the beginnings of sorrows.

Matthew's and Luke's records include the word *pestilences*,[19] and Luke's record also states that "fearful sights and great signs shall there be from heaven."[20] Despite these troubling circumstances, Luke's account states, "Be not terrified: for these things must first come to pass; but the end is not by and by."[21]

Some of the specific events Jesus was referring to here came at the time of His death. There was darkness over all the earth, the veil of the temple in Jerusalem was rent,[22] there was an earthquake, and rocks broke into pieces.[23] In the Americas (included in the "divers places" in Matthew 24:7 and Mark 13:8),

---

18. Rom. 1:29–32.
19. Matt. 24:7; Luke 21:11.
20. Luke 21:11.
21. Luke 21:9.
22. See Luke 23:44–45.
23. See Matt. 27:51.

there were tempests, earthquakes, fires, whirlwinds, upheavals, and thick darkness, resulting in the destruction of mountains, cities, and the wicked.[24]

Josephus wrote that closer to the time of Jerusalem's destruction, there was "a star resembling a sword, which stood over the city, and a comet that continued a whole year."[25] He also wrote of a "prodigious storm in the night when the Idumeans were at the gate of Jerusalem, with the utmost violence, and very strong winds, with the largest showers of rain and continual lightnings, terrible thunderings, and amazing concussions and bellowings of the earth that was in an earthquake."[26]

An example of the prophesied troubles is Jerusalem's increasing corruption. As one example, Josephus recorded that in about AD 48, the Jews' affairs

> grew worse and worse continually; for the country was again filled with robbers and imposters, who deluded the multitude. . . . These robbers went up to the city, as if they were going to worship God, while they had daggers under their garments; and, by thus mingling themselves among the multitude, they slew Jonathan . . . and mingling themselves among the multitude, they slew certain of their enemies . . . and slew others not only in remote parts of the city, but in the temple itself also. . . . And it seems to me to have been the reason why God, out of his hatred to these men's wickedness, rejected our city; and as for the temple, he no longer esteemed it sufficiently pure for him to inhabit therein, but brought the Romans upon us, and threw a fire upon the city to purge it; and brought upon us, our wives, and children, slavery.[27]

Further, Josephus explained that after King Agrippa appointed Ismael as the high priest, sedition arose

> between the high priests and the principal men of the multitude of Jerusalem. . . . And there was nobody to reprove them; but these disorders were after a licentious manner in the city, as if it had no government over it. And such was the impudence and boldness that had seized on the high priests, that they had the hardness to send their servants into the thrashing-floors, to take away those tithes that were due to the priests,

24.   See 3 Ne. 8.
25.   Josephus, *Wars*, 6.6.2.
26.   Josephus, *Wars*, 4.4.5.
27.   Josephus, *Antiquities*, 20.8.5.

insomuch that it so fell out that the poorer sort of the priests died for want. To this degree did the violence of the seditious prevail over all right and justice.[28]

As examples of wars, in the decades following Christ's death, the Roman Empire forcefully expanded into Europe, the Near East, and northern Africa. Additionally, there was civil strife and turmoil in Rome. Emperor Caligula was assassinated, as was Nero's father, Claudius. Rome was burned in AD 64. Moreover, Jerusalem fell to Rome in AD 70,[29] and Masada fell to Rome three years later.

Jesus Teaches That the Gospel Will Be Preached among All Nations (Matt. 24:14; Mark 13:10)[30]

Jesus then gave the sixth sign: that before Jerusalem was destroyed, the Apostles would have an opportunity to take the gospel to the then-known world:

Mark 13:10. And the gospel must first be published among all nations.

Notwithstanding the great calamities Jesus prophesied of, the Apostles were to bear witness of Christ throughout the world. They would have sufficient time to accomplish their responsibility of spreading the gospel in accordance with Heavenly Father's plan.

Jesus Teaches about the Abomination of Desolation (Matt. 24:15; Mark 13:14; Luke 21:20; JS—M 1:12)

Next, Jesus gave the seventh sign:

Joseph Smith—Matthew 1:12. When you, therefore, shall see the abomination of desolation, spoken of by Daniel the prophet, concerning the destruction of Jerusalem, then you shall stand in the holy place; whoso readeth let him understand.

28. Josephus, *Antiquities*, 20.8.8.
29. See note 2 at the end of this chapter for an account of the events leading up to and during the destruction of Jerusalem.
30. Joseph Smith's translation of Matthew 24 does not include preaching the gospel to the world as a sign preceding the destruction of Jerusalem and the temple. He included this item among the signs given of the Lord's Second Coming (see v. 31). Nevertheless, this duty may also have been a sign preceding the destruction of Jerusalem and the temple.

The abomination of desolation spoken of would consist of the desecration and destruction of Jerusalem's temple.[31] Jesus taught that upon seeing the abomination of desolation, Christians were to "stand in the holy place." The scriptures do not explain where this holy place was located. It is worth considering some possibilities, for the underlying principles may be applicable to the latter days, when the abomination of desolation will once again occur. The holy place likely was not the temple because it is doubtful that the presumably large number of Christians could all gather in the temple, especially without other Jews taking notice and taking action against the Christians, possibly even to the point of physical violence.[32] Moreover, as Dummelow explained, soon after Titus's army had encompassed Jerusalem, "the Zealots seized the Temple."[33]

The holy place may have been the Christians' homes. It is possible that, perhaps by the power of the priesthood, the homes of the Christians were sanctified as holy places. A similar situation occurred when the Lord told the Israelites to place the blood of a lamb around the doors of their houses so that the Israelites' firstborn sons would be passed over and only the firstborn of the Egyptians would be killed.[34]

It is also possible that the holy place was a location designated by one or more of the Apostles as a safe place in which Christians could gather to receive prophetic guidance and direction. Christ's statement concerning the holy place may even have been a direction for the Apostles, or at least one of them, to designate a place and dedicate it for the gathering of the Christians during the destruction of Jerusalem. Such a place was likely outside of Jerusalem.

Insight regarding what may have occurred at the holy place can be found in Daniel's prophecy, of which the Savior spoke. Daniel's prophecy is as follows: "And after threescore and two weeks shall Messiah be cut off, but not for himself: and the people of the prince that shall come shall destroy

---

31.   The temple in Jerusalem had been destroyed at least twice before: first by the Babylonian armies of Nebuchadnezzar shortly before 600 BC and then by the Seleucid armies of Antiochus IV Epiphanes in approximately 170 BC. In both cases, the temple had been desecrated. (See 2 Kgs. 25; vol. 1., pp. 58, 61–62, in this series; Maccabees 1, 1:21–43.)

32.   Many Jews persecuted Christians (see Lyon, *Apostasy to Restoration*, pp. 54–56).

33.   Dummelow, *Bible Commentary*, p. 703.

34.   See Ex. 12:3–13.

the city and the sanctuary; and the end thereof shall be with a flood, and unto the end of the war desolations are determined. And he shall *confirm the covenant* with many for one week: and in the midst of the week he shall cause the sacrifice and the oblation to cease, and for the overspreading of abominations he shall make it desolate, even until the consummation, and that determined shall be poured upon the desolate."[35] According to Daniel, the covenant would be confirmed. Given that Christ gave the instruction "stand in the holy place" to the Apostles, it is possible that at least one of the Apostles was among those who "confirm[ed] the covenant" or at least participated in the covenant.[36]

Presumably, the covenant was in part a covenant of protection. The covenant may also have included a confirmation or renewal of the Abrahamic covenant, which included promises that Christ would watch over Abraham's posterity, that they would receive the gospel and the priesthood, that they would be blessed "above measure," and that through their ministry Christ's name would be known on the earth forever.[37] Whatever was included in the covenant that Daniel referred to, the covenant was important to make at that time, for shortly thereafter, temple sacrifices and offerings would cease and then the Roman army would destroy the temple, making the abomination of desolation complete.[38]

Jesus Teaches That Those Who Are Steadfast Will Be Saved (Matt. 24:13; Mark 13:13; JS—M 1:11)

Jesus had warned His Apostles of false Christs and false prophets. He had warned the Apostles that they would be persecuted, hated, and betrayed. He had warned of great iniquity. Now He gave the following reassurance:

Matthew 24:13. But he that shall endure unto the end, the same shall be saved.

---

35.   Dan. 9:26–27, italics added; see also Dan. 11:31; 12:11.

36.   If one of the Apostles was involved, it could not have been Peter or James, since they were killed prior to the siege and destruction of Jerusalem. Andrew had likely also been killed by this time. It is certain that John was still alive (see John 21:21–23).

37.   Abr. 2:9; see also Abr. 1:18–19; 2:8, 10–11.

38.   Christ also stated that an abomination of desolation was one of the signs that would precede His Second Coming (see JS—M 1:32).

This promise was also given by various prophets in the Book of Mormon,[39] and the Lord has given it in the latter days as well.[40]

Jesus Teaches That Christians Would Need to Flee to the Mountains (Matt. 24:16–22; Mark 13:14–20; Luke 21:21–24; JS—M 1:13–21)

Jesus then taught that Christians in Judea, which included Jerusalem, would need to flee to the mountains in order to avoid the tribulations that would precede the destruction of the city:

> **Joseph Smith—Matthew 1:13–21.** Then let them who are in Judea flee into the mountains; let him who is on the housetop flee, and not return to take anything out of his house; neither let him who is in the field return back to take his clothes; and wo unto them that are with child, and unto them that give suck in those days; therefore, pray ye the Lord that your flight be not in the winter, neither on the Sabbath day; for then, in those days, shall be great tribulation on the Jews, and upon the inhabitants of Jerusalem, such as was not before sent upon Israel, of God, since the beginning of their kingdom until this time; no, nor ever shall be sent again upon Israel. All things which have befallen them are only the beginning of the sorrows which shall come upon them. And except those days should be shortened, there should none of their flesh be saved; but for the elect's sake, according to the covenant, those days shall be shortened. Behold, these things I have spoken unto you concerning the Jews.

Luke's record refers to those "in the midst of it,"[41] presumably referring to those in Jerusalem. Luke's account then states, "Let not them that are in the countries enter thereinto."[42] In other words, Christians who lived outside of Jerusalem were not to enter the city the Passover season in which the Roman armies were at Jerusalem.[43]

The people's flight was to be so rapid that those on their housetops were not to spend the time required to gather anything in their houses; those working in the fields were not to return home to pack clothes before

39. See 1 Ne. 22:31; 2 Ne. 9:24; 31:16, 20; 33:4; Omni 1:26; 3 Ne. 15:9; Morm. 9:29.
40. See D&C 14:7; 18:22.
41. Luke 21:21.
42. Luke 21:21.
43. Many Jews traveled to Jerusalem for the Passover that year and were allowed into the city by the Roman army.

leaving. Leaving quickly would be especially hard for nursing mothers, and their double burden would provide an opportunity for others to serve. They were to pray that they would not need to flee in the winter; this prayer was honored, for Titus's army came in early spring. They were also to pray that they would not be required to travel on the Sabbath. The destruction of Jerusalem by the Roman army would be only the beginning of sorrows, for the surviving Jews would be scattered throughout much of the world.

Then Jesus gave the great promise that the days of destruction would be shortened "for the elect's sake, according to the covenant" that Christ would make with them. The Christians would have enough time to escape.

Many Christian Jews Are Saved

Many of the Christian Jews did escape prior to the final Roman siege of Jerusalem. Unfortunately, there is no scriptural record regarding where they went or what happened to them. Third-century scholars Eusebius and Epiphanius referred to a traditional belief that before the Romans destroyed Jerusalem, the Jerusalem Christians were warned to flee to Pella, which is in the mountainous region of the Decapolis, northeast of Jerusalem. However, because of the lack of records written by Christians at the time they fled Jerusalem, it is uncertain when they left and where they went.

Eusebius wrote, "Before the war began, members of the Jerusalem church were ordered by an oracle given by revelation to those worthy of it to leave the city and settle in a city of Perea called Pella. Here they migrated from Jerusalem, as if, once holy men had deserted the royal capital of the Jews and the whole land of Judea, the judgment of God might finally fall on them for their crimes against Christ and his apostles, utterly blotting out all that wicked generation."[44]

Epiphanius wrote, "This sect of Nazoraeans is to be found in Beroea near Coelesyria, in the Decapolis near Pella, and in Bashanitis at the place called Cocabe—Khokhabe in Hebrew. For that was its place of origin, since all the disciples had settled in Pella after their remove from Jerusalem—Christ having told them to abandon Jerusalem and withdraw from it because of the siege it was about to undergo. And they settled in Peraea for this reason and,

---

44.   Eusebius, *Missions and Persecutions*, bk. 3, p. 82.

as I said, lived their lives there. It was from this that the Nazoraean sect had its origin."[45] Epiphanius also wrote, "Practically all who had come to faith in Christ had settled in Peraea then, in Pella, a town in the Decapolis."[46]

According to Clarke, who examined the writing of both Eusebius and Epiphanius, "it is very remarkable that not a single Christian perished in the destruction of Jerusalem."[47] However, that statement may have been an exaggeration and presumes that all Christians were united, faithful, and willing to leave their families if necessary.

The Righteous Will Be Spared in the Last Days

Following Jesus's death, natural disasters destroyed many cities and people in the Americas, but most of the righteous were spared.[48] The escape of the Christians before the siege of Jerusalem and the preservation of the majority of the righteous in the Americas after Jesus's death are types and shadows of His preservation of the righteous from the destruction that will occur prior to His Second Coming. Many scriptures testify of this preservation. For example, Nephi prophesied: "Wherefore, he will preserve the righteous by his power, even if it so be that the fulness of his wrath must come, and the righteous be preserved, even unto the destruction of their enemies by fire. Wherefore, the righteous need not fear; for thus saith the prophet, they shall be saved, even if it so be as by fire."[49] As another example, the Lord told Joseph Smith, "For they that are wise and have received the truth, and have taken the Holy Spirit for their guide, and have not been deceived—verily I say unto you, they shall not be hewn down and cast into the fire, but shall abide the day."[50]

The Lord has also said that in the last days, His people should establish a New Jerusalem as a place of refuge and safety: "And with one heart and with one mind, gather up your riches that ye may purchase an inheritance which shall hereafter be appointed unto you. And it shall be called the New

45.   Epiphanius, *Panarion*, p. 129.
46.   Epiphanius, *Panarion*, p. 132.
47.   See Clarke, *Commentary*, vol. 5, pp. 228–229.
48.   See 3 Ne. 9:11, 13; 10:12–14.
49.   1 Ne. 22:17.
50.   D&C 45:57.

Jerusalem, a land of peace, a city of refuge, a place of safety for the saints of the Most High God; and the glory of the Lord shall be there, and the terror of the Lord also shall be there, insomuch that the wicked will not come unto it, and it shall be called Zion. And it shall come to pass among the wicked, that every man that will not take his sword against his neighbor must needs flee unto Zion for safety. And there shall be gathered unto it out of every nation under heaven; and it shall be the only people that shall not be at war one with another."[51]

Just as Christian Jews were protected by heeding the voice of the Lord, people today can be protected by heeding His word, which comes through those who are called and sustained as prophets, seers, and revelators. The Lord has said, "What I the Lord have spoken, I have spoken, and I excuse not myself; and though the heavens and the earth pass away, my word shall not pass away, but shall all be fulfilled, whether by mine own voice or by the voice of my servants, it is the same."[52]

Notes to Chapter 54

1. Farrar's description of the temple in Jerusalem. Farrar provided the following description of the temple:

And now Jesus left the Temple for the last time; but the feelings of the Apostles still clung with the loving pride of their nationality to that sacred spot. They stopped to cast upon it one last lingering gaze, and one of them was eager to call His attention to its goodly stones and priceless offerings—those nine gates overlaid with gold and silver, and the one of solid Corinthian brass yet more precious; those graceful and towering porches; those polished and beveled blocks forty cubits long and ten cubits high, testing to the toil and munificence of so many generations; those double cloisters and stately pillars; that lavish adornment of sculpture and arabesque; those alternate blocks of red and white marble, recalling the crest and hollow of

51.   D&C 45:65–69.
52.   D&C 1:38.

the sea-waves; those vast clusters of golden grapes, each cluster as large as a man, which twined their splendid luxuriance over the golden doors. They would have Him gaze with them on the rising terraces of courts—the Court of the Gentiles with its monolithic columns and rich mosaic, above this the flight of fourteen steps which led to the Court of the Women; the flight of fifteen steps which led to the Court of the Priests; then, once more, the twelve steps which led to the final platform crowned by the actual Holy, and Holy of Holies which the Rabbis fondly compared for its shape to a couchant lion, and which, with its marble whiteness and golden roofs, looked like a glorious mountain whose snowy summit was gilded by the sun. It is as though they thought the loveliness and magnificence of this scene would intercede with Him, touching His heart with mute appeal. But the heart of Jesus was sad. To Him the sole beauty of a temple was the sincerity of its worshippers, and no gold or marble, no brilliant vermillion or curiously-carven cedar-wood, no delicate sculpturing or votive gems, could change for Him a den of robbers into a House of Prayer.[53]

2. Synopsis of events preceding the Roman siege and destruction of Jerusalem in AD 70. As recorded in Deuteronomy 28:15–68, the Lord told Moses that if the time came that Israel "wilt not hearken unto the voice of the Lord thy God, to observe to do all his commandments and his statutes which I command thee this day; that all these curses shall come upon thee, and overtake thee."[54] Certainly, the curses included Assyria's capture and dispersal of the northern ten tribes, Babylon's capture of Jerusalem and desecration of the temple, and the Seleucid Empire's capture of Jerusalem. These curses were followed by the curse of Rome destroying Jerusalem in AD 70. This note summarizes the events leading up to and during the destruction of Jerusalem and the temple. The Lord's prophecy about curses following disobedience is applicable today, and the discussion of Rome's destruction of Jerusalem may help people better understand the severity of the curses and have a greater desire to be obedient.

The beginning of the conflict. The Jews detested being ruled by the Roman government. This hatred boiled over into rebellion "owing to the arbitrary action of the procurators Felix, Festus, Albinus, and Gessius Florus, who by

---

53. Farrar, *Life of Christ*, pp. 515–516.
54. Deut. 28:15.

their exactions drove the Jews into open revolt. In the year 66 began that heroic war which ended with the destruction of the Second Temple and of the national existence of the Jews."[55]

Florus loved money, hated the Jews, and cared little for their religion and for religious rights. As Roman procurator, he ruled Judea from AD 64 to 66. The Jewish rebellion against Rome began in Caesarea, a city on the coast of the Mediterranean Sea.[56] Caesarea contained a Jewish synagogue on land that the Jews desired to buy. The landowner refused to sell the land to the Jews. Instead, he sold the land to others, and they began building shops, leaving only a narrow entrance to the synagogue. The Jews tried to stop the construction of these shops, and tensions increased between the Jews and others of the city. Consequently, the Jews sought the assistance of Florus and paid him eight talents to intervene. He promised he would help but instead left the city.[57]

The next day, a man in Caesarea who desired to instigate a fight with the Jews brought a barrel to the entrance of the synagogue, turned the barrel over, and sacrificed birds on it, polluting the synagogue. The Jews were incensed and took their book of the law to a neighboring city. Thirteen of the principal Jews in the city made an appeal to Florus. Rather than assisting them, he imprisoned them for taking their book of the law out of the city.[58]

Thereafter, Florus "blew up the war [which was in its initial stages] into a flame."[59] He directed some people, presumably soldiers, to go to Jerusalem and take seventeen talents out of the temple's treasury, pretending that Caesar wanted them. The Jews were again incensed, and they reprimanded Florus. He demanded that those who were speaking against him be brought before him. Some Jews spoke with Florus and begged forgiveness for those who had spoken against him. Florus became furious that the seditious men were not exposed. He therefore sent his soldiers to "plunder the Upper Market Place, and to slay such as they met with."[60] As a result, thirty-six

---

55. *Jewish Encyclopedia*, s.v. "Nero."
56. See *HarperCollins Bible Dictionary*, s.v. "Caesarea."
57. See Josephus, *Wars*, 2.14.4.
58. See Josephus, *Wars*, 2.14.5.
59. Josephus, *Wars*, 2.14.6.
60. Josephus, *Wars*, 2.14.8–9.

hundred men, women, and children (including infants) were killed. Some were whipped and then crucified.[61] The result was an explosive Jewish revolt.

Subsequently, non-Jews in Caesarea confronted the Jews there and in about one hour's time had killed twenty thousand Jews. Florus caught some Jews who fled the city, and he sent them to the galleys as slaves.[62]

The war reached as far south as the Nile Delta and Alexandria in Egypt, where a large number of Jews resided. Cestius Gallus sent his army to these two areas, and his soldiers unmercifully killed fifty thousand Jews.[63] Rebellion and consequent wars also sprung up throughout much of Galilee:

> Under all the procurators, good and bad alike, there were clashes and the land seethed with rebellion. The most serious opposition came from Galilee where the Zealots became the leaders. They were extremists who shrank from nothing to bring down their heathen masters. Their watchword was: "No God but Yahweh, no tax but to the Temple, no friend but the Zealot." The crucifixions which followed every unsuccessful flouting of imperial power only had the effect of arousing avengers, who fought on until they too hung in agony on a public gibbet.
>
> Ultimately Roman patience was thoroughly exhausted, and the procurators introduced measures of barbarous severity. Soldiers slew on the slightest provocation. Eminent Jewish leaders were crucified, whole villages were razed. All in vain. A fever of martyrdom seemed to seize upon the harassed people. Fanatics went up and down the country, wild-eyed and frantic, prophesying the end of the world, and the advent of the Messiah. Multitudes were ready to follow every impossible visionary who claimed inspiration from heaven. Zealots rushed to their deaths crying out in hysterical exaltation. What was one to do with such a nation? The Romans were frankly bewildered. They had dealt with many turbulent peoples, but with none so contrary—so insanely intractable.[64]

As an example of Rome's barbarism, Cestius joined his army with soldiers sent by Antiochus and Agrippa. They marched to Zebulon in Galilee and found the city deserted of men, who had fled to the mountains. Cestius

---

61. See Josephus, *Wars*, 2.14.9.
62. See Josephus, *Wars*, 2.18.1.
63. See Josephus, *Wars*, 2.18.8.
64. Sachar, *History of the Jews*, p. 117.

permitted his soldiers to plunder the city and then set it on fire.[65] His army then went to Joppa, south of Caesarea, and killed eighty-four hundred Jews.[66]

Cestius also took his army to Lydda and burned that city.[67] When Cestius and his army went to Jerusalem, they laid siege to the city, then entered and undermined the temple wall. For some unknown reason, he then left the city. Some of the remaining Jews fought a guerrilla war against the departing Roman army and caused them to flee amid many casualties and great embarrassment.[68] The Jews then prepared for all-out war. Upon learning of the Jews' success against Cestius and his army, Nero decided to appoint Vespasian to lead the Roman army in punishing the Jews for their rebellion.[69]

Vespasian's war efforts. Vespasian and his troops traveled to Jotapata, which he desired to take because he had heard that the largest part of the Jewish army in Galilee was in that city.[70] This Jewish army was led by Josephus. Vespasian's army soon began the siege of the city.

Among the Roman soldiers were archers, those who could hurl stones (presumably with slings), and those with swords and spears. The army also had engines that could sling large stones and large arrows. Vespasian directed his soldiers to create banks against the city's walls so that battering rams could weaken and ultimately destroy the walls. In the siege, Vespasian was wounded with an arrow.[71] The siege lasted forty-seven days. In spite of the valiant efforts of the Jews, the Romans finally forced their way into the city.[72]

Josephus's surrender. Josephus escaped into a cistern connected to a cave, in which forty other Jews were hiding. This hiding place was discovered, and a Roman soldier whom Josephus knew promised that Josephus's life would be spared if he agreed to surrender. The Jews with Josephus threatened to kill him if he chose to surrender, and they planned to kill themselves as well. He escaped only by convincing them to kill each other according to the lots they drew. Josephus somehow, by luck or arrangement, was the next

---

65. See Josephus, *Wars*, 2.18.9.
66. See Josephus, *Wars*, 2.18.10.
67. See Josephus, *Wars*, 2.19.1.
68. See Josephus, *Wars*, 2.19.7, 9.
69. See Josephus, *Wars*, 3.1.1–3.
70. See Josephus, *Wars*, 3.7.3.
71. See Josephus, *Wars*, 3.7.22.
72. See *Jewish Encyclopedia*, s.v. "Josephus."

to last or the last to be killed, and after the others had killed each other, he convinced the other surviving Jew to surrender too.[73]

Josephus was then taken to Vespasian. Josephus's life was spared because of his great valor and because he asserted that he had a prophetic gift. He told Vespasian that the latter would succeed Nero as emperor. Ultimately, Josephus was given freedom; adopted Vespasian's family name, Flavius; was given land; and was with Titus during the siege of Jerusalem.[74]

The continuing wars in Galilee and Judea. Even Samaria did not escape the Roman armies. Members of the Samaritan army assembled on top of their holy mountain, Gerizim. They had some provisions but little water. Ultimately, the Roman commander Cerealis, 600 horsemen, and 3,000 footmen prevailed. Approximately 11,600 Samaritans were slain.[75]

One of the last Galilean cities to be taken by Roman armies was Gischala. Those remaining in the city ultimately let Titus into the city, and the rebellion was put down. [76] Josephus wrote, "And thus was all Galilee taken; but this not till after it had cost the Romans much pains before it could be taken by them."[77]

Of the wars in Galilee, the *Jewish Encyclopedia* states the following:

> A terrible punishment awaited the conquered. Galilee was entirely depopulated; 6,000 youths were sent to Nero to work on the Isthmus of Corinth; 1,200 old men were killed; and the remaining Jews, more than 30,400 in number, were sold as slaves, servitude being also the fate of those who were given to Agrippa (ib. iii. 10, § 10). There now remained only the fortress of Gamala, whose defenders repulsed the Romans so disastrously that Vespasian in person had to urge his soldiers on. The fortress was reduced at last, however, and the Romans massacred 4,000 Jews, the rest preferring death by their own hands. In the meantime the fort of Itabyrion at Tabor had surrendered, while the city of Giscala was reduced by Titus, so that Galilee was entirely subdued by Vespasian.[78]

---

73. See *Jewish Encyclopedia*, s.v. "Josephus;" see also Josephus, *Wars*, 3.8.1–2, 7.
74. See *Jewish Encyclopedia*, s.v. "Josephus."
75. See Josephus, *Wars*, 3.7.32.
76. See Josephus, *Wars*, 4.2.1–5.
77. Josephus, *Wars*, 4.2.5.
78. *Jewish Encyclopedia*, s.v. "Vespasian."

Internal strife and corruption in Jerusalem. Before the Romans' siege of Jerusalem began, there was great strife and corruption among various factions in the city, and these circumstances greatly contributed to Jerusalem's downfall. For example, there was a bitter dispute between those, including John of Gischala, who favored war with Rome and those who desired peace.[79] As another example, groups of robbers went about the countryside raping women. These robbers came into Jerusalem, which had "become a city without a governor."[80] Other robbers also came to the city. The robbers measured their courage by raping woman, murdering men, and plundering the city. They imprisoned and then killed some of the more prominent leaders in the city and appointed new high priests.[81] The central government was rapidly falling.

The Zealots and robbers gained control of the temple. In response, Ananus, the oldest high priest, planned to lead the majority of the people against the Zealots to take back the temple. Ananus and Jesus the son of Gamala reproached the people for their sloth in failing to fight against the Zealots. John of Gischala pretended to be a friend to Ananus and the general populace, but he actually was a secret agent for the Zealots.

By befriending Ananus and other leaders, John learned of their plans to overthrow the Zealots and take back the temple. He then reported these plans to the Zealots. John claimed that Ananus had invited the Romans to come into the city. Of course, this lie outraged the Zealots. John then wrote a letter to the Idumeans, whose territory was south of Judea, telling them the same lie. The Idumeans were furious because they feared that the Romans would attack their land after attacking Jerusalem. As a result, twenty thousand Idumean soldiers marched toward Jerusalem under four commanders.[82] When the soldiers arrived at the walls of Jerusalem, they encountered a severe storm. Ananus gave the guards in Jerusalem permission to sleep, assuming the storm would deter the Idumeans from trying to enter. However, some of the Zealots sawed open the gates to the city and let the Idumeans in. Once in, the Roman soldiers assisted the Zealots in leaving the

---

79. See Josephus, *Wars*, 4.3.2.
80. Josephus, *Wars*, 4.3.3.
81. See Josephus, *Wars*, 4.3.4–6.
82. See Josephus, *Wars*, 4.4.1–2.

temple so that they could fight against members of the general populace, who were outside the temple walls.[83]

A battle ensued, and Josephus recorded that "now the outer temple was all of it overflowed with blood; and that day, as it came on, saw eight thousand five hundred dead bodies there."[84] The Idumeans went after the priests, including Ananus and Jesus, and slew them.

Josephus also wrote, "I should not mistake if I said that the death of Ananus was the beginning of the destruction of the city, and that from this very day may be dated the overthrow of her wall, and the ruin of her affairs, whereon they saw their high priest, and the procurer of the preservation slain in the midst of the city."[85]

The armies of Vespasian deemed the sedition among the Jews to be a great advantage to the Romans. Vespasian agreed but decided not to go in haste to Jerusalem but to let the Jews continue to fight among themselves.[86]

Titus's war efforts. In the meantime, Nero died and Vespasian returned to Rome, became emperor, and designated his son Titus as the commander of the Roman army assigned to take Jerusalem.[87] Titus gathered his forces at Caesarea before beginning the assault on Jerusalem.[88]

The internal sedition and strife among the Jews continued to expand. A Zealot named Eleazar was angry with John. The result was that the Zealots split into factions, one under the command of Eleazar and one under the command of John. A third faction was under the command of the "tyrant Simon, the son of Gioras, whom the people had invited in" because they hoped he would assist them in their defense against the other two factions.[89] Many battles occurred among these three factions, and robbers continued to murder, rape, and plunder. At this time, many Jews were coming to Jerusalem from other nations for the Passover, and they too were killed, some even while offering sacrifice at the altar.

---

83. See Josephus, *Wars*, 4.4.5–7.
84. Josephus, *Wars*, 4.5.1.
85. Josephus, *Wars*, 4.5.2.
86. See Josephus, *Wars*, 4.6.2.
87. See Josephus, *Wars*, 4.11.5.
88. See Josephus, *Wars*, 4.11.5.
89. Josephus, *Wars*, 5.1.3; see also 5.1.2

Regarding what was happening in Jerusalem, Josephus lamented: "O most wretched city . . . for thou couldst be no longer a place fit for God, nor couldst thou longer continue in being, after thou hadst been a sepulcher for the bodies of thine own people, and hadst made the holy house itself a burying-place in this civil war."[90]

The conflict continued, and John set fire to the houses that stored the corn and other provisions the people had laid up against the coming Roman siege. He apparently did so out of spite for the internal strife and so that if the Romans were successful, they would not find food in the city. Simon retaliated by setting on fire other houses that held provisions. Thus, all the places around the temple where provisions were stored were destroyed.[91] These actions set the stage for a famine in Jerusalem, which would cost many lives and perhaps contributed to the city's destruction.

The siege of Jerusalem. Titus began his siege by surrounding the city with six Roman legions at about the time of the Passover in AD 70.[92] *Encyclopedia Britannica* states, "Since that action coincided with Passover, the Romans allowed pilgrims to enter the city but refused to let them leave—thus strategically depleting food and water supplies within Jerusalem."[93]

After surveying the city, Titus ordered that his soldiers move closer to the city. He then commanded his army to cut down all the trees, hedges, and walls that people had erected around their homes outside the city walls. He also ordered that all the hollow places be filled in and that all rocks be removed so that the area between his army and the city wall was level.[94]

Jerusalem was fortified along the perimeter with an outer wall, a middle wall, and an inner wall, except in places that were unpassable; in those places, there was only one wall.[95] The outer wall was ten cubits wide and twenty cubits high and had battlements and turrets on top.[96] Many of the stones forming the outer wall were white marble, and each stone was approximately

90. Josephus, *Wars*, 5.1.3.
91. See Josephus, *Wars*, 5.1.4.
92. See Josephus, *Wars*, 5.1.6.
93. *Encyclopedia Britannica*, s.v. "siege of Jerusalem," accessed August 4, 2022, https://www.britannica.com/event/Siege-of-Jerusalem-70.
94. See Josephus, *Wars*, 5.3.2.
95. See Josephus, *Wars*, 5.4.1.
96. See Josephus, *Wars*, 5.4.2.

twenty cubits in length, ten in breadth, and five in depth.[97] The outer wall
had sixty towers, the middle wall had forty towers, and the inner wall had
ninety towers.[98] The tower of Antonia was located at the northwest corner
of the temple court and was forty cubits high.[99] The city was divided into
three areas: the upper city, the temple mount, and the lower city. Simon and
the Idumeans controlled the upper city, and John controlled the temple.[100]
Fighting among the factions in the city continued, even with Titus and
his army camped close to the city walls. Josephus observed, "The sedition
destroyed the city, and the Romans destroyed the sedition."[101]

Titus ordered his men to set on fire the homes outside the city's outer
wall and to bring in timber and dirt to raise banks around the outer wall at
places he designated. The Jews shot arrows and threw stones at the soldiers
building the banks. The Romans used engines to throw stones and shoot
large arrows at the Jews on the wall and in the city. Josephus reported that
the stones hurled by the Roman engines weighed about 66 pounds, [102] and
Sachar stated that some of the stones weighed approximately 125 pounds.[103]
Further, the engines could throw the stones more than thirteen hundred
feet.[104] Some of the stones were blackened so they were hard to see at night.

Once the banks were completed, Titus ordered that his soldiers bring
the battering rams to the outer wall in three places and start working to
bring down the wall. These efforts motivated the factions of Jews to unite in
hurling torches at the battering rams and shooting arrows at the soldiers.[105]

Titus ordered his soldiers to make three towers with metal plates on the
front so that his soldiers could be somewhat protected while trying to kill
Jews on the city walls. One tower fell, but the Roman soldiers gathered in

97.   See Josephus, *Wars*, 5.4.4.
98.   See Josephus, *Wars*, 5.4.3.
99.   See Josephus, *Wars*, 5.5.8.
100. See Josephus, *Wars*, 5.6.1.
101. Josephus, *Wars*, 5.6.1.
102. See Josephus, *Wars*, 5.6.3.
103. See Sachar, *History of the Jews*, p. 119.
104. See Josephus, *Wars*, 5.6.3.
105. See Josephus, *Wars*, 5.6.4.

the other two towers and were able to kill or wound many Jews while being protected from the Jews' arrows.[106]

Eventually, the Roman soldiers breached one of the weakest areas of the outer wall.[107] Five days later, the soldiers made a narrow breach in the second wall, but the soldiers were forced to leave the city because they could not defend the small area that they had taken.[108] Titus then ordered that two additional banks be built.[109] The work on these banks was greatly hindered by the Jews, and Titus sent Josephus to speak to the Jews and persuade them to surrender.[110]

Some decided to surrender to the Roman army, and a number of those who were about to desert to the Romans were killed by other Jews.[111] Of the Jews who left without surrendering, some were captured by the Romans and crucified next to the walls of the city, and others' hands were cut off.[112]

Meanwhile, the famine was growing more and more intense, and the only food available were the small amounts that had been hidden from the robbers. Apparently, some of the Jews planned to desert the city, and they swallowed gold coins so they would have money if their escape proved successful. Approximately two thousand Jewish deserters were killed, and their stomachs were cut open in order to obtain the swallowed coins. Titus was appalled and threatened to put to death any who sought for gold in this manner.[113]

Titus ordered additional banks to be raised, one of which was near the tower of Antonia. Titus then ordered that a battering ram be brought up to the wall. Meanwhile, inside the wall near the tower of Antonia, John had his men dig a trench under the wall and support it with large beams. He daubed these beams with pitch and bitumen and then set them on fire. Because of the fire, the beams gave way and the bank and battering ram were destroyed.[114] Jews also burned battering rams at other locations.

---

106. See Josephus, *Wars*, 5.7.1–2.
107. See Josephus, *Wars*, 5.7.2.
108. See Josephus, *Wars*, 5.8.1–2.
109. See Josephus, *Wars*, 5.9.2.
110. See Josephus, *Wars*, 5.9.4.
111. See Josephus, *Wars*, 5.10.1–2.
112. See Josephus, *Wars*, 5.11.1.
113. See Josephus, *Wars*, 5.13.4–5.
114. See Josephus, *Wars*, 5.11.4.

Next, Titus ordered a wall to be built around much of the city to prevent the Jews from sneaking out or receiving supplies.[115] Food was so scarce that some people searched the sewers and the dunghills of cattle for things to eat.[116] Many people died because of the lack of food.[117] Some of the bodies of the dead were cast down from the walls into the valleys. When Titus saw dead bodies with "thick putrefaction running about them, he gave a groan; and spreading out his hands to heaven, called God to witness that this was not his doing: and such was the sad case of the city itself."[118] Josephus reported that at least six hundred thousand of those who had died were thrown out of the city gates and that many more were lying in heaps in large houses.

The capture of Jerusalem. There were two main strongholds in Jerusalem. One was the Antonia Fortress. This fortress was built on the northeastern side of the city, near the temple mount and the pool of Bethesda. This tower was prominent during Jesus's time and was used by Roman soldiers to view those on the temple mount. This area was the general location where the banks and Roman battering ram had been destroyed by John and his followers. The ram were repaired, and Titus once again ordered that a battering ram be brought to the wall.

The battering ram weakened the wall, and the Roman soldiers finally succeeded in removing four of its stones. Because John had undermined the wall, the ground gave way and the part of the wall by the battering ram suddenly fell.[119] The middle wall was weaker than the first, and it was breached.

At about three o'clock in the morning, fifteen Roman soldiers snuck through the ruins of the walls to the Antonia Fortress, cut the throats of Jewish guards, took possession of the city's inner wall, and ordered the trumpeter to sound his trumpet. Roman soldiers then forced their way through to the fortress's tower, took possession of it, and forced the Jews to the temple.[120] Titus gave orders to "dig up the foundations of the tower of Antonia, and make him a ready passage for his army to come up."[121]

---

115. See Josephus, *Wars*, 5.12.1.
116. Josephus, *Wars*, 5.13.6.
117. See Josephus, *Wars*, 5.12.3.
118. See Josephus, *Wars*, 5.12.3–4.
119. See Josephus, *Wars*, 6.1.3.
120. See Josephus, *Wars*, 6.1.7.
121. Josephus, *Wars*, 6.2.1.

Titus called on Josephus to plead with the Jews to surrender.[122] Titus also called on the Jews to surrender or to at least move the battle away from the temple: "I do not force you to defile this your sanctuary; and if you will but change the place where on you will fight, no Roman shall either come near your sanctuary, or offer any affront to it; nay, I will endeavor to preserve you your holy house, whether you will or not."[123] The Jews interpreted both Josephus's and Titus's words as fear and therefore fought all the harder.

To convey the desperate nature of the Jews' situation in the city when the Roman soldiers entered, Josephus presented a horrific account of a Jewish widow who was daily raped by Roman soldiers; these soldiers also stole what little food she had. The woman had a young son who was still nursing, and the famine was so terrible that both the woman and her son were starving. She concluded that her condition was worse than death and that there was no hope for her son. Out of desperation, she killed him, roasted him, and ate a portion of his flesh. When the Roman soldiers discovered what she had done, many of them pitied the woman and the Jews in general. However, Titus believed that his efforts to take the city were excused before God, and he used this incident to demonstrate that the Jews were not fit to live and also to justify the belief that their entire country should be destroyed.[124]

The capture of the temple. Titus then ordered that battering rams be brought to the inner wall, which surrounded the temple. When the Roman battering rams failed to breach the wall, Titus ordered his soldiers to set fire to the temple gates.[125] After two days of fire, Titus ordered his army to advance into the temple courts, a portion of which had been set fire by the Jews to stop the Roman soldiers. After the soldiers entered, one of them picked up some burning material, was lifted on the shoulders of another, and threw the burning material into a window of the temple. The flames spread through the temple.[126]

Josephus recorded, "While the holy house was on fire, everything was plundered that came to hand, and ten thousand of those that were caught

---

122. Josephus, *Wars*, 6.2.2.
123. Josephus, *Wars*, 6.2.4.
124. See Josephus, *Wars*, 6.3.4.
125. See Josephus, *Wars*, 6.4.1.
126. See Josephus, *Wars*, 6.4.5, 7.

were slain; . . . children, and old men, and profane persons, and priests, were all slain in the same manner."[127] Josephus added, "It is God therefore, it is God himself who is bringing on this fire, to purge that city and temple by means of the Romans, and is going to pluck up this city, which is full of your pollutions."[128]

Afterward, the Romans brought their ensigns (i.e., idols on poles) into the temple and offered sacrifices to the ensigns.[129] Many of the temple's treasures were delivered to Titus. The desecration of the temple was complete.

The Roman army continued to destroy the city's walls, set fires, and kill any Jews who were found.[130] Some Jews fled to subterranean caverns. When these Jews were found, they were killed by the soldiers, including through causing the caverns to collapse on the Jews inside.[131]

In the eastern portion of the city, the Jews had built large and secure towers; ultimately, the Jews decided to relinquish the towers. Titus inspected the towers and said, "We have certainly had God for our assistant in this war, and it was no other than God that ejected the Jews out of these fortifications; for what could the hands of men, or any machines do towards overthrowing these towers!"[132] These towers were left standing as a monument to Titus's good fortune in taking Jerusalem.

Josephus estimated that 97,000 Jews were taken captive; many of the captives were sold as slaves to labor in Egyptian mines or were taken to Roman provinces to be killed for sport in amphitheaters.[133] Josephus estimated that approximately 1.1 million people perished in the siege, either because they were murdered or starved; many of them had come to Jerusalem from surrounding areas for the Passover and the Feast of Unleavened Bread.[134] Approximately 40,000 others were released.[135]

---

127. Josephus, *Wars*, 6.5.1.
128. Josephus, *Wars*, 6.2.1.
129. See Josephus, *Wars*, 6.6.1.
130. See Josephus, *Wars*, 6.6.3.
131. See Josephus, *Wars*, 6.9.4.
132. Josephus, *Wars*, 6.9.1.
133. See Josephus, *Wars*, 6.9.2–3.
134. See Josephus, *Wars*, 6.9.2.
135. Josephus, *Wars*, 6.8.2.

After the city had been burned, Titus "gave orders that they should now demolish the entire city and temple, but should leave as many of the towers standing as were of the greatest eminency . . . and so much of the wall as enclosed the city on the west side . . . but for all the rest of the wall, it was so thoroughly laid even with the ground by those that dug it up to the foundation, that there was left nothing to make those that came thither believe it had ever been inhabited. This was the end which Jerusalem came to."[136] The Jewish rabbi Maimonides said, "The very foundations of the temple were digged up, according to the Roman custom . . . that the saying might be fulfilled, 'Zion shall be ploughed as a field.'"[137]

---

136. Josephus, *Wars*, 7.1.1.
137. Clarke, *Commentary*, vol. 5, p. 226; see also Jer. 26:18.

Chapter 55

SIGNS OF JESUS'S SECOND COMING

(Tuesday)

This chapter explores Jesus's answer to the second question His Apostles posed Tuesday on the Mount of Olives: "What shall be the sign of thy coming, and of the end of the world?"[1] In this chapter, Joseph Smith—Matthew will be quoted frequently because this translation contains significant differences from Matthew 24 and thereby provides additional insight about the signs Jesus gave of His Second Coming.

There Will Be False Christs and False Prophets (Matt. 24:23–24; Mark 13:5–6, 21–23; JS—M 1:21–22)

Jesus began His discussion of the signs of His Second Coming by warning about false Christs and false prophets:

Joseph Smith—Matthew 1:21–22. And again, after the tribulation of those days which shall come upon Jerusalem, if any man shall say unto you, Lo, here is Christ, or there, believe him not; for in those days there shall also arise false Christs, and false prophets, and shall show great signs and wonders, insomuch, that, if possible, they shall deceive the very elect, who are the elect according to the covenant.

---

1.   Matt. 24:3. Because there are more signs of Jesus's Second Coming than just the ones discussed in this chapter, the purpose of this chapter is not to present an analysis of all the signs and events of His Second Coming. Further, this chapter does not present a thorough analysis of each of the signs Jesus mentioned, in part because many other resources also address aspects of the signs of Jesus's Second Coming.

According to one list, in the last few centuries more than forty people have claimed to be Jesus or the Messiah.[2] One example is Ann Lee (1736–1784). She was the founder and leader of the Shakers, and her followers believed that Christ had returned to earth as Lee.[3] As another example, William W. Davies (1833–1906), who was the leader of a church called the Kingdom of Heaven, claimed to be the reincarnation of Michael (or Adam). When Davies's son Arthur was born, Davies declared that the infant was Christ reincarnated.[4] As a further example, leaders of numerous splinter groups of The Church of Jesus Christ of Latter-day Saints have claimed to receive prophetic guidance.

As the time of the Lord's Second Coming draws nearer, there may be more false Christs. Nephi prophetically warned about false Christs in the latter days when he stated that the Lord's words, including those in the Book of Mormon, will help convince people of the true Messiah so they can distinguish Him from false Christs: "For they [the Lord's words] shall be given them for the purpose of convincing them of the true Messiah, who was rejected by them; and unto the convincing of them that they need not look forward any more for a Messiah to come, for there should not any come, save it should be a false Messiah which should deceive the people; for there is save one Messiah spoken of by the prophets, and that Messiah is he who should be rejected of the Jews."[5]

It is important to be aware of those who may be false Christs and how they may try to deceive people. As a single example, false Christs may include religious leaders who try to take the place of Christ or Heavenly Father in forgiving sin. False Christs may lead people to believe in false doctrine and therefore be disobedient to true principles. Additionally, when people learn that a person who claimed to be Jesus Christ is not, they may be reluctant to believe in the true Christ, His Atonement, and the resurrection of humankind. Consequently, their eternal progression may be hindered. False Christs are thus an affront to Heavenly Father's merciful plan of salvation and to Christ's role in that plan.

---

2. See Wikipedia, s.v. "List of Messiah Claimants," last modified July 28, 2022, 20:31, http://en.wikipedia.org/wiki/List_of_messiah_claimants.

3. See D&C 49, section heading.

4. See Wikipedia, s.v. "William W. Davies," last modified March 2, 2022, 22:58, http://en.wikipedia.org/wiki/William_W._Davies.

5. 2 Ne. 25:18.

Similarly, false prophets can lead to a lack of faith, for if one prophesies of a coming event and that event does not come about, then people's faith in revelation and in God may be diminished. As an Old Testament example, Hananiah claimed to be a prophet and prophesied of peace between the Jews and Nebuchadnezzar of Babylon. Peace did not come as Hananiah had prophesied, and the Jews' faith in God was diminished. The Lord directed Jeremiah to tell Hananiah, "The Lord hath not sent thee; but thou makest this people to trust in a lie."[6]

False prophets include not only those who falsely claim to be prophets but also Latter-day Saints who claim to receive revelation for the Church or a group beyond their sphere of stewardship. These individuals might have the greatest likelihood of deceiving and leading away even the elect.[7]

False prophets also include those who prophecy of the exact date, time, place, or circumstances of Christ's return. For example, many prophesied that Christ would return in the year AD 2000. However, as Christ told the Apostles, only Heavenly Father knows the day and the hour of the Second Coming.[8]

If there are false Christs and false prophets, presumably there are also false churches and other people who profess false doctrine. Indeed, Elder McConkie asserted that false Christs are churches and belief systems: "A false Christ is not a person. It is a false system of worship, a false church, a false cult that says: 'Lo, here is salvation; here is the doctrine of Christ. Come and believe thus and so, and ye shall be saved.' It is any concept or philosophy that says that redemption, salvation, sanctification, justification, and all of the promised rewards can be gained in any way except that set forth by the apostles and prophets."[9]

Christ warned that false Christs and false prophets will "show great signs and wonders, insomuch, that, if possible, they shall deceive the very elect, who are the elect according to the covenant." Christ did not describe what those great signs and wonders will be. Perhaps they will become more

---

6.   Jer. 28:15; see also vv. 1–14. Another example of a false prophet in the Old Testament is Shemaiah (see Jer. 29:31–32).

7.   Those who claim divine revelation beyond their stewardship or who challenge the principles revealed by the Lord's authorized prophets risk losing the guiding influence of the Holy Ghost and thus risk losing their testimonies and ultimately their membership in the Church.

8.   See JS—M 1:40.

9.   McConkie, *Millennial Messiah*, p. 48.

apparent as the time for Christ's return draws nearer. Importantly, whatever they are, they will be so impressive that the elect may be deceived by them.

Christ specified who the elect are: the "elect according to the covenant." The Hebrew word for *elect* is *eklektos*, which means "chosen."[10] The elect are therefore the Lord's chosen people. They become chosen because they obey God's commandments and keep their covenants with Him.[11]

Presumably, the covenant that Christ was referring to is the Abrahamic covenant, and the elect are heirs to that covenant either through direct lineage or by adoption.[12] Therefore, the elect are those who keep the commandments and their covenants and are or become of the lineage of Abraham. As Christ warned, even these people may be deceived.

Satan is at the heart of false Christs, false prophets, false churches, and false doctrine. Satan desired in the premortal world and still desires today to exalt himself above all that is of God, and he does so by seeking the honor and glory of God[13] and by claiming to be the god of the world. As part of Satan's efforts, he strives to convince people to pridefully claim to be the Messiah or a prophet. As 2 Thessalonians 2:1–4 states, "Let no man deceive you by any means: for that day shall not come, except there come a falling away first, and that man of sin be revealed, the son of perdition; who opposeth and exalteth himself above all that is called God, or that is worshipped; so that he as God sitteth in the temple of God, shewing himself that he is God."[14]

There Will Be Wars and Rumors of Wars (Mark 13:7–8; Luke 21:9–10, 25; JS—M 1:23, 28–29)

Next, Jesus taught that wars and rumors of wars would be a sign preceding His coming:

Joseph Smith—Matthew 1:23, 28–29. Behold, I speak these things unto you for the elect's sake; and you also shall hear of wars, and rumors of wars; see that ye be not troubled, for all I have told you must come to pass; but the

---

10.   Young, *Analytical Concordance*, s.v. "elect."
11.   See Ex. 19:5; Deut.14:2; 26:18; Ps. 135:4.
12.   See D&C 84:33–41; McConkie, *Mormon Doctrine*, pp. 217–218.
13.   See Moses 4:1–3.
14.   2 Thess. 2:1–4.

end is not yet. . . . And they shall hear of wars, and rumors of wars. Behold I speak for mine elect's sake; for nation shall rise against nation, and kingdom against kingdom.

During the last several hundred years, there has not been a time without war occurring somewhere in the world.[15] Today, with global and almost instantaneous news coverage, there are reports of wars and rumors of wars almost daily. Nations great and small continue to arm themselves for war.

As Luke 21:25 states, along with the wars there will be "distress of nations, with perplexity." For those involved in wars, great distress comes from the loss of life, the loss of homes and cities, and the overthrow of governments. Among other things, there is great perplexity about what to do when governments fall or are about to fall or when homes and cities are destroyed. There is great perplexity about how to conclude and avoid wars. There is also great perplexity about how to limit the number of weapons, especially those capable of causing mass destruction. There is great perplexity about whether and how to live in peace and recognize basic human values, especially in times of great social and political divide. Sometimes there is even great perplexity about how to deal with notions such as moral equivalence. The distress and perplexity will continue as wars and rumors of wars continue until the Lord's Second Coming.

The Great Sign of Jesus's Second Coming Will Appear (Matt. 24:27, 30; Mark 13:26; Luke 21:27; JS—M 1:24–26, 36)

Next, Jesus taught that though some people will claim He has returned to a remote location on the earth, His return will not be hidden but will be visible to all:

Joseph Smith—Matthew 1:24–26. Behold, I have told you before; wherefore, if they shall say unto you: Behold, he is in the desert; go not forth: Behold,

---

15. For multiple lists of wars, see *Encyclopedia Britannica*, s.v. "list of wars," accessed July 30, 2021; Wikipedia, s.v. "outline of wars," last modified May 19, 2022, 12:17, https://en .wikipedia.org/wiki/Outline_of_war#Wars. The Lord revealed to Joseph Smith, "Verily, thus saith the Lord concerning the wars that will shortly come to pass, beginning at the rebellion of South Carolina, which will eventually terminate in the death and misery of many souls: And the time will come that war will be poured out upon all nations, beginning at this place." (D&C 87:1–2.)

he is in the secret chambers; believe it not; for as the light of the morning cometh out of the east, and shineth even unto the west, and covereth the whole earth, so shall also the coming of the Son of Man be.

Jesus then gave the great sign of His Second Coming:

Mark 13:26. And then shall they see the Son of man coming in the clouds with great power and glory.[16]

Joseph Smith—Matthew 1:36. And, as I said before, after the tribulations of those days, and the powers of the heavens shall be shaken, then shall appear the sign of the Son of Man in heaven, and then shall all the tribes of the earth mourn; and they shall see the Son of Man coming in the clouds of heaven, with power and great glory.

Jesus referred to the desert and secret chambers, which may be actual places and also metaphors for all places that are not populated and are relatively hidden. Jesus declared that His return will not occur in such places. Instead, He declared, His coming will be "as the light of the morning [which] cometh out of the east, and shineth even unto the west." He also said that He will come down from the clouds with power and glory.[17] When He appears, the whole world will see the sign of His coming in the heavens, and "every knee shall bow" before Him.[18] In the latter days, the Lord has said the following about the great sign of His coming: "And angels shall fly through the midst of heaven, crying with a loud voice, sounding the trump of God, saying: Prepare ye, prepare ye, O inhabitants of the earth; for the judgment of our God is come. Behold, and lo, the Bridegroom cometh; go ye out to meet him. And immediately there shall appear a great sign in heaven, and all people shall see it together."[19] It is unknown whether those on the earth will hear angels playing trumpets and announcing the Savior's return.

When He returns, His power and glory will be so great that mountains will "flow down at [His] presence."[20] His apparel will be red, "like him that

---

16. See also Luke 21:27. The inspiration for the cover of each of the volumes in this series of books comes from this great sign of the Second Coming.
17. See Matt. 24:30; Mark 13:26; Luke 21:27; JS—M 1:36; see also D&C 34:7.
18. D&C 88:104; see also Isa. 45:23; Rom. 14:11; Phil. 2:10; Mosiah 27:31; D&C 76:110; 138:23.
19. D&C 88:92–93; see also Rev. 1:7; D&C 101:23.
20. D&C 133:40, 44.

treadeth in the wine-vat,"[21] and His brightness and glory will eclipse the brightness of the sun, moon, and stars. As Doctrine and Covenants 133:49 states, "And so great shall be the glory of his presence that the sun shall hide his face in shame, and the moon shall withhold its light, and the stars shall be hurled from their places." Likewise, Isaiah 60:19–20 explains, "The sun shall be no more thy light by day; neither for brightness shall the moon give light unto thee: but the Lord shall be unto thee an everlasting light, and thy God thy glory. Thy sun shall no more go down; neither shall thy moon withdraw itself: for the Lord shall be thine everlasting light, and the days of thy mourning shall be ended."

Jesus then taught that when the great sign of His coming appears, His people should look up:

> **Luke 21:28.** And when these things begin to come to pass, then look up, and lift up your heads; for your redemption draweth nigh.

Jesus's disciples should look up because He will come from the heavens in clouds of glory.[22] The instruction to look up also has symbolic meanings. For example, Christ was lifted upon the cross so that all people can look up to Him for redemption.[23] Looking up to Christ means repenting so that His Atonement can take away the burden of sin in people's lives and so that they can become better. Looking up also means looking beyond the minutia of daily life and seeing the divine potential within each person. Looking up helps people see what they lack and how they need to improve. Looking up also helps people recognize those who are in need and how to reach out to them.

Somewhat ironically, people often look up to Heavenly Father while on their knees and with their heads bowed, eyes closed, hearts broken, and spirits contrite, desiring to spiritually see and to be guided and taught. Looking up to Father in Heaven helps people see those things that are of most worth, both now and in eternity.

---

21.   D&C 133:48.

22.   Similarly, when Jesus visited the Americas after His Resurrection, the Nephites looked up and saw Him descend from heaven (see 3 Ne. 11:8).

23.   See 3 Ne. 27:14–15.

Looking up has symbolic meaning beyond seeing with the eyes. In Doctrine and Covenants 35:26, the Lord counseled, "Lift up your hearts and be glad, your redemption draweth nigh." Rather than looking down and considering the challenges of life, especially the difficult conditions in the world preceding Christ's Second Coming, Christ's disciples should lift up their heads and hearts. Looking up with the eyes and heart gives people perspective on life when all feels dark and dreary. Looking up involves having hope amid despair and feeling joy instead of sorrow. By looking up, there can be a bright future instead of darkness and there can be forgiveness and peace instead of ill will and strife.

Christ promised that when He returns, He "will wipe away tears from off all faces."[24] The righteous who are living and the righteous who are dead will be caught up to meet Christ as He descends in the clouds of glory.[25] To be caught up, people will likely need to first look up. Therefore, the righteous should look up for the great signs of His coming. There will be rejoicing as the righteous look up, are caught up, and are with Jesus and righteous loved ones who have passed on.

Christ desires that all people look up to heaven and receive a witness that He is indeed the Only Begotten Son of God. He will return to the earth and usher in the Millennium. Therefore, looking up is important counsel that refers to daily life and also to a marvelous event in the future.

Many of the Elect Will Be Gathered Before Jesus Returns (Matt. 24:28; JS—M 1:27)

Jesus then taught that many of the elect will be gathered before His Second Coming. To illustrate, He gave a parable involving eagles:

Joseph Smith—Matthew 1:27. And now I show unto you a parable. Behold, wheresoever the carcass is, there will the eagles be gathered together; so likewise shall mine elect be gathered from the four quarters of the earth.

Eagles are majestic and powerful birds, fast of flight, sharp eyed, and strong. They are among the birds at the top of the avian food chain. Eagles

---

24.   Isa. 25:8.
25.   See D&C 88:96–98.

are, therefore, an apt metaphor for the elect. This metaphor is also apt because eagles are seen in many parts of the world. Perhaps eagles were flying overhead as Jesus told this parable and He pointed to them as He spoke.

In the parable, the eagles are gathered around a source of food. Similarly, the elect are gathering from the four quarters of the earth to partake of spiritual food. The Lord's elect generally gather together in congregations to partake of the sacrament, which represents and reminds people of the body and blood of Christ, both of which He sacrificed for all people. The elect also gather to be taught, to minister to others, and to be ministered to. Another way the elect gather is by coming together to listen to prophets, apostles, and other Church leaders during general conferences. Further, the elect gather in temples and other places where ordinances are performed and covenants are made.

In part, the elect are gathering because of the great missionary effort of The Church of Jesus Christ of Latter-day Saints. Just as eagles are powerful, those who take the gospel to the world must be spiritually powerful. Those who want to serve a mission need to develop spiritual power prior to serving. They obtain additional power by being set apart by priesthood authority and by receiving their temple endowment. Further, just as eagles are swift, so must be missionaries. As the Lord has said, "Send ye swift messengers, yea, chosen messengers."[26] Missionaries should not waste away their time. The Lord's work is too important, and their time as missionaries is relatively short.

Eagles have excellent long-distance vision, enabling them to see things that are not discernable to the unaided human eye. Similarly, Church members have the gift of the Holy Ghost to help guide them through perils, see what should be done, and recognize who they should help and who is prepared to receive the gospel. Additionally, those who are prepared to hear and receive the gospel will be able to see the truth.

Eagles were also used as a metaphor by Isaiah; he wrote that people who "wait upon the Lord shall renew their strength; they shall mount up with wings as eagles; they shall run, and not be weary; and they shall walk and not faint."[27] The Hebrew word for *wait* is *qavah*, which means to "expect, look

---

26. D&C 124:26.
27. Isa. 40:31.

for, hope."[28] As people are gathered in the last days, they will look for and hope for the Savior's return and be strengthened in their efforts to stand fast in obedience and service to others.

Isaiah also prophesied that the Lord "will lift up an ensign to the nations from far, and will hiss unto them from the end of the earth: and, behold, they shall come with speed swiftly."[29] This verse suggests that some of those in the last days will have not only increased strength but also the ability to be gathered to Zion, in all places it has been established,[30] as quickly as they reasonably can.

Famines, Pestilences, and Earthquakes Will Occur (Mark 13:8; JS—M 1:29)

Jesus also prophesied that famines, pestilences, and earthquakes will occur prior to His Second Coming:

Joseph Smith—Matthew 1:29. There shall be famines, and pestilences, and earthquakes, in divers places.[31]

Similarly, in the book of Revelation, John recorded: "And I beheld when he [Christ] had opened the sixth seal, and, lo, there was a great earthquake . . . and every mountain and island were moved out of their places."[32]

The Lord also discussed this sign in a revelation to Joseph Smith:

And after your testimony cometh wrath and indignation upon the people. For after your testimony cometh the testimony of earthquakes, that shall cause groanings in the midst of her, and men shall fall upon the ground and shall not be able to stand. And also cometh the testimony of the voice of thunderings, and the voice of lightnings, and the voice of tempests, and the voice of the waves of the sea heaving themselves beyond their bounds. And all things shall be in commotion.[33]

---

28. Young, *Analytical Concordance*, s.v. "wait."
29. Isa. 5:26; see also 2 Ne. 15:26.
30. See D&C 97:21.
31. See also Morm. 8:30; D&C 43:25; 45:33; 88:89.
32. Rev. 6:12, 14.
33. D&C 88:88–91.

One can simply look at the daily news to see evidence of this sign; an internet search will lead to lists of earthquakes that have occurred in the past twenty-four hours. The frequency and intensity of natural disasters may increase as the day of the Lord's return approaches.

These challenging events can cause tremendous turmoil, loss of possessions, injury, and even death, but these events have been prophesied to occur and should not cause bitterness or diminished testimony. These events provide opportunities to serve others and are a reminder to be prepared for what may come. An important message in this prophecy is to be prepared both physically and spiritually, for "if ye are prepared ye shall not fear."[34]

Iniquity Will Abound, and People's Love Will Wax Cold (JS—M 1:30)

Jesus next taught that iniquity and a lack of love will abound before He returns:

Joseph Smith—Matthew 1:30. And again, because iniquity shall abound, the love of men shall wax cold; but he that shall not be overcome, the same shall be saved.

Iniquity is rampant, and immorality is visible everywhere. They are regularly portrayed in movies and on television. Pornography is readily available on the internet and via other media. Reports of shootings, stabbings, and lootings are common. Some people no longer look to God or observe the Sabbath day. Deceit is common. Corruption and greed abound in business, with the focus not on what is right or just but on how much advantage a person can obtain. A further major issue in today's world is the illegal use of drugs, which can lead to crime, illness, disability, and even death. Iniquity is also manifest in numerous other ways, and it prevents the influence of the Holy Ghost, decreases love and balance in life, and prompts people to justify their unrighteous conduct.

It is important to note that Christ stated iniquity leads to a lack of love. Often, iniquity is motivated by pride and self-gratification, which are the antithesis of godly love. God's love for His children is so great "that He

---

34. D&C 38:30.

gave His only begotten Son."[35] This love is what all people should strive to achieve. Christ warned that iniquity may decrease love for God and others, for when people commit iniquity, they lose the influence of the Holy Ghost and may rationalize their actions, which may lead to diminished belief in God. Nevertheless, Christ's Atonement is always available and enables repentance and the ability to overcome sin.

The lack of love for others is manifest in many ways. It is prominent in terrorism, war, shootings, ethnic and gender disputes, riots, looting, and gang violence. It is often seen in politics and when people are publicly castigated for past mistakes. Sometimes the lack of love for others is manifest in discord between family members and between disaffected members of religions and their ecclesiastical leaders.

Amid today's abounding iniquity, to be prepared for Christ's Second Coming people must be "unspotted from the world"[36] and have their garments washed "white in the blood of the Lamb."[37]

There are many simple things people can do to be spiritually prepared for the Lord's return. Examples include regularly praying, studying the scriptures, attending the temple, serving others, and striving to be obedient. Another simple but important step is described in Doctrine and Covenants 59:9: "And that thou mayest more fully keep thyself unspotted from the world, thou shalt go to the house of prayer and offer up thy sacraments upon my holy day."[38]

Further, the Light or Spirit of Christ helps people to discern good from evil[39] and persuades people to do good and avoid iniquity.[40] In addition, the Holy Ghost teaches people of truth,[41] thereby helping them avoid error. The Holy Ghost also sanctifies people[42] and shows them what they should do,[43] including what they should do to spiritually prepare for the Lord's return.

---

35. John 3:16.
36. James 1:27.
37. Rev. 7:14; see also 1 Ne. 12:10; Alma 5:21; 13:11; 3 Ne. 27:19.
38. D&C 59:9.
39. See Moro. 7:16.
40. See D&C 11:12.
41. See Moro. 10:4–5.
42. See 3 Ne. 27:20.
43. See 2 Ne. 32:5.

The Gospel Will Be Preached throughout the World (JS—M 1:31)

Jesus also explained that before He returns to the earth, the gospel will be preached throughout the world:

Joseph Smith—Matthew 1:31. And again, this Gospel of the Kingdom shall be preached in all the world, for a witness unto all nations, and then shall the end come, or the destruction of the wicked.

This prophecy is expanded on in the book of Revelation, in which John stated the following: "And I saw another angel fly in the midst of heaven, having the everlasting gospel to preach unto them that dwell on the earth, and to every nation, and kindred, and tongue and people. Saying with a loud voice, Fear God, and give glory to him; for the hour of his judgment is come: and worship him that made heaven, and earth, and the sea, and the fountains of waters."[44]

Similarly, in the latter days the Lord has declared, "And now, verily saith the Lord, that these things might be known among you, O inhabitants of the earth, I have sent forth mine angel flying though the midst of heaven, having the everlasting gospel, who hath appeared unto some and hath committed it unto man, who shall appear unto many that dwell on the earth. And this gospel shall be preached unto every nation, and kindred, and tongue, and people."[45]

Presumably, the angel that John and the Lord referred to is Moroni, who holds the keys of the Book of Mormon.[46] The Book of Mormon will eventually go to all the peoples of the earth.

Missionaries for the Church are now teaching in many parts of the world and are recognizable wherever they go. The Book of Mormon is being translated into an ever-increasing number of languages. Nevertheless, there are still very large populations of people who have not yet heard of the restored gospel. In some parts of the world, many people have not even heard about Christ. Clearly, there is still much work to do.

Christ will be actively involved in this important effort. He has said, "For I will show unto the children of men that I am able to do mine own work."[47]

---

44. Rev. 14:6–7.
45. D&C 133:36–37.
46. See D&C 27:5.
47. 2 Ne. 27:21.

He will hasten missionary work "in its time,"[48] and He will prepare people from all over the world to receive the gospel.[49] Christ will guide this great and most important effort. Of course, His disciples must also put forth great effort and must be patient. James, the Lord's brother, gave the following insightful instruction: "Be patient therefore, brethren, unto the coming of the Lord. Behold, the husbandman waiteth for the precious fruit of the earth, and hath long patience for it, until he receive the early and latter rain."[50]

The Abomination of Desolation Will Occur Again (JS—M 1:32)

Jesus then turned His discussion to the abomination of desolation, presumably in Jerusalem, at the time of His return:

Joseph Smith—Matthew 1:32. And again shall the abomination of desolation, spoken of by Daniel the prophet, be fulfilled.

Daniel's prophecy about the abomination of desolation is as follows:

Daniel 9:25–27. Know therefore and understand, that from the going forth of the commandment to restore and to build Jerusalem unto the Messiah the Prince shall be seven weeks, and threescore and two weeks: the street shall be built again, and the wall, even in troublous times. And after threescore and two weeks shall Messiah be cut off, but not for himself: and the people of the prince that shall come shall destroy the city and the sanctuary; and the end thereof shall be with a flood, and unto the end of the war desolations are determined. And he shall confirm the covenant with many for one week: and in the midst of the week he shall cause the sacrifice and the oblation to cease, and for the overspreading of abominations he shall make it desolate, even until the consummation, and that determined shall be poured upon the desolate.

Daniel 11:31. And they shall pollute the sanctuary of strength, and shall take away the daily sacrifice, and they shall place the abomination that maketh desolate.[51]

---

48.   See D&C 88:73.
49.   See D&C 43:23–25.
50.   James 5:7.
51.   See also Dan. 12:11.

As discussed at length in chapter 54 of this volume, Daniel's prophecy was fulfilled when the Romans destroyed Jerusalem in AD 70. The temple was desecrated and demolished. The temple has not been rebuilt, and the site is under the control of Palestinian Authority.[52]

In Joseph Smith—Matthew 1:32, Jesus was stating that Daniel's prophecy about the abomination of desolation would be fulfilled again, this time as a sign of Jesus's return to the earth. Since the previous abomination of desolation was the destruction of Jerusalem and the temple, it is reasonable to assume that the fulfillment of Daniel's prophecy in the latter days will at least in part involve similar destruction. Presumably, for the abomination of desolation to once again occur, the temple in Jerusalem must be rebuilt and then will be desecrated once again. However, Christ's meaning is uncertain.

Though the abomination of desolation will occur again, Christ's disciples will be protected, as they were when the Roman army arrived at Jerusalem in AD 70.[53] This assurance is given in Zechariah 14:1–5, which describes the abomination of desolation and Christ's protection of the righteous in Jerusalem:

> Behold, the day of the Lord cometh, and thy spoil shall be divided in the midst of thee. For I will gather all nations against Jerusalem to battle; and the city shall be taken, and the houses rifled, and the women ravished; and half of the city shall go forth into captivity, and the residue of the people shall not be cut off from the city. Then shall the Lord go forth, and fight against those nations, as when he fought in the day of battle. And his feet shall stand in that day upon the mount of Olives, which is before Jerusalem on the east, and the mount of Olives shall cleave in the midst thereof toward the east and toward the west, and there shall be a very great valley; and half of the mountain shall remove toward the north, and half of it toward the south. And ye shall flee to the valley of the mountains; for the valley of the mountains shall reach unto Azal: yea, ye shall flee, like as ye fled from before the earthquake in the days of Uzziah king of Judah: and the Lord my God shall come, and all the saints with thee.

Presumably, the abomination of desolation will come upon the wicked. Therefore, it is essential that Jesus's disciples share the gospel and encourage

---

52. See *Encyclopedia Britannica*, s.v. "Palestinian Authority," accessed August 5, 2022, http://www.britannica.com/topic/Palestinian-Authority.

53. See chapter 54 in this volume.

people to embrace it, "that their souls may escape the wrath of God, the desolation of abomination which awaits the wicked, both in this world and in the world to come."[54]

The Sun and Moon Will Be Dark, the Stars Will Fall, and the Powers of Heaven Will Be Shaken (Matt. 24:29; Mark 13:24–25; Luke 21:25–26; JS—M 1:33)

Jesus next prophesied that the sun will be dark, the moon will not shine, and the stars will fall from the sky:

Matthew 24:29. Immediately after the tribulation of those days shall the sun be darkened, and the moon shall not give her light, and the stars shall fall from heaven, and the powers of the heavens shall be shaken.

Luke 21:25–26. And there shall be signs in the sun, and in the moon, and in the stars; and upon the earth distress of nations, with perplexity; the sea and the waves roaring; men's hearts failing them for fear, and for looking after those things which are coming on the earth: for the powers of heaven shall be shaken.

Certainly, the sun will not stop producing light, the moon will not stop reflecting the sun's light, and stars will not fall from the sky. Rather, events will take place that cause the sun and moon to appear to be dark and the stars to appear to fall. Christ is not the only one who has prophesied about the sun, moon, and stars as signs of the Second Coming. For example, Isaiah prophesied: "For the stars of heaven and the constellations thereof shall not give their light: the sun shall be darkened in his going forth, and the moon shall not cause her light to shine."[55] Additionally, the Lord told Joseph Smith that "the moon shall be turned into blood . . . and there shall be greater signs in heaven above and in the earth beneath."[56] In many scriptures, the signs regarding the sun, moon, and stars are referred to together,[57] possibly indicating a common cause of these events.

---

54.   D&C 88:85.
55.   Isa. 13:10; see also 2 Ne. 23:10.
56.   D&C 29:14; see also 34:9; 45:42.
57.   See Isa. 13:10; Ezek. 32:7; Joel 2:10, 31; 3:15; Matt. 24:29; Mark 13:24–25; Luke 21:25; JS—M 1:33; Acts 2:20; 2 Ne. 23:10; Hel. 14:20; D&C 29:14; 34:9; 45:42; 88:87; 133:49.

Importantly, Christ told His Apostles that the signs regarding the sun, moon, and stars would occur "immediately after the tribulation." The tribulation Christ referred to includes wars and rumors of wars, famines, pestilences, earthquakes, iniquity, the lack of love, and the abomination of desolation. Whether these tribulations will be the cause of the signs is unknown.

Significantly, Jesus stated that not only will the sun and moon appear to be darkened and the stars will appear to fall from heaven but that the "powers of the heavens shall be shaken." Certainly, the word *heavens* here does not refer to the place where God dwells but, rather, to the sky and perhaps beyond. Isaiah prophetically wrote, "Therefore I will shake the heavens, and the earth shall remove out of her place, in the wrath of the Lord of hosts, and in the day of his fierce anger. And it shall be as the chased roe, and as a sheep that no man taketh up."[58] Isaiah also wrote, "The earth shall reel to and fro like a drunkard, and shall be removed like a cottage. . . . Then the moon shall be confounded, and the sun ashamed, when the Lord of hosts shall reign in mount Zion, and in Jerusalem, and before his ancients gloriously."[59]

Enoch likewise wrote about this sign preceding Christ's Second Coming: "Before that day the heavens shall be darkened, and a veil of darkness shall cover the earth; and the heavens shall shake, and also the earth; and great tribulations shall be among the children of men, but my people will I preserve."[60]

Similarly, the Lord told Joseph Smith, "For not many days hence and the earth shall tremble and reel to and fro as a drunken man; and the sun shall hide his face, and shall refuse to give light; and the moon shall be bathed in blood; and the stars shall become exceedingly angry, and shall cast themselves down as a fig that falleth from off a fig tree."[61]

It is unclear when or how these prophesied events will transpire; however, it is evident that Christ will be directly involved. Certainly, when these signs appear, they will be recognizable.

---

58. Isa. 13:13–14.
59. Isa. 24:20, 23.
60. Moses 7:61.
61. D&C 88:87.

People's Hearts Will Fail Them Because of Fear (Luke 21:26)

Jesus then explained that because of the great tribulations on the earth and in the heavens, people's hearts will fail them:

Luke 21:26. Men's hearts failing them for fear, and for looking after those things which are coming on the earth: for the powers of heaven shall be shaken.

The idea of people's "hearts failing them for fear" is also described in Isaiah 13:6–9: "Howl ye; for the day of the Lord is at hand; it shall come as a destruction from the Almighty. Therefore shall all hands be faint, and every man's heart shall melt: And they shall be afraid: pangs and sorrows shall take hold of them; they shall be in pain as a woman that travaileth: they shall be amazed one at another; their faces shall be as flames. Behold, the day of the Lord cometh, cruel both with wrath and fierce anger, to lay the land desolate: and he shall destroy the sinners thereof out of it." Isaiah also foresaw a time when many people would hide in the clefts of rocks because of fear.[62]

In the latter days, the righteous do not need to fear, for they "shall not perish"[63] but will be preserved by the Lord's power,[64] as were the majority of the righteous Nephites and Lamanites when Jesus died.[65]

When Jesus Returns, People Will Mourn (Matt. 24:30; JS—M 1:36)

Jesus then explained that when He returns, people will mourn:

Matthew 24:30. And then shall appear the sign of the Son of man in heaven: and then shall all the tribes of the earth mourn, and they shall see the Son of man coming in the clouds of heaven with power and great glory.

The righteous might mourn for those who failed to repent. The righteous might also mourn for the same reason that the people in the Americas did following the terrible destruction that occurred when Christ died: "There was great mourning and howling and weeping among all the people continually;

---

62.   See Isa. 2:19–21; see also D&C 88:91. Perhaps the destruction of the wicked Lamanites and Nephites at Christ's death (see 3 Ne. 8–9) is a type and shadow of what will take place when Christ returns.

63.   1 Ne. 22:19.

64.   See 1 Ne. 22:17, 22.

65.   See 3 Ne. 9:11, 13.

yea, great were the groanings of the people, because of the darkness and the great destruction which had come upon them."[66] The people's mourning turned to joy after Christ appeared, and the righteous in the last days will have great reason to rejoice when Christ returns.

Those who are wicked will mourn because they disbelieved, failed to repent, and perhaps even fought against the gospel and those who do believe. They will also mourn because the prophesies regarding wars, famines, pestilences, earthquakes, and the heavens have been fulfilled. The wicked will mourn for their loved ones who are wicked and perhaps were killed. The wicked will also mourn because of the effects of iniquity and the lack of love for one another in the world. This mourning may be similar to that of the people in the Book of Mormon after the destruction that occurred at Christ's death: "They were heard to cry and mourn, saying: O that we had repented before this great and terrible day, and had not killed and stoned the prophets, and cast them out; then would our mothers and our fair daughters, and our children have been spared."[67]

The Remainder of the Elect Will Be Gathered After Jesus Returns (Matt. 24:31; Mark 13:27; JS—M 1:37)

Next, Jesus explained that after He returns, the remainder of the elect will be gathered:

Mark 13:26–27. And then shall they see the Son of man coming in the clouds with great power and glory. And then shall he send his angels, and shall gather together his elect from the four winds, from the uttermost part of the earth to the uttermost part of heaven.

It is significant that angels in heaven will be directly involved in gathering the remainder of the elect. The scriptures contain little information about who these angels are and the nature and extent of their ministries.[68] However, angels have been involved in the Restoration of the gospel, including the restoring of priesthood keys, which has enabled the gathering of Israel to take

---

66. 3 Ne. 8:23.

67. 3 Ne. 8:25.

68. Much of the information that is available about these angels is found in Revelation 8–10 and 16.

place. These angels include Moroni, who delivered the gold plates to Joseph Smith;[69] John the Baptist, who conferred upon Joseph Smith and Oliver Cowdery the Aaronic priesthood;[70] Peter, James, and John, who conferred upon Joseph Smith and Oliver Cowdery the Melchizedek Priesthood;[71] Moses, who conferred upon Joseph Smith the keys of the gathering of Israel;[72] and Elias (possibly Noah)[73] and Elijah, who conferred upon Joseph Smith the keys of the power to turn the hearts of the fathers to the children and the hearts of the children to the fathers.[74] All of these angels have contributed to and may continue to contribute to gathering the elect. Christ may have also been referring to other angels who have contributed to or will yet contribute to the Restoration and the gathering of the elect.[75]

Insight regarding certain angels' involvement may come from Doctrine and Covenants 77:11. This verse records Joseph Smith's question and the Lord's answer regarding the Apostle John's vision of the Lamb of God on Mount Zion with "an hundred forty and four thousand, having his Father's name written in their foreheads":[76]

Q. What are we to understand by sealing the one hundred and forty-four thousand, out of all the tribes of Israel—twelve thousand out of every tribe?

A. We are to understand that those who are sealed are high priests, ordained unto the holy order of God, to administer the everlasting gospel; for they are they who are ordained out of every nation, kindred, tongue, and people,

---

69. See Smith, *History of the Church*, vol. 1. pp. 11–16, 18; D&C 27:5.
70. See D&C 13; Smith, *History of the Church*, vol. 1, pp. 39–41.
71. See Smith, *History of the Church*, vol. 1, pp. 40–41.
72. See D&C 110:11.
73. See D&C 27:6; 110:11; Luke 1:19; Smith, *Teachings*, p. 157.
74. See D&C 110:13–16; 27:9.
75. See Sarah Jane Weaver, "President Nelson Teaches New Mission Leaders How 'Repeated, Miraculous Tutoring' Prepared Joseph Smith for His Calling," *Church News*, June 24, 2021, https://www.thechurchnews.com/leaders-and-ministry/2021-06-24/president-nelson-mission-leadership-seminar-joseph-smith-2-217463; see also Larry C. Porter, "Visions of Joseph Smith," in *Encyclopedia of Mormonism*, ed. Daniel H. Ludlow, vol. 4, p. 1515. In addition, the Apostle John and the Three Nephites, who are not angels but translated beings, continue their ministry of gathering the elect before Christ returns (see John 21:22–23; 3 Ne. 28:4–10, 27–32; D&C 7; Smith, *History of the Church*, vol. 1, p. 176).
76. Rev. 14:1.

by the angels to whom is given power over the nations of the earth, to bring as many as will come to the church of the Firstborn.[77]

It is not certain that these 144,000 will be angels; perhaps some will be mortals at the time. Other angels may come from heaven, as Enoch saw in vision: "Angels descend[ed] out of heaven, bearing testimony of the Father and Son; and the Holy Ghost fell on many."[78] Further, Joseph Smith said that "men and angels are to be co-workers in bringing to pass this great work."[79]

Importantly, Jesus stated that not only the elect on the earth will be gathered but also the elect in heaven will be gathered. All who are alive and all who have ever lived will be given the opportunity to accept the gospel,[80] the central features of which are Christ and His Atonement. Some of those in the spirit world who have accepted the gospel have been called to take the gospel message to others there and to prepare for Christ's return.

Jesus's Prophecies about the Signs of the Second Coming Will Be Fulfilled

The accounts in Matthew, Mark, and Luke use identical language to convey the immutable truth that Christ's prophecies about the events preceding His Second Coming will certainly come to pass: "Heaven and earth shall pass away: but my words shall not pass away."[81] The Joseph Smith—Matthew account contains amplification: "Although, the days will come, that heaven and earth shall pass away; yet my words shall not pass away, but all shall be fulfilled."[82] The fundamental principle that all of Christ's words will be fulfilled should be kept firmly in mind and heart and should be evidenced in people's conduct as the Second Coming of the Lord draws ever nearer.[83]

During the challenges and turmoil before Christ returns, those who follow Christ can find peace in knowing that God will help them, just as

---

77. D&C 77:11.
78. See Moses 7:27.
79. Smith, *History of the Church*, vol. 2, p. 260.
80. See D&C 138.
81. Matt. 24:35; Mark 13:31; Luke 21:33.
82. JS—M 1:35.
83. Some have speculated about what will cause the various signs Jesus gave of His Second Coming; however, such speculation is to no avail. What is important is that He who created the earth will fulfill His words in His own way and in His own time.

He helped Helaman and his soldiers during battle: "God did visit us with assurances that he would deliver us . . . [and] speak peace to our souls, and . . . grant unto us great faith, and . . . cause us that we should hope for our deliverance in him."[84]

---

84.   Alma 58:11.

Chapter 56

JESUS'S COUNSEL TO WATCH AND BE READY

(Tuesday)

After Jesus told the Apostles some of the signs of His Second Coming, He instructed them to watch and be ready for His coming. In teaching about the timing of His coming, He used a fig tree as an example and explained that only Heavenly Father knows the day and hour that Jesus will return. He also taught that in contrast to the righteous, the wicked will not be prepared for nor recognize the signs of His coming. The wicked will be punished for their wickedness, whereas the righteous will receive eternal rewards.

Parable of the Fig Tree (Matt. 24:32; Mark 13:28; Luke 21:29–31; JS—M 1:38–39)

Jesus began His instruction about the timing of His return by using the metaphor of a fig tree:

Joseph Smith—Matthew 1:38–39. Now learn a parable of the fig tree— When its branches are yet tender, and it begins to put forth leaves, you know that summer is nigh at hand; so likewise, mine elect, when they shall see all these things, they shall know that he is near, even at the doors.

The metaphor was particularly apt because earlier on this day and on the day before, Jesus had taught His Apostles various principles by referring to a fig tree.[1] There may have been one or more fig trees where Jesus and His

---

1. See Matt. 21:18–20; Mark 11:12–14, 20–21; see also chapters 50 and 51 in this volume.

Apostles were now gathered on the Mount of Olives. In Joseph Smith— Matthew, Jesus refers to "the fig tree," whereas in Luke's account, Jesus refers to not only "the fig tree" but "all the trees,"[2] suggesting that other trees were also in the area. Perhaps Jesus pointed to a nearby tree whose branches were beginning to bud because it was early spring.

Jesus told His Apostles that when a tree's branches begin to bud, summer is approaching. Likewise, when the signs of the Second Coming begin to appear, the elect will recognize that Jesus will soon return. Luke's account adds, "Ye see and know of your own selves that summer is now nigh at hand."[3] In other words, each person is individually responsible for watching for and understanding the signs and for being prepared for Christ's return to the earth. This parable also implies that there will be some period between when the signs begin to appear and when He returns to the earth, just as trees begin to bud several months before the summer leaves come.

Jesus stated that when the elect[4] see the signs of His coming, they will know that His return is near, "even at the doors." He used the plural word *doors*. It is reasonable to assume that this word refers to the elect all over the world who are watching for the signs of the Lord's return and who understand that His coming is soon approaching.

Implicitly, Jesus was also teaching that in the last days, in order to know and understand the signs of His return, each person needs to study the scriptures because they describe many of the prophesied signs. Additionally, people need spiritual discernment from the Holy Ghost in order to more fully understand what has been written about the signs of the Second Coming.

Only God Knows the Day and Hour of Jesus's Second Coming (Matt. 24:36; Mark 13:32; JS—M 1:40)

Jesus next stated that God alone knows when Jesus will return. Implied in this statement is that God alone will determine when Jesus returns, when the wicked will be destroyed, and when the Millennium will be ushered in.

---

2.   Luke 21:29.
3.   Luke 21:30.
4.   For a discussion of who the elect are, see page 116 in this volume.

In making this statement, Jesus was tacitly affirming that God's hand is over all things.

Joseph Smith—Matthew 1:40. But of that day, and hour, no one knoweth; no, not the angels of God in heaven, but my Father only.

Christ may have knowledge of the economy of the earth, the future of humankind, and the specific timing of events to come, but He implied that even He does not know the day and hour of His return. That knowledge belongs only to Heavenly Father, who will determine when Christ will return.[5]

An important principle regarding Heavenly Father's timing was stated by James, one of Jesus's brothers: "Be patient therefore, brethren, unto the coming of the Lord. Behold, the husbandman waiteth for the precious fruit of the earth, and hath long patience for it, until he receive the early and latter rain."[6] A husbandman is "one that plows and cultivates land,"[7] and he must wait for crops to mature and be ready for harvesting. So that crops can grow, they need to be watered, such as by "early and latter rain."[8] Therefore, James may have been counseling people to be patient, just as a husbandman must wait for his crops.

Alternatively, James may have been using the word *husbandman* to refer to God, who figuratively planted His children on the earth.[9] Just as crops are precious to the husbandman, Heavenly Father's children are precious to Him.[10] Likewise, just as a husbandman watches over his crops, God lovingly[11] watches over each of His children. Father in Heaven will wait patiently for those who should receive the gospel to have that opportunity before His Beloved Son returns. Further, the "latter rain" may refer to the latter days. Presumably, the hour, day, and year of the Lord's coming are of much less

---

5.   See also Acts 1:7.

6.   James 5:7.

7.   *Merriam-Webster,* s.v. "husbandman," accessed August 5, 2022, https://www.merriam-webster.com/dictionary/husbandman.

8.   For a discussion of "early and latter rain," see Clarke, *Commentary,* vol. 3, p. 825; see also Deut. 11:14.

9.   In Jesus's analogy about a vine, the husbandman is the Father, and the fruit are His children. See chapter 62 of this volume for discussion of this analogy.

10.   See Isa. 13:12; 2 Ne. 23:12; Jacob 5:61, 74; D&C 109:43.

11.   See John 3:16.

importance than how, when, and under what circumstances people will hear the gospel, be tested, and hopefully qualify for eternal life.

Jesus Compares the Last Days to the Days of Noah (Matt. 24:37–39; JS—M 1:41–43)

In further instructing the Apostles, Jesus used the conditions of Noah's day as a type and shadow of the conditions that will prevail in the days before His second advent:

> **Joseph Smith—Matthew 1:41–43.** But as it was in the days of Noah, so it shall be also at the coming of the Son of Man; for it shall be with them, as it was in the days which were before the flood; for until the day that Noah entered into the ark they were eating and drinking, marrying and giving in marriage; and knew not until the flood came, and took them all away; so shall also the coming of the Son of Man be.

In Noah's day, terrible wickedness prevailed: "And God saw that the wickedness of man was great in the earth, and that every imagination of the thoughts of his heart was only evil continually."[12] People indulged in worldly appetites and were not apprehensive about the future. Given Jesus's statement, it seems that in Noah's time there was a degree of prosperity and complacency. Perhaps the conditions were similar to those Jesus had described in the parable of the rich man, who said to himself, "Soul, thou hast much goods laid up for many years; take thine ease, eat, drink and be merry."[13] The people in Noah's day apparently did not think their lives were in jeopardy. Rather, they went about their daily activities, "eating and drinking, marrying and giving in marriage." They presumably scoffed at Noah and the great ark he was building. They refused to change their lives until it was too late.

Christ made it clear that in the last days, wickedness will again be prevalent. Regarding this wickedness, Peter wrote the following: "There shall come in the last days scoffers, walking after their own lusts."[14] Paul likewise taught of wickedness in the last days:

---

12. Gen. 6:5; see also vv. 11–12.
13. Luke 12:19; see also Isa. 22:13; 1 Cor. 15:32; Eccl. 8:15; 2 Ne. 28:21.
14. 2 Pet. 3:3.

This know also, that in the last days perilous times shall come. For men shall be lovers of their own selves, covetous, boasters, proud, blasphemers, disobedient to parents, unthankful, unholy, without natural affection, trucebreakers, false accusers, incontinent, fierce, despisers of those that are good, traitors, heady, highminded, lovers of pleasures more than lovers of God; having a form of godliness, but denying the power thereof. . . . Led away with divers lusts, ever learning, and never able to come to the knowledge of the truth.[15]

Each form of wickedness mentioned in the scriptures above is evident in the world today, and each is a sign that Christ's return is not far distant. Despite these signs, many people today, like the wicked in Noah's day, fail to repent and prepare for what has been prophesied to come. To the wicked, Jesus's return will be unexpected; in contrast, to the righteous who watch for the signs Jesus has given, His return will be anticipated and glorious.

The Righteous and the Wicked Will Be Divided (Matt. 24:40–41; JS—M 1:44–45)

Jesus then illustrated His point by using an example from ordinary life: people working in the field and grinding at the mill:

Joseph Smith—Matthew 1:44–45. Then shall be fulfilled that which is written, that in the last days, two shall be in the field, the one shall be taken, and the other left; two shall be grinding at the mill, the one shall be taken, and the other left.

The phrase "then shall be fulfilled that which is written" presumably refers to the writings of a prophet, though the Old Testament does not contain the prophesy Jesus mentioned. The idea being conveyed is that the righteous and the wicked will be divided. Nephi likewise prophesied that in the latter days, "the Lord God shall cause a great division among the people, and the wicked will he destroy; and he will spare his people, yea, even if it so be that he must destroy the wicked by fire."[16]

---

15. 2 Tim. 3:1–5, 7; see also Rom. 1:25–32; 2 Ne. 28.
16. 2 Ne. 30:10; see also the parable of the wheat and the tares (Matt. 13:24–30, 36–43; D&C 86).

The statement that one person will be taken and the other will be left can have dual meanings. The statement may mean that those who are wicked will be taken and destroyed by fire, while the righteous will be spared. The statement may also mean that the righteous will be taken, in that they will be caught up to join Christ as He descends to the earth, as described in the Doctrine and Covenants:

> And there shall be silence in heaven for the space of half an hour; and immediately after shall the curtain of heaven be unfolded, as a scroll is unfolded after it is rolled up, and the face of the Lord shall be unveiled; and the saints that are upon the earth, who are alive, shall be quickened and be caught up to meet him. And they who have slept in their graves shall come forth, for their graves shall be opened; and they also shall be caught up to meet him in the midst of the pillar of heaven—they are Christ's, the first fruits, they who shall descend with him first, and they who are on the earth and in their graves, who are first caught up to meet him; and all this by the voice of the sounding of the trump of the angel of God.[17]

Regardless of which meaning of *taken* is intended, what is important is that the righteous will be spared and even blessed beyond measure when Jesus returns in glory.

Jesus Directs All to Watch and Be Ready for His Return
(Matt. 24:42–44; Mark 13:33; JST Luke 21:36; JS—M 1:46–48)

To further illustrate the need to watch and be ready, Jesus gave another parable:

> **Joseph Smith—Matthew 1:46–48.** And what I say unto one, I say unto all men; watch, therefore, for you know not at what hour your Lord doth come. But know this, if the good man of the house had known in what watch the thief would come, he would have watched, and would not have suffered his house to have been broken up, but would have been ready. Therefore be ye also ready, for in such an hour as ye think not, the Son of Man cometh.

This parable focuses on a good person. Nevertheless, he slacks in watching. The verb *watch* means not only to see but also to be attentive and

---

17. D&C 88:95–98.

keep guard.[18] In the parable, if the good man had known in which watch[19] the thief[20] would come, the good man would have prevented a burglary, which very well may have occurred at night when members of the household were sleeping.

Spiritually, to watch is to not only be aware of the signs that the Savior and His prophets have given of His coming but also be prepared, both physically and spiritually. Watching also involves searching the scriptures and treasuring up the words of Christ, including regarding the signs of His coming. As He told the Apostles, "Whoso treasureth up my word, shall not be deceived."[21] Further, watching involves serious regular introspection and effort to weed out anything that is preventing someone from being clean.

In the parable, the house was broken up; the house may be a metaphor for the family. Marriage is a serious and sacred obligation, and spouses need to be attentive to each other. Likewise, watching over children is a sacred obligation. Parents are responsible for teaching their children,[22] guarding them from evil in the world, and preparing them to meet the challenges they will face in their lives. If parents are not vigilant in teaching their children, they risk spiritually losing their children. Even in the best of homes, it is possible that children will stray, but the chances decrease when parents are vigilant and notice signs of spiritual decline.

After concluding the parable, Jesus highlighted the importance of watching and being ready for His Second Coming, "for in such an hour as ye think not, the Son of Man cometh." Just as the wicked people in Noah's time did not expect a fatal flood to come when it did, the Savior will return to the earth at a time when those who are worldly do not expect Him to come.

---

18.   See *Merriam-Webster*, s.v. "watch," accessed August 5, 2022, http://www.merriam-webster.com/dictionary/watch.

19.   "The proper Jewish reckoning recognized only three [night] watches. . . . These would last respectively from sunset to 10 P.M., from 10 P.M. to 2 A.M., and from 2 A.M. to sunrise." (Smith, *Bible Dictionary*, s.v. "watches of the night.")

20.   See also 2 Pet. 3:10.

21.   JS—M 1:37.

22.   See D&C 68:25.

Jesus Teaches about Being a Faithful, Wise Servant (Matt. 24:45–51; Mark 13:34–36; JS—M 1:49–54)

Jesus next presented a parable about servants in a household:

Joseph Smith—Matthew 1:49–54. Who, then, is a faithful and wise servant, whom his lord hath made ruler over his household, to give them meat in due season? Blessed is that servant whom his lord, when he cometh, shall find so doing; and verily I say unto you, he shall make him ruler over all his goods. But if that evil servant shall say in his heart: My lord delayeth his coming, and shall begin to smite his fellow-servants, and to eat and drink with the drunken, the lord of that servant shall come in a day when he looketh not for him, and in an hour that he is not aware of, and shall cut him asunder, and shall appoint him his portion with the hypocrites; there shall be weeping and gnashing of teeth.

In the parable, the household represents members of the Church, and the servants represent the Apostles, the Seventy, and all other Church members who are called to serve. They are to diligently serve in their various callings and fulfill their stewardships, whether small or great. If they remain diligent, they will receive an eternal reward: that of becoming rulers in God's heavenly kingdom.

They will not receive a reward if they become slothful or apathetic in their service or cease to look to the Lord, justifying their inaction with the belief that He will not return until much later. In the parable, Jesus described these unrighteous servants as "smiting" others. The word *smiting* may refer to physical or emotional harm or may symbolize a lack of love, compassion, and mercy or the desire to gain material advantage. In the parable, Jesus also described the wicked servant as eating and drinking with the drunk. This behavior may symbolize a person's focus on the material things of the world and lack of awareness of his or her spiritual well-being. Even members of the Church can fall, and Jesus taught that slothful servants will eventually be cut off from the kingdom of heaven and will dwell with the hypocrites.

Certainly, disciples' ministries do not end when they die, nor does their obligation to be faithful and wise servants cease. There will be much for them to do in the spirit world, serving the Lord in ways that have not yet been fully revealed, teaching others the gospel, and preparing for the Lord's return. The prophet Joseph F. Smith saw in vision some of those who were laboring in the spirit world:

> And as I wondered, my eyes were opened, and my understanding quickened, and I perceived that the Lord went not in person among the wicked and the disobedient who had rejected the truth, to teach them; but behold, from among the righteous, he organized his forces and appointed messengers, clothed with power and authority, and commissioned them to go forth and carry the light of the gospel to them that were in darkness, even to all the spirits of men; and thus was the gospel preached to the dead. And the chosen messengers went forth to declare the acceptable day of the Lord and proclaim liberty to the captives who were bound, even unto all who would repent of their sins and receive the gospel. . . . I beheld that the faithful elders of this dispensation, when they depart from mortal life, continue their labors in the preaching of the gospel of repentance and redemption, through the sacrifice of the Only Begotten Son of God, among those who are in darkness and under the bondage of sin in the great world of the spirits of the dead.[23]

It is significant that in the parable about the servants, it was the evil servant who stated that the lord delayed his return.[24] Wicked servants fail to heed the warnings of the apostles and prophets and fail to understand the signs that scriptures give of the Lord's return.

The parable emphasizes that if people are not vigilant and adopt worldly habits because of the belief that Christ's Second Coming has been delayed, these people will not be prepared for the Lord's return. Consequently, they will lose their eternal reward and will weep and gnash their teeth.

Jesus Warns about Excess (Luke 21:34–36)

Luke's account alone includes the following counsel that Jesus gave to His Apostles while speaking to them on the Mount of Olives:

Luke 21:34–36. And take heed to yourselves, lest at any time your hearts be overcharged with surfeiting, and drunkenness, and cares of this life, and so

---

23.   D&C 138:29–31, 57.

24.   For other examples of people believing that Christ's coming has been delayed, see 3 Ne. 29:2; D&C 45:26.

that day come upon you unawares. For as a snare shall it come on all them that dwell on the face of the whole earth. Watch ye therefore, and pray always, that ye may be accounted worthy to escape all these things that shall come to pass, and to stand before the Son of man.

Jesus was teaching His Apostles about the need for introspection and correction. Jesus used the word *hearts* as a metaphor. Symbolically, a person's heart represents the core of who he or she is—his or her "innermost character, feelings, or inclinations."[25] The feelings of the heart frequently motivate an individual's actions. *Surfeiting* means "an overabundant supply: excess," "an intemperate or immoderate indulgence in something," or "disgust caused by excess."[26] In speaking of surfeit, Jesus gave the example of drunkenness, which may mean intoxication by alcohol or by worldly things; another example of surfeit is drug addiction.

By warning about surfeit, Jesus was teaching the Apostles—and, by extension, all people—to not let their hearts (i.e., their emotions and character) be ruled by excess emotion and thereby be overcome by the things of the world. Rather, people should follow Jesus's teachings, including to pray regularly, repent, and be obedient, in order to be watching and ready for His return.

Jesus Teaches That the Wicked Will Be Destroyed (JS—M 1:55)

Expanding on the idea just taught, Jesus repeated part of a prophecy that He had given, as Jehovah, to Moses:

Joseph Smith—Matthew 1:55. And thus cometh the end of the wicked, according to the prophecy of Moses, saying: They shall be cut off from among the people; but the end of the earth is not yet, but by and by.

Jesus was presumably referring to the prophecy He gave Moses about those who were sexually immoral[27] and those who worshipped idols.[28] Of course,

---

25. *Merriam-Webster*, s.v. "heart," accessed August 8, 2022, http://www.merriam-webster.com/dictionary/heart.

26. *Merriam-Webster*, s.v. "surfeit," accessed August 8, 2022, http://www.merriam-webster.com/dictionary/surfeit.

27. See Lev. 20:17.

28. See Deut. 17:2–5.

wickedness also has many other forms. Jesus made clear that the wicked will be destroyed. Therefore, people need to not only watch but also avoid the evils and excesses of the world in order to be clean when Jesus returns.

Jesus Teaches That All of His Words Will Be Fulfilled (Matt. 24:35; Mark 13:31; Luke 21:33; JS—M 1:35)

By way of warning, Jesus next told His Apostles that all His words would come to pass:

Joseph Smith—Matthew 1:35. Although, the days will come, that heaven and earth shall pass away; yet my words shall not pass away, but all shall be fulfilled.

Insight regarding Jesus's words is found in 2 Peter 3:9–14:

The Lord is not slack concerning his promise, as some men count slackness; but is longsuffering to us-ward, not willing that any should perish, but that all should come to repentance. But the day of the Lord will come as a thief in the night; in the which the heavens shall pass away with a great noise, and the elements shall melt with fervent heat, the earth also and the works that are therein shall be burned up. Seeing then that all these things shall be dissolved, what manner of persons ought ye to be in all holy conversation and godliness, looking for and hasting unto the coming of the day of God, wherein the heavens being on fire shall be dissolved, and the elements shall melt with fervent heat? Nevertheless we, according to his promise, look for new heavens and a new earth, wherein dwelleth righteousness. Wherefore, beloved, seeing that ye look for such things, be diligent that ye may be found of him in peace, without spot, and blameless.[29]

There is no way to really understand how the earth and heavens will pass away, for humankind has no frame of reference for such events. However, these events will presumably be dramatic and recognized by many. Likewise, there is no way to fully understand how the righteous will be spared amid great destruction. Therefore, faith is required. With that faith, people can heed Peter's admonition: "Wherefore, beloved, seeing that ye look for such things, be diligent that ye may be found of him in peace, without spot, and blameless."

---

29.   See also Heb. 1:10–11; Rev. 21:1; 3 Ne. 26:3; Morm. 9:2; D&C 101:25; 130:9.

All People Need to Watch and Be Ready

An additional consideration related to the imperative to watch and be prepared is that Christ has said He will come quickly. For example, the Lord repeated this idea multiple times in the vision that the Apostle John saw of events in the last days.[30] Likewise, the Lord repeatedly told Joseph Smith that He would come quickly.[31] The final time that the Doctrine and Covenants records the Lord making this statement was on July 23, 1837.[32] More than 180 years have gone by, and the Lord has not come, leading to the question of what the Lord meant when he used the word *quickly*. Possibly, He meant that He is coming quickly in terms of heaven's reckoning of time or in relation to the length of the earth's existence. Alternatively, the word may not mean that He is coming soon but, rather, that after the final signs prior to His coming occur, He will come suddenly. For example, the Apostle John was told the following in vision: "Therefore shall her plagues come in one day."[33] It is therefore imperative that people watch for the signs of His coming so they are ready when He suddenly appears.

Watching and being ready can be challenging because while climbing up the steep, rugged mountain trails of life, people will not be able to see the grand vistas that God, through His Son, has created—the full view can be seen only after reaching the summit. Climbing takes time, effort, and the willingness to continue even when tired, bruised from stumbling over rocks, and scratched by brush along the way. People need to lift their eyes and hearts to the summit of Christ and the plan of salvation and be ever sensitive to the whisperings of the Holy Spirit. By doing so, people will gain a greater understanding of the grand plan not only for this world but for each individual and will recognize the signs of the Lord's coming.

---

30. See Rev. 3:11; 22:7, 12, 20.
31. See D&C 33:18; 34:12; 35:27; 39:24; 41:4; 49:28; 51:20; 54:10; 68:35; 87:8; 88:126; 99:5; 112:34.
32. See D&C 112:34.
33. Rev. 18:8.

In regard to the Lord's Second Coming, the inspired words in the first verse of the "Battle Hymn of the Republic" are poignant:

> Mine eyes have seen the glory of the coming of the Lord;
> He is trampling out the vintage where the grapes of wrath are stored.
> He hath loosed the fateful lightning of his terrible, swift sword;
> His truth is marching on.[34]

Jesus's simple instruction to watch[35] is an apt conclusion to this portion of His discussion with the Apostles the final Tuesday of His life. The instruction to watch is applicable to all in mortality and to those who have passed on. Whether in this life or the next, if people watch and are faithful, they will rejoice when they see the coming of the Lord.

---

34. Julia Ward Howe, "Battle Hymn of the Republic," *Hymns,* no. 60.
35. See Mark 13:37.

Chapter 57

THE PARABLE OF THE TEN VIRGINS

(Tuesday₁)

To further illustrate the importance of watching and being ready for the Second Coming, Jesus gave the parable of the ten virgins. This parable is one of Jesus's most frequently discussed parables. It has deep meaning and significant implications for those in the last days who believe in Christ and await His glorious return to the earth.

Jesus Gives the Parable of the Ten Virgins (Matt. 25:1–13)

The Gospel of Matthew is the only Gospel that gives an account of this parable, and Joseph Smith's translation of Matthew 25:1 identifies the context of this parable as "at that day, before the Son of Man comes." The parable is as follows:

> **Matthew 25:1–13.** Then shall the kingdom of heaven be likened unto ten virgins, which took their lamps, and went forth to meet the bridegroom. And five of them were wise, and five were foolish. They that were foolish took their lamps, and took no oil with them: but the wise took oil in their vessels with their lamps. While the bridegroom tarried, they all slumbered and slept. And at midnight there was a cry made, Behold, the bridegroom cometh; go ye out to meet him. Then all those virgins arose, and trimmed their lamps. And the foolish said unto the wise, Give us of your oil; for

---

1.   Some scholars are of the opinion that Jesus gave the parable of the ten virgins on Wednesday (see, for example, Edersheim, *Life and Times of Jesus the Messiah*, pp. 772–796).

our lamps are gone out. But the wise answered, saying, Not so; lest there be not enough for us and you: but go ye rather to them that sell, and buy for yourselves. And while they went to buy, the bridegroom came; and they that were ready went in with him to the marriage: and the door was shut. Afterward came also the other virgins, saying, Lord, Lord, open to us. But he answered and said, Verily I say unto you, I know you not. Watch therefore, for ye know neither the day nor the hour wherein the Son of man cometh.

The main purpose of this parable is to emphasize the need for individuals to always be spiritually prepared, not only to be ready for the Lord's Second Coming but also to be worthy to enter the kingdom of heaven. The following sections provide insight about various components of the parable.

The Kingdom of Heaven

This parable begins similar to several of Jesus's other parables: "Then shall the kingdom of heaven be likened unto . . ."[2] Jesus was indicating that the parable would provide insight into the requirements to enter the kingdom of heaven.

The Wedding

During Jesus's day, Jewish weddings typically took place in the late afternoon or at night. Prior to the wedding, it was common for the bridegroom to go the home of the bride, accompanied by some of his friends in a festive procession. The bridegroom, the bride, and the others in the procession would then go to his home, his parents' home, or some other designated place for the wedding and associated festivities. Friends of the bride would watch for the procession to appear on its way to the location of the wedding and would join the procession, using their lamps to light the way.[3]

Metaphorically, the bridegroom represents the Lord, and the bride represents the Lord's Church,[4] although the bride is not directly mentioned in the parable. In this parable, the bridegroom "tarried" before arriving where the ten virgins were waiting. Edersheim postulated that the bridegroom was

---

2.   See, for example, Matt 13:24; 18:23; 20:1; 22:1–2.
3.   See Talmage, *Jesus the Christ*, p. 536; Edersheim, *Life and Times of Jesus the Messiah*, p. 788; Trench, *Notes on the Parables*, p. 85.
4.   See Rev. 19:7–9; see also D&C 33:17; 65:3; 88:92; 109:73–74; 133:10, 19.

traveling from a distant place,—those who waited for him did not know
the precise time he would come, and when he did come, someone called
out, "The bridegroom cometh." Metaphorically, that faraway place could
be heaven, for Jesus ascended to heaven after His forty-day ministry in
Jerusalem following His Resurrection and He will descend from heaven
when He returns to the earth for His Second Coming., Although the exact
timing of the bridegroom's arrival was unknown beforehand, all those in
the wedding party were well aware that he would come that night. It seems
that the ten virgins were either at or close by the place where the marriage
would take place, for there is no mention of the virgins traveling with the
procession. Rather, the parable states that when the bridegroom arrived, the
five virgins who were there to meet him "went in with him to the marriage."

The Ten Virgins

In the parable, the ten people waiting for the bridegroom were virgins,
suggesting that these individuals were morally pure and had a degree of
faith., Therefore, the virgins in this parable represent those who believe in
Christ, are members of Christ's Church, and are waiting for Him to return
and usher in the Millennium.

The fact that there were ten virgins is significant. According to Edersheim,
"ten was the number required to be present at any office or ceremony,
such as at the benedictions accompanying the marriage-ceremonies.", In
addition, according to Trench, "Wherever there were ten Jews living in one
place, there was a congregation, and there a synagogue ought to be built.",
Dummelow stated that this number was "chosen because among the Jews it
was a complete number.",

The virgins may have been young; if so, this parable may be particularly
applicable to the youth of the Church as they prepare for the Lord's return
throughout their lives, not knowing when He will come.

---

5.   See Edersheim, *Life and Times of Jesus the Messiah*, pp. 788–789.
6.   See Acts 1:1–11.
7.   See Trench, *Notes on the Parables*, p. 85.
8.   Edersheim, *Life and Times of Jesus the Messiah*, p. 788.
9.   Trench, *Notes on the Parables*, p. 85.
10. Dummelow, *Bible Commentary*, p. 705.

The Lamps and Vessels

Regarding the lamps that the virgins carried, Edersheim stated the following: "The 'lamps'—not 'torches'—which the Ten Virgins carried, were of well-known construction. . . . The lamps consisted of a round receptacle for pitch or oil for the wick. This was placed in a hollow cup or deep saucer . . . which was fastened by a pointed end into a long wooden pole, on which it was borne aloft."[11] Additionally, according to the *HarperCollins Bible Dictionary*, oil lamps "had two basic parts: a receptacle for the oil and a wick inserted into the oil whose protruding end would burn. Olives provided the main source of oil in the Near East; various materials, including flax, served as wicks."[12]

Each virgin brought her own lamp; however, only five brought vessels— that is, containers—filled with extra oil.[13] Extra oil was important because lamps in Jesus's day needed to be regularly replenished with oil in order to keep burning. The five who did not bring vessels did not have enough oil to keep their lamps burning when the bridegroom arrived. These foolish virgins could not borrow oil, nor did they have time to purchase more.

It is doubtful that the foolish virgins did not have extra oil because they forgot to bring vessels. Rather, they likely incorrectly assumed they would have sufficient oil in their lamps, believing the bridegroom would come in the early evening, or they may have thought they could acquire oil from others, such as the five wise virgins. The five foolish virgins did not diligently prepare, particularly for a situation in which the groom not only arrived later than expected but also suddenly, meaning that they did not have adequate time to acquire the needed oil.

---

11.   Edersheim, *Life and Times of Jesus the Messiah*, p. 788.

12.   *HarperCollins Bible Dictionary*, s.v. "lamp." Olives are also associated with Christ's Atonement, as He atoned for the sins of humankind in an olive grove. Gethsemane means "olive press." (See *HarperCollins Bible Dictionary*, s.v. "Gethsemane.")

13.   Edersheim postulated, "It seems scarcely likely that these lamps had been lighted while waiting in the bridal house, where the Virgins assembled, and which, no doubt, was festively illuminated. Many practical objections to this view will readily occur. The foolishness of the five Virgins therefore consisted, not (as commonly supposed) *in their want of perseverance*—as if the oil had been consumed before the Bridegroom came, and they had only not provided themselves with sufficient extra-supply—but in *the entire absence of personal preparation*, having brought no oil of their own in their lamps." (Edersheim, *Life and Times of Jesus the Messiah*, p. 789.)

Just as lamps need to be regularly replenished with oil, people need to regularly replenish their spiritual strength so that they can meet all of life's challenges and shine their light, as Jesus admonished: "Let your light so shine before men, that they may see your good works, and glorify your Father which is in heaven."[14]

The Oil

In Jesus's day, the first step in turning olives into oil involved soaking them in water, for the purpose of cleaning them and removing their bitterness. They were then crushed and placed in baskets, and the oil dripped into a storage vat. Sometimes they were also crushed in a large grooved stone press; with this method, the olives were placed on a large stone and then another large stone was rolled on top.[15]

Oil was used for various purposes, not just as fuel for lamps, and these uses add insight about the parable's symbolism. Oil was used to anoint and sanctify Aaron and his sons prior to their receipt of the holy priesthood: "And he [Moses] poured of the anointing oil upon Aaron's head, and anointed him, to sanctify him"[16] and to hallow him.[17] The Hebrew word for *sanctify* and *hallow* is *qadesh*, which means to "separate, set apart."[18] *Sanctification* means to set "something apart for holy use or consecrating a place or person, or thing to God."[19] *Hallow* means "to make holy or to set apart for special service."[20] Oil was also used to anoint the tabernacle of the congregation and some of its altars and vessels.[21] Additionally, oil was used

---

14.   Matt. 5:16.

15.   See *HarperCollins Bible Dictionary*, s.v. "oil."

16.   Lev. 8:12. "Ezek. 36:22–27 describes this process [sanctification] in three steps: first, the people are purified from their old sinfulness and idolatry by being sprinkled with clear water; second, the Lord gives them a 'new heart: (cf. 11:19; Jer. 31:31–34); and, third, the Spirit of the Lord is put in the human heart. The result of this divine sanctification is a person freed from the 'evil inclination' of the human heart and obedient to the will of God." (*HarperCollins Bible Dictionary*, s.v. "sanctification.")

17.   See Ex. 29:1.

18.   Young, *Analytical Concordance*, s.vv. "sanctify," "hallow."

19.   *HarperCollins Bible Dictionary*, s.v. "sanctification."

20.   *HarperCollins Bible Dictionary*, s.v. "hallow."

21.   See Ex. 30:22–29.

to anoint some kings[22] and prophets.[23] Oil was also used when ceremonially cleaning those who had been healed of leprosy.[24] Further, olive oil was used in New Testament times and is used today when administering to the sick.[25]

The oil in the virgins' lamps and vessels may also symbolize a person becoming sanctified, hallowed, and worthy to welcome Christ when He comes and to qualify to enter the kingdom of heaven.[26] Therefore, the oil may represent who a person is—his or her character and righteousness— which cannot be loaned or given away. The oil may also represent the Holy Spirit, which sanctifies people.[27]

The Lord has stated the following regarding having sufficient spiritual strength in the last days: "And I give unto you . . . a commandment that you assemble yourselves together, and organize yourselves, and prepare yourselves, and sanctify yourselves; yea, purify your hearts, and cleanse your hands and your feet before me, that I may make you clean; that I may testify unto your Father, and your God, and my God, that you are clean from the blood of this wicked generation; that I may fulfil this promise, this great and last promise, which I have made unto you, when I will."[28]

The Virgins' Sleeping While the Bridegroom Tarried

Because the bridegroom's coming was delayed, the ten virgins fell asleep before he arrived. Sleeping may symbolize that in the last days, even Church members may not be fully ready for Christ's return and even some of the elect may be deceived.[29]

The virgins' sleeping and then being awoken may also symbolize that Christ will come suddenly and when not expected. The bridegroom's sudden

---

22.   See 1 Sam. 10:1; 16:1–3; 1 Kgs. 1:39.

23.   See 1 Kgs 19:16.

24.   See Lev. 14:2, 10, 12, 15–18.

25.   See Mark 6:13; James 5:14; D&C 42:44.

26.   This sanctification often comes through the ministration of the Holy Ghost (see 3 Ne. 27:20; Dummelow, *Bible Commentary*, p. 705).

27.   See 2 Thess. 2:13; 1 Pet. 1:2; Rom. 15:16; 3 Ne. 27:20; Dummelow, *Bible Commentary*, p. 705.

28.   D&C 88:74–75.

29.   See JS—M 1:22.

coming is a warning that people need to be spiritually prepared, even when most people are figuratively asleep and think He will not return today.

The Bridegroom's Arrival

In the parable, the bridegroom arrived at midnight, a time at which many people likely did not think that he would come. Similarly, Christ has taught that "in such an hour as ye think not the Son of man cometh."[30] Just as the virgins needed to be prepared for the groom's arrival, whenever it occurred, people need to be prepared for Christ's Second Coming, whenever it occurs.

In the parable, someone cried out when the bridegroom was coming near. Similarly, the Apostle John saw in vision that angels will cry mightily before Christ returns. The following verses mention two of these angels:

And he cried mightily with a strong voice, saying, Babylon the great is fallen, is fallen, and is become the habitation of devils, and the hold of every foul spirit, and a cage of every unclean and hateful bird. For all nations have drunk of the wine of the wrath of her fornication, and the kings of the earth have committed fornication with her, and the merchants of the earth are waxed rich through the abundance of her delicacies. And I heard another voice from heaven, saying, Come out of her, my people, that ye be not partakers of her sins, and that ye receive not of her plagues. For her sins have reached unto heaven, and God hath remembered her iniquities. . . . Alas, alas, that great city Babylon, that mighty city! for in one hour is thy judgment come.[31]

Additionally, Paul told the Thessalonian Saints, "For the Lord himself shall descend from heaven with a shout, with the voice of the archangel, and with the trump of God."[32] It is important to note that in the parable and in John's vision, the cry went out before the arrival of the bridegroom (symbolizing Christ). There was time to trim lamps but not to purchase oil.

The parable does not state what the bridegroom was doing while he tarried. Similarly, little is known about what Christ is doing before He returns. He is certainly engaged in the world of spirits, supervising the work there, and in providing guidance to His prophets on the earth.[33] Moreover, Christ

---

30. Matt. 24:44; see also JS—M 1:48.
31. Rev. 18:2–5, 10.
32. 1 Thess. 4:16.
33. See D&C 138:18–19, 30.

may be involved in the work occurring on other worlds He helped create, as He implied in a parable He gave to Joseph Smith.[34]

In the parable of the bridegroom, he arrived later than is typical for a marriage celebration. Symbolically, this delay may indicate that there will be a significant period between Christ's Resurrection and His Second Coming. An additional implication may be that there will be a significant period between the Restoration of Christ's Church on the earth and His return. No matter how long or how short the interval, it is a time to spiritually prepare for His return. As Amulek in the Book of Mormon taught, "For behold, this life is the time for men to prepare to meet God; yea, behold the day of this life is the day for men to perform their labors."[35]

The Virgins' Trimming of Their Lamps

When the virgins awoke, each trimmed her lamp, which involved trimming the wick so that the flame would burn brighter. This process was typically accompanied by adding oil to the lamp so that the flame would continue to burn. Likewise, as the Savior's return draws near, the wick within each person needs to be trimmed and the lamp needs to be filled with spiritual oil so that the person's flame burns bright and continues burning until Christ's return.

The Foolish Virgins' Request for Oil

The five foolish virgins saw that their lamps had gone out and therefore asked the wise virgins to share their oil. The wise virgins answered that they would not because they did not have sufficient oil for themselves and the foolish virgins; the foolish virgins would have to buy oil. As previously explained, the oil symbolizes a person's character and righteousness and therefore cannot be given to someone else. People can shine their light so that others may see but cannot give oil to others.

While the five foolish virgins were buying oil, the bridegroom arrived. The five wise virgins entered the location of the wedding with the bridegroom, and then the door was closed. When the five foolish virgins arrived and asked the lord (i.e., the bridegroom) to open the door, he replied, "I know you not,"

---

34. See D&C 88:51–61; Sperry, *Doctrine and Covenants Compendium*, p. 430.
35. Alma 34:32.

and he did not permit them to enter. The wording of the lord's response is slightly different in Joseph Smith's translation of Matthew 25:12: "Verily I say unto you, Ye know me not." This wording clarifies that the foolish virgins were the ones who lacked knowledge. They had failed to come to know the lord. Likewise, Christ certainly knows all of God's children, and they are responsible for coming to know Him and qualifying to enter the kingdom of heaven. As the parable also taught, it is difficult or even impossible to immediately develop the character required to enter the kingdom of heaven, particularly if people have spent their entire lives not preparing.[36]

Tests

This parable is not just about being spiritually prepared for the Lord's return; the parable is also about having sufficient spiritual strength to withstand the tests of the dark night of mortality. Christ, as the firstborn spirit son of God in the premortal world, made it clear that a purpose of this earth life is to be tested and tried:

> And there stood one among them that was like unto God, and he said unto those who were with him: We will go down, for there is space there, and we will take of these materials, and we will make an earth whereon these may dwell; and we will prove them herewith, to see if they will do all things whatsoever the Lord their God shall command them; and they who keep their first estate shall be added upon; and they who keep not their first estate shall not have glory in the same kingdom with those who keep their first estate; and they who keep their second estate shall have glory added upon their heads for ever and ever.[37]

Presumably, all the virgins were tested by the spiritually sleeping world. So are all of God's children who have come to the earth.

Blessings for the Spiritually Prepared

In the parable, the five wise virgins received the opportunity to be with the bridegroom and enjoy the wedding and likely a wedding feast. Likewise,

---

36. See Alma 34:32–35.
37. Abr. 3:24–26.

those who are spiritually prepared will have the opportunity to be with Christ when He returns:

> And at that day, when I shall come in my glory, shall the parable be fulfilled which I spake concerning the ten virgins. For they that are wise and have received the truth, and have taken the Holy Spirit for their guide, and have not been deceived—verily I say unto you, they shall not be hewn down and cast into the fire, but shall abide the day. And the earth shall be given unto them for an inheritance; and they shall multiply and wax strong, and their children shall grow up without sin unto salvation. For the Lord shall be in their midst, and his glory shall be upon them, and he will be their king and their lawgiver.[38]

If the ten virgins had not previously attended a wedding and accompanying feast, they could not have comprehended the joy that awaited them at the upcoming wedding. Likewise, the righteous cannot fully comprehend the joy that awaits them upon entering the kingdom of heaven.

Judgment of the Unprepared

The five foolish virgins were separated from the five wise virgins when the bridegroom came. Similarly, the righteous will be divided from the unrighteous shortly before the Savior's return. The Lord told the Prophet Joseph Smith that when He returns to the earth, "there will be foolish virgins among the wise; and at that hour cometh an entire separation of the righteous and the wicked; and in that day will I send mine angels to pluck out the wicked and cast them into unquenchable fire."[39] At that day, as the prophet Abinadi said in the Book of Mormon, "the wicked [will] be cast out, and they shall have cause to howl, and weep, and wail, and gnash their teeth; and this because they would not hearken unto the voice of the Lord; therefore the Lord redeemeth them not."[40]

Trust

A further principle that can be learned from this parable regards trust. The five wise virgins could be trusted to have enough oil for their lamps

---

38.   D&C 45:56–59.
39.   D&C 63:53–54.
40.   Mosiah 16:2.

even after the bridegroom arrived. The bridegroom, and likely the bride, presumably trusted that the virgins would be waiting for the bridegroom to come. Similarly, the virgins trusted that the bridegroom would come. Likewise, people need to trust that Jesus will return and, because of this trust, live righteously and let their lights shine. Jesus trusts His disciples to be obedient as they await His return.

Of course, all people make mistakes, and their supply of oil and the brightness of their lights may vary at times. Through diligent effort and Christ's Atonement, they can replenish their oil and shine brightly again. This parable, however, indicates that repentance cannot be put off until the end.

Faith

A corollary to being spiritually prepared is to have faith. Sometimes, trials such as illnesses, accidents, and even willful acts of harm occur without warning. At such times, maintaining faith is necessary. Further, priesthood blessings and other prayers of faith need to be given when there is little or no time for further spiritual preparation. By continually exercising faith, people will be better prepared when challenges come without warning.

Be Prepared

At the end of this parable, Jesus said: "Watch therefore, for ye know neither the day nor the hour wherein the Son of man cometh." People should watch by assessing their spiritual strength and worthiness. People should watch by determining how they can help others to acquire sufficient spiritual oil. And people should watch by looking for the signs of Christ's glorious Second Coming.

Though this parable is presented as a warning—a warning to be spiritually prepared—Jesus gave it out of His and God's love and desire that God's children be worthy to welcome Jesus when He returns and to be worthy to enter the kingdom of heaven.

Chapter 58

JESUS'S CONCLUDING INSTRUCTION ON THE LAST TUESDAY OF HIS LIFE

(Tuesday[1])

While on the Mount of Olives in the afternoon on the last Tuesday of Jesus's life, He taught His Apostles of the signs of His Second Coming and gave the parable of the ten virgins, through which He taught of the importance of being spiritually prepared for His return. He concluded His instruction by giving the Apostles the parable of the talents and by using a metaphor involving sheep and goats to teach about the importance of serving others. Jesus then told His Apostles of His impending betrayal and death. Soon after, Judas met with the chief priests and agreed to assist in their plot to take Jesus's life.

Jesus Gives the Parable of the Talents (Matt. 25:14–30)

After Jesus gave the parable of the ten virgins,[2] He proceeded to give the parable of the talents. Though he told the parable to His Apostles, the lessons from the parable are applicable to everyone. Comparing the parable of the ten virgins, the parable of the talents, and the parable of the ten

---

1.   Some scholars are of the opinion that Jesus's teachings in Matthew 24 and 25 were given on Wednesday (see, for example, Edersheim, *Life and Times of Jesus the Messiah*, pp. 772–796).

2.   See Matt. 25:1–13.

pounds (which Jesus had given less than a week earlier)[3] may help individuals more fully understand each of these parables and the overall messages Christ was conveying. The parable of the ten virgins addresses being spiritually prepared for the coming of the Lord. The parables of the talents and the pounds address diligently serving the Lord prior to His Second Coming. The parable of the ten virgins focuses on wedding guests, presumably symbolizing members of the Church, whereas the parables of the ten pounds and the talents focus on the servants, presumably symbolizing servants of the Lord. The parable of the ten virgins contains the warning that those who are not spiritually prepared for the Savior's return will not be numbered among His chosen people. The parables of the talents and the ten pounds include the warning that if individuals do not put their talents to use in building up God's kingdom, then those talents will be taken away at the Final Judgment, to the great sorrow of these individuals.

The parable of the talents teaches that servants of the Lord must use their God-given talents, whatever they are and whatever the servants' circumstances are, to further the work of the Lord.[4] In the parable, the servants who increased their talents received great blessings; the servant who hid his talent was condemned.

The parable of the talents is discussed below. The text is separated into sections for ease of discussion.

The Man

The parable begins as follows:

Matthew 25:14–15. For the kingdom of heaven is as a man travelling into a far country, who called his own servants, and delivered unto them his goods. And unto one he gave five talents, to another two, and to another one; to every man according to his several ability; and straightway took his journey.

The man who traveled a great distance is later called a lord, and he symbolizes Jesus, who would be crucified a little more than two days later and would go to more than one far country after being resurrected. Specifically, Jesus went to heaven to be with His Father, to spirit paradise to preach the

---

3.   See Luke 19:11–27.
4.   See McConkie, *Mortal Messiah*, vol. 3, p. 469; see also D&C 4:2; 58:27; 60:13; 64:33–34.

gospel there,[5] to the Americas to teach the Nephites,[6] and to the locations of the "other sheep" of the house of Israel.[7] He may have also visited other worlds or kingdoms.[8]

The Servants

In the parable, before the lord left he called his servants and gave them talents according to their abilities. The servants symbolize the Apostles, whom Jesus called and ordained, as well as other people who serve God. Just as the lord left his servants in charge of his goods, Christ would leave His Church in the care of the Apostles after His death. The servants may also symbolize all those who believe in Christ and follow Him, for the parable is applicable to all who are called to serve the Lord, in whatever generation and whatever locality they may be.

The Goods

In the parable, goods are synonymous with talents. In another sense, the goods in the parable may symbolize God's authority to watch over and care for His Church. Alternatively, the goods may symbolize God's children, since they are of the greatest value to both God and Jesus.

Talents and Abilities

The lord gave one of his servants five talents, another servant two talents, and yet another servant one talent. According to the *HarperCollins Bible Dictionary*, in Jesus's day a talent "was a large unit of money equal to 6,000 *drachmae* or *denari*. Thus, 1 talent was roughly equal to what a typical worker would make over a sixteen-year period. . . . Five talents was more than an average worker could hope to earn in a lifetime."[9] The servants in

---

5.   See D&C 138:18–19.
6.   See 3 Ne. 11:1–28:12.
7.   See 3 Ne. 16:1–3.
8.   In Doctrine and Covenants 88:51, the Lord states that He will liken the kingdoms in the heavens "to a man having a field, and he sent forth his servants into the field to dig." The man then visits each of his servants (i.e., kingdoms) in turn (see D&C 88:52–59). The Lord may have been indicating that he will visit different worlds, and the "far country" referenced in the parable of the talents may be understood to include people on other worlds.
9.   *HarperCollins Bible Dictionary*, s.v. "talent."

the parable did not own the talents; rather, the talents and any interest the servants obtained from investing the talents were the lord's.[10] The fact that large amounts were entrusted to the servants in this parable may have helped the Apostles understand the enormity of their responsibility, the great value of God's children to Him and to Jesus, and the magnitude of the blessings for faithful and diligent service.

The talents may symbolize gifts that Heavenly Father bestows upon His children. These gifts include the gifts of the Spirit, such as wisdom, knowledge, and faith. Other gifts of the Spirit include the ability to heal, to work miracles, to prophesy, to discern spirits, and to speak and interpret foreign languages. Of course, there are many other spiritual gifts as well. All spiritual gifts contribute to the complete operation and administration of the Church and to the edification of the Saints.[11]

The talents might also symbolize other gifts. Some people are talented in running businesses, leading others, or diligently following leaders. Some people have the gift of great intelligence. Other gifts might involve having skills in banking, electrical wiring, computer technology, construction, or science. Some people have gifts related to physical abilities. Just as there is a great variety of gifts, the magnitude of gifts can vary greatly.

The number of talents each servant received in the parable was presumably based on the servant's ability to manage what was entrusted to him. Heavenly Father knows all of His children and their various talents, in terms of objective number and subjective degree of ability. He also knows each person's circumstances, challenges, and weaknesses. God uses His complete knowledge and wisdom when endowing His children with talents and allowing His children to experience mortality in the circumstances best suited to help His children progress eternally. What God expects of His children is that they increase their talents, whatever they may be, by diligently and faithfully serving Him. This truth is the heart of the parable of the talents.

Implicitly, the lord in the parable was making an agreement— symbolically, a covenant—with his servants. They were to diligently serve

10.   In Jesus's time, slaves and servants were often allowed to trade on their lord's account and then share their profits with the lord (see Trench, *Parables of Our Lord*, p. 92).

11.   See 1 Cor. 12:1–11, 28.

the lord, and in turn he would reward them. The lord would not break this agreement; only the servants could break the agreement, by their lack of diligence.

The Servants' Increasing or Burying of the Talents

The parable then explains what the servants did with the talents they had received:

Matthew 25:16–18. Then he that had received the five talents went and traded with the same, and made them other five talents. And likewise he that had received two, he also gained other two. But he that had received one went and digged in the earth, and hid his lord's money.

The servants who received five and two talents, respectively, put in the effort required to double the number of talents they had received. The servant who received one talent simply buried the money.

All three servants presumably had an equal opportunity to increase the number of talents they had received and thereby fulfill their responsibility as the lord's servants to increase what the lord had entrusted to them. Further, nothing in the parable indicates that the servants could not more than double the amounts that were entrusted to them.

Some of the Apostles would have a bounteous harvest, and some would have more modest success. However, all had the responsibility to work, serve diligently, and increase their talents, as did the servants in the parable. Presumably, the Apostles recognized they were each given talents to use and improve according to God's knowledge of the Apostles. All that was required was that they serve diligently and faithfully, according to their God-given abilities.

The same is true with missionaries today. They have different opportunities and experiences as they serve in different countries and in differing circumstances. Some missionaries have the opportunity to baptize many people, whereas other missionaries baptize only a few. However, all missionaries have an obligation to improve their talents, including their faith and commitment, according to their abilities and circumstances. The same obligation applies to all others who serve the Lord, whatever their abilities and circumstances.

The Lord's Request for an Accounting

The lord then asked his servants to give an accounting of what they had done with the talents:

Matthew 25:19. After a long time the lord of those servants cometh, and reckoneth with them.

In the parable, the lord returned "after a long time."[12] Symbolically, the "long time" may be the period between Christ's death and His Second Coming and Final Judgment. In the parable, when the lord returned, he asked his servants for an accounting of what they had done with the talents. Likewise, the Lord's Second Coming will be a day of reckoning and judgment for all people.

The Bestowal of Blessings and Condemnation

The servants who had received five and two talents, respectively, reported their results to the lord:

Matthew 25:20–23. And so he that had received five talents came and brought other five talents, saying, Lord, thou deliveredst unto me five talents: behold, I have gained beside them five talents more. His lord said unto him, Well done, thou good and faithful servant: thou hast been faithful over a few things, I will make thee ruler over many things: enter thou into the joy of thy lord. He also that had received two talents came and said, Lord, thou deliveredst unto me two talents: behold, I have gained two other talents beside them. His lord said unto him, Well done, good and faithful servant; thou hast been faithful over a few things, I will make thee ruler over many things: enter thou into the joy of thy lord.

The servants who had received five and two talents, respectively, had each doubled the number of talents the lord had entrusted to these servants. The servant given five talents may have been expected to produce greater returns than the servant given two, for "where much is given, much is required."[13] The five talents and two talents of increase were minimal compared to the rewards that the lord promised these two faithful servants, for the lord

---

12. Similarly, the bridegroom in the parable of the ten virgins tarried and did not arrive until midnight.

13. D&C 82 section heading; see also D&C 82:3; Luke 12:48.

promised that since they had "been faithful over a few things," he would make them "ruler[s] over many things." Even though the lord had given the first two servants different numbers of talents and the servants had earned different numbers of talents, the lord's acknowledgement of their efforts and the reward that he gave was the same. The lord rewarded their diligence.

Similarly, all who keep their covenants with the Lord and serve Him diligently are promised the same reward: entrance into the celestial kingdom and the presence of the Lord, as well as "all that [the] Father hath."[14] The number of talents given or earned is not pertinent to the eternal reward that the Lord offers. Those who inherit the celestial kingdom will be "equal in power, and in might, and in dominion."[15] Of course, a complete understanding of the breadth, depth, and scope of these eternal blessings is impossible to grasp during mortality. What joy will fill the hearts of those who hear Christ say to them, "Well done, thou good and faithful servant"!

The Slothful Servant

Next, the servant who received one talent reported to the lord:

Matthew 25:24–25. Then he which had received the one talent came and said, Lord, I knew thee that thou art an hard man, reaping where thou hast not sown, and gathering where thou hast not strawed: And I was afraid, and went and hid thy talent in the earth: lo, there thou hast that is thine.

The servant who received one talent buried it in the earth, squandering his opportunities to increase the number of talents he had been entrusted with. Whether he was lazy or wanted to focus his efforts on other things is unstated in the parable. As Howick observed, the slothful servant had "performed no labor, shown no devotion, and exemplified no faithfulness in the use of his talent. He had completely wasted his opportunity."[16] Consequently, all he could return to the lord was one dirt-encrusted talent. Just as the lord expected the servant to use the talent for the lord's benefit, God wants His children to use the talents He has given them, including to serve others. People should not bury their talents.

---

14. D&C 84:38.
15. D&C 76:95.
16. Howick, *Life of Jesus the Messiah*, p. 264.

This servant failed to take responsibility for his inactions and instead blamed the lord and criticized him, saying he was a "hard man, reaping where [he had] not sown" and gathering what he had not harvested. The servant's criticism of the lord may have been in reality a reflection of the servant's own life, as is often the case when a person wrongfully blames another. The slothful servant was in effect saying that the lord was not a just man, did not care for his possessions, did not care about his servants' actions, and cared only about obtaining more possessions. The servant imputed unrighteousness and greed to the lord, who bestowed the talent in the first place. The slothful servant was entirely mistaken about the work to which he was called: the servant's responsibility was to increase his talent, not bury it. Symbolically, the slothful servant had a false view of the character of God and Christ. The slothful servant is somewhat like those whom Paul described as having "tasted the good word God" but then falling away.[17] Of these people Paul wrote, "But that which beareth thorns and briers is rejected, and is nigh unto cursing; whose end is to be burned."[18]

The slothful servant's attitude may have been somewhat like Satan's attitude in the premortal world when he rebelled against God for not agreeing to give Satan honor. The slothful servant was also implying that he desired a reward like the other servants received even though he had not put forth effort and been diligent—a perspective that Satan influences people to have in order to deceive them.

Symbolically, the third servant in the parable was in a sense denying the Atonement by fearing failure and therefore not trying to increase what the Lord had given him. He did not understand that Christ, through His atoning sacrifice, makes up for the deficiencies of those who repent, even if they have fewer talents than others and regardless of their circumstances. Further, even those who try to increase their talents fall short, and Christ's Atonement makes up for these shortcomings. Christ's Atonement is one of the greatest of all the gifts that anyone may receive, for it allows all to progress and even learn from mistakes and failures. The Atonement also compensates for any perceived injustices regarding the number or magnitude

---

17. See Heb. 6:5; see also vv. 4, 6–7.
18. Heb. 6:8.

of talents a person receives from God. The marvelous gift of the Atonement is far greater than any talents that are given.

The servant may have incorrectly thought that since comparatively little was entrusted to him, the lord did not trust the servant as much as the other servants. The slothful servant may have thought that it did not matter much if he increased his single talent, for the increase would likely be small compared with the increases of the other servants' talents. Symbolically, this servant failed to understand that even a single talent has great worth in the sight of God and can bring forth much good. As the Lord has said, "If it so be that you should labor all your days in crying repentance unto this people, and bring, save it be one soul unto me, how great shall be your joy with him in the kingdom of my Father!"[19] Note that the reward for bringing one soul unto the Lord is entrance into the kingdom of heaven, which is the same reward given to the servants who doubled their talents. Moreover, symbolically, the slothful servant lacked faith in the Lord and did not believe that the Lord would be fair, for the servant said that the lord was a hard man and desired an increase even though he did not directly assist in the effort.

The slothful servant also sought to justify his actions by saying he was afraid. Presumably, he was afraid to fail because he perceived the lord to be a hard man. Sometimes, people are asked to serve but are unwilling to because they are afraid. They may be afraid that they are not good enough or that they will be perceived by others as not having enough gospel knowledge or experience. Jesus made it clear in this parable that people should not refuse to serve out of fear to try, even if they think they have little ability.

God is not a hard man. He loves and is mindful of all His children, is involved in their lives, and wants them to speak to Him through prayer. He understands His children's challenges, fears, and weaknesses. He loves all of His children and will strengthen them if they ask for His assistance. He has provided a merciful plan of salvation, at the center of which are the Atonement of Christ, the gift of repentance and forgiveness, and the resurrection of all people. God has also provided the Holy Ghost to inspire, guide, and bring peace in times of turmoil. God has instituted the family unit and the Church to provide help and support and has given each of His

---

19. D&C 18:15.

children talents. Likewise, Christ is not a hard man. He loves and understands all people and is ready to help. He has said, "Take my yoke upon you, and learn of me; for I am meek and lowly in heart: and ye shall find rest unto your souls."[20]

The Lord's Condemnation of the Slothful Servant and Further Reward for the Servant with Ten Talents

The lord then condemned the slothful servant and gave a further reward to the servant who had increased his original five talents to ten:

> **Matthew 25:26–30.** His lord answered and said unto him, Thou wicked and slothful servant, thou knewest that I reap where I sowed not, and gather where I have not strawed: thou oughtest therefore to have put my money to the exchangers, and then at my coming I should have received mine own with usury. Take therefore the talent from him, and give it unto him which hath ten talents. For unto every one that hath shall be given, and he shall have abundance: but from him that hath not shall be taken away even that which he hath. And cast ye the unprofitable servant into outer darkness: there shall be weeping and gnashing of teeth.

The lord responded by telling the servant that he was both wicked and slothful and that he knew when he accepted the talent that the lord expected the servant to improve upon that talent. The servant did not understand that putting one's talents to use in the service of the lord would have an influence on others. Just as the lord in the parable expected the servant to make use of the talent, the Lord expects all people to magnify their talents and thereby let their light shine in the lives of others. If the slothful servant had put to use the single talent entrusted to him and had doubled it, presumably he would have received the same reward as the other two servants received.

The lord then commanded that the slothful servant's one talent be taken from him, leaving him with nothing. Similarly, when faith and other spiritual gifts are not used, they may diminish and eventually no longer be present. The slothful servant was then cast into outer darkness. Likewise, those who are slothful and wicked will lose the light of the gospel, and when the Lord

---

20. Matt. 11:29.

returns, they will weep and gnash their teeth.[21] Rebelling against God is spiritually dangerous.

The talent that was taken away from the slothful servant was given to the servant who had increased his five talents to ten. Similarly, those who are faithful will receive an increase beyond what they expected and even beyond their comprehension.[22] Because God is just, the bestowal of talents may also be affected by how valiant people were in the premortal world.[23] This servant had demonstrated that he could amplify the talents the lord had given the servant, and the results benefited not just the lord but also the servant. Moreover, since the talent was taken from the slothful servant and given to the servant who initially received five, the parable may be implying that the principle of increasing talents will continue in the next life.

As the Apostles listened to Jesus give this parable, they may have considered the fact that the chief priests, scribes, and Pharisees in Jerusalem had buried the talents the Lord had entrusted to them. The Apostles may have also gained a greater understanding of the need to serve the Lord and magnify their callings, regardless of their weaknesses and the challenges they faced.

A fundamental principle in the parable of the talents is the importance of using God-given talents in diligently and faithfully serving the Lord. A similar principle is found in Doctrine and Covenants 84, in which the Lord speaks about entering into the oath and covenant of the priesthood and magnifying one's callings.[24] In the parable of the talents, the servants who increased their talents received the rewards of being made "ruler[s] over many things" and being invited to enter "into the joy of [the] lord." Similarly, in Doctrine and Covenants 84, the Lord states that those who are faithful and magnify their callings will receive "all that my Father hath."[25] In the parable, the servant who did not fulfill his responsibilities was cast into outer darkness, and Doctrine and Covenants 84 states that those who break and

---

21. Several other scriptures contain similar references. See, for example, the following in the New Testament: Matt. 8:12; 13:42, 50; 22:13; 24:51; Luke 13:28.
22. See D&C 76:62–70; D&C 130:9–11.
23. See Abr. 3:22–23; Alma 13:3; McConkie, *Mortal Messiah*, vol. 3, p. 470.
24. See D&C 84:33.
25. D&C 84:38.

turn away from the oath and covenant of the priesthood "shall not have forgiveness of sins in this world nor in the world to come."[26]

Jesus Will Separate the Sheep from the Goats (Matt. 25:31–46)

Jesus continued His instruction by using a metaphor involving sheep and goats, confirming that a final judgment will come to all. The following is Matthew's account:

Matthew 25:31–46. When the Son of man shall come in his glory, and all the holy angels with him, then shall he sit upon the throne of his glory: and before him shall be gathered all nations: and he shall separate them one from another, as a shepherd divideth his sheep from the goats: and he shall set the sheep on his right hand, but the goats on the left. Then shall the King say unto them on his right hand, Come, ye blessed of my Father, inherit the kingdom prepared for you from the foundation of the world: for I was an hungred, and ye gave me meat: I was thirsty, and ye gave me drink: I was a stranger, and ye took me in: naked, and ye clothed me: I was sick, and ye visited me: I was in prison, and ye came unto me. Then shall the righteous answer him, saying, Lord, when saw we thee an hungred, and fed thee? or thirsty, and gave thee drink? When saw we thee a stranger, and took thee in? or naked, and clothed thee? Or when saw we thee sick, or in prison, and came unto thee? And the King shall answer and say unto them, Verily I say unto you, Inasmuch as ye have done it unto one of the least of these my brethren, ye have done it unto me. Then shall he say also unto them on the left hand, Depart from me, ye cursed, into everlasting fire, prepared for the devil and his angels: for I was an hungred, and ye gave me no meat: I was thirsty, and ye gave me no drink: I was a stranger, and ye took me not in: naked, and ye clothed me not: sick, and in prison, and ye visited me not. Then shall they also answer him, saying, Lord, when saw we thee an hungred, or athirst, or a stranger, or naked, or sick, or in prison, and did not minister unto thee? Then shall he answer them, saying, Verily I say unto you, Inasmuch as ye did it not to one of the least of these, ye did it not to

---

26.   D&C 84:41. Of course, though only men enter into the oath and covenant of the priesthood, both men and women are expected to enter into baptismal and temple covenants with God. Likewise, the conditions that determine the degree of glory a person will obtain are the same for men and women (see D&C 76).

me. And these shall go away into everlasting punishment: but the righteous into life eternal.

Jesus began by implicitly affirming that He is the Son of God and will return to the earth in glory. He then told the Apostles that when He comes, "all the holy angels [will come] with Him." Insight regarding this statement is available in a marvelous revelation that Joseph Smith received: "And the saints that are upon the earth, who are alive, shall be quickened and be caught up to meet him. And they who have slept in their graves shall come forth, for their graves shall be opened; and they also shall be caught up to meet him in the midst of the pillar of heaven—they are Christ's, the first fruits, they who shall descend with him first, and they who are on the earth and in their graves, who are first caught up to meet him."[27]

Jesus also declared that when He comes, He will "sit upon the throne of his glory" as the "King of kings, and Lord of lords."[28] This event will be wondrous to behold. The throne of His glory will also be the throne of His judgment, for Heavenly Father has committed all judgment to His Only Begotten Son.[29]

Jesus next used the metaphor of a shepherd whose flocks consisted of sheep and goats. The sheep represent the righteous, and the goats represent the wicked. Jesus said He would put the sheep at His right hand and put the goats at His left hand. The right hand symbolizes preeminence, righteousness, blessings, strength, and divine acceptance.[30] For example, various scriptures state that when the resurrected Christ ascended into heaven, He sat on the right hand of God.[31] As Stephen was being stoned to death, he saw the heavens open and Christ stand on the right hand of God.[32] Additionally, when Christ comes to the earth again, He will be seen "sitting on the right hand of power."[33]

---

27. D&C 88:96–98.
28. Rev. 19:16.
29. See John 5:22.
30. See, for example, Gen. 48:13–20; Ps. 110:1; 118:16; Matt. 22:44; Mark 16:19; Acts 2:33; 7:54–56; Rom. 8:34; Eph. 1:20–21; Col. 3:1; Heb. 10:12–13; 1 Pet. 3:21–22.
31. See Heb. 1:3; 8:1; 10:12; 12:2; 1 Pet. 3:22; D&C 20:24; 76:20, 23.
32. See Acts 7:55–56.
33. Matt. 26:64; Mark 14:62; see also Luke 22:69.

As a further example of the symbolism of the right hand, the Lord directed that the sacrificial blood of a ram be put on "the tip of the right ear," "upon the thumb of their right hand," and upon the right big toe of Aaron and his sons as part of hallowing them before they received the priesthood.[34] In terms of the right hand symbolizing strength, various scriptures state that God's right hand overcame Israel's enemies.[35]

In this metaphor, Christ implicitly stated that all nations will gather before Him and that He will divide the sheep from the goats, meaning that He will judge the people. As Christ told the Nephites, "And even unto the great and last day, when all people, and all kindreds, and all nations and tongues shall stand before God, to be judged of their works, whether they be good or whether they be evil—if they be good, to the resurrection of everlasting life; and if they be evil, to the resurrection of damnation; being on a parallel, the one on the one hand and the other on the other hand, according to the mercy, and the justice, and the holiness which is in Christ, who was before the world began."[36] The metaphor also illustrates the justice that God and Christ will exercise in the Final Judgment by dividing the sheep and the goats.[37]

The metaphor of the sheep and the goats can be viewed as part of a larger discourse that also includes the parables of the ten virgins and the talents, and considering this larger discourse can lead to a more complete understanding of people's responsibilities. As Talmage wrote, "The absolute certainty of the Christ coming to execute judgment upon the earth, in the which every soul shall receive according to his deserts, is the sublime summary of this unparalleled discourse."[38]

After Jesus finished presenting the metaphor of the sheep and the goats, He stated that the king (Jesus) will say, "Come, ye blessed of my Father, inherit the kingdom prepared for you from the foundation of the world." Jesus then gave examples of who will be on His right hand and who will be on His left

---

34.   Ex. 29:20; see also Lev. 8:23.
35.   See Ex. 15:6, 12; Isa. 62:8.
36.   3 Ne. 26:4–5.
37.   The parable of the wheat and the tares also refers to the righteous and the wicked being divided at the day of judgment (see Matt. 13:24–30; D&C 86).
38.   Talmage, *Jesus the Christ*, p. 543.

hand. Those who will be on His right hand have fed the hungry, given water to the thirsty, provided lodging to strangers, clothed the naked, and comforted the sick and imprisoned. Through serving others, these individuals have served Jesus, for as He explained, "Verily I say unto you, Inasmuch as ye have done it unto one of the least of these my brethren, ye have done it unto me."[39] Those on Jesus's right hand are judged by their righteous works, as James taught.[40]

In contrast, those who will be on Jesus's left hand have chosen not to serve others. Perhaps they thought they did not have time to help, or perhaps they simply did not care. Perhaps they were too concerned about their own lives to consider the needs of others. Those on Jesus's left hand did not realize that by serving others, they would be serving Him. By not serving others, they were also missing an opportunity to come to know Jesus, for as King Benjamin taught, "How knoweth a man the master whom he has not served, and who is a stranger unto him, and is far from the thoughts and intents of his heart?"[41] Those who have not served Jesus by serving others will be cast off "into everlasting fire, prepared for the devil and his angels." What a sharp contrast between these two groups: those on Jesus's right hand will be called "blessed of my Father" and will inherit eternal life in the kingdom of heaven, whereas those on Jesus's left hand will be cursed and consigned to "everlasting punishment."

Though not expressly stated, Christ was indicating that those who will be on His right hand are those who love others as He and God love all people. Those who will be on Christ's right hand are mindful of and minister to those who are downtrodden and are otherwise in need of help. In giving examples of love and service in daily life, Christ may have been helping the Apostles to further understand the breadth of His and God's love for all humankind. Christ wanted His Apostles to understand that they were not to merely testify of Him but were to develop Christlike love[42] and provide humble, nonjudgmental, and unselfish service to others.

---

39.   See also Mosiah 2:17.

40.   See James 2:14–26.

41.   Mosiah 5:13.

42.   Earlier on this day, Jesus had taught: "Thou shalt love the Lord thy God with all thy heart, and with all thy soul, and with all thy mind. This is first and great commandment. And the second is like unto it, Thou shalt love thy neighbor as thyself. On these two commandments hang all the law and the prophets." (Matt. 22:37–39; see also Luke 10:27–28.)

Christ has set the example of selflessly serving. He came to this earth from the realms of glory so that He could serve others, particularly by atoning and dying for all of God's children. Christ did so because He loves all people. All people need to strive to have Christlike love for others.

Wonderful examples of how to serve others can be found in the hymn "Have I Done Any Good," by Will L. Thompson:

> Have I done any good in the world today?
> Have I helped anyone in need?
> Have I cheered up the sad and made someone feel glad?
> If not, I have failed indeed.
> Has anyone's burden been lighter today
> Because I was willing to share?
> Have the sick and the weary been helped on their way?
> When they needed my help was I there?
>
> There are chances for work all around just now,
> Opportunities right in our way.
> Do not let them pass by, saying, "Sometime I'll try,"
> But go and do something today.
> 'Tis noble of man to work and to give;
> Love's labor has merit alone.
> Only he who does something helps others to live.
> To God each good work will be known.
>
> [Chorus]
>
> Then wake up and do something more
> Than dream of your mansion above.
> Doing good is a pleasure, a joy beyond measure,
> A blessing of duty and love.[43]

First and foremost, people should love God and Jesus and have faith in them. The next priority is to love and have charity for others, for "charity never faileth."[44] Certainly, each person needs to determine how to best serve family members. Mothers in particular excel in this area, with their lives often filled with service to family members. People should also find ways to reach

---

43.   Will L. Thompson, "Have I Done Any Good?," *Hymns*, no. 223.
44.   1 Cor. 13:8; Moro. 7:46.

out to others who are in need. The Church of Jesus Christ of Latter-day Saints provides wonderful opportunities for all to serve others in multiple ways. Whether serving in administrative, teaching, or ministering positions, all people can serve others. As Thompson wrote, "There are chances for work all around just now."

Many today are absorbed with working and seeking fun and pleasure. Work is not intrinsically bad—earning a living is essential. If, however, working and making money become more important than family, religious responsibilities, and service to others, eternal progression can be seriously hindered. Similarly, fun and pleasure are not innately evil; in fact, they are necessary for mental and emotional health and for strong family relationships. However, when fun and pleasure regularly distract people from family or religious responsibilities, people might not develop Christlike characteristics and serve others. People need to maintain balance in their lives. Even when engaging in work and fun, it is worth asking, "How do I treat others?" "What can I do for someone else?" "Am I focused only on making money or having fun?" "Do I follow the Savior's example in how I live?"

Of course, individuals cannot accomplish everything themselves, and they should not try to. Working together in the service of others not only helps those in need but also lifts those who serve together. As a Quaker proverb states, "Thee lift me, and I lift thee, and together we ascend."[45] Moreover, people should not berate themselves because they are less than perfect or cannot provide all the help that is seemingly required, even when assisted by others, for sometimes problems are simply too big to solve. For example, hunger in a city often cannot be totally eliminated, but it can be reduced by helping at least one person.

Jesus Tells His Apostles That He Will Be Betrayed and Crucified (Matt. 26:1–2)

From almost the beginning of Jesus's public ministry, He had alluded to His death. For example, after he cleansed the temple in Jerusalem during the first Passover of His ministry, He had said: "Destroy this temple, and in

---

45.   Some people attribute this proverb to John Greenleaf Wittier.

three days I will raise it up."[46] Soon afterward, Jesus told Nicodemus: "And as
Moses lifted up the serpent in the wilderness, even so must the Son of man
be lifted up."[47] When teaching disciples of John the Baptist in Capernaum,
Jesus said: "But the days will come, when the bridegroom shall be taken from
them."[48] Jesus alluded to the manner of His death when He spoke of the need
for people to take up their crosses and follow Him.[49] In His Bread of Life
sermon, Jesus spoke of giving His flesh "for the life of the world."[50] In the
parable of the good shepherd, Jesus said He would lay down His life for His
sheep.[51] Following the glorious experience on the Mount of Transfiguration,
Jesus told His Apostles: "The Son of man shall be betrayed into the hands
of men: and they shall kill him, and the third day he shall be raised again."[52]
Further, as Jesus rode triumphantly into Jerusalem, He told the Apostles:
"Behold, we go up to Jerusalem; and the Son of man shall be betrayed unto
the chief priests and unto the scribes, and they shall condemn him to death,
and shall deliver him to the Gentiles to mock, and to scourge, and to crucify
him: and the third day he shall rise again."[53] Earlier in the day that Jesus
gave the parable of the talents, He had given the parable of the wicked
husbandmen, in which the vineyard owner's son, who symbolized Jesus, was
killed at the husbandmen's direction.[54] Now, Jesus told His Apostles that the
Son of Man would soon be betrayed and crucified:

Matthew 26:1–2. And it came to pass, when Jesus had finished all these
sayings, he said unto his disciples, Ye know that after two days is the feast of
the passover, and the Son of man is betrayed to be crucified.

One can only wonder what thoughts and feelings filled the Apostles'
minds and hearts as they heard the one they loved and revered as the Son of
God state that He would soon be crucified. Though they likely did not fully
comprehend what would shortly come to pass and how it would occur, they

46. John 2:19; see also Edersheim, *Life and Times of Jesus the Messiah*, p. 798.
47. John 3:14.
48. Matt. 9:15.
49. See Matt. 10:38.
50. John 6:51.
51. See John 10:11, 15.
52. Matt. 17:22–23.
53. Matt. 20:18–19.
54. See Matt. 21:39.

were presumably filled with varied and deep emotions, such as anxiety about what would befall Him and what they should do after His death.

The Chief Priests, Scribes, and Elders Plot to Kill Jesus (Matt. 26:3–5; Mark 14:1–2; Luke 22:1–2)

Whereas the Apostles (except Judas) greatly loved Jesus, the chief priests, scribes, and elders hated Him, and they conspired to plot Jesus's death. The following is Matthew's record:

> **Matthew 26:3–5.** Then assembled together the chief priests, and the scribes, and the elders of the people, unto the palace of the high priest, who was called Caiaphas, and consulted that they might take Jesus by subtilty, and kill him. But they said, Not on the feast day, lest there be an uproar among the people.

Those who gathered at Caiaphas's palace must have done so by invitation and with the purpose of discussing how to bring about Jesus's death. Most of those present presumably were members of the priestly council and leading members of the Sanhedrin, and some may have directly supervised the temple.[55] Notwithstanding their role as keepers of the law, they sought Jesus's death.

They consulted together regarding how to take Jesus quietly. They decided not to take Him during the daytime on the Feast of the Passover because they wanted to avoid "an uproar among the people" and they knew that any uprising would be greatly frowned upon by Pilate, who had the authority to order that Jesus be killed and who could administer vengeance upon the Jewish leaders if they caused disorder or their actions resulted in Jews rebelling against Rome. Those gathered at Caiaphas's palace also likely discussed what charges they should make against Jesus in order to persuade Pilate to crucify Jesus.

Judas Iscariot Conspires to Betray Jesus (Matt. 26:14–16; Mark 14:10–11; Luke 22:3–6)

Presumably while Jesus and the Apostles were in Bethany on Wednesday, Judas journeyed back to Jerusalem. The reason Judas may have given for

---

55. See Edersheim, *Life and Times of Jesus the Messiah*, p. 802.

departing is unknown. Since Judas "had the bag,"[56] meaning he was in charge
of the Apostles' money, he may have said he was going to Jerusalem to make
arrangements to purchase a lamb for the Passover meal so that it could
pass Levitical inspection prior to the lamb being sacrificed on Thursday.[57]
Whatever the reason, Judas met with the chief priests and agreed to betray
Jesus "for thirty pieces of silver." The following is Matthew's account:

> **Matthew 26:14–16.** Then one of the twelve, called Judas Iscariot, went unto
> the chief priests, and said unto them, What will ye give me, and I will deliver
> him unto you? And they covenanted with him for thirty pieces of silver. And
> from that time he sought opportunity to betray him.

It is unknown what motivated Judas to betray Jesus, whom Judas had
associated with for the last three years. However, Joseph Smith's translation
of Mark 14:10 states that Judas "turned away from him [Jesus], and was
offended because of his words."[58] Judas's disaffection from Jesus likely
developed over time and may have had multiple causes. For example, Judas
may have expected the Messiah to take political power, according to traditional
Jewish beliefs, and was upset that Jesus refused to do so.[59] Judas may not
have grasped Jesus's deeper meaning when He told a multitude in or near
Capernaum that He was the Bread of Life and that those who ate His flesh
and drank His blood would have eternal life.[60] Judas may have been upset
about not being asked to accompany Jesus to the Mount of Transfiguration[61]
and about Jesus's statement that the Apostles lacked sufficient faith to cast
an evil spirit out of a boy.[62] Judas may have wanted Jesus to perform a great
miracle or show a sign from heaven to prove He was the Messiah, as the
Pharisees and Sadducees had requested.[63] Judas may have been upset that

---

56. John 12:6.
57. See Edersheim, *Life and Times of Jesus the Messiah*, p. 810.
58. JST Mark 14:31.
59. For example, after Jesus fed five thousand in Galilee, some people in the multitude
wanted to force Him to become king; He refused and withdrew from the multitude (see
John 6:15). For a detailed discussion of potential reasons Judas betrayed Jesus, see Edersheim,
Life and Times of Jesus the Messiah, pp. 800–801.
60. See John 6:26, 53–58.
61. See Matt. 17:1; Mark 9:2.
62. See Matt. 17:14–21; Mark 9:17–29.
63. See Matt. 16:1–4.

some of the other Apostles wondered who was greatest among them,[64] and he may have even stolen from the bag, claiming he cared for the poor.[65] The root cause may have been pride, a lack of spiritual conversion, or a critical nature. He may also have been greedy, as suggested by John's statement that Judas "was a thief."[66] He certainly lacked faith in Jesus and in God.

Whatever the causes of Judas's disaffection from Christ, Luke's record suggests that Judas's disaffection reached its zenith the last few days of Jesus's mortal life: "Then entered Satan into Judas surnamed Iscariot, being of the number of the twelve, and he went his way, and communed with the chief priests and captains, how he might betray him unto them."[67]

This action was the blackest and most hypocritical deed ever committed, because Judas was an Apostle and had associated with Jesus for the last three years. As Talmage wrote, "Let it be said that before Judas sold Christ to the Jews, he had sold himself to the devil; he had become Satan's serf, and did his master's bidding."[68]

One can only imagine the perplexity that must have appeared on the faces of the chief priests as Judas said, "What will ye give me, and I will deliver him unto you?" Standing before them was not their friend but a despicable traitor to Jesus—a traitor who could help them achieve their goal of killing Jesus and a traitor who wanted money in exchange for his assistance. Mark's and Luke's records indicate that the chief priests were glad when Judas offered to help them.[69] They agreed to pay him "thirty pieces of silver," fulfilling Zechariah's prophecy.[70] Thirty pieces of silver was the amount set forth in Exodus 21:32 to pay as recompense for the injury or death of a slave.[71] In the current context, the thirty pieces of silver was being paid to secure the blood of the "great and last sacrifice"—Jesus Christ, the Son of God.[72] Presumably, the thirty pieces of silver that Judas

---

64. See Luke 9:46; see also Matt. 20:20–28.
65. See John 12:6.
66. John 12:6.
67. Luke 22:3–4.
68. Talmage, *Jesus the Christ*, p. 550.
69. See Mark 14:11; Luke 22:5.
70. See Zech. 11:12–13.
71. See also Edersheim, *Life and Times of Jesus the Messiah*, p. 803.
72. Alma 34:10, 14.

would receive was taken directly or indirectly from the temple treasury—obviously a completely inappropriate use of temple money. The scriptures do not indicate when Judas was paid the blood money; however, the money presumably was not paid until the betrayal was complete, since the crafty Jews were unlikely to pay for a foul deed that had not yet been performed.

It is worth contemplating Judas's betrayal in the context of the instruction Jesus had given while on the slopes of the Mount of Olives. Jesus had warned the Apostles of the coming destruction of Jerusalem and had promised protection to those who fled when they saw the Roman army approaching. He had taught signs of His Second Coming and had warned to watch for them. He had taught the parable of the ten virgins, which included the warning that those who are not prepared will lose eternal blessings. He had given the parable of the talents, which included the warning to not bury talents, and had explained that He would separate the sheep and the goats. Judas had been amply warned, but he chose not to heed the warnings. His fall is an additional warning to all who are called to serve. Judas fell even though he was one of the Twelve Apostles. No matter the positions people hold, they can fall if they do not have sufficient spiritual oil.

Tuesday Is Concluded

In conclusion, while on the slopes of the Mount of Olives, Christ taught about the need to understand and watch for the signs of His Second Coming and the need to be spiritually and physically prepared. He taught about the need for people to use and increase their talents and to diligently serve. Additionally, He taught that people need to love God and to love and serve others. All these things are hard to do fully. In the final analysis, however, God is both just and merciful and will reward all people in the next life according to how they lived in mortality.

As daylight was waning and the shadows of the evening were upon Jesus, He walked with His disciples on the road toward Bethany, which had become almost a second home to Him. Bethany was a place where He could be with those who loved and revered Him instead of with those who challenged His every word and sought to take His life. He would spend this night and the next day with His friends. When He walked on this road on Thursday,

He would be traveling to Jerusalem for the Passover meal, followed by His atoning sacrifice, Judas's betrayal of Him, His arrest and subjection to multiple trials, and His Crucifixion. For now, He could be somewhat distant from the noise, congestion, and filth of the city, all of which were likely greater during the Passover season. He may have spent a few hours of rest and communion with His Father. For the last time in mortality, He may have gazed at the stars and the moon and contemplated the workmanship of His hands. He might have taken time to feel the grass of the hillsides under His feet and to look at the trees, rocks, hills, and birds. In Bethany that night and the next day, He may have spent some time alone under the olive trees or in the fields, seeking peace and strength to face what was to come.

Chapter 59

THE PASSOVER MEAL
(Thursday Evening)

As Jesus's final Passover arrived, He desired to eat the paschal meal with His Apostles in a home in Jerusalem.[1] This meal was the last meal Jesus would eat in mortality. Although not fully understood by the Jews, the purpose of the Passover was much more than to remember God's deliverance of the Israelites from Egyptian bondage; the Passover also symbolized the Lamb of God, whose Atonement and death would deliver all people from the bondage of sin and death.

During this Passover meal, Jesus instituted the sacred ordinances of the washing of feet and of the sacrament. Also during the meal, Jesus told the Apostles that one of them would betray Him. Soon afterward, Judas left the group so he could complete his betrayal of Jesus.

Jesus Asks Peter and John to Arrange Plans for the Passover Meal (Matt. 26:17–19; Mark 14:12–16; Luke 22:7–13)

Sometime on Thursday, the first day of the Festival of Unleavened Bread,[2] Jesus instructed Peter and John to make preparations for the Passover meal. The following is Luke's account:

Luke 22:7–13. Then came the day of unleavened bread, when the passover must be killed. And he sent Peter and John, saying, Go and prepare us the passover, that we may eat. And they said unto him, Where wilt thou that we prepare? And he said unto them, Behold, when ye are entered into the

---

1. For a discussion of the Passover, see note 1 at the end of this chapter.
2. See Mark 14:12; Luke 22:7.

city, there shall a man meet you, bearing a pitcher of water; follow him into the house where he entereth in. And ye shall say unto the goodman of the house, The Master saith unto thee, Where is the guestchamber, where I shall eat the passover with my disciples? And he shall shew you a large upper room furnished: there make ready. And they went, and found as he had said unto them: and they made ready the passover.

It is not clear why Jesus asked Peter and John and not the other Apostles to make preparations for the Passover. Perhaps Jesus asked Peter because he was the chief Apostle. As for John, perhaps he knew or at least recognized the owner of the home where the Passover meal was to be eaten.

After Jesus instructed Peter and John to prepare for the Passover meal, they asked where they should go to do so. The two Apostles might have asked, in part, because the meal could have been eaten in Bethany or some other city.[3] Jesus responded by indicating that they should go to Jerusalem and that after they arrived, they would meet a man (likely a servant) holding a pitcher of water. They were to follow him until he entered a house, and then they were to enter the house too.

It is unclear why Jesus did not identify the location or the name of the owner of the house. Perhaps Judas was present and Jesus did not want Judas to know the meal's location beforehand, since Judas might have shared the information with the chief priests; in turn, the chief priests might have arranged for Jesus to be arrested before the conclusion of the Passover meal and what Jesus intended to accomplish during it. Whatever the reason, the method through which Peter and John found the location Jesus intended would be a small miracle.

Jesus apparently was confident that Peter and John would fulfill their assignment, and the two Apostles presumably had faith that events would unfold as Jesus said they would. Faith was certainly needed because at the time of the Passover, the city was crowded with approximately two hundred thousand people,[4] meaning that it might not be easy to see the man carrying the pitcher of water.

---

3.   Edersheim explained that "for ecclesiastical purposes, Bethphage and Bethany seem to have been included in Jerusalem" (Edersheim, *Life and Times of Jesus the Messiah*, p. 805).

4.   See Seely, "The Last Supper according to Matthew, Mark, and Luke," *Life and Teachings of Jesus Christ*, vol. 3, ed. Holzapfel and Wayment, pp. 83–84.

When Peter and John entered the house, they were to tell the owner, "The Master saith unto thee, Where is the guestchamber, where I shall eat the passover with my disciples?" It is reasonable to assume that the owner of the house already was or would become a disciple, since Jesus referred to him as a *goodman* and since he apparently knew whom Peter and John were referring to when they used the word *Master*.[5]

Jesus did not instruct the two Apostles to ask for the upper room; rather, Jesus was humbly asking for only a common guest room.[6] Yet, Jesus knew that the owner of the house would make available the best room—a large, furnished upper room—and He told His Apostles such.

Peter and John did as Jesus directed. As they entered the city, possibly early in the afternoon, they would have seen the multitude, including travelers who were there to participate in the Passover and the Festival of Unleavened bread. The Apostles would also have seen the temple courts thronged by worshippers and seen the priest's court filled with priests and Levites dressed in white robes.

While in the city, Peter and John found the man carrying the pitcher of water. They followed him, entered the house, and asked the owner to use his guest room for the paschal meal. Instead of showing the Apostles the guest room, he showed them the upper room, which was already "furnished," presumably meaning that it was already prepared to be used for the Passover meal, with the table set and cushions positioned for people to recline on. Likely, the owner felt joy at making his home available to Jesus and His Apostles for the Passover, and this joy presumably increased if the owner saw Jesus and the Twelve enter his home. Perhaps the owner will be forever blessed for what he did for the Savior of the world on that day.

Presumably, Peter and John needed to prepare the meal by obtaining the lamb; presenting it for sacrifice; and then roasting it and acquiring wine,[7]

---

5.   For a discussion of who the owner might have been, see note 2 at the end of this chapter.

6.   For a discussion of the nature of a guest room, or "guestchamber," see Edersheim, *Life and Times of Jesus the Messiah*, pp. 807–808.

7.   Although the Gospels mention only two cups of wine, four cups of wine was standard at Passover meals (see Smith, *Bible Dictionary*, s.v. "Passover").

cakes of unleavened bread, bitter herbs, and vinegar to dip the herbs in. Regarding the sacrifice of the lamb, Edersheim stated the following:

> Before the incense was burnt for the Evening Sacrifice, or yet the lamps in the Golden Candlestick were trimmed for the night, the Paschal-Lambs were slain. The worshippers were admitted in three divisions within the Court of the Priests. . . . A threefold blast from the Priests' trumpets intimated that the Lambs were being slain. . . . While this [the sacrificing of the lambs] was going on, the Hallel (Ps. 113–118)[8] was being chanted by the Levites. . . . Only the first line of every Psalm was repeated by the worshippers; while to every other line they responded by a Halleluyah, till Ps. 118 was reached, when, besides the first, these three lines were also repeated:
>
> Save now, I beseech Thee, Lord:
>
> O Lord, I beseech Thee, send no prosperity.
>
> Blessed be He that cometh in the Name of the Lord.[9]

It is well worth the time for a person to read and ponder the words of the entire Hallel and to consider his or her own faith and commitment. The words of the Hallel that were chanted would likely have had a profound effect on Peter and John. The words "Save now, I beseech Thee" may have reminded Peter and John of Jesus's triumphal entry into Jerusalem just days before, because the multitude had shouted, "Hosanna"[10] (which means "save, we pray thee"[11]) and "Blessed is he that cometh in the name of the Lord."[12]

After the lamb had been slain, skinned, cleaned, and the inmost parts removed and prepared for burning on the altar, the lamb would have been placed on two staves, which Peter and John would have rested on their shoulders and carried back to the house where the paschal meal was to be eaten. When they arrived, they would have placed the lamb on a pomegranate spit over a fire for roasting.[13] Then they would have prepared everything else, if it had not already been prepared.

---

8.   See note 3 at the end of this chapter, which includes portions of Psalms 113–118.

9.   Edersheim, *Life and Times of Jesus the Messiah*, pp. 810–811.

10.   See Matt. 21:9; Mark 11:9-10; John 12:13.

11.   Young, *Analytical Concordance*, s.v. "hosanna"; see also *HarperCollins Bible Dictionary*, s.v. "hosanna"; Smith, *Bible Dictionary*, s.v. "hosanna."

12.   Matt. 21:9; Mark 11:9–11; see also Luke 19:38; John 12:13.

13.   For a discussion of the roasting of the paschal lamb, see note 4 at the end of this chapter.

The Last Supper Begins (Matt. 26:20; Mark 14:17; Luke 22:14–18)[14]

Jesus and all the Apostles except for Peter and John likely left Bethany for Jerusalem in the late afternoon. They descended the slopes of the Mount of Olives, crossed the Kidron Valley, and ascended the steep path into Jerusalem. This occasion was the last time in mortality that Jesus would make this journey. He knew what He must do, what He would soon face, and what He must soon accomplish for all humankind.

As they walked, Jesus may have seen spring flowers and groves of olive trees. He may have seen the last rays of the sun lighting the temple and its spires. He may have seen the clouds turning pink and orange as the sun was setting. As the small group came into the city, they surely saw throngs of people dressed in festive attire; tents where travelers were staying for the Passover; and men coming down from the temple mount, ready to roast their sacrificed paschal lambs. The group likely smelled smoke and parts of the paschal lambs being burned on the temple altar.

Jesus may have felt deep melancholy as He walked toward the house where He would partake of His last Passover meal. During His ministry, He wanted to draw the Jews to Him, but most had rejected Him.[15] Jesus likely also felt the divine within Him give Him the strength to endure what He soon would face. Because of His love for all, He would offer Himself as the true Passover Lamb. As John the Baptist had said three years earlier, "Behold the Lamb of God, which taketh away the sin of the world."[16]

As Jesus and the Apostles reached the house where they would eat the Passover meal, the first three stars may have been visible and the men might have heard the sounds of trumpets on the temple mount ringing out to all Jerusalem that the Passover had begun. After entering the house, Jesus and the Apostles climbed the stairs to the upper room—perhaps the

14. Seely explained that "the phrase 'Last Supper' never occurs in the New Testament. It is a phrase that is descriptive of the fact that this occasion was the last time the Savior would eat with His Apostles in mortality. . . . Paul refers to the commemoration of the sacrament as the 'Lord's supper.'" (Seely, "The Last Supper according to Matthew, Mark, and Luke," *Life and Teachings of Jesus Christ*, vol. 3, ed. Holzapfel and Wayment, p. 60n1.)

15. See Matt. 23:37; Luke 13:34.

16. John 1:29; see also Edersheim, *Life and Times of Jesus the Messiah*, p. 811.

same room where three days later He would appear to His Apostles as the resurrected Lord.[17]

Luke's record gives the most complete account of the beginning of the Passover meal:

> **Luke 22:14–18.** And when the hour was come, he sat down, and the twelve apostles with him. And he said unto them, With desire I have desired to eat this passover with you before I suffer: for I say unto you, I will not any more eat thereof, until it be fulfilled in the kingdom of God. And he took the cup, and gave thanks, and said, Take this, and divide it among yourselves: for I say unto you, I will not drink of the fruit of the vine, until the kingdom of God shall come.

In alignment with Jewish custom, Jesus and the Apostles would have reclined on couches arranged on three sides of a short-legged rectangular table.[18] Each person would have rested on one hand or elbow and kept his other hand free in order to eat. Their feet would have faced away from the table. The seating area was shaped somewhat like a horseshoe, and Jesus may have been in the center position.[19] John was likely on Jesus's right side, and Judas was likely on Jesus's left side. Peter likely rested on the pillow facing or next to John.[20]

After Jesus sat down at the table, He told the Apostles that He wanted to eat His final Passover meal with them, whom He loved, before He fulfilled His mortal mission. This occasion was an opportunity not only to eat the paschal meal but also to give further instruction and complete sacred ordinances.

Jesus then took a cup of wine and offered a prayer of gratitude. Jesus's prayer might have been the one commonly offered by Jews at the start of the Passover meal: "Blessed art Thou, Jehovah our God, Who has created the fruit of the Vine!"[21] He then instructed His Apostles to drink the wine. Jesus next stated that He would "not drink of the fruit of the vine, until the kingdom of God shall come."

---

17. See Luke 24:36–39; Edersheim, *Life and Times of Jesus the Messiah*, p. 813; Farrar, *Life of Christ*, p. 532.

18. The table and surrounding couches were called a triclinium.

19. See Farrar, *Life of Christ*, p. 532.

20. For a discussion of the placement of John, Judas, and Peter at the table, see note 5 at the end of this chapter.

21. Edersheim, *Life and Times of Jesus the Messiah*, p. 817.

The Apostles Contend about Who Is Greatest (Luke 22:24–30)

Luke's record then states that the Apostles debated which of them was the greatest. Jesus responded by teaching them the difference between worldly honor and authority on the one hand and honor in His kingdom on the other hand.

> **Luke 22:24–30.** And there was also a strife among them, which of them should be accounted the greatest. And he said unto them, The kings of the Gentiles exercise lordship over them; and they that exercise authority upon them are called benefactors. But ye shall not be so: but he that is greatest among you, let him be as the younger; and he that is chief, as he that doth serve. For whether is greater, he that sitteth at meat, or he that serveth? is not he that sitteth at meat? but I am among you as he that serveth. Ye are they which have continued with me in my temptations. And I appoint unto you a kingdom, as my Father hath appointed unto me; that ye may eat and drink at my table in my kingdom, and sit on thrones judging the twelve tribes of Israel.

The contention may have been the result of Judas claiming the seat to the left of Jesus or claiming precedence over the other Apostles because he had the money bag. Similar contention had occurred among the Apostles some months earlier, when Salome, the mother of James and John, asked Jesus if her two sons could sit on his right and left hands in the kingdom of heaven.[22] Jesus took that occasion to teach Salome and His Apostles much the same lesson as He again taught during this last Passover meal. Repeating instruction is valuable, especially given the passage of time and changes in circumstances.

Jesus explained that in the world, kings exercise authority over their subjects; in contrast, in the Lord's kingdom, the greatest should humbly serve and not seek recognition or exercise dominion over others. Jesus then used His own life as an example of selfless service. He did not seek to obtain wealth or position or to be served by others; He came into this world to serve all people and make possible their eternal life.

Christ then assured His Apostles that because they had been with Him during His temptations, He would appoint them a place in His kingdom, which He had received from His Father. The Apostles would have a place

---

22. See Matt. 20:20–28; Mark 10:35–45.

at Christ's figurative table and would have the authority to judge the twelve tribes of Israel.

Jesus Declares That One of the Apostles Will Betray Him
(Matt. 26:21–25; Mark 14:18–21; Luke 22:21–23; John 13:18–19, 21–30)

Likely while Jesus and the Apostles ate the Passover meal, Jesus declared that one of the Apostles would betray Him.[23] The following is Matthew's account:

> **Matthew 26:21–25.** And as they did eat, he said, Verily I say unto you, that one of you shall betray me. And they were exceeding sorrowful, and began every one of them to say unto him, Lord, is it I? And he answered and said, He that dippeth his hand with me in the dish, the same shall betray me. The Son of man goeth as it is written of him: but woe unto that man by whom the Son of man is betrayed! it had been good for that man if he had not been born. Then Judas, which betrayed him, answered and said, Master, is it I? He said unto him, Thou hast said.

Jesus's declaration that one of the Apostles would betray Him caused them, perhaps with the exception of Judas, to feel great sorrow. One can only imagine their thoughts and introspection. Humbly and perhaps with disbelief in their voices, they asked: "Lord, is it I?" They did not point accusing fingers at each other. Jesus responded by explaining that the Apostle who dipped his hand in the dish with Jesus would betray Him.[24] That reply must not have given the Apostles comfort, for they all had dipped into the dish.

Jesus then stated that "the Son of man goeth as it has been written of him"—Jesus was presumably referring to prophecies about His death. He then added a sorrowful warning to the one who would betray Him: it would have been better for the betrayer if he had never been born. Melancholy

---

23.   Matthew's and Mark's records indicate that Jesus made this declaration while the group ate; John's record indicates that Jesus made the declaration after Jesus had washed the Apostles' feet (see Matt. 26:21; Mark 14:18; John 13:1–18).

24.   Jesus was likely referring to dipping bitter herbs in a "broth made of vinegar and bruised fruit." The bitter herbs were "emblematic of the sojourn in Egypt." (Dummelow, *Bible Commentary*, p. 810.)

likely settled over the group, for Jesus had said not only that one of the Apostles would betray Him but that He would be killed.

Judas then asked, "Master, is it I?" In asking the question, Judas was being hypocritical, audacious, and shameless—he had already conspired to betray Jesus for thirty pieces of silver. Though Judas presumably asked because he did not want to arouse suspicion, did he really think that he could deceive the Savior of the world?

With divine knowledge, Jesus responded, apparently only in the hearing of Judas: "Thou hast said." Judas may have heard sorrow in Jesus's voice as He declared that Judas was the one who would betray Him. In a way, Jesus may have been warning Judas and giving him a chance to repent, but Judas would not.

John's account provides additional insight regarding Jesus's declaration that one of the Apostles would betray him. According to John's account, Jesus said: "I speak not of you all: I know whom I have chosen: but that the scripture may be fulfilled, He that eateth bread with me hath lifted up his heel against me."[25] Of course, Jesus was stating that Judas would figuratively lift his heel against Jesus by betraying Him. Jesus may have also been referring to Genesis 3, which states that God placed enmity between Satan and the seed of Eve. Satan would have power to bruise the heel of Eve's seed—that is, Christ. But Christ would bruise Satan's head.[26] Satan bruised Christ's heal by entering Judas and influencing him to betray Jesus to Jewish leaders.[27] Christ would soon bruise Satan's head by completing the Atonement and being resurrected. Christ will again bruise Satan's head when He returns to the earth at His Second Coming. Ultimately, He will triumph over all evil.[28] Additionally, Christ may have been referencing Psalm 41, in which David stated, "Yea, mine own familiar friend, in whom I trusted, which did eat of my bread, hath lifted up his heel against me."[29]

John's record also states that Jesus told the Twelve of His impending betrayal and death so that when it came to pass, the Apostles would "believe

---

25. John 13:18.
26. See Gen. 3:15.
27. See John 13:27.
28. See Rev. 20:1–10.
29. Ps. 41:9.

that I am he."[30] Jesus's prophecy can likewise be a witness to people in the latter days, helping them to believe.

Jesus Washes the Apostles' Feet (John 13:3–17, 20)

In Jesus's day, it was customary for people entering a house to remove their sandals so that they did not track dust and dirt onto the white floor mats.[31] Jesus and the Apostles would have followed this custom, particularly since their feet would have been covered with the dust and dirt of their journey from Bethany to the house in Jerusalem. It was also customary for a household servant to wash guests' feet after they removed their sandals. However, Jesus's and the Apostles' feet were apparently not washed after entering the house. Given the generosity of the house's owner, it is possible that he had offered to have the guests' feet washed but that Jesus had declined since He knew that He would wash the Apostles' feet. Or perhaps the owner had left so that Jesus and the others could be alone and had provided a basin filled with water and a towel. Whatever the circumstances, Jesus washed the Apostles feet. The following is John's account:

> **John 13:3–17, 20.** Jesus knowing that the Father had given all things into his hands, and that he was come from God, and went to God; He riseth from supper, and laid aside his garments; and took a towel, and girded himself. After that he poureth water into a basin, and began to wash the disciples' feet, and to wipe them with the towel wherewith he was girded. Then cometh he to Simon Peter: and Peter saith unto him, Lord, dost thou wash my feet? Jesus answered and said unto him, What I do thou knowest not now; but thou shalt know hereafter. Peter saith unto him, Thou shalt never wash my feet. Jesus answered him, If I wash thee not, thou hast no part with me. Simon Peter saith unto him, Lord, not my feet only, but also my hands and my head. Jesus saith to him, He that is washed needeth not save to wash his feet, but is clean every whit: and ye are clean, but not all. For he knew who should betray him; therefore said he, Ye are not all clean. So after he had washed their feet, and had taken his garments, and was set down again, he said unto them, Know ye what I have done to you? Ye call me Master and Lord: and ye say well; for so I am. If I then, your Lord and

---

30.   John 13:19.
31.   See Farrar, *Life of Christ*, p. 533.

Master, have washed your feet; ye also ought to wash one another's feet. For I have given you an example, that ye should do as I have done to you. Verily, verily, I say unto you, The servant is not greater than his lord; neither he that is sent greater than he that sent him. If ye know these things, happy are ye if ye do them. . . . Verily, verily, I say unto you, He that receiveth whomsoever I send receiveth me; and he that receiveth me receiveth him that sent me.

John stated that Christ knew "that the Father had given all things into his hands, and that he was come from God, and went to God." What strength and confidence Christ must have felt from knowing that His life had been approved by His Father. It is impossible to grasp the full import of John's words and to know what transpired between Heavenly Father and His Only Begotten Son. What is clear is that Heavenly Father committed all judgment to His Son[32] and that "this earth will be Christ's."[33]

Jesus rose, removed His outer garment, and tied a towel around His waist. Then He poured water into a container and may have knelt in preparation to wash His Apostles' feet. If He did kneel, this humble act was a gesture the Apostles would likely never forget. Presumably, all of the Apostles watched as Jesus approached each Apostle in turn and proceeded to wash his feet. Imagine the tenderness with which the Lord took each Apostle's feet, bathed them with water, and then gently dried them with the towel. Washing the feet of a guest was the work of slaves,[34] but this Passover evening, Christ— the greatest of all—washed the Apostle's feet. Presumably, each of the Apostles except for Peter sat in silent awe and reverence at Jesus's gracious and humble act of love and service. Presumably, none of the Apostles had volunteered to offer this act of kindness to Jesus or the others. Jesus was providing an example for the Apostles and teaching them to likewise be humble servants. Jesus was also instituting a priesthood ordinance—though the Apostles likely did not understand the full significance of their feet being washed.[35] He was also fostering oneness between the Apostles and with their

---

32. See John 5:22.

33. D&C 130:9.

34. See Farrar, *Life of Christ*, p. 534; Edersheim, *Life and Times of Jesus the Messiah*, p. 821.

35. For a discussion of the ordinance of washing of feet, see note 6 at the end of this chapter.

Lord and Master by washing and drying all of the Apostles' feet. Jesus later referenced this unity in what is known as the Intercessory Prayer.[36]

When Jesus approached Peter, he asked whether Jesus was going to wash his feet also, perhaps implying that Peter should instead wash Jesus's feet. Jesus answered, "What I do thou knowest not now; but thou shalt know hereafter." In response, Peter said that he would never allow Jesus to wash his feet. Jesus responded by stating that if He did not wash Peter's feet, Peter would have no part with Jesus. Jesus was likely implying that Peter's glory in the kingdom of heaven would be diminished if Jesus did not wash Peter's feet. Peter then asked that not only his feet be washed but also his hands and head. In response, Jesus told Peter that only his feet needed to be washed in order for him to be "clean every whit."

Christ then told the Apostles, "Ye are clean, but not all." The Savior of the world was pronouncing that all of the Apostles—except Judas—were clean. They were clean through their faithfulness; the ordinance of the washing of feet; and His Atonement, which He would soon complete. The eleven clean Apostles must have deeply pondered the meaning of Christ's words and actions. They likely realized that Christ was not referring to their feet being washed but to their souls being cleansed.

Though Jesus knew Judas was a traitor, He washed this Apostle's soiled feet. But neither Jesus's gentle hands, which had healed so many, nor the water could cleanse Judas of the devil's influence, which had entered Judas's heart. Therefore, in a way, Judas was acting hypocritically by allowing Jesus to wash his feet.

After Jesus finished washing the Apostles' feet, He put His outer garments on again and sat down. Then He asked, "Know ye what I have done to you?" Apparently without waiting for a reply, Jesus acknowledged that they called him Master and that they were correct. He then stated that if He, the Master, had washed their feet, then they should wash each other's feet. He had set the example. The eleven must be purified and serve, not seek to be served.

Jesus then stated that just as servants are not greater than their lord, neither is Jesus greater than His Father. As always, Jesus was giving honor and

---

36. See John 17.

glory to God. Jesus also explained that if they understood this relationship between Him and God, what had been done for the Apostles, and in turn what they should do, they would be happy. Further, Jesus stated that those who would accept the Apostles' and other disciples' testimonies would believe in Jesus and God. Jesus was implying that the Apostles were to help others believe in Him and follow His teachings and thereby come unto God.

Jesus Institutes the Sacrament (Matt. 26:26–29; Mark 14:22–25; Luke 22:19–20)

As this special Passover meal was concluding, Jesus instituted the second priesthood ordinance that the Apostles needed before He died: the sacrament. This ordinance included eating bread and drinking wine in remembrance of Jesus's body, which would be sacrificed, and His blood, which would be shed, as part of His infinite atoning sacrifice.[37] The following is Matthew's account:

> **Matthew 26:26–29.** And as they were eating, Jesus took bread, and blessed it, and brake it, and gave it to the disciples, and said, Take, eat; this is my body. And he took the cup, and gave thanks, and gave it to them, saying, Drink ye all of it; for this is my blood of the new testament, which is shed for many for the remission of sins. But I say unto you, I will not drink henceforth of this fruit of the vine, until that day when I drink it new with you in my Father's kingdom.

Imagine being in the room with Jesus and the Twelve and witnessing the presumably humble yet divine spirit with which Jesus took the bread, broke it,[38] and blessed it. Jesus then gave the bread to His Apostles to eat and said, "This is my body which is given for you: this do in remembrance of me."[39] One can only imagine what the Twelve thought and felt as they each took a piece of bread. Each piece was unique in shape, just as each of the Apostles was unique in abilities. The same is true of all people, and all people can be uniquely blessed by the Lord's Spirit as they partake of the sacramental emblems.

---

37. For a detailed discussion of Christ's Atonement being infinite, see Callister, *Infinite Atonement*, pp. 63–65.

38. JST Matt. 26:22 indicates that Jesus broke the bread before He blessed it.

39. Luke 22:19.

Additional insight comes from Joseph Smith's translations of the accounts in Matthew and Mark. Joseph Smith's translation of Matthew 26:26 in part states, "Take, eat; this is in remembrance of my body which I give a ransom for you." Joseph Smith's translation of the corresponding verse in Mark states, "Take it, and eat. Behold, this is for you to do in remembrance of my body; for as oft as ye do this ye will remember this hour that I was with you."[40]

Jesus then gave thanks for the cup of wine (and presumably also blessed it). A cup is a wonderful symbol of Christ atoning in Gethsemane and on the cross, where He voluntarily gave His life. The word cup appears numerous times in the Old Testament, and of particular significance is the use of cup in Psalm 116:13. This verse, which is part of the Hallel and which Jesus and the Apostles likely sang during the Passover meal, states: "I will take the cup of salvation, and call upon the name of the Lord." Jesus also used the word cup in relation to His Atonement and Crucifixion. For example, while experiencing the anguish of the Atonement, Jesus prayed, "If it be possible, let this cup pass from me."[41] Afterward, when speaking of His coming death on the cross, Jesus said to Peter, "The cup which my Father hath given me, shall I not drink it?"[42]

Christ explained that the wine in the cup represented His "blood of the new testament"[43]—that is, the new covenant.[44] This new covenant involves remembering Christ's body, which He gave as a "ransom,"[45] and His blood, which He "shed for many."[46] Christ is the Messiah of the new testament, or new covenant, and all must look to Him, believe in Him, and follow Him in order to receive exaltation. As Christ said to the Nephites in the Book of Mormon, "Behold, I am he that gave the law, and I am he who covenanted with my people Israel; therefore, the law in me is fulfilled, for I have come

40.   JST Mark 14:20–21.
41.   Matt. 26:39; see also Mark 14:36; Luke 22:42.
42.   John 18:11.
43.   See also Luke 22:20.
44.   See Dummelow, *Bible Commentary*, p. 710; Talmage, *Jesus the Christ*, p. 554; see also Matt. 26:28 in the following versions of the Bible: New International Version, New Living Translation, English Standard Version, Berean Study Bible, New King James Version, New American Standard Bible, World English Bible, and Young's Literal Translation.
45.   JST Matt. 26:26.
46.   JST Mark 14:24.

to fulfil the law; therefore it hath an end."[47] In part, the law that Christ fulfilled was the law of sacrificing animals. Joseph Smith's translation of Matthew 26:28 specifies that Christ's blood was "shed for as many as shall believe on my name, for the remission of their sins."[48]

Jesus invited all of His Apostles—including Judas—to partake of the bread and wine. Presumably, Judas partook of the sacramental emblems.[49] If he did, he did so with hypocrisy in his heart. As Jesus later taught the Nephites, "Whoso eateth and drinketh my flesh and blood unworthily eateth and drinketh damnation to his soul."[50] Judas's partaking of the sacramental emblems and then betraying Jesus would bring him damnation.

In administering the sacrament, Jesus likely passed the broken bread and then the cup of wine to the Apostle at one of His sides, and then that Apostle passed the emblems to the next Apostle, and so on. In this simple way, they served each other and thereafter may have been reminded of the importance of unity and service to others.

Obviously, Jesus had not transmuted His body into the bread or His blood into the wine. The Apostles understood that the sacramental bread and wine were symbols. As the Apostles partook of the sacrament, they may have remembered Jesus's Bread of Life sermon, in which He twice declared that He was "the bread of life"[51] and once declared that He was the "living bread."[52] Jesus had also said, "Whoso eateth my flesh, and drinketh my blood, hath eternal life; and I will raise him up at the last day,"[53] that they "dwelleth in me, and I in him,"[54] and that they "shall live by me."[55]

According to Joseph Smith's translations of Matthew's and Mark's accounts, Jesus also stated that the bread and wine were to be partaken in remembrance of His body and blood.[56] This truth has been reiterated

---

47.   3 Ne. 15:5.

48.   JST Matt. 26:24; see also Alma 11:40–41.

49.   See Mark 14:23; see note 7 at the end of this chapter for a discussion of whether Judas partook of the sacrament.

50.   3 Ne. 18:29; see also Morm. 9:29; D&C 46:4.

51.   John 6:35, 48.

52.   John 6:51.

53.   John 6:54.

54.   John 6:56.

55.   John 6:57.

56.   See JST Matt. 26:22, 24; JST Mark 14:21–24.

multiple times, including by the resurrected Lord when visiting the Nephites, by Paul when writing to the Corinthians, by Moroni when writing in the Book of Mormon, and by the Lord in the latter days.[57]

According to Joseph Smith's translation of Matthew 26, Jesus taught that the Apostles—and, by extension, the Church—should continue to observe the ordinance of the sacrament: "And I give unto you a commandment, that ye shall observe to do the things which ye have seen me do, and bear record of me even unto the end."[58] Joseph Smith's translation of Mark 14 adds, "For of me ye shall bear record unto all the world."[59] It is reasonable to assume that during the Passover meal or later on, Jesus taught the Apostles the wording that priesthood holders should use as they bless the bread and wine, just as He later taught the wording to the Nephites and to Joseph Smith.[60]

There is no doubt that the Apostles not only long remembered receiving the sacrament for the first time but also reflected many times afterward on the deep meanings of the ordinances of the sacrament and of the washing of feet. These ordinances gave the Apostles added spiritual strength to serve missions throughout the then-known world following Jesus's death.

After Jesus administered the sacrament, He explained that He would not partake of the sacramental emblems again "until that day when I shall come and drink it new with you in my Father's kingdom," presumably meaning after He returns for His Second Coming.[61] Joseph Smith's translation of Luke 22:16 states, "For I say unto you, I will not any more eat thereof, until it be fulfilled which is written in the prophets concerning me. Then I will partake with you, in the kingdom of God."

Just as Jesus and the Apostles presumably sung a portion of the Hallel during the Passover meal, members of The Church of Jesus Christ of Latter-day Saints sing a hymn before the sacrament in order to help them feel the Spirit of the Lord. Today, the sacred ordinance of the sacrament is the most regularly performed ordinance in the Church, and the associated covenants are renewed more regularly than are any others. Perhaps a reason is that

---

57. See 3 Ne. 18:7, 11; 1 Cor. 11:23–25; Moro. 4:3; 5:2; 6:6; D&C 20:75–79.
58. JST Matt. 26:25.
59. JST Mark 14:23.
60. See Moro. 4:1, 3; 5:2; D&C 20:77, 79.
61. JST Matt 22:29; see also D&C 27:5–13.

almost the entire focus of this ordinance is on Jesus and His sacrifice. The sacrament is a time to think of Jesus voluntarily offering His body and blood for each of God's children. Partaking of the sacrament has blessed the lives of many, both in the past and today, providing the opportunity to renew covenants, commit to improve, and receive the guidance of the Holy Ghost. It is important for all who partake of the sacred emblems of the sacrament to remember Jesus's sacrifice; to remember and keep His commandments; and to remember and feel the sweet and quiet testimony of the Holy Spirit that Jesus is the Christ, the Son of God.

Jesus Reveals Who Will Betray Him, and Judas Departs (John 13:23–30)

Before the meal concluded, Peter asked John, who was next to Jesus, to inquire further about who would betray Jesus. The following is John's account:

> **John 13:23–30.** Now there was leaning on Jesus' bosom one of his disciples, whom Jesus loved. Simon Peter therefore beckoned to him, that he should ask who it should be of whom he spake. He then lying on Jesus' breast saith unto him, Lord, who is it? Jesus answered, He it is, to whom I shall give a sop, when I have dipped it. And when he had dipped the sop, he gave it to Judas Iscariot, the son of Simon. And after the sop Satan entered into him. Then said Jesus unto him, That thou doest, do quickly. Now no man at the table knew for what intent he spake this unto him. For some of them thought, because Judas had the bag, that Jesus had said unto him, Buy those things that we have need of against the feast; or, that he should give something to the poor. He then having received the sop went immediately out: and it was night.

In response to John's question, Jesus stated that the betrayer was the Apostle whom Jesus would give a sop—presumably a piece of bread[62]— after he dipped it, likely in the vinegar prepared for the paschal meal. Jesus then dipped a sop, handed it to Judas, and said to him, "That thou doest, do quickly." Joseph Smith's translation of the corresponding verse in Mark states, "And he said unto Judas Iscariot, What thou doest, do quickly; but

---

62. Smith explained the following regarding sop: "In eastern lands the meat with the broth is brought to the table in a bowl. Meat is taken from the bowl with the fingers, and the broth or gruel is then soaked up with a piece of bread held in the fingers. This is called a 'sop.'" (Smith, *Bible Dictionary*, s.v. "sop.")

beware of innocent blood."[63] Perhaps Jesus was, in part, mercifully giving Judas one last chance to repent of the evil he conspired to enact. Jesus knew Judas would betray Him, and Judas knew that Jesus knew. Yet Judas did not repent. One of the Twelve had fallen and had fallen completely—a sad warning to all.

Presumably, the exchange between Jesus and John was not heard by the others at the table, with the possible exception of Peter. The other Apostles would not have known that Jesus's passing the sop to Judas had any significance. They did hear Jesus tell Judas to complete an undisclosed task quickly, and John recorded that some of the Apostles thought Jesus was telling Judas to purchase more items for the meal, whereas other Apostles thought that Jesus was directing Judas to give something to those who were poor.

John recorded that after Judas had eaten the sop that Jesus had passed to him, Satan once again entered into Judas. Judas had been an Apostle for approximately three years, and John had presumably gotten to know Judas well. Perhaps with sadness, John ended his account of this incident by stating that Judas "went immediately out: and it was night." In using the word night, John may not only have been referring to the time but also alluding to Judas's spiritual condition. Judas was filled with the powers of darkness, and in that darkness he left the house so he could betray Jesus. The evil in Judas's heart and the knowledge that Judas would betray Jesus may have caused a feeling of gloom in John. One of the Twelve had fallen! Moreover, John knew that Jesus was the "true Light, which lighteth every man that cometh into the world"[64] and that "shineth in darkness"[65] but that Judas would soon assist in taking the Light from the world. However, Jesus still had much to do before being taken. First, He would spend some precious time with the rest of the Apostles, instructing, edifying, and strengthening them.

Christ began His mortal ministry by entering into the priesthood ordinance of baptism, "to fulfill all righteousness."[66] Near the end of His mortal ministry, He instituted the priesthood ordinance of the sacrament. Through partaking of the sacrament, His disciples covenanted to always

---

63. JST Mark 14:28.
64. John 1:9.
65. John 1:5.
66. 2 Ne. 31:5.

remember Him, to take His name upon themselves, and to keep His commandments, "that they may always have His Spirit to be with them."[67]

Notes to Chapter 59

1. The Passover during Jesus's ministry. The Passover is a "religious festival commemorating God's deliverance of the Jews from [Egyptian] slavery."[68] Luke's Gospel states that Jesus's parents went to Jerusalem every year to celebrate the Passover.[69] When Jesus was twelve, He attended the Passover with his parents and later was found in the temple with the "doctors,"[70] hearing them teach and asking them questions.[71] Three Passovers occurred during Jesus's ministry. For the first one, Jesus traveled to Jerusalem, and while there He drove the money changers from the temple.[72] For the second Passover, Jesus apparently was in Galilee.[73] For the third, Jesus traveled to Jerusalem with His Apostles.[74]

The Lord's command regarding the Passover and the accompanying Feast of Unleavened Bread is set forth in the book of Leviticus: "In the fourteenth day of the first month at even is the Lord's passover. And on the fifteenth day of the same month is the feast of unleavened bread unto the Lord: seven days ye must eat unleavened bread."[75] The Feast of Unleavened Bread "was celebrated for seven days beginning on the fifteenth day of the month of Nisan[76] . . . [and] was later combined with the Passover," creating an eight-day celebration.[77] The Passover began at the time the first three stars appeared

---

67. D&C 20:77.
68. *HarperCollins Bible Dictionary*, s.v. "Passover."
69. See Luke 2:41.
70. The title of doctor was given to those who were experts in the law and taught the law (see Smith, *Bible Dictionary*, s.v. "doctor").
71. See Luke 2:46.
72. See John 2:13–16.
73. See John 6:1–4.
74. See John 13:1.
75. Lev. 23:5–6.
76. Nisan in the Jewish calendar corresponds with part of March and part of April (see *HarperCollins Bible Dictionary*, p. 115).
77. See *HarperCollins Bible Dictionary*, s.v. "Unleavened Bread, Festival of."

on the fourteenth day of the first month (Nisan[78]) and ended when the first
three stars appeared on the fifteenth day of Nisan.[79] No leavened bread was
to be eaten for seven days, and no work was to be performed.[80] Thus, the
day before the Passover meal, members of the household carefully searched
throughout the house for leaven and then destroyed any they found.[81]

The Passover meal included roasted lamb, unleavened bread, and bitter
herbs and was to be eaten quickly. The lamb had to be a male that was in its
first year of life and that was unblemished.[82] The lamb had to be slain and
roasted before sunset on Thursday,[83] and no bones of the lamb could be
broken when it was being killed.[84] The lamb was slain by a representative of
the family or group who would eat the Passover, and the blood of each slain
lamb was sprinkled on the foot of the altar by one of numerous priests.[85]
The lamb was a reminder of when the Israelites had spread the blood of
lambs on lintels and door posts so that God would pass by the firstborn
sons of the Israelites and would kill only the firstborn of the Egyptians.[86]
Although unrecognized by the Jews, eating the lamb during the Passover
may have been symbolic of internalizing the sacrifice of the Son of God.

---

78.   According to Jewish reckoning, one day ended and a new day began at sundown
(see Talmage, *Jesus the Christ*, p. 551).

79.   See Edersheim, *Life and Times of Jesus the Messiah*, p. 805; see also Talmage, *Jesus
the Christ*, p. 550.

80.   See Ex. 12:15, 16, 18.

81.   See Edersheim, *Life and Times of Jesus the Messiah*, p. 805.

82.   See Ex. 12:5, 8–11.

83.   See Smith, *Bible Dictionary*, s.v. "Passover"; see also Mark 14:12; Luke 22:7. Seely
stated that "during the Passover, Jerusalem was crowded and busy with the activities of
the festival. Hundreds of thousands of faithful Jews from all over the world converged on
Jerusalem to sacrifice their lambs at the temple and to eat their Passover meal within the
confines of the holy city. Jeremias estimates that Jerusalem at the time of Jesus probably
had a population of 20,000 to 30,000 and concludes from a careful study of the ancient
sources that there could have been as many as 180, 000 pilgrims at Passover." (Seely, "The
Last Supper according to Matthew, Mark, and Luke," *Life and Teachings of Jesus Christ*, vol.
3, ed. Holzapfel and Wayment, pp. 83–84.) Consequently, a very large number of lambs were
sacrificed at the Passover, requiring a large number of temple priests and perhaps Levites (see
HarperCollins Bible Dictionary, s.v. "Levites"). Because of the large number of lambs to be
slain, the process of killing the lambs may have begun on Wednesday.

84.   See Ex. 12:46; see also John 19:36.

85.   See Seely, "The Last Supper according to Matthew, Mark, and Luke," *Life and
Teachings of Jesus Christ*, vol. 3, ed. Holzapfel and Wayment, p. 85.

86.   See Ex. 12:12–13, 21–22.

The unleavened bread symbolized the haste in which the Israelites departed from Egypt,[87] and the bitter herbs symbolized the bitterness of bondage the Israelites had suffered in Egypt.[88] The Passover was to be eaten each year,[89] and at that time the Israelite children were to be taught of the Lord's deliverance from Egyptian bondage.[90]

2. Possible owner of the home where Jesus ate the Passover meal. Edersheim speculated that the owner of the house was the father of Mark, the Gospel writer.[91] This assumption is based on the fact that Mark's family home was large enough to accommodate various disciples following Peter's imprisonment.[92] Additionally, only Mark's Gospel records that a young man (presumably Mark) wearing only a linen cloth had followed Jesus to Gethsemane and then fled, leaving the linen cloth behind, to escape the soldiers who had come to arrest Jesus.[93] If the Passover meal was held at Mark's house, Judas and the soldiers may have first gone to the house and, not finding Jesus there, then gone to Gethsemane. If Mark witnessed the temple guards seeking Jesus, he may have followed them to Gethsemane.

3. The Hallel. The *HarperCollins Bible Dictionary* (s.v. "Hallel") states that during the Passover, the Hallel "is sung in two parts, Pss. 113–14 before the seder and Pss. 115–18 after. This may have been the 'hymn' that Jesus and his disciples are said to have sung at the Last Supper." The following portions of the Hallel give praise to the Lord and refer to covenants and commitments:

> **Psalm 113:1–4.** Praise ye the Lord. Praise, O ye servants of the Lord, praise the name of the Lord. Blessed be the name of the Lord from this time forth and for evermore. From the rising of the sun unto the going down of the same the Lord's name is to be praised.

> **Psalm 114:1, 3, 7–8.** When Israel went out of Egypt, the house of Jacob . . . the sea saw it, and fled: Jordan was driven back. The mountains skipped like

---

87. See Ex. 12:17.
88. See Ex. 1:14.
89. See Ex. 12:14.
90. See Ex. 12:26–27; 13:8.
91. See Edersheim, *Life and Times of Jesus the Messiah*, pp. 849–850.
92. See Acts 12:1–17.
93. See Mark 14:51–52.

rams, and the little hills like lambs. . . . Tremble, thou earth, at the presence of the Lord, at the presence of the God of Jacob; which turned the rock into a standing water, the flint into a fountain of waters.

Psalm 115:1, 12, 18. Not unto us, O Lord, not unto us, but unto thy name give glory, for thy mercy, and for thy truth's sake. . . . The Lord hath been mindful of us: he will bless us; he will bless the house of Israel. . . . But we will bless the Lord from this time forth and for evermore. Praise the Lord.

Psalm 116:1, 8, 12–14, 17–19. I love the Lord, because he hath heard my voice and my supplications. . . . For thou hast delivered my soul from death, mine eyes from tears, and my feet from falling. I will walk before the Lord in the land of the living. . . . What shall I render unto the Lord for all his benefits toward me? I will take the cup of salvation, and call upon the name of the Lord. I will pay my vows unto the Lord now in the presence of all his people. . . . I will offer to thee the sacrifice of thanksgiving, and will call upon the name of the Lord. I will pay my vows unto the Lord now in the presence of all his people, in the courts of the Lord's house, in the midst of thee, O Jerusalem. Praise ye the Lord.

Psalm 117:1–2. O praise the Lord, all ye nations: praise him, all ye people. For his merciful kindness is great toward us: and the truth of the Lord endureth for ever. Praise ye the Lord.

Psalm 118:1, 6, 14–17, 19–22, 24–25, 27–29. O give thanks unto the Lord; for he is good: because his mercy endureth for ever. . . . The Lord is on my side; I will not fear: what can man do unto me? . . . The Lord is my strength and song, and is become my salvation. The voice of rejoicing and salvation is in the tabernacles of the righteous: the right hand of the Lord doeth valiantly. The right hand of the Lord is exalted: the right hand of the Lord doeth valiantly. I shall not die, but live, and declare the works of the Lord. . . . Open to me the gates of righteousness: I will go into them, and I will praise the Lord: This gate of the Lord, into which the righteous shall enter. I will praise thee: for thou hast heard me, and art become my salvation. The stone which the builders refused is become the head stone of the corner. . . . This is the day which the Lord hath made; we will rejoice and be glad in it. Save now, I beseech thee, O Lord. . . . God is the Lord, which hath shewed us light: bind the sacrifice with cords, even unto the horns of the altar. Thou art my God, and I will praise thee: thou art my God, I will exalt thee. O give thanks unto the Lord; for he is good: for his mercy endureth for ever.

4. The roasting of the paschal lamb. Edersheim described the roasting of the paschal lamb as follows:

According to Jewish ordinance, the Paschal Lamb was roasted on a spit made of pomegranate wood, the spit passing right through from the mouth to vent. Special care was to be taken that in roasting the lamb did not touch the oven, otherwise the part touched had to be cut away. This can scarcely be regarded as an instance of Rabbinical punctiliousness. It was intended to carry out the idea that the lamb was to be undefiled by any contact with foreign matter, which might otherwise have adhered to it. For everything here was significant, and the slightest deviation would mar the harmony of the whole. If it had been said, that not a bone of the Paschal Lamb was to be broken, that it was not to be "sodden at with water, but roast with fire—his head with his legs, and with the purtenance thereof," and that none of it was to "remain until the morning," all that had not been eaten being burnt with fire—such ordinances had each a typical object. Of all other sacrifices, even the most holy, it alone as not to be "sodden," because the flesh must remain pure, without the admixture even of water. Then, no bone of the lamb was to be broken; it was to be served up entire—none of it was to be left over; and those who gathered around it were to form one family. All this was intended to express that it was to be a complete and unbroken sacrifice, on the ground of which there was complete and unbroken fellowship with the God who had passed by the blood-sprinkled doors, and with those who together formed but one family and one body. "The cup of blessing which we bless, is it not the communion of the blood of Christ? The bread which we break, is it not the communion of the body of Christ? For we, being many, are one bread and one body; for we are all partakers of that one bread."[94]

5. The placement of John, Judas, and Peter at the table during the Last Supper. Edersheim presented the following reasoning for assuming that John sat at Jesus's right side, that Judas sat at Jesus's left side, and that Peter sat facing or next to John:

This [John's location] explains how when Christ whispered to John by what sign to recognize the traitor, none of the other disciples heard it. It also explains, how Christ would first hand to Judas the sop, which formed part of

---

94. Edersheim, *Temple: Its Ministry and Services*, pp. 182–183.

the Paschal ritual, beginning with him as the chief guest at the table, without thereby exciting special notice. Lastly, it accounts for the circumstance that, when Judas, desirous of ascertaining whether his treachery was known, dared to ask whether it was he, and received the affirmative answer, no one at [the] table knew what had passed. But this could not have been the case, unless Judas had occupied the place next to Christ; in this case, necessarily at His left, or the post of chief honour. As regards Peter, we can quite understand how, when the Lord with such loving words rebuked their self-seeking and taught them of the greatness of Christian humility, he should, in his petuosity of shame, have rushed to take the lowest place at the other end of the table. Finally, we can now understand how Peter could beckon to John, who sat at the opposite end of the table, over against him, and ask him across the table, who the traitor was.[95]

6. The ordinance of washing feet. As the Prophet Joseph Smith was establishing the school of the prophets, he received divine instruction about the priesthood ordinance of washing feet:

> And ye shall not receive any among you into this school save he is clean from the blood of this generation; and he shall be received by the ordinance of the washing of feet, for unto this end was the ordinance of the washing of feet instituted. And again, the ordinance of washing feet is to be administered by the president, or presiding elder of the church. It is to be commenced with prayer; and after partaking of bread and wine, he is to gird himself according to the pattern given in the thirteenth chapter of John's testimony concerning me. Amen.[96]

Joseph Smith said of this ordinance, "The house of the Lord must be prepared, and the solemn assembly called and organized in it, according to the order of the house of God: and in it we must attend to the ordinance of washing of feet. It was never intended for any but official members. It is calculated to unite our hearts, that we may be one in feeling and sentiment, and that our faith may be strong, so that Satan cannot overthrow us, nor have any power over us here."[97]

---

95. Edersheim, *Life and Times of Jesus the Messiah*, p. 816.
96. D&C 88:138–141; see also 124:37–39.
97. Smith, *Teachings*, p. 91.

7. The questions of whether Jesus washed Judas's feet and of whether he partook of the sacrament. The order in which certain parts of the Last Supper occurred is difficult to determine based on the scriptural record, and therefore it is unclear which parts Judas participated in. Matthew's and Mark's records state that Jesus instituted the sacrament during the Passover meal.[98] Mark recorded that "all" drank of the sacramental wine,[99] implying that Judas was present for the sacrament. John's account indicates that Jesus washed the feet of the Apostles before He passed the sop to Judas,[100] suggesting that Jesus washed Judas's feet.

Various scholars have suggested that because Satan had entered Judas's heart, Jesus would have not allowed Judas to partake of the sacrament. Other scholars have stated that Jesus allowed Judas to partake of the sacrament to seal his condemnation or to give him one more opportunity to abandon his evil designs. Given Jesus's infinite love and justice, it seems likely that He allowed Judas to partake of the sacrament as an opportunity to repent and also allowed Judas to use his agency to fill his evil cup to the brim.[101]

---

98. See Matt. 26:26; Mark 14:22.
99. Mark 14:23.
100. See John 13:1–30.
101. See Talmage, *Jesus the Christ*, pp. 573–574.

Chapter 60

A NEW COMMANDMENT

(Thursday)

After Judas left the Passover meal, Jesus continued to instruct His other Apostles. He gave them "a new commandment"—to love one another—and taught that after He died, those who believed in Him would be scattered but that He would appear to them in Galilee. Jesus then told Peter that he would deny knowing Jesus, and then He warned the Apostles about the challenges they would soon face.[1]

Jesus Says That He and God Are Glorified (John 13:31–33)

Jesus began His instruction to the Apostles by focusing not on the darkness of His impending betrayal and death but on His and His Father's glory. The following is John's account:

> **John 13:31–33.** Therefore, when he [Judas] was gone out, Jesus said, Now is the Son of man glorified, and God is glorified in him. If God be glorified in him, God shall also glorify him in himself, and shall straightway glorify him. Little children, yet a little while I am with you. Ye shall seek me: and as I said unto the Jews, Whither I go, ye cannot come; so now I say to you.

Presumably, Christ wanted His Apostles to more completely understand His relationship with His Father and the fact that Christ would shortly

---

1.   The location where Jesus gave this instruction is unknown. According to Mark's record, Jesus gave some of this instruction after He and the Apostles left the home (see Mark 14:26). According to John's record, Jesus and the Apostles did not go to Gethsemane until after Jesus gave the instruction contained in John 13–17 (see John 18:1). Edersheim believed that much of Jesus's final instruction occurred in the upper room (see Edersheim, *Life and Times of Jesus the Messiah*, p. 829).

complete the work He had come to earth to perform. He had promised in the premortal world to complete this work, telling His Father: "Thy will be done, and the glory be thine forever."[2] This work would involve atoning for all humankind, dying on the cross, and being resurrected, and in doing so He would overcome the world and glorify God. In turn, God would glorify His Only Begotten Son. This knowledge would help give the Apostles confidence to move forward.

Then, likely tenderly, Jesus referred to His Apostles as little children. They were little, or young, in the sense that they were still comparatively inexperienced in the gospel and had not yet received the gift of the Holy Ghost. Additionally, perhaps they could not fully comprehend the grand purpose of this earth life, the importance of their mission, and the glory they would ultimately receive. Moreover, Jesus loved them just as He loved little children.[3]

Jesus next stated that He would be with the Apostles for only a short time. Indeed, that very night Jesus would be arrested, and early the next morning He would be tried and crucified. Following His resurrection, He would be with them for only forty days.

Jesus also told them that they could not go where He was going. They could not atone with Him in Gethsemane, stand with Him during the illegal trials He would be subjected to, or be crucified with Him on the cross. They could not ascend with Him to His Father or go with Him to the Nephites in America. They were to continue their mortal ministries of taking His gospel throughout their region of the world.

Jesus Gives a New Commandment (John 13:34–35)

Christ then gave His Apostles "a new commandment": to "love one another." The following is John's account:

John 13:34–35. A new commandment I give unto you, That ye love one another; as I have loved you, that ye also love one another. By this shall all men know that ye are my disciples, if ye have love one to another.

---

2.   Moses 4:2.
3.   See Matt. 19:13–15.

This commandment is absolute and does not come with any exceptions. The fundamental truth underlying this commandment is that God loves His children. His love for His children is the reason that His work and glory are to "bring to pass the immortality and eternal life of man."[4] John wrote that "God is love"[5]—that is, He is the embodiment of love. As the Savior stated, "For God so loved the world, that he gave his only begotten Son."[6] This love was evident in Nephi's vision of the Tree of Life. Nephi afterward stated that "the love of God . . . sheddeth itself abroad in the hearts of the children of men; wherefore, it is the most desirable above all things. And he [an angel] spake unto me, saying: Yea, and the most joyous to the soul."[7] The love of God is supreme and infinite—infinite in that He loves all of His children and in that the magnitude of His love is unbounding. God's love can lift people out of discouragement and even despair and can help people switch their focus from the material things of the world to a desire to be more like God's Beloved Son.

Though Jesus stated that the command to love others was new, He had taught this commandment before. For example, as Jehovah He had told the Israelites in the wilderness that "thou shalt love thy neighbor as thyself."[8] This commandment was well-known to the Jews during Jesus's day, as evidenced by the fact that when a lawyer[9] asked Jesus what he needed to do to inherit eternal life, Jesus asked him what the law said and the lawyer responded, "Thou shalt love the Lord thy God with all thy heart, and with all thy soul, and with all thy strength, and with all thy mind; and thy neighbor as thyself." Jesus then told the lawyer, "Thou hast answered right: this do, and thou shalt live."[10] This discussion gave rise to the parable of the good Samaritan. As another example, in Jesus's Sermon on the Mount, He taught: "Ye have heard that it hath been said, Thou shalt love thy neighbor, and hate thine enemy. But I say unto you, Love your enemies, bless them that curse you, do

---

4.   Moses 1:39.
5.   1 John 4:8.
6.   John 3:16.
7.   1 Ne. 11:21–23.
8.   Lev. 19:18.
9.   The word *lawyer* was used in the New Testament to refer to an "expert in the Torah, i.e., the law of god, or simply the scriptures" (*HarperCollins Bible Dictionary*, s.v. "lawyer").
10.   Luke 10:27–28.

good to them that hate you, and pray for them which despitefully use you, and persecute you."[11] Additionally, when another lawyer asked Jesus "which [was] the great commandment in the law," Jesus responded: "Thou shalt love the Lord thy God with all thy heart, and with all thy soul, and with all thy mind. This is the first and great commandment. And the second is like unto it, Thou shall love thy neighbor as thyself. On these two commandments, hand all the law and the prophets."[12]

Considering that the commandment was not new, the question arises as to why Jesus referred to the commandment as being new. Clarke provided a partial answer: "Now Christ more than fulfilled the Mosaic precept; he not only loved his neighbor as himself, but he loved him more than himself, for he laid down his life for men. In this he called upon the disciples to imitate him; to be ready on all occasions to lay down their lives for each other. This was, strictly, a new commandment: no system of morality ever prescribed any thing so pure and disinterested as this. Our blessed Lord has outdone all the moral systems in the universe in two [precepts]: 1. Love your enemies; 2. Lay down your lives for each other."[13] Jesus may have also used the word *new* because this commandment was part of the higher law that He introduced in the Sermon on the Mount.[14]

After Jesus commanded the Apostles to love one another, He specified that the love His Apostles were to have for others is the same love that He had for the Apostles.[15] Jesus demonstrated His love in many ways, including by leaving the realms of glory and coming to live on the earth as a mortal. Because of His love for all people, He was born in a lowly stable in arid Bethlehem in the meridian of time, without the benefit of modern conveniences. He lived a humble life, often with no place to call home,[16] and He traveled lengthy distances by foot on dusty roads.

11.　Matt. 5:43–44.

12.　Matt. 22:36–40; see also Mark 12:28–31.

13.　Clarke, *Commentary*, vol. 3, p. 620.

14.　Christ taught this same precept to the Nephites in America (see 3 Ne. 12:43–44).

15.　The Greek word for *love* that Christ used in both instances is *agapaō* (or *agape*) (see Young, *Analytical Concordance*, s.v. "love"). This word refers to the highest form of love. As Christ declared, this form of love is the love He possesses.

16.　See Matt. 8:20.

Jesus also demonstrated His love through how He treated people. He healed the sick and infirm;[17] gave sight to the blind;[18] and restored life to the daughter of Jairus,[19] to the son of the widow from Nain,[20] and to His beloved friend Lazarus.[21] In restoring life to Lazarus, "Jesus wept."[22] He also forgave people, such as a man with palsy[23] and a woman who had committed adultery.[24]

Further, Jesus demonstrated His love through what He taught. In the Sermon on the Mount, Jesus praised those who possess characteristics associated with love, including mourning, such as for those who are in need; being merciful; and being peacemakers.[25] He also taught that people should turn the other cheek, make wrongs right, go the extra mile, be generous, love and pray for enemies,[26] and not judge others.[27] Jesus taught that people should consider all others to be neighbors and should love them.[28]

Jesus would soon demonstrate His love by suffering beyond human comprehension in Gethsemane. He also meekly suffered pain as He was scourged and crowned with thorns. He then bled and died in agony on the cross so that all people might be drawn to Him.[29] His suffering caused Him "to tremble because of pain, and to bleed at every pore, and to suffer both body and spirit—and would that [He] might not drink the bitter cup, and shrink."[30] As Jesus told His Apostles, "Greater love hath no man than this, that a man lay down his life for his friends."[31]

Jesus then told the Apostles that the love they demonstrated would be a sign that they were His disciples. Perhaps Jesus was implying that the world

17. See, for example, Matt. 8:14–16; Mark 2:10–12; 3:1–6; Luke 17:11–19.
18. See, for example, Matt. 9:27–30; Mark 8:22–24; John 9:2–6.
19. See Mark 5:40–42.
20. See Luke 7:11–16.
21. See John 11:43–44.
22. John 11:35.
23. See Matt. 9:2.
24. See John 8:11.
25. See Matt. 5:4–9.
26. See Matt. 5:39–44.
27. See Matt. 6:14–15; 7:1–5. Jesus, as Jehovah, taught similar principles to Moses (see Lev. 19:9–18).
28. See Matt. 22:34–40; Mark 12:28–34; Luke 10:25–37.
29. See 3 Ne. 27:14–15.
30. D&C 19:18.
31. John 15:13.

would be observing what the Apostles did and said, to determine whether the Apostles were true followers of Christ.

In stark contrast with Christ is Satan, who fosters hate instead of love and fosters rage instead of peace. Whereas Christ taught people to turn the other cheek and to forgive others, Satan encourages people to be critical of and harshly judge others. Whereas Christ taught that people should selflessly serve others and go the extra mile, Satan wants people to think only of themselves.

Love is at the center of selflessness. Perfect love is also called *charity*. Charity is the "pure love of Christ."[32] In this phrase, the word *of* can signify two things: first, love for Christ that is pure; second, Christlike love for others. Christ has taught that people need to be filled with "charity towards all men."[33] According to Paul, charity will never fail.[34] By having charity, the Apostles would feel peace and joy.

Loving God, Christ, and others can not only bring peace and joy but also help people move forward in their lives with confidence: Confidence that God does not upbraid.[35] Confidence that they live the way Jesus taught that they should live. Confidence that they are good people. Confidence in the promise of joy in this life and in the life to come. Confidence that eventually they will develop the perfect love that God and Christ have.

Jesus Teaches That His Disciples Will Be Offended and Scattered (Matt. 26:31–32; Mark 14:27–28)

Jesus then told His Apostles that they would "be offended because of [Him]":

Matthew 26:31–32. Then saith Jesus unto them, All ye shall be offended because of me this night: for it is written, I will smite the shepherd, and the sheep of the flock shall be scattered abroad. But after I am risen again, I will go before you into Galilee.

---

32. Moro. 7:47.
33. D&C 121:45.
34. See 1 Cor. 13:8; Moro. 7:46.
35. See James 1:5.

The Greek word for *offend* as used in Matthew's record is *skandalizō*, meaning "to cause to stumble."[36] Some Bible versions translate this word as "fall away"[37] or "abandon your faith."[38] In explaining why the Apostles would stumble or fall away, Christ referenced a prophecy of Zechariah: "Awake, O sword, against my shepherd, and against the man that is my fellow, saith the Lord of hosts: smite the shepherd, and the sheep shall be scattered: and I will turn mine hand upon the little ones."[39] Christ was telling the Apostles that after He was put to death, they would not immediately know what they should do—as scattered sheep, they would lack clear direction. Christ had ordained them, had instructed them for approximately three years, and had told them to take the gospel to the world, but He had not organized them and other disciples as a church. Christ presumably wanted them to know that they would be scattered, so that when they were on their own, they would not be surprised or despair and would be better prepared to move forward with faith and confidence.

Presumably, Jesus was also implicitly telling the Apostles that their faith would be tested as never before. They would see Jesus arrested, wrongfully accused, illegally tried, convicted, mocked, scourged, and crucified. Following Jesus's death, some disciples may have lost their faith, thinking that if Jesus was the Son of God, He could have saved Himself. The Apostles needed to have faith that Jesus would be resurrected—the first person in the history of the world to ever live again. After Jesus's Resurrection, all of the Apostles except, of course, for Judas received a personal witness that He indeed had risen from the dead.[40]

Jesus Tells Peter That He Will Deny Three Times That He Knows Jesus (Matt. 26:33–35; Mark 14:29–31; Luke 22:31–34; John 13:36–38)

In response to Jesus's statement that the Apostles would be offended, Peter boldly declared that he never would. With a firm understanding of

---

36.   Young, *Analytical Concordance*, s.v. "offend."
37.   See Matt. 26:31 in the New International Version, English Standard Version, and International Standard Version.
38.   See Matt. 26:31 in the New Living Translation.
39.   Zech. 13:7.
40.   See Luke 24:36–40; John 20:19–20, 24–29.

what would transpire, Jesus explained that Peter would three times deny knowing Him. The following are Matthew's and Luke's accounts:

> **Matthew 26:33–35.** Peter answered and said unto him, Though all men shall be offended because of thee, yet will I never be offended. Jesus said unto him, Verily I say unto thee, That this night, before the cock crow, thou shalt deny me thrice. Peter said unto him, Though I should die with thee, yet will I not deny thee. Likewise also said all the disciples.

> **Luke 22:31–34.** And the Lord said, Simon, Simon, behold, Satan hath desired to have you, that he may sift you as wheat: but I have prayed for thee, that thy faith fail not: and when thou art converted, strengthen thy brethren. And he said unto him, Lord, I am ready to go with thee, both into prison, and to death. And he said, I tell thee, Peter, the cock shall not crow this day, before that thou shalt thrice deny that thou knowest me.

Jesus responded to Peter by stating that Satan wanted to sift Peter as wheat. In Jesus's time, sifting wheat involved vigorously shaking it to separate the wheat kernels from the chaff. Satan wanted to shake Peter hard enough that his faith would be shattered and he would blow away, just as the chaff does. Presumably, Jesus wanted to impress on Peter's mind that Satan was real and that Satan knew of Peter's potential and wanted to spiritually destroy him. Therefore, Peter needed to be constantly on guard.

No doubt, Peter firmly believed he would never falter, even if others did. Christ had named him Cephas, which means "a stone."[41] Peter had walked a few steps on the water with Christ and had accompanied Him to the Mount of Transfiguration. But Christ knew Peter better than Peter knew himself. Christ knew of Peter's impetuousness and, more importantly, knew of his strengths and potential. Satan also knew Peter and his weaknesses, just as Satan knows other people's weaknesses. Nevertheless, Peter could overcome Satan's temptations through Christ's help, just as all other children of God can.

To provide encouragement, Jesus told Peter that He had prayed for Peter so that his faith would not fail. Even if Peter faltered, he did not need to fail. Peter would learn from his mistake. By doing so, presumably he would better understand the Atonement; would have greater empathy for others, enabling

---

41. John 1:42.

him to better help them with their own weaknesses; and would be more fit to serve in the kingdom of God.

Jesus next told Peter that when he was converted, he should strengthen his brethren. This instruction may have initially puzzled Peter. Peter likely thought he was already absolutely converted; he had declared that Jesus was the Christ, the Son of God. Peter likely wondered how his conversion could be stronger. But over the next few days, during which he would falter, he would come to learn that his conversion and commitment could be strengthened. His conversion was likely strengthened when he saw the resurrected Lord and when he received the gift of the Holy Ghost. Peter would become a stone, as Jesus had called him.

Peter, thinking he would never falter, told Jesus: "I am ready to go with thee, both into prison, and to death." Matthew's account indicates that the other Apostles likewise said they would. In response to Peter, Jesus explained that before a rooster crowed the next morning, Peter would deny three times that he knew Jesus.[42] Jesus's words must have cut Peter to the very core, and he may have wondered how he could ever deny that he knew Jesus.

Jesus Warns the Apostles about Challenges They Will Face (Luke 22:35–38)

Jesus then warned the Apostles that they needed to be prepared for what was to come:

> **Luke 22:35–38.** And he said unto them, When I sent you without purse, and scrip, and shoes, lacked ye any thing? And they said, Nothing. Then said he unto them, But now, he that hath a purse, let him take it, and likewise his scrip: and he that hath no sword, let him sell his garment, and buy one. For I say unto you, that this that is written must yet be accomplished in me, And he was reckoned among the transgressors: for the things concerning me have an end. And they said, Lord, behold, here are two swords. And he said unto them, It is enough.

Jesus began by reminding His Apostles that when they had served their previous missions, they had traveled without purse, scrip, or shoes but they

---

42. Mark 14:30 states that Jesus said the rooster would crow twice: "Even in this night, before the cock crow twice, thou shalt deny me thrice."

had nevertheless lacked nothing. In contrast, after Jesus was no longer with the Apostles, they would be responsible for obtaining food and clothing and taking care of their other basic needs, perhaps with help from others. Jesus stated that in addition to needing purses and scrips, the Apostles would need swords. Jesus used the word sword as a metaphor. The Apostles would face persecution from the chief priests, from those they sent, and from the Romans, and these groups would seek to take the Apostles' lives. The Apostles needed to be wise, humble, and prepared and to always seek spiritual protection. By relying on God and the Holy Ghost, the Apostles would be able to fulfill their mortal missions.

Some of the Apostles may not have fully grasped Jesus's meaning, thinking the sword was a literal sword, for they replied, "Here are two swords." Jesus responded, "It is enough," presumably indicating that their thinking was incorrect. Jesus certainly did not need physical weapons to protect Himself or them, and neither did they. Instead of relying on physical swords, they needed to rely on God's protection as had the Old Testament prophet Elisha, who told his servant when faced with a great Syrian army, "Fear not: for they that be with us are more than they that be with them."[43] The Apostles needed to rely on the priesthood authority they had received and on the "sword of the Spirit, which is the word of God."[44]

To further help the Apostles understand and be prepared for what was to come, Jesus referred to part of the following prophesy of Isaiah: "Therefore will I divide him a portion with the great, and he shall divide the spoil with the strong; because he hath poured out his soul unto death: and he was numbered with the transgressors; and he bare the sin of many, and made intercession for the transgressors."[45] Christ, as Jehovah, had shown Isaiah that He would atone for the sins of humankind and would be crucified between two thieves on the cross.

Love Is an Eternal Principle

Jesus commanded the Apostles to love others as He did. That commandment applies to all of God's children and is eternal. Similarly,

---

43. 2 Kgs. 6:16.
44. Eph. 6:17.
45. Isa. 53:12.

charity, or the pure love of Christ, will endure forever.[46] In speaking of charity, Mormon taught: "Pray unto the Father with all the energy of heart, that ye may be filled with this love, which he hath bestowed upon all who are true followers of his Son, Jesus Christ."[47] As Christ said to His Apostles, "By this shall all men know that ye are my disciples, if ye have love one to another." Disciples of Christ should be lights to the world by loving others, even in the midst of apostasy, disregard for God's commandments, hate, anger, and political and social division.

---

46.   See Moro. 7:47.
47.   Moro. 7:48.

Chapter 61

JESUS'S TEACHINGS ABOUT THE COMFORTERS

(Thursday after the Passover Meal)

Following the Passover meal, Jesus had told His Apostles that after He died, they would be as sheep without a shepherd and that they would be offended—that is, stumble. In addition, He had told Peter that by the next morning, he would deny three times that he knew Jesus. In light of what Jesus had said, He then told the Apostles not to be troubled and He explained that there are many mansions in heaven. He also counseled them to have faith in Him because He is the way, the truth, and the life. He affirmed His relationship with His Father, counseled the Apostles to be obedient, and promised them that the comforters—Jesus and the Holy Ghost—would come to the Apostles after Jesus's death. He also spoke of what is commonly referred to today as the Second Comforter. He then promised them His peace and once again honored His Father.

Jesus Tells the Apostles to Not Be Troubled (John 14:1–4)

Jesus's words about what would shortly come to pass surely caused concern in the Apostles. Jesus, who had led and taught them for approximately three years, would soon no longer be with them. They may have wondered what they should individually and collectedly do. They had been ordained as Apostles and had been told to take the gospel to the world. But how could they do so after Jesus was gone? In response to the Apostles' concern, Jesus counseled His Apostles to not be troubled:

John 14:1–4. Let not your heart be troubled: ye believe in God, believe also in me. In my Father's house are many mansions: if it were not so, I would have told you. I go to prepare a place for you. And if I go and prepare a place for you, I will come again, and receive you unto myself; that where I am, there ye may be also. And whither I go ye know, and the way ye know.

Jesus's counsel to the Apostles was to continue to believe in Him and in God. No matter the challenges they would encounter, the foundational principle that would guide them was faith—deep and abiding faith in God and in His Beloved Son. If the Apostles had faith, God would hear and answer their prayers and Jesus would watch over them. If they had faith, they would be valiant, would endure their trials, would grow, and would accomplish the work assigned to them. Faith would bring them hope, including that they could be forgiven when they fell short.

Jesus's counsel to not be troubled but to believe is wonderful counsel for all of humankind. The optimism that Jesus was encouraging in the Apostles is also present in the lyrics of the hymn "Let Us All Press On":

> Let us all press on in the work of the Lord,
> That when life is o'er we may gain a reward;
> In the fight for right let us wield a sword,
> The mighty sword of truth.

> We will not retreat, though our numbers may be few
> When compared with the opposite host in view;
> But an unseen pow'r will aid me and you
> In the glorious cause of truth.

> If we do what's right we have no need to fear,
> For the Lord, our helper, will ever be near;
> In the days of trial his Saints he will cheer,
> And prosper the cause of truth.

> [Chorus]

> Fear not, though the enemy deride,
> Courage, for the Lord is on our side.

We will heed not what the wicked may say,
But the Lord alone we will obey.[1]

Jesus presented one of the reasons that the Apostles should not be troubled and should believe: they would receive an eternal reward. Jesus explained that His Father's house contains many mansions[2] and that He was going "to prepare a place" in heaven for the Apostles. Regarding the reference to mansions, Joseph Smith taught the following: "My text is on the resurrection of the dead, which you will find in the 14th chapter of John— 'In my Father's house are many mansions.' It should be—'in my Father's Kingdom are many Kingdoms,' in order that ye may be heirs of God and joint heirs with me. . . . There are mansions for those who obey a celestial law, and there are other mansions for those who come short of the law, every man in his own order."[3] Because the Apostles had proved faithful, they would qualify to enter Heavenly Father's highest kingdom of glory.

Jesus was implicitly teaching His Apostles what He later told Joseph Smith: "Thine adversity and thine afflictions shall be but a small moment; and then, if thou endure it well, God shall exalt thee on high."[4] After the Apostles inherited celestial glory, "their joy [would] be full forever."[5] What He taught the Apostles at this time likely gave them hope after Jesus's death and helped them maintain an eternal perspective, particularly when persecutions came, difficulties arose in leading the Church, and other challenges occurred.

Offering further comfort, Jesus told the Apostles that He would visit them after He died. He would witness that He had been resurrected, and He would further prepare them to lead the Church and share the gospel. Jesus then stated that He had previously told them where He was going. Presumably He was referring to teaching the Apostles about His death, Resurrection, and return to His Father. He also told them they knew the way—that is, they knew the way to obtain eternal life.

---

1.   Evan Stephens, "Let Us All Press On," *Hymns*, no. 243.
2.   Implicit in Christ's statement about many mansions is that there are varying degrees of reward in heaven, and they are given based on a person's righteousness.
3.   Smith, *History of the Church*, vol. 6, p. 365.
4.   D&C 121:7–8.
5.   2 Ne. 9:18.

Jesus Declares That He Is the Way, the Truth, and the Life (John 14:5–6)

In response to Jesus's instruction, Thomas asked where Jesus was going and how the Apostles could "know the way." The following is John's account:

John 14:5–6. Thomas saith unto him, Lord, we know not whither thou goest; and how can we know the way? Jesus saith unto him, I am the way, the truth, and the life: no man cometh unto the Father, but by me.

Thomas was likely stating that even though Jesus had told them where He would be, they did not fully understand what heaven is. Thomas and the others had no frame of reference with which to fully comprehend the nature of the eternal realms of glory. Then, he in effect asked how the Apostles could be sure of the way to inherit eternal life if they did not fully comprehend heaven.

Jesus's response was simple and direct. Unlike the rabbis, He did not present lengthy and elaborate rules or a checklist to follow in order to find the way to a heavenly reward. In addition, Jesus did not tell Thomas and the others that the way was through learning or worldly success. Rather, He simply said, "I am the way, the truth, and the life: no man cometh unto the Father, but by me." To come to know God and eventually return to His presence, people need to have faith that Jesus is the Son of God, embrace His commandments and other teachings, and live them.

The Way

Jesus stated that He is the way, and indeed faith in Him and His teachings is the first principle in obtaining eternal life with Heavenly Father and Jesus. As Alma 11:40–41 states, Jesus "shall come into the world to redeem his people; and he shall take upon him the transgressions of those who believe on his name; and these are they that shall have eternal life, and salvation cometh to none else."[6] Similarly, in latter-day revelation, the Lord stated that those who will inherit the celestial kingdom "are they who received the testimony of Jesus, and believed on his name."[7]

---

6. Alma 11:40–41.
7. D&C 76:51.

Jesus had previously taught that He is the Good Shepherd, that He knows His sheep, and that they know Him.[8] Jesus had also taught that He is the keeper of the gate and that those who attempt to enter the sheepfold by some other way than by Him are thieves.[9] Similarly, in 2 Nephi 9:41, Jacob taught that "the keeper of the gate is the Holy One of Israel; and he employeth no servant there; and there is none other way save it be by the gate; for he cannot be deceived, for the Lord God is his name." Jesus alone will be the one to admit people into the kingdom of heaven.

Jesus is also the way in that He taught and showed by example how people need to live in order to obtain eternal life. For example, He taught through word and example the importance of love, humility, and service to others.

The Truth

Jesus said He is the truth. During the time the Apostles had been with Jesus, they had heard Him teach in the synagogues; in the temple in Jerusalem; on hillsides; by the sea; and on dusty roads in Galilee, Tyre, Sidon, Decapolis, Perea, and Judea. His words were truth, for He is the Word of God.[10] Jesus taught the truth with divine authority, unlike the scribes and Pharisees,[11] and that truth resonates with those who believe in Him.

More than just speaking the truth, Jesus embodied truth. As He has said in the latter days, "Truth is knowledge of things as they are, and as they were, and as they are to come."[12] Jesus had that knowledge. He had the knowledge to create this earth and worlds without number under Heavenly Father's direction.[13] Jesus turned water into wine and stilled the raging storm with only His word. He revealed to Joseph Smith, "For the word of the Lord is truth, and whatsoever is truth is light, and whatsoever is light is Spirit, even the Spirit of Jesus Christ. And the Spirit giveth light to every man that cometh into the world."[14] The Lord later told Joseph Smith, "He that ascended up on high, as also he descended below all things, in that he

---

8.   See John 10:14.
9.   See John 10:1.
10.   See John 1:1.
11.   See Matt. 7:29; Mark 1:22.
12.   D&C 93:24.
13.   See Moses 1:33.
14.   D&C 84:45–46.

comprehended all things, that he might be in all and through all things, the light of truth; which truth shineth. This is the light of Christ."[15]

Jesus has more knowledge than is contained in all the books in all the libraries of the world. His knowledge is beyond human comprehension. A person cannot truly have faith in Jesus without believing that what He taught is true. Jesus prayed that the Apostles would be "sanctified through the truth"[16]—truth that came from Jesus's example and teachings and truth that came from God and the Holy Ghost.

The Life

Jesus also taught that He is the life. Similarly, Jesus had taught the women at the well in Samaria that the water he would give was a "well of water springing up into everlasting life."[17] To people near Capernaum, He had taught that He was the "bread of life."[18] To Martha, He had taught, "I am the resurrection, and the life: he that believeth in me, though he were dead, yet shall he live: and whosoever liveth and believeth in me shall never die."[19]

He is the life because, under the direction of Heavenly Father, Jesus created worlds without number and brought life to them.[20] Jesus is also the life in that only through His Resurrection can all of humankind be resurrected[21] and only through His atoning sacrifice can people gain eternal life. As the Apostle John said of Jesus, "in him [is] life."[22]

Jesus States, "I Am in the Father, and the Father in Me" (John 14:7–14)

After Jesus explained that if the Apostles knew Him, they would also know His Father, then Philip asked Jesus to show the Apostles His Father.

---

15. D&C 88:6–7.
16. John 17:19.
17. John 4:14.
18. John 6:35, 48; see also v. 51.
19. John 11:25–26.
20. See Moses 1:32–33; D&C 93:9–10.
21. See 1 Cor. 15:22.
22. John 1:4.

This request gave Jesus further opportunity to teach the Apostles. The following is John's account:

> **John 14:7–14.** If ye had known me, ye should have known my Father also: and from henceforth ye know him, and have seen him. Philip saith unto him, Lord, shew us the Father, and it sufficeth us. Jesus saith unto him, Have I been so long time with you, and yet hast thou not known me, Philip? He that hath seen me hath seen the Father; and how sayest thou then, Shew us the Father? Believest thou not that I am in the Father, and the Father in me? The words that I speak unto you I speak not of myself: but the Father that dwelleth in me, he doeth the works. Believe me that I am in the Father, and the Father in me: or else believe me for the very works' sake. Verily, verily, I say unto you, He that believeth on me, the works that I do shall he do also; and greater works than these shall he do; because I go unto my Father. And whatsoever ye shall ask in my name, that will I do, that the Father may be glorified in the Son. If ye shall ask any thing in my name, I will do it.

The greatest revelation of the nature and character of Heavenly Father is His Son, Jesus Christ. As Paul explained, Jesus is "the brightness of his [God's] glory, and the express image of his person, and uphold[s] all things by the word of his power."[23] Whereas all people's bodies are patterned after Heavenly Father's body,[24] Jesus looks like Heavenly Father. Therefore, since the Apostles had seen Jesus, they knew what Heavenly Father looked like. Further, Jesus had Heavenly Father's character. They were of one heart and mind. They were one in goodness and holiness and one in purpose: "to bring to pass the immortality and eternal life of man."[25] Moreover, Jesus taught what He had heard from His Father.[26]

Philip knew Jesus, but he desired more: to see the Father. Philip presumably wanted to have more than just faith in God; he wanted a sure knowledge of God. Jesus explained that it was not necessary for the Apostles to see God, because the Apostles were with Jesus and Jesus was "in the Father, and the Father in [Jesus]." Jesus counseled Philip to believe

---

23. Heb. 1:3.
24. See Gen. 1:27; 5:3; Moses 2:26–27; Abr. 4:27.
25. Moses 1:39.
26. See John 8:26, 28, 38, 40.

the words that He had spoken—words that would lead to eternal life.[27] For
several years, Philip had walked and spoken with Jesus, felt of His spirit,
heard His spiritually deep words, and seen His miracles. Philip understood
the difference between Jesus's teachings and those of the scribes, Pharisees,
and rabbis. Philip had seen Jesus's words change lives and lift others to a
higher spiritual plain. Everything Jesus had said and done was according
to Heavenly Father's directions. Talmage explained the following regarding
Jesus's reply to Philip: "So absolutely were the Father and the Son of one
heart and mind, that to know either was to know both; nevertheless, the
Father could be reached only through the Son."[28]

In effect, Jesus asked Philip and the others to simply believe in Him—
believe that He is in the Father and that the Father is in Jesus in the sense
that They have the same purpose and characteristics. They are one,[29] not
physically but in Their desire to bring to pass the immortality and eternal life
of God's children through accomplishing God's merciful plan of salvation.
God and Jesus are also one in Their infinite love for all of humankind.

Jesus then stated that those who believe in Him would be able to perform
great works like Jesus's—and even greater works, because Jesus would return
to His Father. He would not sleep eternally in the earth or even merely go to
heaven. Rather, He would go to His Father in the realms of glory and there
reside with Him. Regarding Jesus's statement that those who believed in Him
would be able to perform great works, they would be able to do so because
the Holy Ghost would strengthen, inspire, and guide them,[30] enabling them
to perform great miracles and testify of Jesus with power, causing many
people to believe.[31]

Christ also stated that He would glorify His Father by doing what the
Apostles asked for in Christ's name. Heavenly Father would be glorified
because of the Apostles' faith in Christ and their righteous prayers.
Additionally, Christ's answers to the Apostles' requests would help the

27. See John 6:68.
28. Talmage, *Jesus the Christ*, p. 559.
29. See John 17:20–23.
30. See John 14:16–17; 15:26.
31. See John 15:26–27.

Apostles witness of Him and thereby lead many to believe in Him. God gains in glory when His children qualify for eternal life.

Further, Jesus told the Apostles that if they prayed in His name, He would grant their righteous desires. For the first time in recorded scripture, Jesus specified that people should pray to Heavenly Father in Jesus's name, and this direction remains in effect today. Jesus knew that His Apostles would not ask amiss,[32] and consequently He would not only grant their requests but also assist in bringing people to Him.[33] Jesus said that in doing so, He would be glorying His Father. Perhaps granting the Apostles' requests would glorify Heavenly Father because it meant the Apostles had faith in Jesus and were striving to be righteous. Additionally, through granting the Apostles' requests, the Apostles would be better able to witness of Jesus and therefore bring more people unto Jesus and God, thereby glorifying God.[34]

People today have reason to be grateful for Thomas's and Philip's questions, for they elicited profound responses from the Savior.

Jesus Directs the Apostles to Keep the Commandments (John 14:15)

Having spoken again of faith, Jesus then succinctly emphasized obedience:

John 14:15. If ye love me, keep my commandments.

Jesus concisely gave His Apostles an important reason to keep His commandments. His commandments are the essence of everything He had taught, and if His Apostles kept these commandments, they would be able to develop the character required to return to the presence of God. In addition, keeping the commandments would bring the Apostles peace and confidence as they served in God's kingdom on earth for the rest of their mortal lives. Keeping the commandments would help them have the faith—not only in God and Christ but also in themselves and their worthiness—that they would need in order to face what lay ahead. Keeping the commandments would entitle them to inspiration from the Holy Ghost, who would further teach

---

32. See, for example, 2 Ne. 4:35; see also 3 Ne. 19:24.

33. In the latter days, the Lord has said: "And whoso receiveth you, there I will be also, for I will go before your face. I will be on your right hand and on your left, and my Spirit shall be in your hearts, and mine angels round about you, to bear you up" (D&C 84:88).

34. See Moses 1:39.

and guide them. Keeping the commandments would allow them to have confidence that their prayers would be heard and appropriately answered. Keeping the commandments would also give them confidence to stand in the presence of God after they finished their mortal missions.

Jesus Said the Apostles Would Receive Another Comforter (John 14:16–17)

Jesus then told His Apostles that they would be given "another Comforter":

> **John 14:16–17.** And I will pray the Father, and he shall give you another Comforter, that he may abide with you for ever; even the Spirit of truth; whom the world cannot receive, because it seeth him not, neither knoweth him: but ye know him; for he dwelleth with you, and shall be in you.

The words *another Comforter* imply there was a first Comforter. For the Apostles, the first Comforter was Jesus during His mortal ministry.[35] When the Apostles were burdened with the cares of the world, they presumably turned to Jesus for spiritual direction and comfort. He not only was their friend but also spoke words of eternal life, which can give comfort and peace. For the Apostles, the other comforter was the Holy Ghost, and Jesus was teaching the Apostles about this third member of the Godhead.

John the Baptist had prophesied of the coming of the Holy Ghost: "I indeed baptize you with water unto repentance: but he that cometh after me is mightier than I, whose shoes I am not worthy to bear: he shall baptize you with the Holy Ghost, and with fire."[36] The word fire is sometimes included when referring to people being baptized with the Holy Ghost[37] because the Holy Ghost refines and purifies. When Christ taught the Nephites following His Resurrection, He emphasized the importance of the Holy Ghost's refining and purifying power when Christ commanded all people to be baptized in His name, "that ye may be sanctified by the reception of the Holy Ghost, that ye may stand spotless before me at the last day."[38] Likewise,

---

35. For other individuals, the First Comforter is the Holy Ghost.
36. Matt. 3:11.
37. See, for example, 2 Ne. 31:13; 3 Ne. 9:20; 19:13–14.
38. 3 Ne. 27:20.

Jesus had taught Nicodemus of the need to be baptized with water and the Spirit in order to enter the kingdom of heaven.[39]

In telling the Apostles about the "other Comforter," Jesus used the phrase "the Spirit of truth." This title describes one of the missions of the Holy Ghost.[40] He would teach the Apostles truth as directed by Heavenly Father and would bring to their remembrance what Jesus had taught and the miracles He had performed. As Moroni in the Book of Mormon taught, "And by the power of the Holy Ghost ye may know the truth of all things."[41] In the Holy Ghost's role as a comforter, He could bring the Apostles peace and comfort no matter what trials they faced.

Jesus stated that the Holy Ghost would dwell in the Apostles. In the latter days, Joseph Smith expanded on this teaching by explaining that "the Holy Ghost has not a body of flesh and bones, but is a personage of Spirit. Were it not so, the Holy Ghost could not dwell in us."[42] Similarly, Jesus explained that the Holy Ghost could abide with them. Soon the Apostles would be given the right to the constant companionship of this member of the Godhead,[43] contingent upon their obedience. Importantly, Christ used the word *forever* to describe the length of time the Holy Ghost could be with the Apostles. *Forever* may refer to the rest of their mortal lives, or it may mean that the Holy Ghost would be with them during mortality and also in the spirit world following the completion of their mortal missions. If the latter is the intended meaning, perhaps one reason the gift of the Holy Ghost is given through a Melchizedek priesthood ordinance is so that this gift will continue to be valid beyond mortality.

Jesus then taught His Apostles that unlike Him, who had walked openly among the Jews, neither the Jews nor the world more broadly would see or know the Holy Ghost. The world would not see or know the Holy Ghost for various reasons, including unbelief and wickedness. In contrast, because the

---

39.   See John 3:5.

40.   See note 1 at the end of this chapter for a discussion of the attributes of the Holy Ghost.

41.   Moro. 10:5.

42.   D&C 130:22.

43.   See John 20:19–22 for an account of Jesus conferring upon the Apostles the gift of the Holy Ghost.

Apostles did believe and were righteous, they would come to know the Holy Ghost, for He would dwell with them.

Jesus Says He Will Not Leave His Apostles Comfortless (John 14:18–19)

Next, Jesus said that He would not leave the Apostles comfortless:

John 14:18–19. I will not leave you comfortless:[44] I will come to you. Yet a little while, and the world seeth me no more; but ye see me: because I live, ye shall live also.

Following Christ's death, the Apostles would receive comfort in multiple ways. For example, Christ provided comfort through appearing to His Apostles many times. He first appeared to Peter[45] and then to all of the Apostles except Thomas.[46] One week later, He appeared to all eleven Apostles.[47] He also met His Apostles at the Sea of Galilee and ate with them and taught them.[48] Likewise, He appeared to the eleven Apostles on a Galilean mountain and directed them to teach all nations.[49] Whereas Jesus would visit the Apostles after His Resurrection, He would not reveal Himself and speak to all the Jews and those in surrounding nations—the world would not see Him. In addition to Christ providing comfort, the Apostles received comfort through the Holy Ghost, perhaps particularly after He poured His Spirit upon them on the day of Pentecost.[50]

Jesus also told the Apostles, "Because I live, ye shall live also." In other words, Jesus was stating that because He would be resurrected, so would the Apostles. The Apostles would likely have a greater understanding of and appreciation for the resurrection after Christ appeared to them following His Resurrection.

---

44. Many other Bible versions use the word *orphans* instead of *comfortless*. See, for example, the New International Version, the New Living Translation, the English Standard Version, the Berean Literal Bible, the New King James Version, the New American Standard Bible, the Christian Standard Bible, the New Revised Standard Version, and the World English Bible.
45. See Luke 24:34; see also 1 Cor. 15:5.
46. See Luke 24:29, 36–43; John 20:19–21.
47. See John 20:24–29.
48. See John 21.
49. See Matt. 28:16–20.
50. See Acts 2.

Jesus Refers to the Second Comforter (John 14:20–24)

Jesus then stated that those who keep the commandments and love Him will be loved by Him and the Father and that They will manifest Themselves to these individuals:

> **John 14:20–24.** At that day ye shall know that I am in my Father, and ye in me, and I in you. He that hath my commandments, and keepeth them, he it is that loveth me: and he that loveth me shall be loved of my Father, and I will love him, and will manifest myself to him. Judas saith unto him, not Iscariot, Lord, how is it that thou wilt manifest thyself unto us, and not unto the world? Jesus answered and said unto him, If a man love me, he will keep my words: and my Father will love him, and we will come unto him, and make our abode with him. He that loveth me not keepeth not my sayings: and the word which ye hear is not mine, but the Father's which sent me.

Though Christ would not remain among the Jews after His Resurrection, He said that He would manifest Himself to those who loved Him and therefore kept His commandments. Judas[51] then asked Christ how He would do so. In response, Christ said that He and His Father would come to these individuals and would "make [their] abode with [them]." Christ was referring to people having their calling and election made sure and receiving the Second Comforter.[52] Joseph Smith explained the following regarding the Second Comforter:

> It is no more nor less than the Lord Jesus Christ Himself; and this is the sum and substance of the whole matter; that when any man obtains this last Comforter, he will have the personage of Jesus Christ to attend him, or appear unto him from time to time, and even He will manifest the Father unto him, and they will take up their abode with him, and the visions of the heavens will be opened unto him, and the Lord will teach

---

51. Luke 6:16 and Acts 1:13 in the King James Version and some other versions of the Bible refer to this Judas as the brother of James; however, many other versions of the Bible (e.g., New International Version, New Living Translation, English Standard Version, New King James Version, New American Standard Bible, Christian Standard Bible, and New Revised Standard Version) identify Judas as the son of James. Matthew 10:3 refers to this Judas as Lebbaeus, whose surname was Thaddaeus. For additional discussion, see *HarperCollins Bible Dictionary*, s.v. "Judas."

52. See note 2 at the end of this chapter for a discussion of a person having his or her calling and election made sure and receiving the Second Comforter.

him face to face, and he may have a perfect knowledge of the mysteries of the Kingdom of God.[53]

Joseph Smith also taught what qualifies a person to have his or her calling and election made sure and to receive the Second Comforter:

After a person has faith in Christ, repents of his sins, and is baptized for the remission of his sins and receives the Holy Ghost, (by the laying on of hands), which is the first Comforter, then let him continue to humble himself before God, hungering and thirsting after righteousness, and living by every word of God, and the Lord will soon say unto him, Son, thou shalt be exalted. When the Lord has thoroughly proved him, and finds that the man is determined to serve Him at all hazards, then the man will find his calling and his election made sure, then it will be his privilege to receive the other Comforter, which the Lord has promised the Saints, as is recorded in the testimony of St. John, in the 14th chapter, from the 12th to the 27th verses.[54]

Further insight regarding what qualifies people to have their calling and election made sure and to receive the Second Comforter may come from Doctrine and Covenants 121:44–45: "Let thy bowels also be full of charity towards all men, and to the household of faith, and let virtue garnish thy thoughts unceasingly; then shall thy confidence wax strong in the presence of God; and the doctrine of the priesthood shall distil upon thy soul as the dews from heaven. The Holy Ghost shall be thy constant companion, and thy scepter an unchanging scepter of righteousness and truth; and thy dominion shall be an everlasting dominion, and without compulsory means it shall flow unto thee forever and ever."[55]

Presumably, God and Christ will not only appear to and teach individuals whose calling and election is made sure but will also be in all their thoughts and actions and even their souls.[56] In Christ's Intercessory Prayer, He prayed that the Apostles and all others who believe in Him would become one with each other and with Christ and Heavenly Father, that they could be made perfect.[57]

---

53. Smith, *Teachings*, pp. 150–151.
54. Smith, *Teachings*, pp. 150–151.
55. D&C 121:45–46.
56. Smith, *Teachings*, p. 151.
57. See John 17:20–23; see also chapter 63 in this volume.

A glimpse of what receiving the Second Comforter entails may come from attending the temple. Temples are dedicated as earthly houses of the Father and the Son. Those who are found worthy are invited into Their holy house. There, these individuals receive instruction, participate in ordinances, and make covenants under the direction and in the presence of those representing the Father and the Son. Those who attend may experience unity with each other and with those in the spirit world who accept the ordinances performed on their behalf. The Spirit of the Lord is there, and those who attend can be uplifted and refined.

Jesus States That the Holy Ghost Will Come to the Apostles (John 14:25–26)

Next, Jesus again told His Apostles that Heavenly Father would send them the Holy Ghost:

John 14:25–26. These things have I spoken unto you, being yet present with you. But the Comforter, which is the Holy Ghost, whom the Father will send in my name, he shall teach you all things, and bring all things to your remembrance, whatsoever I have said unto you.

The Apostles had likely sought for the gift of the Holy Ghost, and Jesus told them that they would soon receive it. Jesus also specified that the Holy Ghost would be sent by Heavenly Father in Jesus's name. Likewise, in The Church of Jesus Christ of Latter-day Saints, the Holy Ghost is given in the name of Jesus Christ and under the direction established by Heavenly Father through His Son.

Of great significance is that Jesus then told the Apostles that the Holy Ghost would teach them all things—not only about what they each should do and where they should go but also about the kingdom of heaven. The Holy Ghost would be their guide as they ministered to the peoples of the world. The Holy Ghost would inspire the Apostles regarding what words to say when giving priesthood blessings and counsel to people. The Holy Ghost would inspire the Apostles regarding whom to call to various positions in the Church. The Holy Ghost would also guide the Apostles in making other administrative decisions—decisions that would benefit the young Church and its members. The Holy Ghost would also guide the Apostles in what to say when bearing witness of Jesus to others, including kings.

Jesus also said that the Holy Ghost would "bring all things to your remembrance, whatsoever I have said unto you." This special gift was a marvelous promise to the eleven Apostles. Remembering Jesus's words would be essential as they recorded the Savior's words or recounted the Savior's words so other people could record the words. Without this blessing, the Gospels of Matthew, Mark, Luke, and John would not contain as many of Jesus's words as these Gospels do.

Jesus Promises the Apostles Peace (John 14:27)

Jesus then gave His Apostles peace:

John 14:27. Peace I leave with you, my peace I give unto you: not as the world giveth, give I unto you. Let not your heart be troubled, neither let it be afraid.

Understandably, the Apostles were troubled about what would soon happen to Jesus. They were also concerned for themselves, for others who believed in Jesus, and perhaps for the Jews overall because they were ruled by Rome. The Apostles needed reassurance, and Jesus now blessed them with peace—peace that only the Prince of Peace could give.[58]

Insight regarding the word *peace* may come from understanding its meanings in various languages used during Jesus's mortal life. The Greek word for *peace* as used in John 14:27 is *eirene*, which can imply "unity" and "concord."[59] The Hebrew word for *peace* is *shalom*, which means "completeness."[60] Though Jesus and the Apostles likely did not regularly speak Hebrew,[61] perhaps they thought of the word *shalom* when Jesus spoke about giving the Apostles peace. Therefore, perhaps Jesus was indicating

58.   Isa. 9:6. Jeffrey R. Holland wrote, "As a prince is a king-in-waiting, a son tutored under his father to take the latter's place eventually, so Jesus was a Prince to Elohim, anticipating the time when He would rise from the prince's position at the Father's feet to stand with Him as a rightful heir at His side. It is significant that the title Prince is, with only rare exception, linked with peace, as if that were to be the chief characteristic and quality of the kingdom of heaven." (Holland, *Witness for His Names*, p. 122.)

59.   Young, *Analytical Concordance*, p. 736.

60.   Young, *Analytical Concordance*, p. 736.

61.   "Jesus probably spoke a dialect of Aramaic" (*HarperCollins Bible Dictionary*, s.v. "Aramaic").

that the peace He gave would help the Apostles to be unified with each other and to become individually complete.

Jesus may have also been giving His Apostles peace through His commandment to love one another, for loving others brings peace to the one giving love as well as to the person being loved. Expressing love can drive away contention. Likewise, peace can come through praying to Heavenly Father, who loves all His children, and receiving answers from Him.

Just as the Apostles were concerned about what lay ahead, all people today experience concern and fear at points in their lives, whether because of adversity that they or a loved one is experiencing or because of some other reason. Jesus offers peace to those in the latter days who are troubled, just as He offered peace to His Apostles to prepare them for the valleys they would descend and the mountains they would climb.

Jesus Teaches That God Is Greater than Jesus (John 14:28)

Jesus then reminded the Apostles that He would leave them but later come to them again and that God is greater than Jesus:

John 14:28. Ye have heard how I said unto you, I go away, and come again unto you. If ye loved me, ye would rejoice, because I said, I go unto the Father: for my Father is greater than I.

Jesus did not want the Apostles to sorrow about his impending death and the events that would lead up to it; rather, He wanted them to rejoice. They should rejoice as did the angels who appeared to shepherds near Bethlehem at the time of Jesus's birth. The Apostles had many reasons to rejoice: Because Jesus would be fulfilling His mortal mission and thereby overcoming the world.[62] Because if Jesus did not atone, was not crucified, and was not resurrected, the purpose of this earth life would be frustrated. And because, as Jesus told the Apostles, He would return to His Father.

Though what Jesus was about to do was central to the plan of salvation, He was forever humble and always gave the glory to His Father. Jesus told the Apostles, "My Father is greater than I." Griggs observed, "We should not overlook the end of John 14:28, where Jesus simply observed that His

---

62. See John 16:33; D&C 50:41.

Father is greater than He. Because of the many times Jesus said that He was one with His Father and that He and the Father were in and with each other, that statement is a powerful reminder that Jesus did not claim to be equal with His Father. Jesus often stated that He was sent into the world by His Father and that He spoke the words and accomplished the works He had been given to say and do. This verse reiterates the relationship between God and Jesus found often in the Fourth Gospel."[63]

Christ's statement that His Father is greater is also an unequivocal statement that Jesus and His Father are separate beings. Though they may be one in love and purpose, they are separate individuals. Those who believe that They are the same substance do not understand Christ's statement here, for how could He be greater than Himself?

Jesus Explains That He Told of Coming Events So His Apostles Would Believe (John 14:29)

Jesus then explained that He told the Apostles of upcoming events so that when they occurred, the Apostles' testimonies of Him and His divinity would be further strengthened and the Apostles would not stumble:

John 14:29. And now I have told you before it come to pass, that, when it is come to pass, ye might believe.

The same is true today. Numerous prophecies have been given about the events that will transpire prior to and at the Second Coming of Christ. These prophecies have been given that people today will believe and will not stumble.

Jesus Declares That "the Prince of This World Cometh" (John 14:30)

Next, Jesus again stated that He would not be with His Apostles much longer, and He referred to Satan's role in His death:

John 14:30. Hereafter I will not talk much with you: for the prince of this world cometh, and hath nothing in me.

Satan would soon make his final attempt to thwart Heavenly Father's plan by stopping Christ's Atonement and instigating His unlawful arrest,

---

63. Griggs, "The Last Supper According to John," *Life and Teachings of Jesus Christ,* vol. 3, ed. Holzapfel and Wayment, p. 120.

trials, and Crucifixion. Christ knew Satan and his plan. Christ also knew that Satan had no power over Him. He had defeated Satan's schemes before,[64] and He knew He would do so again in these final hours. Likewise, Christ wanted His Apostles to know that He would be victorious.

Jesus Loves His Father (John 14:31)

Jesus's final message in this discourse to His Apostles is that He loves and honors His Father:

John 14:31. But that the world may know that I love the Father; and as the Father gave me commandment, even so I do. Arise, let us go hence.

Christ's words "I love the Father" can easily be passed over as a statement of fact and lacking in the depth of feeling that Christ must have been expressing for His Father. God and His Only Begotten Son have a special and unique relationship, the depth of which is difficult, if not impossible, for mortals to fully comprehend. Christ loves His Father, and that love is reciprocated.

Jesus had declared His love for His Father and would soon demonstrate this love by completing the Atonement and voluntarily giving up His life. Through these acts and His Resurrection, He would complete the core components of Heavenly Father's plan of salvation for His children. Jesus would accomplish what His Father had sent Jesus to the earth to do.[65]

After Jesus declared His love for His Father, Jesus said to His Apostles, "Arise, let us go hence." They then departed for Gethsemane.

Notes to Chapter 61

1. The attributes of the Holy Ghost. Talmage wrote the following:

The Holy Ghost is associated with the Father and the Son in the Godhead. In the light of revelation, we are instructed as to the distinct personality of the Holy Ghost. He is a being endowed with the attributes and powers

---

64. See Matt. 4:1–11; Luke 4:1–13.
65. 3 Ne. 27:13.

of deity, and not a mere force, or essence. The term Holy Ghost and its common synonyms, Spirit of God, Spirit of the Lord, or simply Spirit, Comforter, and Spirit of Truth, occur in the scriptures with plainly different meanings, referring in some cases to the person of God the Holy Ghost, and in other instances to the power or authority of this great Personage, or to the agencies through which he ministers. . . . The Holy Ghost undoubtedly possesses personal powers and affections; these attributes exist in Him in perfection. Thus, He teaches and guides, testifies of the Father and the Son, reproves for sin, speaks, commands, and commissions, makes intercession for sinners, is grieved, searches and investigates, entices and knows all things. These are not figurative expressions, but plain statements of the attributes and characteristics of the Holy Ghost. That the Spirit of the Lord is capable of manifesting Himself in the form and figure of man, is indicated by the wonderful interview between the Spirit and Nephi, in which He revealed Himself to the prophet, questioned him concerning his desires and belief, instructed him in the things of God, speaking face to face with the man. "I spake unto him," says Nephi, "as a man speaketh: for I beheld that he was in the form of a man; yet nevertheless, I knew that it was the Spirit of the Lord; and he spake unto me as a man speaketh with another."[66]

2. Calling and election made sure and the Second Comforter. It is not the author's place to state whether the original Apostles (excluding Judas) had their calling and election made sure and received the Second Comforter. However, a revelation to Joseph Smith provides insight: "Wherefore, I now send upon you another Comforter, even upon you my friends, that it may abide in your hearts, even the Holy Spirit of promise; which other Comforter is the same that I promised unto my disciples, as is recorded in the testimony of John. This Comforter is the promise which I give unto you of eternal life, even the glory of the celestial kingdom; which glory is that of the church of the Firstborn, even of God, the holiest of all, through Jesus Christ his Son."[67]

---

66. Talmage, *Articles of Faith*, pp. 159–160.
67. D&C 88:3–5; compare 2 Pet. 1:19.

Chapter 62

THE FINAL DISCOURSE
(Thursday after the Passover Meal)

After Jesus gave the instruction recorded in John 14, He told the eleven Apostles, "Arise, let us go hence."[1] The location where Jesus gave the next portions of His instruction is unknown, but it was likely a private place and perhaps outside of Jerusalem and on the way to Gethsemane.[2] This portion of Jesus's instruction is an extension of the prior portion and is somewhat repetitive, likely for emphasis.

Jesus began this portion of His instruction with a marvelous analogy. He then taught of the greatest love a person can have, told the Apostles of His love for them, and warned them that others would hate them. Jesus then spoke again of the Holy Ghost and the Apostles' eternal reward. Jesus also affirmed that He came from the Father, told the Apostles that their sorrow would be turned into joy, and counseled them to be of good cheer. Additionally, Jesus once again counseled the Apostles to pray, especially since He said they would be scattered.

Jesus States That He Is the True Vine (John 15:1–11)

Jesus started His instruction by presenting an analogy, perhaps while pointing to grape vines if any were visible:

John 15:1–11. I am the true vine, and my Father is the husbandman. Every branch in me that beareth not fruit he taketh away: and every branch that beareth fruit, he purgeth it, that it may bring forth more fruit. Now ye are

---

1.   John 14:31.

2.   This assumption is based on the fact that almost everyone in Jerusalem, including those from other countries, would have been involved in the Passover, making it difficult to find a private place in Jerusalem.

clean through the word which I have spoken unto you. Abide in me, and I in you. As the branch cannot bear fruit of itself, except it abide in the vine; no more can ye, except ye abide in me. I am the vine, ye are the branches: He that abideth in me, and I in him, the same bringeth forth much fruit: for without me ye can do nothing. If a man abide not in me, he is cast forth as a branch, and is withered; and men gather them, and cast them into the fire, and they are burned. If ye abide in me, and my words abide in you, ye shall ask what ye will, and it shall be done unto you. Herein is my Father glorified, that ye bear much fruit; so shall ye be my disciples. As the Father hath loved me, so have I loved you: continue ye in my love. If ye keep my commandments, ye shall abide in my love; even as I have kept my Father's commandments, and abide in his love. These things have I spoken unto you, that my joy might remain in you, and that your joy might be full.

In this analogy, Christ is the vine. His Father is the husbandman of a vineyard, which symbolizes the earth and humankind. The fact that in the analogy God is a husbandman—that is, a farmer[3]—implies that He is actively involved in all that takes place on the earth, including in each of His children's lives. The vine's branches, which bear fruit, are the Apostles and others who believe in Christ and serve in His Church.

Talmage discussed the significance of Jesus being the vine:

A grander analogy is not to be found in the world's literature. Those ordained servants of the Lord were as helpless and useless without Him as a bough severed from the tree. As the branch is made fruitful only by virtue of the nourishing sap it receives from the rooted trunk, and if cut away or broken off withers, dries, and becomes utterly worthless except as fuel for the burning, so those men, though ordained to the Holy Apostleship, would find themselves strong and fruitful in good works, only as they remained in steadfast communion with the Lord. Without Christ what were they, but unschooled Galileans, some of them fishermen, one a publican, the rest of undistinguished attainments, and all of them weak mortals? As branches of the Vine they were at that hour clean and healthful, through the instructions

---

3.   A husbandman is someone who "plows and cultivates land" and who is "a specialist in a branch of farm husbandry" (*Merriam-Webster*, s.v. "husbandman," accessed August 9, 2022, https://www.merriam-webster.com/dictionary/husbandman).

and authoritative ordinances with which they had been blessed, and by the reverent obedience they had manifested.[4]

Christ specified that He is not only *a* vine but *the true* vine. Indeed, He is the *only* true vine. He is the "stem of Jesse" that Isaiah referred to.[5] Christ, the Son of God, is the true vine in that He enables eternal life. He is the only true vine in that eternal life is available only through Him. Christ's analogy about being the true vine somewhat parallels two analogies He had previously presented. First, Christ told a woman at a well in Sychar, "Whosoever drinketh of the water that I shall give him shall never thirst; but the water that I shall give him shall be in him a well of water springing up into everlasting life."[6] Second, Christ told Jews in Capernaum, "I am the bread of life: he that cometh to me shall never hunger; and he that believeth on me shall never thirst. . . . He that eateth of this bread shall live for ever."[7] Christ gave these three analogies to different groups—a Samaritan, a gathering of Jews, and the faithful eleven Apostles—which indicates that His teachings and atoning sacrifice are for all people. Christ is the true vine for all.

Both water and bread (i.e., food) are essential for a person to live, just as a vine is essential in order for water and nutrients to flow to grape branches, enabling them to grow and produce fruit. Likewise, Christ provides the spiritual nutrients that people need in order to flourish spiritually, do good works, and be a light to others (i.e., bear fruit).

Of significance, Jesus stated that the husbandman would purge the fruitful branches.[8] The Greek word for *purge* as used in John 15 is *kathairō*, which means "to cleanse."[9] Further, *Merriam-Webster* defines *purge* as to "clear of guilt," to "free from moral or ceremonial defilement," and "to get rid of."[10] By purging the fruitful branches, the husbandman would make

4.   Talmage, *Jesus the Christ*, p. 561.
5.   See Isa. 11:1; D&C 113:1.
6.   John 4:14.
7.   John 6:35, 58. Bread and water are also used symbolically in the sacrament prayers (see Moro. 4:3; 5:2; D&C 20:77, 79).
8.   Compare Jacob 5.
9.   Young, *Analytical Concordance*, s.v. "purge."
10.   *Merriam-Webster*, s.v. "purge," accessed August 9, 2022, https://www.merriam-webster.com/dictionary/purge.

the grape vines even more fruitful. In stating that the husbandman was the one who purged the branches, Christ was once again indicating that His Father is not distant or uninterested in the lives of His children; rather, He is personally involved in cleansing and refining them so that they can become even better and serve Him even more effectively. For example, under God's authority, Christ had washed the eleven Apostles' feet and pronounced these Apostles "clean every whit."[11] Now, in giving this analogy, Christ once again declared that the eleven Apostles were clean. Hearing Christ say these words was surely a great blessing for the Apostles.

The branches in this allegory are God's children, and they can bear various types of fruit. For example, people can bear the fruit of personal faith, obedience, and testimony; when they make mistakes, they can access the Atonement of Christ to be cleansed and better able to spiritually assist others. Additionally, people can bear fruit by helping family members and others to come unto Christ. Further, people can bear fruit by performing sacred saving ordinances for those who are deceased.

All people need constant spiritual nourishment, but just as grapes begin as small buds, particular help should be given to youth as they begin life's journey and find their way through the difficult teenage years. Youth need to learn of God and Jesus Christ, develop testimonies of Them, and learn the importance of choosing the right. Some youth feel they are inadequate. Some feel they are not accepted or are treated cruelly by their peers. Depression can also beset youth. Often, they simply need good friends and others to talk with, but good friends are sometimes difficult to find, just as some soil in the vineyard is better than other soil. Some youth have physical, mental, or emotional challenges. There are almost as many needs for help as there are people.

Of course, bringing forth fruit is not limited to helping someone learn about the Church and be baptized and receive the gift of the Holy Ghost. As James stated, "Pure religion and undefiled before God and the Father is this, To visit the fatherless and widows in their affliction, and to keep himself unspotted from the world."[12]

---

11. John 13:10. Presumably, they were not only forgiven for their sins and shortcomings but also cleansed from the sins of their generation.

12. James 1:27.

In this analogy, Christ used the word *abide* eight times and the word *abideth* one time. For example, He stated: "Abide in me, and I in you. As the branch cannot bear fruit of itself, except it abide in the vine; no more can ye, except ye abide in me." The Greek word for *abide* is *menō*, which means to "remain or continue."[13] In using *abide*, Jesus was emphasizing the need to continually be one with Him, just as the branches and the fruit in the analogy are always with the vine; if the branches and fruit had not been connected to the vine, they would have quickly withered and died. The Apostles and others called to serve could not effectively serve in the Lord's Church and kingdom on their own. They needed Christ as their companion, for Christ said in this analogy: "For without me ye can do nothing."

Jesus gave some keys to abiding in Him. He counseled His Apostles to allow His words to abide in them, which the Apostles could do by continually studying His words. The Apostles also needed to pray. They would not ask amiss in their prayers as long as they continued to love Jesus, have faith in Him, and remain obedient to His teachings. Because the Apostles would not ask amiss, Heavenly Father would honor their petitions. The Apostles also needed to serve with the love that Jesus demonstrated and with love for Him and God. The Apostles were to pattern their love after Jesus's love for them and Heavenly Father's love for His Only Begotten Son. Jesus also counseled the Apostles to keep His commandments. In doing so, they would abide in His love. By abiding in Jesus, the Apostles would "bear much fruit" and thereby glorify Heavenly Father. The same is true for all people. Jesus also warned that those who do not abide in Him and do not bring forth fruit will wither and will be burned.[14]

Christ then said that He had told the Apostles these things "that my joy might remain in you, and that your joy might be full." That is, Christ's joy derived from loving His Father and His Father loving Him, and the joy Christ felt because of the eleven Apostles' faithfulness would be with them forever and they too would have joy. *Merriam-Webster*'s first definition for *joy* is "the emotion evoked by well-being, success, or good fortune or by

---

13. Young, *Analytical Concordance*, s.v. "abide."

14. Dummelow posited that angels will be the ones who cast the withered branches into the fire (see Dummelow, *Bible Commentary*, p. 801). The warning about the wicked being burned is also included in Jesus's parable of the wheat and the tares (see Matt. 13:24–30, 36–43).

the prospect of possessing what one desires."[15] In a religious context, the joy that Christ spoke of to His eleven Apostles is defined as "the explicit association of joy with the person of Jesus and an emphasis on the perfect (or completed) joy of those secure in their loving relationship with him and one another."[16] In a more expanded and eternal sense, Lehi in the Book of Mormon taught, "Men are, that they might have joy."[17]

All too frequently, life's challenges make it difficult for people to experience joy. The process of learning to respond to life's challenges with joy begins with awareness that God is at work in people's lives and that He has an eternal purpose for why people experience trials. People learn from falling and failing, and the process of overcoming and rising above challenges can bring joy in life. With the proper attitude, people can also find joy in others' successes. Joy can also come from family relationships and from small kindnesses that are given or received. Joy can come from seeing others gain faith, repent, accept the gospel, and make covenants. Further, the joy that Christ spoke of is not limited to this life; this joy is also associated with eternal life. This joy is eternal because of Heavenly Father's love for His children and because of His plan of salvation, at the core of which are Christ's Atonement and Resurrection.

Jesus Teaches, "Greater Love Hath No Man This, That a Man Lay Down His Life for His Friends" (John 15:12–13)

Jesus next spoke about love:

John 15:12–13. This is my commandment, That ye love one another, as I have loved you. Greater love hath no man than this, that a man lay down his life for his friends.

One of the last and perhaps one of the most important principles that Jesus emphasized while instructing His Apostles before His death was that of love—His and God's love for all people and the need for all people to love each other and God and Jesus. Earlier in the evening, Jesus had given

15.   *Merriam-Webster*, s.v. "joy," accessed August 9, 2022, https://www.merriam-webster.com/dictionary/joy.
16.   *HarperCollins Bible Dictionary*, s.v. "joy."
17.   2 Ne. 2:25.

the commandment to "love one another," as recorded in John 13:34. In John 14, the word *love* and its derivatives are used ten times; in John 15, the word *love* and its derivatives are used another ten times.

In John 15:13, Christ used Himself as the supreme example of love by stating, "Greater love hath no man than this, that a man lay down his life for his friends." The next day, Christ would demonstrate this kind of love by laying down His life for all humankind. The Apostle John, having learned well Jesus's teachings about love, later wrote the following:

> Beloved, let us love one another: for love is of God; and every one that loveth is born of God, and knoweth God. He that loveth not knoweth not God; for God is love. In this was manifested the love of God toward us, because that God sent his only begotten Son into the world, that we might live through him. Herein is love, not that we loved God, but that he loved us, and sent his Son to be the propitiation for our sins. Beloved, if God so loved us, we ought also to love one another. . . . If we love one another, God dwelleth in us, and his love is perfected in us. . . . And we have known and believed the love that God hath to us. God is love; and he that dwelleth in love dwelleth in God, and God in him. Herein is our love made perfect, that we may have boldness in the day of judgment: because as he is, so are we in this world. There is no fear in love; but perfect love casteth out fear: because fear hath torment. He that feareth is not made perfect in love. We love him, because he first loved us. If a man say, I love God, and hateth his brother, he is a liar: for he that loveth not his brother whom he hath seen, how can he love God whom he hath not seen? And this commandment have we from him, That he who loveth God love his brother also.[18]

The love of Heavenly Father and Christ for humankind must be felt in order to be understood. Heavenly Father and Christ's love for each person can be felt by recognizing the blessings They provide. Their love can also be felt through hearing the whisperings of the Holy Ghost, through studying, through serving, and through attending the temple. Additionally, Their love can be felt through partaking of the sacrament, participating in other sacred ordinances, considering Christ's sacrifices for humankind, sincerely praying to Heavenly Father, and seeing His mercy unfold.

---

18. 1 John 4:7–12, 16–21.

Jesus Says That His Apostles Are His Friends (John 15:14–17)

Jesus then told His Apostles that they were not His servants but His friends:

John 15:14–17. Ye are my friends, if ye do whatsoever I command you. Henceforth I call you not servants; for the servant knoweth not what his lord doeth: but I have called you friends; for all things that I have heard of my Father I have made known unto you. Ye have not chosen me, but I have chosen you, and ordained you, that ye should go and bring forth fruit, and that your fruit should remain: that whatsoever ye shall ask of the Father in my name, he may give it you. These things I command you, that ye love one another.

Jesus had taught His beloved Apostles for approximately three years. Jesus and the Apostles had walked together along the dusty roads of Galilee, Perea, and Judea. They had experienced great adversity and great joy together. Earlier in the evening, Jesus had told the Apostles that He would soon die. Now, He called them His friends. One can only imagine what emotions filled the Apostles as they heard Jesus speak these words, perhaps for the last time. Not only did Jesus love them, but He also liked them and liked being with them. He told them that He had taught them what He had heard from His Father. A lesson that can be learned from Jesus's statement is that being friends with those a person serves with in the Church and in other places can be valuable.

Jesus also reminded the Apostles that they had not chosen Him but that He had chosen them. After choosing them, He had laid His hands on each of their heads and ordained them and blessed them. Because they were ordained, they were to bring forth fruit and their fruit would remain. He also promised them that what they asked Heavenly Father for in Jesus's name would be given to them; Jesus made this promise because He knew they would not ask amiss. Additionally, He once again commanded them to love one another.

Just as Jesus called the original Apostles His friends, He called many early latter-day Church members His friends.[19] It is worth the time for people today to consider whether they are friends of Jesus.

---

19.   See D&C 84:63, 77; 88:3, 62, 117; 93:45, 51; 94:1; 98:1; 100:1; 103:1; 104:1; 105:26; 109:6.

Jesus Teaches That the Apostles Will Be Hated, Just as Jesus and God Are Hated (John 15:18–25)

Jesus had just taught the Apostles about loving one another and had told them that they were His friends. Now, in contraposition, He told them that they would be hated, just as He and Heavenly Father are hated:

> **John 15:18–25.** If the world hate you, ye know that it hated me before it hated you. If ye were of the world, the world would love his own: but because ye are not of the world, but I have chosen you out of the world, therefore the world hateth you. Remember the word that I said unto you, The servant is not greater than his lord. If they have persecuted me, they will also persecute you; if they have kept my saying, they will keep yours also. But all these things will they do unto you for my name's sake, because they know not him that sent me. If I had not come and spoken unto them, they had not had sin: but now they have no cloak for their sin. He that hateth me hateth my Father also. If I had not done among them the works which none other man did, they had not had sin: but now have they both seen and hated both me and my Father. But this cometh to pass, that the word might be fulfilled that is written in their law, They hated me without a cause.

One may wonder what went through the Apostles' minds when Jesus told them that they would be hated. No one wants to be hated; generally, people have an innate desire to be accepted, respected, appreciated, and loved. However, by telling the Apostles of what would occur, He was preparing them so that they would be better able to face the persecution and remain strong amid persecution.

In telling the Apostles that they would be hated by the world, Jesus also offered some comfort and strength by stating that He understood: He knew well what it felt like to be hated and persecuted, and He understood that those who hated Him hated the Father also. In other words, the Apostles were not alone—they were in very good company. However, in facing persecution, they must always remember that they were not greater than Jesus was and did not suffer as much as He did.

Jesus told His Apostles that they would be hated because He had chosen them to be His special witnesses, meaning they were no longer "of the world," including the Jews' religious and political factions. Many Jews hated and persecuted Jesus because they would not believe that He was the Son of God, notwithstanding His teachings and miracles. These Jews, particularly religious leaders, were wicked and no longer sought to follow God. Additionally, many religious leaders were jealous of Jesus's miracles, which these leaders could not perform, and feared that people would follow Jesus because of His miracles. Therefore, the only real cause against Jesus was His challenge to the Jews' pride, greed, and corruption, and this reason was not a justifiable cause. What the Psalmist wrote had come to pass: "They that hate me without a cause are more than the hairs of mine head: they that would destroy me, being mine enemies wrongfully, are mighty."[20] Jesus explained that the Jews who rejected Him and His Father would be held accountable for doing so, for these Jews had rejected Jesus and His Father after hearing Jesus teach and seeing or hearing of His many miracles.

In the world today, hatred and rejection of God, Christ, and religion are ever increasing. Many people desire to take God, Christ, and Christianity out of everything and strive to do so through being vocal in the media and in the courts. As Nephi prophesied, it seems there is an ever-widening divide between the righteous and those who mock religion.[21] Today, disciples of Christ face persecution, just as the original Apostles did. Amid the persecution, disciples of Christ can look forward to receiving an eternal reward if they endure well the challenges they face.[22]

Jesus Teaches That the Holy Ghost Will Testify of Jesus (John 15:26–27)

Next, Jesus once again told His Apostles that the Comforter—that is, the Holy Ghost—would come:

John 15:26–27. But when the Comforter is come, whom I will send unto you from the Father, even the Spirit of truth, which proceedeth from the Father, he shall testify of me: and ye also shall bear witness, because ye have been with me from the beginning.

---

20.   Ps. 69:4.
21.   See 2 Ne. 30:10; see also D&C 63:54; 86.
22.   See Matt. 10:22; 24:13; Mark 13:13; 1 Ne. 13:37; 31:20; 3 Ne. 15:9; 27:16; D&C 10:69; 50:5; 53:7; 101:35; 121:8.

In addition to calling the Holy Ghost the comforter, Christ referred to the Holy Ghost as the Spirit of Truth. As the Spirit of Truth, the Holy Ghost would testify of Christ. The Apostles, who had been with Christ from the beginning of His ministry, were directed to likewise bear witness of Christ. Presumably, as the Apostles testified of Christ, their witness would pierce the hearts of those who would spiritually listen and the Holy Ghost would confirm the Apostles' witness.

Jesus Explains That He Is Teaching His Apostles So They Will Not Stumble (John 16:1–4)

Jesus then explained why He was telling His Apostles about what would soon occur:

> **John 16:1–4.** These things have I spoken unto you, that ye should not be offended. They shall put you out of the synagogues: yea, the time cometh, that whosoever killeth you will think that he doeth God service. And these things will they do unto you, because they have not known the Father, nor me. But these things have I told you, that when the time shall come, ye may remember that I told you of them. And these things I said not unto you at the beginning, because I was with you.

Even though Jesus was likely weighed down with the knowledge that He would experience the anguish of the Atonement later that evening and would be crucified the following day, He was concerned for His Apostles, whom He loved and who were His friends. He wanted to prepare them for what was to come.

In John 16, Jesus continued to focus on the era that would begin after His death. He continued to teach His Apostles of Heavenly Father and of the Holy Ghost—the Comforter—and His mission and influence in their lives. In essence, Jesus was teaching of the three members of the Godhead in that He was also teaching about Himself as He taught of God and the Holy Ghost. The first article of faith, penned by Joseph Smith in the latter days, states: "We believe in God, the Eternal Father, and in His Son, Jesus Christ, and in the Holy Ghost."[23] Jesus could not give more important foundational

---

23. Articles of Faith 1:1; see also Smith, *History of the Church*, vol. 4, pp. 535–541.

instruction to the Apostles or to anyone than about the Godhead. That the Godhead consists of three distinct individuals is a foundational principle of Church members' faith and a guiding principle of life, and the Apostles needed to understand this principle above all else.

Jesus had previously warned His Apostles about being offended—that is, stumbling—and now He again explained that He did not want His Apostles to stumble.[24] He also identified events that could cause the Apostles to stumble: Jews would expel the Apostles from synagogues and would even seek to kill the Apostles. These wicked Jews would do so because they had rejected the truth and therefore did not know God or His Beloved Son. This knowledge of what would occur was surely unsettling for the Apostles, but when Jesus's words were fulfilled, the Apostles could draw strength from the fact that Jesus had warned them and knew that they could overcome the trials they would experience.

Jesus Says That He Must Leave So That the Holy Ghost Can Come (John 16:5–12)

The Apostles were likely troubled by many of the things Jesus had taught during and after the Passover meal. The Apostles did not precisely know what was to come and when and how it would happen. Jesus told them He was going to His Father, but they likely had no frame of reference regarding heaven. In the solemnity of the moment, they may not have dared ask further.

Perceiving the Apostles' troubled feelings, Jesus taught them further:

John 16:5–12. But now I go my way to him that sent me; and none of you asketh me, Whither goest thou? But because I have said these things unto you, sorrow hath filled your heart. Nevertheless I tell you the truth; it is expedient for you that I go away: for if I go not away, the Comforter will not come unto you; but if I depart, I will send him unto you. And when he is come, he will reprove the world of sin, and of righteousness, and of judgment: of sin, because they believe not on me; of righteousness, because I go to my Father, and ye see me no more; of judgment, because the prince

---

24. See Matt. 26:31–32; see chapter 60 of this volume for discussion of the meaning of *offended*.

of this world is judged. I have yet many things to say unto you, but ye cannot bear them now.

Jesus had likely known that sorrow would fill the Apostles' hearts as He once again told them that His death was imminent. Nevertheless, they needed to know the truth and be prepared. In like manner, people today need to know the truth and be prepared for what is to come, and they can learn the truth through the scriptures and the teachings of modern-day prophets.

As Jesus explained, as long as He was on the earth, Heavenly Father would not send the Holy Ghost. Jesus could not teach His Apostles everything during the time they were with Him, but the Holy Ghost would come and teach them all things.[25] The Holy Ghost indeed did come after Jesus's death; the first recorded instance was on the day of Pentecost, fifty days after Jesus was crucified.[26] On this day, the following occurred:

> They [the eleven Apostles[27]] were all with one accord in one place. And suddenly there came a sound from heaven as of a rushing mighty wind, and it filled all the house where they were sitting. And there appeared unto them cloven tongues like as of fire, and it sat upon each of them. And they were all filled with the Holy Ghost, and began to speak with other tongues, as the Spirit gave them utterance. And there were dwelling at Jerusalem Jews, devout men, out of every nation under heaven. Now when this was noised abroad, the multitude came together, and were confounded, because that every man heard them speak in his own language.[28]

In stating that the Holy Ghost would come, Jesus referred to the Holy Ghost by His title of Comforter and explained that He would "reprove the world of sin, and of righteousness, and of judgment." *Reprove* has several meanings, including "to scold or correct usually gently or with kindly intent."[29] Additionally, the Greek word for *reprove* is *elegchō*, which means

25. See John 14:26.
26. Jesus died on the Passover, which was fifty days before the Pentecost (see *HarperCollins Bible Dictionary*, s.v. "Pentecost").
27. See Talmage, *Jesus the Christ*, p. 651.
28. Acts 2:1–7.
29. See *Merriam-Webster*, s.v. "reprove," accessed August 9, 2022, https://www.merriam-webster.com/dictionary/reprove.

"to convict"[30]—that is, "to convince of error or sinfulness."[31] Thus, one meaning of Jesus's statement may be that the Holy Ghost would discern and quietly correct a person's thoughts and actions. He would help the person distinguish between truth and error[32] and encourage repentance and righteousness. Through repenting, the individual would feel the peace that the Comforter and Christ offer.

Christ's statement may also be an oblique reference to a role the Holy Ghost may have when the entire world is judged and the earth is cleansed before the Millennium is ushered in. The Holy Ghost may be a part of this process of judging the wicked and the righteous and therefore determining whether they will be spared. The Holy Ghost cannot be deceived.[33]

Another possible meaning of Jesus's statement is that the Holy Ghost will certify Jesus's judgment of people at the day of final judgment. The Holy Ghost might search the souls of all people and determine whether they are unrepentant and therefore sinful or are repentant and therefore righteous.

After stating that the Holy Ghost would reprove the world, Christ made it clear that Satan, the prince of this world, had already been judged; by implication, so had those spirits that followed him. Satan had attempted to cause Christ to fall and would shortly attempt to cause Him to shrink from the Atonement and Crucifixion, thus thwarting Heavenly Father's plan. Nevertheless, Christ overcame Satan and his temptations, judged Satan, and will again judge Satan when He returns to the earth. Because Christ spoke of the Holy Ghost reproving, or convicting, the world of sin and Satan being judged, presumably there would be two witnesses before God against Satan and his followers. Christ could have said more concerning the convicting mission of the Holy Ghost, but perhaps Christ

---

30. Young, *Analytical Concordance*, s.v. "reprove"; see also the following versions of the Bible, which set forth the same meaning: New Living Translation, English Standard Version, Berean Study Bible, Berean Literal Bible, New American Standard Bible, International Standard Version, New American Stand Standard Version, English Revised Version, and Young's Literal Translation.
31. See *Merriam-Webster*, s.v. "convict," accessed August 9, 2022, https://www.merriam-webster.com/dictionary/convict.
32. See John 16:13; 1 John 4:6; 1 Cor. 2:12–14.
33. See McConkie, *Mormon Doctrine*, p. 362.

chose not to because the eleven Apostles would not understand or did not need to know.

Jesus Teaches That the Holy Ghost Will Guide People to Truth (John 16:13–15)

Jesus then instructed the Apostles regarding other aspects of the mission of the Holy Ghost:

> **John 16:13–15.** Howbeit when he, the Spirit of truth, is come, he will guide you into all truth: for he shall not speak of himself; but whatsoever he shall hear, that shall he speak: and he will shew you things to come. He shall glorify me: for he shall receive of mine, and shall shew it unto you. All things that the Father hath are mine: therefore said I, that he shall take of mine, and shall shew it unto you.

Once again, Jesus referred to the Holy Ghost as the Spirit of Truth. This name is fitting because one of His missions is to reveal truth to people.[34] The truth that He reveals comes from Heavenly Father and is what Heavenly Father instructs the Holy Ghost to teach and to testify of. Jesus explained that the Holy Ghost would not only teach the Apostles truth but also show them things that would occur in the future. These things the Apostles needed to clearly understand. They needed instruction from the Holy Ghost in order to lead the young Church. They needed to understand that the Holy Ghost would give them vision regarding the future and enable them to know in advance what the fledgling Church would need to understand in order to face the challenges that would come. The Apostles needed to understand that the Holy Ghost would guide them regarding where they should go, whom they should speak to, and what they should say. The Holy Ghost would also guide them in making administrative decisions, in teaching members of the Church, and in counseling those who needed help. The Apostles needed to learn to trust the inspiration that came through Him.

Christ further explained that the Holy Ghost would show the Apostles marvelous things concerning the glory of Christ and the glory that awaits those who are faithful.

---

34. See Moro. 10:5.

Jesus Says That the Apostles' Sorrow Will Turn into Joy (John 16:16–22)

Christ then said that His Apostles soon would not see Him because He would return to His Father but that shortly afterward they would see Him again and that their sorrow would be replaced by joy:

> **John 16:16–22.** A little while, and ye shall not see me: and again, a little while, and ye shall see me, because I go to the Father. Then said some of his disciples among themselves, What is this that he saith unto us, A little while, and ye shall not see me: and again, a little while, and ye shall see me: and, Because I go to the Father? They said therefore, What is this that he saith, A little while? we cannot tell what he saith. Now Jesus knew that they were desirous to ask him, and said unto them, Do ye inquire among yourselves of that I said, A little while, and ye shall not see me: and again, a little while, and ye shall see me? Verily, verily, I say unto you, That ye shall weep and lament, but the world shall rejoice: and ye shall be sorrowful, but your sorrow shall be turned into joy. A woman when she is in travail hath sorrow, because her hour is come: but as soon as she is delivered of the child, she remembereth no more the anguish, for joy that a man is born into the world. And ye now therefore have sorrow: but I will see you again, and your heart shall rejoice, and your joy no man taketh from you.

The Apostles were puzzled by Jesus's statement that they would not see Him for a short time and that they would then see Him again. Jesus recognized their confusion. To expand on what He had just said, He told the Apostles that soon they would sorrow, whereas the world would rejoice (presumably at His death), but the Apostles would rejoice when they saw Jesus again. To help them more fully understand, Jesus used the analogy of a woman being in pain while delivering a child and then forgetting the pain and feeling joy as soon as the child is born. Likewise, for a short time after Jesus was crucified, the Apostles would sorrow because Jesus was not with them. But when He appeared to them as a resurrected being, the Apostles would rejoice.

Jesus Tells His Apostles to Pray in His Name to Heavenly Father (John 16:23–27)

During Christ's mortal ministry, the Apostles could readily ask Him questions and learn from Him. Christ now taught that after He returned to Heavenly Father, the Apostles would need to pray to Heavenly Father in Christ's name.

> **John 16:23–27.** And in that day ye shall ask me nothing. Verily, verily, I say unto you, Whatsoever ye shall ask the Father in my name, he will give it you. Hitherto have ye asked nothing in my name: ask, and ye shall receive, that your joy may be full. These things have I spoken unto you in proverbs: but the time cometh, when I shall no more speak unto you in proverbs, but I shall shew you plainly of the Father. At that day ye shall ask in my name: and I say not unto you, that I will pray the Father for you: for the Father himself loveth you, because ye have loved me, and have believed that I came out from God.

Jesus taught that if the Apostles prayed in His name to Heavenly Father, then Heavenly Father would hear and answer their prayers. He would answer the Apostles' prayers because He loved them. He loved them in part because they loved Jesus and believed that He is the Only Begotten Son of God. Receiving answers from Heavenly Father would bring the Apostles joy.

Christ also said that He spoke to the Apostles in proverbs but the time would come when He would no longer speak in proverbs and instead would show them "plainly of the Father," presumably including things regarding His kingdom. A possible reason that Jesus spoke obliquely about various doctrinal matters was to encourage the Apostles to ponder His words and, with the assistance of the Holy Ghost, gain greater understanding for themselves and better remember what they had learned. Just a few days after Christ made this promise to the Apostles, He showed the Apostles His resurrected body and allowed them to feel the prints of the nails in His hands and feet.[35] As a result, they gained a much greater understanding of the resurrection and thus a greater understanding of the nature of Heavenly Father. Moreover, the resurrected Christ taught the Apostles for forty days, and some of His teachings may have regarded the kingdom of heaven.

---

35. See Luke 24:36–40.

Jesus Asks the Apostles Whether They Believe (John 16:28–31)

Jesus then declared that He came from His Father and would return to His Father:[36]

> **John 16:28–31.** I came forth from the Father, and am come into the world: again, I leave the world, and go to the Father. His disciples said unto him, Lo, now speakest thou plainly, and speakest no proverb. Now are we sure that thou knowest all things, and needest not that any man should ask thee: by this we believe that thou camest forth from God. Jesus answered them, Do ye now believe?

In response, the Apostles said that they believed that Jesus was divine. Then, presumably to encourage the Apostles to once again search their hearts, Jesus asked them: "Do ye now believe?" This question seems to be posed to the eleven Apostles both individually and collectively. This profound question is an important question for all people to ponder and answer.

Jesus Teaches the Apostles That They Will Be Scattered (John 16:32)

Next, Jesus once again told His Apostles that they would be scattered:

> **John 16:32.** Behold, the hour cometh, yea, is now come, that ye shall be scattered, every man to his own, and shall leave me alone: and yet I am not alone, because the Father is with me.

Jesus recognized what He would soon face. However, even in this dark time, He desired to make certain that the Apostles were informed of and prepared for what was ahead of them. This desire was fueled by His love and concern for them.

Jesus's statement about the Apostles being scattered and leaving Him must have caused the Apostles to once again be fearful and perplexed. They likely wondered how the scattering would occur. Despite their fear and perplexity, they may have also felt some comfort in Jesus's reassurance that even though they could not be with Him, His Father would be with Jesus. Likewise, as Jesus had previously promised, the Apostles would not be alone,

---

36. This declaration is more evidence of the physical separateness of the Father and the Son, for how could Jesus come from and return to Himself?

for the Holy Ghost would come and He and Heavenly Father would watch over the Apostles.

Jesus Tells the Apostles to Be of Good Cheer (John 16:33)

Jesus then offered words of comfort:

John 16:33. These things I have spoken unto you, that in me ye might have peace. In the world ye shall have tribulation: but be of good cheer; I have overcome the world.

The Apostles were to feel peace because Christ had told them what was to come, and they were to be happy amid tribulation because Christ had overcome the world and so could they. Certainly, it would be difficult for the Apostles to feel peace and be cheerful when Christ was illegally arrested and tried, presented before Pilate, scourged, and then crucified. Nevertheless, they could feel peace because Heavenly Father would always answer their prayers and because the Holy Ghost would provide comfort. They could feel peace because they were Christ's friends and because He would prepare a place for them with Him in the kingdom of His Father. They could feel peace in Christ's Atonement, which would make them clean before Heavenly Father. They could feel peace and also be cheerful because Jesus would appear to them after His Resurrection, providing evidence that He had "overcome the world." These same things can bring people joy and happiness today.

Chapter 63

THE CONCLUDING PRAYER
(Thursday after the Passover Meal)

Following Jesus's final instruction to His eleven Apostles, He lifted His eyes to heaven and prayed to His Father. This tender, holy prayer has been referred to by various names. For example, Farrar called this prayer the "great High-Priestly prayer,"[1] for Jesus was the great high priest.[2] Edersheim referred to this prayer as the "real Lord's Prayer" because it was His "great preparation for His Agony, Cross, and Passion."[3] Many others have referred to this prayer as the Intercessory Prayer because in part of the prayer, Jesus interceded on behalf of His Apostles and others who believe in Him.[4] Certainly, all three names are appropriate, and only Jesus was qualified to offer this prayer, as He had consecrated His entire mortal life to doing the will of His Father and was about to atone for the sins of all humankind.

Jesus's Recorded Prayers

Of course, Jesus had prayed many times before; however, the Gospels contain relatively few references to Jesus praying, and most of these references state that He prayed but do not specify what He said. The scriptures indicate that Jesus prayed immediately following His baptism in the Jordan River,[5] in

---

1. Farrar, *Life of Christ*, p. 550; see also Talmage, *Jesus the Christ*, p. 565.
2. See Heb. 4:14; 5:5; 6:20; 7:26; 8:1.
3. Edersheim, *Life and Times of Jesus the Messiah*, p. 839.
4. See McConkie, *Mortal Messiah*, vol. 4, p. 105.
5. See Luke 3:21.

the wilderness in Galilee,[6] and in a private place near Capernaum.[7] He also prayed all night on a mountainside and thereafter called twelve men to be His Apostles.[8] On a hillside, He taught His disciples how to pray as He gave what is now referred to as the Lord's Prayer,[9] which has inspired millions of people over the centuries. He also prayed as He blessed loaves of bread and fish, with which He fed more than five thousand people near Bethsaida.[10] Afterward, He prayed alone on a mountainside in the same area.[11] In or near Caesarea Philippi, He prayed on a mountainside and then asked His disciples, "Whom say the people that I am."[12] Along the coast of Judea, Jesus blessed young children who were brought to Him.[13] Additionally, He prayed with Peter, James, and John on the Mount of Transfiguration.[14] Jesus also blessed the broken bread and the cup of wine as He instituted the sacrament during His final Passover meal.[15] Further, He prayed to His Father in Gethsemane, asking that, if possible, the burden of the Atonement be removed from Him.[16]

The last recorded words Jesus spoke during His mortal life were on the cross, when He prayed, "My God, my god, why hast thou forsaken me?"[17] Jesus then "cried with a loud voice, and gave up the ghost."[18]

The evening before Jesus was crucified, He offered the Intercessory Prayer in the presence of His eleven Apostles.[19] The record of this prayer is much longer than the records of any of His other prayers. Even so, it is possible that even the record of this prayer is not complete, for some of the things Jesus said to His Father may have been too sacred to record, as

6. See Luke 5:16.
7. See Mark 1:35.
8. See Luke 6:12–13.
9. See Matt. 6:9–13; Luke 11:1–4.
10. See Matt. 14:19; Mark 6:41; Luke 9:16; John 6:11.
11. See Matt. 14:23; Mark 6:46.
12. See Luke 9:18; see also Matt. 16:13; Mark 8:27.
13. See Matt. 19:1, 13–15; Mark 10:1, 13–16; Luke 18:15–17.
14. See Luke 9:28–36; Matt. 17:1–13; Mark 9:2–13.
15. See Matt. 26:26–27; Mark 14:22–23; Luke 22:19–20.
16. See Matt. 26:39; Mark 14:35–36; Luke 22:41–42.
17. Matt. 27:46; Mark 15:34.
18. Mark 15:37; see also Matt. 27:50.
19. See Matt. 26:36–46; Mark 14:32–42; Luke 22:40–46.

was the case when Jesus prayed with the multitude in the Americas prior to blessing the children.[20]

For ease of analysis and discussion, Jesus's Intercessory Prayer is divided into sections in this chapter.

Eternal Life Involves Knowing God and Jesus (John 17:1–5)

In the first five verses, Jesus spoke of glory and what eternal life involves:

John 17:1–5. These words spake Jesus, and lifted up his eyes to heaven, and said, Father, the hour is come; glorify thy Son, that thy Son also may glorify thee: as thou hast given him power over all flesh, that he should give eternal life to as many as thou hast given him. And this is life eternal, that they might know thee the only true God, and Jesus Christ, whom thou hast sent. I have glorified thee on the earth: I have finished the work which thou gavest me to do. And now, O Father, glorify thou me with thine own self with the glory which I had with thee before the world was.

Jesus began His prayer by stating that the hour had come for His infinite atoning sacrifice, first in Gethsemane and then on Golgotha. Jesus then prayed to be glorified by His Father so that Jesus could glorify His Father. In making this statement, Jesus may have been implicitly asking for strength to accomplish what He soon would face.

Jesus then acknowledged that His Father had given Jesus power "over all flesh." That is, no one could take His life, but He could give it willingly.[21] Additionally, He had power "over all flesh" in that He would be resurrected, thereby making possible the resurrection of all humankind. Jesus recognized that His sacrifice was necessary in order for those who believe in Him and keep His commandments to receive eternal life. By atoning for the world and then being resurrected, Jesus would fulfill the commitment He had made in the premortal world and would thus glorify His Father, and His Father would in turn glorify Jesus.[22]

In speaking of eternal life, Christ stated that it involved knowing God and Christ. The following sections provide insight about God and Christ,

---

20. See 3 Ne. 17:11–20.
21. See John 10:18.
22. See Moses 4:2.

to aid in developing an understanding of Them. Much of the world does not understand fundamental truths about the nature of God and Christ and humankind's relationship to Them; however, these truths give meaning and purpose to mortality and to life in the world to come.

Insight about God

God Has Multiple Names

God is often referred to as the Father and is sometimes referred to as Elohim,[23] Man of Holiness,[24] and the Most High God.[25] There is no other God besides Him.[26]

God Has a Physical Body

God has a physical body,[27] and of all His creations on this earth, only human bodies are created "in the image of God."[28] He will not die and cannot be destroyed.

God Is the Supreme Governor and Is Perfect

Joseph Smith taught, "God is the only supreme governor and independent being in whom all fullness and perfection dwell; who is omnipotent, omnipresent and omniscient; without beginning of days or end of life; and that in him every good gift and every good principle dwell; and that he is the Father of lights; in him the principle of faith dwells independently, and he is the object in whom the faith of all other rational and accountable beings

---

23.   See Smith, *Teachings*, pp. 371–372; McConkie, *Mormon Doctrine*, p. 224; see also Talmage, *Jesus the Christ*, p. 36. According to the *HarperCollins Bible Dictionary*, the word *Elohim* is "widely used as a name for God in the Bible." The word is plural in form, perhaps "derive[d] from some original sense of 'gods,' but in the Bible it is employed as a proper noun that takes singular verbs." (*HarperCollins Bible Dictionary*, s.v. "El.")

24.   See Talmage, *Jesus the Christ*, p. 138.

25.   See Gen. 14:18–20; Dan. 4:2; 1 Ne. 11:6; Alma 26:14; 3 Ne. 11:17; D&C 39:19; 76:70; 121:32.

26.   See Moses 1:6.

27.   See D&C 130:22.

28.   Gen. 1:26–27; 9:6; see also 1 John 3:2; Moses 2:26–27; Abr. 4:26–27.

center for life and salvation."[29] God is also eternal[30] and omnipotent.[31] *Merriam-Webster* defines *omnipotence* as "having virtually unlimited authority or influence" and as being almighty.[32] *Merriam-Webster* defines *almighty* as "having absolute power over all."[33] God has power over all His creations, and the heavens and the earth obey His word.[34] His ability to create and have dominion over all His creations is almost beyond human comprehension, particularly when considering the complexities of the universe and of particles, atoms, and molecules.

God is also perfect.[35] He is perfect in wisdom, honesty, mercy, grace, goodness, holiness, righteousness, and justice.[36] He also has perfect love for all His children and other creations.[37] The extent of God's attributes is incomprehensible to humankind and cannot be adequately described by mortals.

God's glory is in part derived from His perfect knowledge of all things. As Talmage stated, God is omniscient,[38] which *Merriam-Webster* defines as "having infinite awareness, understanding, and insight" and being "possessed of universal or complete knowledge."[39] God is the source of all truth. As Talmage also wrote, "To comprehend Himself, an infinite Being, He must possess an infinite mind."[40]

God Directed the Creation of Innumerable Worlds and Sees All of His Creations

God directed the creation of "worlds without number," including this earth. According to Talmage, "there is no part of creation, however remote,

29. *Lectures on Faith*, p. 13.

30. See Moses 1:3; D&C 19:10–11.

31. Talmage, *Articles of Faith*, p. 44.

32. *Merriam-Webster*, s.v. "omnipotent," accessed August 9, 2022, https://www.merriam-webster.com/dictionary/omnipotent.

33. *Merriam-Webster*, s.v. "almighty," accessed August 9, 2022, https://www.merriam-webster.com/dictionary/almighty.

34. Moses 1:33; see also Moses 1:34–38; Isa. 48:13; 1 Ne. 20:13.

35. See Matt. 5:48; 3 Ne. 12:48. The Greek word for *perfect* is *teleios*, which means "ended, complete" (Young, *Analytical Concordance*, s.v. "perfect").

36. See 2 Ne. 9; Smith, *Teachings*, p. 55; Enos 1:6.

37. See 1 Jn. 4:8–9, 16; Matt. 5:48; 1 Ne. 11:16, 22; Talmage, *Articles of Faith*, p. 44.

38. Talmage, *Articles of Faith*, p. 43.

39. *Merriam-Webster*, s.v. "omniscient," accessed January 10, 2022, https://www.merriam-webster.com/dictionary/omniscient.

40. Talmage, *Articles of Faith*, p. 44.

into which God cannot penetrate; through the medium of the Spirit the Godhead is in direct communication with all things at all times."[41] He caused this earth to be created so that His children could gain physical bodies, learn good from evil, repent, be tested, grow, and be refined.[42] As part of His plan of salvation, He provided for the Atonement and the resurrection. God's work and glory is "to bring to pass the immortality and eternal life" of all humankind[43] and His other creations.[44]

God told Moses, "There is no God beside me, and all things are present with me, for I know them all."[45] God can see all of His creations, just as He showed Moses all of the creations on this earth.[46] Isaiah wrote that Christ—and by extension, God—"measured the waters in the hollow of his hand, and meted out heaven with the span, and comprehended the dust of the earth in a measure, and weighed the mountains in scales, and the hills in a balance."[47] As Talmage wrote, "There is no part of creation, however remote, into which God cannot penetrate; through the medium of the Spirit the Godhead is in direct communication with all things at all times."[48]

God Is the Father of All Humankind

God is the Father of all mortals. In 1909, the Church's First Presidency stated, "Man, as a spirit, was begotten and born of heavenly parents, and reared to maturity in the eternal mansions of the Father prior to coming upon the earth in a temporal body to undergo an experience in mortality,"[49] and "all men and women are in the similitude of the universal Father and Mother and are literally the sons and daughters of deity."[50] Similarly, "The Family: A Proclamation to the World" states that each mortal "is a beloved spirit son or daughter of heavenly parents, and, as such, each has a divine

---

41. Talmage, *Articles of Faith*, pp. 42–43.
42. See Moses 4:1–2; 2 Ne. 9:6, 13; Alma 24:14; 34:9; 42:5.
43. Moses 1:39.
44. See Smith, *Teachings*, p. 291.
45. Moses 1:6.
46. Moses 1:4, 7–8, 27–29.
47. Isa. 40:12.
48. Isa. 48:13.
49. Smith, *Man, His Origins, and Destiny*, p. 351.
50. Smith, *Man, His Origins, and Destiny*, p. 351.

nature and destiny."[51] Because God is the Father of all people, all people have the potential to inherit all that He has[52] and to become like Him, including by having posterity throughout eternity.[53]

God Has Infinite Love and Therefore Wants to Communicate with His Children through Prayer

God has infinite love. Jesus taught the following regarding the depth of God's love: "For God so loved the world, that he gave his only begotten Son, that whosoever believeth in him should not perish, but have everlasting life."[54] In speaking of God's love, Nephi said that it "sheddeth itself abroad in the hearts of the children of men; wherefore, it is the most desirable above all things."[55] God's love is also the thing that is "most joyous to the soul."[56]

Because of God's love, He sorrows when His children are disobedient, as the prophet Enoch saw in vision. In this vision, Enoch saw God weep because of the wicked who lived immediately before the flood, even though, as Enoch said, God is "holy, and from all eternity to all eternity[.] And were it possible that man could number the particles of the earth, yea, millions of earths like this, it would not be a beginning to the number of thy creations; and thy curtains are stretched out still; and yet thou art there, and thy bosom is there; and also thou art just; thou art merciful and kind forever."[57]

Additionally, because God loves His children, He is, as Joseph Smith said, more "boundless in His mercies and blessings, than we are ready to believe or receive."[58] Further, because God loves His children, He wants them to communicate with Him through prayer.[59] Prayers offered in faith will not go unheeded.[60]

---

51. "The Family: A Proclamation to the World."
52. See D&C 84:38.
53. See D&C 132:19–24.
54. John 3:16.
55. 1 Ne. 11:22.
56. 1 Ne. 11:23.
57. Moses 7:28–30; see also vv. 31–38; 1 Ne. 8:10–12; 11:21–22. Presumably, God weeps because of the wickedness of His children today too.
58. Smith, *Teachings*, p. 257.
59. See Alma 34:17–19; D&C 19:38; 93:49.
60. See Matt. 7:7; James 1:5.

God Is Glorified through His Creations

God stated that He derives glory through bringing "to pass the immortality and eternal life of man."[61] God also receives glory as well as honor from His other creations. For example, the Apostle John saw in vision that "every creature which is in heaven, and on the earth, and under the earth, and such as are in the sea, and all that are in them, heard I saying, Blessing, and honour, and glory, and power, be unto him that sitteth upon the throne, and unto the Lamb for ever and ever."[62] Regarding John's vision, Joseph Smith stated: "I suppose John saw beings there of a thousand forms, that had been saved from ten thousand times ten thousand earths like this—strange beasts of which we have no conception: all might be seen in heaven. . . . John learned that God glorified Himself by saving all that His hands had made, whether beasts, fowls, fishes or men; and He will glorify Himself with them."[63]

God's Attributes Are Reflected in Christ's Attributes

The most complete representation of God's nature is His Only Begotten Son. As Jesus explained, "I do nothing of myself; but as my Father hath taught me, I speak these things."[64] Jesus judged, served, loved, and forgave as God would judge, serve, love, and forgive. Jesus healed physically and spiritually as God would heal. Just as Jesus demonstrated humility throughout His mortal life, God demonstrates humility; for example, when He has spoken to those on the earth, He has not taken glory for Himself but instead has acknowledged His Son.[65] Further, Jesus is perfect, just as God is perfect, as Jesus acknowledged when He told the Nephites to be perfect as He and His Father are perfect.[66]

---

61.   Moses 1:39.
62.   Rev. 5:13.
63.   Smith, *Teachings*, p. 291.
64.   John 8:28.
65.   See Matt. 3:17; Mark 1:11; Luke 3:22; 3 Ne. 11:7; Smith, *History of the Church*, vol. 1, p. 5.
66.   See 3 Ne. 12:48. Because the volumes in this series explore the many attributes of Jesus, by extension they also explore the attributes of God.

Insight about Belief in and Knowledge of Jesus and God

Those Who Believe in Jesus Will Also Believe in God

Because Jesus and God have the same attributes and because Jesus taught God's words, if a person truly believes in Jesus, he or she will also believe in God. For the same reason, if a person truly believes in God, he or she will also believe in Jesus, given the appropriate opportunity. Jesus said of His role in revealing the Father: "Neither knoweth any man the Father, save the Son, and he to whomsoever the Son will reveal him."[67]

The Holy Ghost Witnesses of Jesus and God

Knowledge of God and Christ is spiritual and must be gained spiritually.[68] This knowledge comes through receiving the witness of the Holy Ghost,[69] and this process can be intensely personal. This knowledge comes as the Holy Ghost inspires an individual to recognize the majesty in God and Christ's creations and Their hand in the universe; to recognize that God has answered this individual's prayers; to feel Their influence; and to recognize that They have watched over this individual, including during trials.

To Know Jesus, People Need to Learn about Him and Acquire His Attributes

To come to know Christ, people need to learn about Him and experience His love and atoning sacrifice in their lives. Christ said, "Take my yoke upon you, and learn of me; for I am meek and lowly in heart: and ye shall find rest unto your souls."[70] People need to figuratively walk where He walked and consider His mighty miracles. People also need to read and ponder His words in the scriptures. People can also learn about Him through worshiping Him in His holy house—the temple—and through participating in the sacred ordinances He established. People can ask Heavenly Father, in Christ's name, for help in learning about Christ and coming unto Him.[71] People can also

---

67. Matt. 11:27.
68. See 1 Cor. 2:9–11.
69. See D&C 20:27; 42:17.
70. Matt. 11:29.
71. See Moro. 10:30, 32.

learn about Christ by keeping His commandments,₇₂ and the covenants they
have made with God.

By learning about Jesus, people will learn about His attributes. By
acquiring these attributes, people will further come to know Him. As King
Benjamin in the Book of Mormon stated, "For how knoweth a man the
master whom he has not served, and who is a stranger unto him, and is
far from the thoughts and intents of his heart?"₇₃ Likewise, Peter taught
that developing Jesus's attributes leads to knowledge of Jesus: "By these
[great and precious promises] ye might be partakers of the divine nature,
having escaped the corruption that is in the world through lust. And beside
this, giving all diligence, add to your faith virtue; and to virtue knowledge;
and to knowledge temperance; and to temperance patience; and to patience
godliness; and to godliness brotherly kindness; and to brotherly kindness
charity. For if these things be in you, and abound, they make you that ye
shall neither be barren nor unfruitful in the knowledge of our Lord Jesus
Christ."₇₄ By developing these attributes, people may also better understand
the value of these attributes and other principles Jesus taught through
example and word. This understanding can also help people to know Jesus.
Likewise, to really know Jesus, one must study the scriptures, which tell of
His dealings with humankind through the millennia and testify of Him.
Additionally, to really know Jesus, people must experience the Atonement
working in their lives. People can come to know Jesus further when a loved
one dies and knowledge of the resurrection brought about by Jesus brings
peace and understanding.

Jesus Prays about the Apostles' Faith and Obedience (John 17:6–10)

In the next part of Jesus's Intercessory Prayer, He spoke to His Father
about the Apostles' faith and obedience:

John 17:6–10. I have manifested thy name unto the men which thou gavest me
out of the world: thine they were, and thou gavest them me; and they have
kept thy word. Now they have known that all things whatsoever thou hast

---

72. See John 14:15.
73. Mosiah 5:13.
74. 2 Pet. 1:4–8; see also Matt. 5–7.

given me are of thee. For I have given unto them the words which thou gavest me; and they have received them, and have known surely that I came out from thee, and they have believed that thou didst send me. I pray for them: I pray not for the world, but for them which thou hast given me; for they are thine. And all mine are thine, and thine are mine; and I am glorified in them.

One can only imagine the depth of Christ's feelings as He prayed to His Father about His Apostles, who were also His friends. Likewise, one can only imagine what Christ's Apostles thought and felt as they heard Christ pray about them. He said that they were God's and that He gave them to Christ—that is, they were with God in the premortal world and were chosen in that realm to be Christ's Apostles on earth. Christ also affirmed to God that they each had kept His word, which Christ had given them. Because the Apostles knew that Jesus is the divine Son of God and the promised Messiah, Jesus acknowledged they also had a testimony and witness of His Father. Jesus gave His Father the honor and glory resulting from the Apostles' righteousness and belief that God had sent Jesus. In so doing, Jesus recognized that He also would be glorified.

Jesus Prays That the Apostles Will Be One (John 17:11–19)

Jesus then prayed that His Father would watch over the Apostles after Jesus died. Further, He prayed that they would be one, as He and His Father are one:

John 17:11–19. And now I am no more in the world, but these are in the world, and I come to thee. Holy Father, keep through thine own name those whom thou hast given me, that they may be one, as we are. While I was with them in the world, I kept them in thy name: those that thou gavest me I have kept, and none of them is lost, but the son of perdition; that the scripture might be fulfilled. And now come I to thee; and these things I speak in the world, that they might have my joy fulfilled in themselves. I have given them thy word; and the world hath hated them, because they are not of the world, even as I am not of the world. I pray not that thou shouldest take them out of the world, but that thou shouldest keep them from the evil. They are not of the world, even as I am not of the world. Sanctify them through thy truth: thy word is truth. As thou hast sent me into the world, even so have I also sent them into the world. And for their sakes I sanctify myself, that they also might be sanctified through the truth.

Heavenly Father and Christ are completely unified in the purpose "to bring to pass the immortality and eternal life of man."[75] Christ had demonstrated this unity throughout His mortal ministry and soon would again demonstrate this unity by atoning in the Garden of Gethsemane and on the cross, after which He was resurrected, enabling the immortality of all people.

The Apostles needed to be likewise unified, including when making decisions for the young Church as it grew in Israel and expanded into other regions. The Lord reemphasized this need for unity when He spoke regarding the Quorum of the Twelve Apostles and the Quorum of the Seventy in this last dispensation: "And every decision made by either of these quorums must be by the unanimous voice of the same; that is, every member in each quorum must be agreed to its decisions, in order to make their decisions of the same power or validity one with the other. . . . The decisions of these quorums, or either of them, are to be made in all righteousness, in holiness, and lowliness of heart, meekness and long-suffering, and in faith, and virtue, and knowledge, temperance, patience, godliness, brotherly kindness and charity."[76]

Jesus also said that none of the Apostles had been lost, except for Judas Iscariot. Further, Jesus said that He was praying in the presence of the eleven Apostles so that they would feel joy, presumably including because of Jesus's declaration to His Father that they were righteous.

Jesus then prayed that His Father would protect the Apostles from evil as they continued their work of teaching the gospel. Moreover, Jesus prayed that His Father would sanctify the Apostles through His words, which Jesus had taught them. His Father's words are truth and lead people to eternal life.

Jesus Prays for Other Believers (John 17:20–23)

Christ next prayed for all who would believe in Him through the words of the Apostles:

John 17:20–23. Neither pray I for these alone, but for them also which shall believe on me through their word; that they all may be one; as thou, Father,

75. Moses 1:39.
76. D&C 107:27, 30.

art in me, and I in thee, that they also may be one in us: that the world may
believe that thou hast sent me. And the glory which thou gavest me I have
given them; that they may be one, even as we are one: I in them, and thou in
me, that they may be made perfect in one; and that the world may know that
thou hast sent me, and hast loved them, as thou hast loved me.

Presumably, Jesus was referring to not only those who heard the Apostles
speak but also to those who heard the Apostles' words from others and to
those who have read the Apostles' words in the scriptures, including people
today. Jesus prayed that all who believe would be unified and made perfect
in unity, just as He and His Father are unified in purpose. In essence, Jesus
was praying that those who believe would develop His and His Father's
attributes. These attributes include recognizing and speaking truth and being
merciful, just, virtuous, humble, temperate, and patient.[77] These attributes
also include having charity, including through "bear[ing] one another's
burdens," "mourn[ing] with those that mourn," and "comfort[ing] those that
stand in need of comfort."[78] Jesus stated that by developing these attributes,
believers would know that God indeed had sent His Son into the world and
that God loves Him and all of humankind.

The unity that Christ prayed for is evident in the Church today in many
ways. For example, Saints meet in unity of faith on the Sabbath. During
sacrament meeting, they partake of the emblems of the sacrament, which
are passed by priesthood holders and then from one member to another
down the rows of pews or chairs. This unity is manifest in people's kindness
and service to others. Unity is evident as priesthood holders stand together
and lay their hands on the heads of those who will be blessed. Unity is
also manifest as those who attend the holy temple are clothed in white and
sit one with another, without regard to position in the Church. Unity is
demonstrated when people serve together in callings so the Church can
operate effectively. Unity is manifest when people teach each other and bear
testimony to one another of the goodness of God and the sacrifice of His
Son. Further, unity is demonstrated when people fast together for spiritual
strength and for others to receive divine help.

---

77.   See 2 Pet. 1:5–7.
78.   Mosiah 18:8–9.

Jesus Prays That the Apostles Will See His Glory (John 17:24–26)

In the final portion of the prayer, Christ again prayed for the Apostles:

John 17:24–26. Father, I will that they also, whom thou hast given me, be with me where I am; that they may behold my glory, which thou hast given me: for thou lovedst me before the foundation of the world. O righteous Father, the world hath not known thee: but I have known thee, and these have known that thou hast sent me. And I have declared unto them thy name, and will declare it: that the love wherewith thou hast loved me may be in them, and I in them.

Jesus asked His Father to enable the Apostles to behold the glory that Jesus had received from His Father. Presumably, Jesus was requesting that the Apostles not only see the glory of His resurrected body when He returned after His death but also behold His glory in the celestial kingdom. Jesus asked these things of His Father because the Apostles believed in Jesus and in His Father. They believed even though most other people did not. Faith and righteousness bring power to see and comprehend spiritual things. Finally, Jesus prayed that God's love for Jesus would also be with the Apostles and that they would be one with Jesus.

After Jesus finished His prayer, He and His Apostles made their way to Gethsemane.[79] There, Jesus would complete the first part of His Atonement for all humankind. Afterward, He would be betrayed by Judas, which would lead to Jesus's Crucifixion, during which He completed His Atonement.

---

79. See John 18:1.

Chapter 64

THE ATONEMENT

(Thursday Evening to Early Friday Morning)

This chapter explores the events immediately before and during Christ's atoning sacrifice in Gethsemane and various aspects of the Atonement and its application in people's lives. The infinite Atonement of Christ is vital to each person's eternal progression. His Atonement and His Resurrection were His greatest miracles and His greatest and most merciful gifts.

Jesus Is the Only One Who Could Atone

Jesus is the only person who could atone for humankind. To better understand why, it is helpful to review several facts about Jesus. He is the first spirit son born of God in the premortal world.[1] Jesus has divine power, which was evidenced in the premortal world as He created "worlds without number,"[2] the sun, the moon, and the stars[3] under the direction of His Father. In the premortal world, Jesus valiantly upheld His Father's plan of salvation and volunteered to redeem humankind by coming to the earth and atoning for all humankind and bringing about the resurrection of all people.[4] As Peter taught, Jesus "was foreordained before the foundation of the world, but was manifest in these last times for you."[5] Note that Peter used the words *for you*, not *to you*. Jesus came to the earth for each of God's mortal children!

---

1. See D&C 93:21; Rom. 8:29; Col. 1:15; see also John 1:1–5.
2. Moses 1:33; see also Moses 1:35; 2:5; D&C 29:30.
3. See D&C 88:7–9.
4. See Moses 4:1–2; 6:62.
5. 1 Pet. 1:20.

Jesus is the Only Begotten Son of God in mortality[6] and came to the earth with divine attributes and authority, including to judge.[7] During His mortal sojourn, He demonstrated His divine authority by commanding the elements. For example, during a storm on the Sea of Galilee, He "rebuked the wind, and said unto the sea, Peace, be still. And the wind ceased, and there was a great calm."[8] At a wedding feast, He turned water into wine,[9] and on multiple occasions He healed the sick and even restored life to the dead.[10] Indeed, He has power over death.[11] As such, no one could cause His death unless He allowed it. As Jesus explained, "No man taketh it [My life] from me, but I lay it down of myself. I have power to lay it down, and I have power to take it again."[12]

Christ is also "the light and life of the world."[13] Speaking in third person, He revealed the following to Joseph Smith concerning His light and power:

He that ascended up on high, as also he descended below all things, in that he comprehended all things, that he might be in all and through all things, the light of truth; which truth shineth. This is the light of Christ. As also he is in the sun, and the light of the sun, and the power thereof by which it was made. As also he is in the moon, and is the light of the moon, and the power thereof by which it was made; as also the light of the stars, and the power thereof by which they were made; and the earth also, and the power thereof, even the earth upon which you stand. And the light which shineth, which giveth you light, is through him who enlighteneth your eyes, which is the same light that quickeneth your understandings; which light proceedeth forth from the presence of God to fill the immensity of space—the light which is in all things, which giveth life to all things, which is the law by which all things are governed, even the power of God who sitteth upon his throne, who is in the bosom of eternity, who is in the midst of all things.[14]

---

6.   See, for example, Luke 1:30–35; John 1:14; 3:16–17; Jacob 4:5, 11; Alma 5:48; D&C 20:21; 76:13, 23–25; 93:11; Moses 1:6; 5:7–9.

7.   See John 5:22, 27.

8.   Mark 4:39.

9.   See John 2:1–11.

10.   See Mark 5:21–43; Luke 7:11–17; John 11:33–44.

11.   See John 5:26.

12.   John 10:15, 17–18.

13.   See Mosiah 16:9; Alma 38:9; 3 Ne. 9:18; 11:11; Ether 4:12.

14.   D&C 88:6–13.

Because Christ's earthly mother was mortal, He was subject to the trials
and challenges of mortality; nevertheless, He was and is perfect. He is perfect
in goodness, compassion, and mercy. He also has perfect love. This love caused
Him to leave His heavenly glory to come to the earth as a mortal and suffer
the agony of the Atonement. Christ is also perfectly sinless and obedient to
His Father.[15] As Christ said in prayer, "Father, behold the sufferings and death
of him who did no sin."[16] Peter likewise taught that Christ is "as of a lamb
without blemish and without spot."[17] Christ was worthy and able in every
way to atone for all humankind, thereby giving all people the opportunity to
progress in accordance with Heavenly Father's plan.

Jesus and the Apostles Go to the Garden of Gethsemane
(Matt. 26:36–38; Mark 14:32–34; Luke 22:39; John 18:1)

After Jesus finished His Intercessory Prayer, He and His Apostles made
their way to the Kidron Valley, which lies between the steep hills of Jerusalem
and the Mount of Olives. They crossed over the Kidron brook,[18] which at
this time in the spring was likely flowing with water.[19] They then went into a
garden[20] called Gethsemane, which is at the foot of the Mount of Olives and
which Jesus and His Apostles had frequented:

Matthew 26:36–38. Then cometh Jesus with them unto a place called
Gethsemane, and saith unto the disciples, Sit ye here, while I go and pray

15.   See D&C 45:4; Heb. 4:14–15; 1 Pet. 2:21–23; John 5:30; 6:38; Mosiah 15:7; 3 Ne. 27:13.
16.   D&C 45:4.
17.   1 Pet. 1:19.
18.   John 18:1 uses the spelling *Cedron*, but *Kidron* is the more common spelling (see
HarperCollins Bible Dictionary, s.v. "Cedron" and "Kidron").
19.   See McConkie, *Mortal Messiah*, vol. 4, p. 123.
20.   Matthew 26:36, Mark 14:32, and Luke 22:40 refer to the location as a "place."
John 18:1 and JST Mark 14:32 refer to the place as a "garden." The Greek word for *garden*
as used in John is *kēpos*, which means a garden, orchard, or plantation (Young, *Analytical
Concordance*, s.v. "garden"). In Jerusalem, a garden was "a plot of cultivated land, often
enclosed by walls made of stones, mud-brick, or hedges. Entrance was normally through a
gate, which could be locked (Song 4:12; 2 Kings 25:4). Located near ample supplies of water,
gardens were lush and desirable pieces of property used for both decorative and utilitarian
purposes (Gen 13:10; Num 24:6; Jer 31:12). Vegetables, spices, fruit trees, and flowers were
grown in them (1 Kgs 21:2; Jer 29:5; Song 4:12–16; Luke 13:19). Gardens were also used as
meeting places for social occasions and for meditation and prayer (Esth 1:5; John 18:1)."
(*HarperCollins Bible Dictionary*, s.v. "garden.")

yonder. And he took with him Peter and the two sons of Zebedee, and began to be sorrowful and very heavy. Then saith he unto them, My soul is exceeding sorrowful, even unto death: tarry ye here, and watch with me.

It is symbolically significant that the Hebrew word for *Gethsemane* means "wine press and oil (farm),"[21] for while in Gethsemane, the awful weight and anguish of the Atonement caused Christ "to bleed at every pore."[22] It is also symbolically significant that Gethsemane is located near the bottom of the Kidron Valley; Christ physically descended the valley to reach Gethsemane, and He also metaphorically descended below all things as He atoned for humankind.

One can only wonder at the thoughts of the Apostles as they walked to the garden with their Lord and Master. They did not fully understand what was about to take place. After arriving in the garden, "the disciples began to be sore amazed, and to be very heavy, and to complain in their hearts, wondering if this be the Messiah."[23] Jesus directed them all to "pray that ye enter not into temptation."[24]

Jesus directed Peter, James, and John to come with Him and told the eight other Apostles to sit where they were. He, Peter, James, and John then went farther into the garden. Joseph Smith's translation states that Jesus then rebuked[25] these three Apostles.[26] Perhaps the reason for the rebuke is that these Apostles did not have a complete understanding of what Jesus was about to do.

According to Mark's account, as they proceeded farther into the garden, Christ "began to be sore amazed."[27] Presumably, Heavenly Father had taught Jesus about what He would endure during the Atonement, but when it came, He was astonished by the magnitude of what He experienced. He told the three Apostles that He had become "exceeding sorrowful, even unto death," and He asked them to remain where they were and watch with Him. That

---

21.   *HarperCollins Bible Dictionary*, s.v. "Gethsemane."

22.   D&C 19:18.

23.   JST Luke 14:36–37.

24.   Luke 22:40.

25.   In Joseph Smith's day, two of the meanings of *rebuke* were "to silence" and "to calm" (see Webster, *An American Dictionary of the English Language*, s.v. "rebuke," accessed August 9, 2022, https://webstersdictionary1828.com/Dictionary/rebuke).

26.   See JST Mark 14:38.

27.   Mark 14:33.

is, He asked them to stay awake and be vigilant.[28] Jesus then walked a short distance away.[29]

Jesus Atones for the World (Matt. 26:39–46; Mark 14:35–42; Luke 22:40–46)

Jesus, the Son of God, then atoned for all humankind. The following is Matthew's account:

> **Matthew 26:39–46.** And he went a little further, and fell on his face, and prayed, saying, O my Father, if it be possible, let this cup pass from me: nevertheless not as I will, but as thou wilt. And he cometh unto the disciples, and findeth them asleep, and saith unto Peter, What, could ye not watch with me one hour? Watch and pray, that ye enter not into temptation: the spirit indeed is willing, but the flesh is weak. He went away again the second time, and prayed, saying, O my Father, if this cup may not pass away from me, except I drink it, thy will be done. And he came and found them asleep again: for their eyes were heavy. And he left them, and went away again, and prayed the third time, saying the same words. Then cometh he to his disciples, and saith unto them, Sleep on now, and take your rest: behold, the hour is at hand, and the Son of man is betrayed into the hands of sinners. Rise, let us be going: behold, he is at hand that doth betray me.

Matthew and the other Gospel writers provided very little detail about what occurred as Jesus took upon Himself the sins of all people and also made up for all their mortal deficiencies and injustices. Perhaps so little has been recorded because what occurred is beyond mortal comprehension and is not for humans to know or understand. As McConkie wrote, "Finite minds can no more comprehend how and in what manner Jesus performed his redeeming labors than they can comprehend how matter came into being, or how Gods began to be."[30] Only Jesus and His Father know and understand exactly what occurred and the extent of Jesus's suffering.

One of the few things the Gospels do indicate is that Jesus prayed. Luke's record states that Jesus "kneeled down, and prayed"; Mark's record states that

---

28. The Greek word for *watch* as used in Matthew 26:38 and Mark 14:34 is *grēgoreō*, which means to "watch, be awake, vigilant" (see Young, *Analytical Concordance*, s.v. "rebuke").

29. See Luke 22:41.

30. McConkie, *Mortal Messiah*, vol. 4. p. 124.

Jesus "fell on the ground, and prayed"; and Matthew's record states that Jesus "fell on his face, and prayed."[31] At a point in Jesus's atoning sacrifice, His sorrow and anguish were so great that as part of His prayer, He pleaded: "O my Father, if it be possible, let this cup[32] pass from me."

The scriptures give some description of the agony associated with Christ's atoning sacrifice. Luke recorded that Christ's "sweat was as it were great drops of blood falling to the ground."[33] Presumably, His agony reached every aspect of His being. Christ told Joseph Smith that this "suffering caused myself, even God, the greatest of all, to tremble because of pain, and to bleed at every pore, and to suffer both body and spirit—and would that I might not drink the bitter cup, and shrink."[34]

Farrar provided the following insight regarding Christ's Atonement:

> It was something far deadlier than death. It was the burden and the mystery of the world's sin which lay heavy on His heart; it was the tasting, in the divine humanity of a sinless life, the bitter cup which sin had poisoned; it was the bowing of Godhead to endure a stroke to which man's apostasy had lent such frightful possibilities. It was the sense, too, of how virulent, how frightful must have been the force of evil in the Universe of God which could render necessary so infinite a sacrifice. It was the endurance, by the perfectly guiltless, of the worst malice which human hatred could devise; it was to experience in the bosom of perfect innocence and love, all that was detestable in human ingratitude, all that was pestilent in human hypocrisy, all that was cruel in human rage. It was to brave the last triumph of Satanic spite and fury, uniting against His lonely head all the flaming arrows of Jewish falsity and heathen corruption—the concentrated wrath of the rich and respectable, the yelling fury of the blind and brutal mob.[35]

---

31.   Luke 22:41; 14:35; Matt. 26:39. Perhaps Christ initially kneeled down and prayed and at a later point fell down and prayed because the intensity of the experience had increased.

32.   According to Talmage, the Old Testament sometimes uses the word *cup* as "a symbolic expression for a bitter or poisonous potion typifying experiences of suffering. See Ps. 11:6; 75:8; Isa. 51:17, 22; Jer. 25:15, 17; 49:12." (Talmage, *Jesus the Christ*, p. 575n8.) Significantly, the author of Psalm 116 uses the word *cup* in connection with *salvation* (see Ps. 116:13). Additionally, when people partake of the water (or wine) of the sacrament, they do so in remembrance of Christ's blood, which was shed in Gethsemane and on the cross (see D&C 20:79; see also Luke 22:19; 3 Ne. 18:7).

33.   Luke 22:44.

34.   D&C 19:18.

35.   Farrar, *Life of Christ*, p. 556.

Christ's Atonement was more severe than what anyone who was only mortal could endure. Joseph Fielding Smith wrote, "A mortal man could not have stood it—that is, a man such as we are. I do not care what his fortitude, what his power, there was no man ever born into this world that could have stood under the weight of the load that was upon the Son of God, when he was carrying my sins and yours and making it possible that we might escape from our sins."[36] In the midst of this agony, Christ reached out to His Father. Every mortal impulse would have been to end the agony, and every impulse of a loving father would have been to remove the pain from his son. Despite the agony Christ was experiencing, He then stated: "Nevertheless not as I will, but as thou wilt." Heavenly Father did not remove the cup,[37] but He sent an angel to strengthen Christ.[38] All people have reason to be eternally grateful to Christ and Heavenly Father for not shrinking from this terrible moment and staying the course through Christ's agony in Gethsemane and later on the cross.

Talmage wrote, "In that hour of anguish Christ met and overcame all the horrors that Satan, 'the prince of this world' could inflict. The frightful struggle incident to the temptations immediately following the Lord's baptism was surpassed and overshadowed by this supreme contest with the powers of evil."[39]

Of the few details that the Gospel writers recorded about Jesus's Atonement, three of the writers included Jesus's pleading to have the bitter cup removed and then accepting His Father's will. Perhaps the Gospel writers included this detail so that people can learn to follow the example of Jesus when pleading with His Father. When people experience anguish, they too should plead with Heavenly Father for help and should strive to be willing to declare, "Nevertheless not as I will, but as thou wilt." Though Heavenly Father may not remove the bitter cup from individuals, He will provide hope, peace, and assistance.

---

36.   Smith, *Gospel Doctrine*, vol. 1, pp. 130–131; see also Callister, *Infinite Atonement*, pp. 135–136.

37.   See Ps. 116:13; 3 Ne. 11:11.

38.   See Luke 22:43. McConkie speculated that this angel was Michael—that is, Adam (McConkie, *Mortal Messiah*, vol. 4, p. 125).

39.   Talmage, *Jesus the Christ*, p. 568.

The length of Christ's suffering is unknown, but the first part may have lasted approximately an hour, for after Christ finished praying the first time, He approached Peter, James, and John and found that they had fallen asleep.[40] Presumably after awaking the three Apostles, He asked Peter: "Couldest not thou watch one hour?"[41] Jesus then told Peter to stay alert and pray so that he would "enter not into temptation: the spirit indeed is willing, but the flesh is weak."[42]

Then Jesus "went away, and prayed, and spake the same words."[43] He then returned to His Apostles and found them asleep once more. It was presumably late at night by now, and the Apostles were understandably tired. He apparently woke them again, and they did not know "what to answer him."[44]

Christ then "went away again, and prayed the third time, saying the same words."[45] Assuming the first atoning experience and prayer lasted one hour and the second and third parts lasted about the same length of time, then His entire atoning experience in Gethsemane lasted approximately three hours. Whatever the length of Christ's suffering, it was sufficient.[46] He arose from His agony triumphant.

Jesus Allows the Apostles to Sleep

Jesus again returned to His Apostles and found them asleep. Unlike the previous times, this time He told them to "sleep on now, and take your rest."[47] After the Apostles slept for a time,[48] Jesus told them: "Rise, let us be going:

---

40.   JST Luke 22:45 indicates that the Apostles were sleeping because "they were filled with sorrow." Before falling asleep, the Apostles may have seen blood on Christ's face, arms, and robe.

41.   Mark 14:37. Alternatively, Christ may have used *hour* to signify a somewhat lengthy period.

42.   Matt. 26:41; see also Mark 14:38. JST Mark 14:43 states that the Apostles, not Jesus, said that the spirit is willing "but the flesh is weak."

43.   Mark 14:39.

44.   Mark 14:40.

45.   Matt. 26:44.

46.   Jesus may have been indicating this idea when He told Peter, "It is enough" (see Mark 14:41).

47.   Mark 14:41.

48.   See JST Mark 14:47.

behold, he is at hand that doth betray me." Judas was about to conclude his conspiracy with the chief priests and members of the Sanhedrin.

The Scriptures Provide Insight about Various Aspects of Jesus's Atonement

The scriptures, in particular the Book of Mormon, provide valuable information about Jesus's Atonement and its relevance in people's lives. Reading these scriptures can increase a person's understanding of the Atonement, but to gain an even deeper understanding, a person must have a testimony that Jesus is the Son of God and must personally experience the Atonement working in his or her life, lifting, cleansing, and providing hope. The following sections discuss concepts related to the Atonement; pondering these and other relevant concepts may help individuals increase their understanding of, appreciation for, and application of the Atonement.[49]

The Crucifixion Is Part of the Atonement

Christ's Atonement includes not only His suffering in Gethsemane but also His Crucifixion on Golgotha.[50] Talmage wrote, "It seems, that in addition to the fearful suffering incident to crucifixion, the agony of Gethsemane had recurred, intensified beyond human power to endure. In that bitterest hour the dying Christ was alone, alone in most terrible reality. That the supreme sacrifice of the Son might be consummated in all its fulness, the Father seems to have withdrawn the support of His immediate Presence, leaving to the Savior of men the glory of complete victory over the forces of sin and death."[51] Likewise, McConkie stated: "All the anguish, all of the sorrow, and all of the suffering of Gethsemane recurred during the final three hours on the cross, the hours when darkness covered the land. Truly there was no sorrow like unto his sorrow, and no anguish and pain like unto that which [He] bore."[52]

---

49. See Callister's *Infinite Atonement* for a more comprehensive discussion of the Atonement.
50. For more discussion about the Crucifixion, see chapter 67 in this volume.
51. Talmage, *Jesus the Christ*, p. 612.
52. McConkie, *Mortal Messiah*, vol. 4, p. 232n22.

To the Nephites, Christ said: "My Father sent me that I might be lifted up upon the cross; and after that I had been lifted up upon the cross, that I might draw all men unto me, that as I have been lifted up by men even so should men be lifted up by the Father, to stand before me, to be judged of their works, whether they be good or whether they be evil."[53] Christ told Joseph Smith, "The Lord your Redeemer suffered death in the flesh; wherefore he suffered the pain of all men, that all men might repent and come unto him."[54]

The Atonement Is Infinite

Christ's Atonement is infinite.[55] *Infinite* means "having no limits."[56] One way the Atonement is infinite is in that it is effective forever.[57] The Atonement is also infinite in that it redeems all of humankind from spiritual death.[58] In other words, the Atonement applies to all people, regardless of their nationality or ethnicity, their gender, their financial status, their intellectual capacity, or any other factor.

Maxwell wrote the following about the Atonement being infinite:

First, . . . only in an "infinite atonement," would mercy overpower the stern demands of justice (see Alma 34:15). . . . Second, the infinite atonement is fully comprehensive in the immortalizing benefits it provides to all of God's children by the grace of God (see Alma 11:40–44). . . . A third dimension may be seen in the infinite intensiveness of Christ's suffering. . . . Thus, in addition to bearing our sins—the required essence of the Atonement—the "how" of which we surely do not understand, Jesus is further described as having come to know our sicknesses, griefs, pains, and infirmities as well. . . . The Atonement, then, was infinite in divineness of the one sacrificed, in the comprehensiveness of its coverage, and the intensiveness—incomprehensible to us—of the Savior's suffering. . . . It may be that the benefits of the Atonement will extend to all of the spirit children of our

---

53.   3 Ne. 27:14.

54.   D&C 18:11.

55.   See 2 Ne. 9:7; 25:16; Mosiah 3:7; Alma 34:10, 12, 14; D&C 19:15–8.

56.   *Merriam-Webster*, s.v. "infinite," accessed August 9, 2022, https://www.merriam-webster.com/dictionary/infinite.

57.   See Isa. 51:6, 8.

58.   See 2 Ne. 9:21.

Father in Heaven, wherever situated. . . . Thus, the Atonement may reach into the universe—even as its blessings and redemptive powers reach into the small universe of each individual's suffering. How infinite, indeed![59]

As Maxwell noted, because the Atonement is infinite, it is reasonable to assume that it applies to Father in Heaven's children in other worlds.[60] The Lord taught Joseph Smith that "by him [Christ], and through him, and of him, the worlds are and were created, and the inhabitants thereof are begotten sons and daughters unto God"[61] and that the Lord "glorifies the Father, and saves all the works of his hands."[62] Further, the headnote to Doctrine and Covenants 76 affirms, "Inhabitants of many worlds are begotten sons and daughters unto God through the atonement of Jesus Christ." Regarding the concept of the universality of the Atonement, McConkie wrote: "Now our Lord's jurisdiction and power extend far beyond the limits of this one small earth on which we dwell. . . . And through the power of his atonement the inhabitants of these worlds, the revelation says, 'are begotten sons and daughters unto God' (D&C 76:24), which means that the atonement of Christ, being literally and truly infinite, applies to an infinite number of earths."[63]

The Atonement Is Necessary Because All People Sin and the Demands of Justice Must Be Satisfied

Adam and Eve's transgression introduced spiritual death—that is, separation from God—into the world.[64] Spiritual death also results when people sin, as all people do.[65] As the Apostle Paul wrote, "All have sinned, and come short of the glory of God."[66] According to the law of justice,

---

59.   Maxwell, *Not My Will, but Thine*, pp. 50–52.
60.   For a discussion of possible reasons this earth was selected as the place where Christ would make His atoning sacrifice, see Callister, *Infinite Atonement*, pp. 97–100. In addition to Callister's analysis, the Lord has revealed that ultimately "this earth will be Christ's" (see D&C 130:9).
61.   D&C 76:24.
62.   D&C 76:43.
63.   McConkie, *Mormon Doctrine*, p. 65.
64.   See Hel. 14:16; D&C 29:41.
65.   See Alma 12:32; Hel. 14:18.
66.   Rom. 3:23; see also Rom. 5:8–12, 19.

which God abides by as a perfectly just being,[67] a penalty must be paid for every sin a person commits.[68] Further, the law prescribes that no one who is unclean "can dwell with God."[69] Therefore, all people would be lost if Jesus had not "satisfied the demands of justice"[70] and "answer[ed] the ends of the law"[71] by atoning for the world. Through the Atonement, Jesus "subject[ed] Himself to the penalty that the law required for [people's] sins"[72] and overcame spiritual death, meaning that people can inherit kingdoms of glory in the next life.

By satisfying the law of justice, Jesus made mercy available to those who repent.[73] As Alma explained, "The plan of mercy could not be brought about except an atonement should be made; therefore God himself atoneth for the sins of the world, to bring about the plan of mercy, to appease the demands of justice, that God might be a perfect, just God, and a merciful God also."[74] It is important to note that because Jesus paid the price for all people's sins, it would be unjust for an individual to require those who have wronged the individual to also pay the price. All people need to forgive.

The Atonement Cleanses and Sanctifies Those Who Believe in Jesus and Repent

In the Book of Mormon, Amulek stated that Jesus would "take upon him the transgressions of those who believe on his name; and these are they that shall have eternal life, and salvation cometh to none else. Therefore the wicked remain as though there had been no redemption made, except it be the loosing of the bands of death; for behold, the day cometh that all shall rise from the dead and stand before God, and be judged according to their works."[75] Similarly, Christ told the Nephites that "no unclean thing can enter into his [God's] kingdom; therefore nothing entereth into his rest save it be

---

67. See Deut. 32:3–4; Ps. 89:14; Isa. 45:21; Zeph. 3:5; Zech. 9:9; Rev. 15:3–4. The fact that God is perfectly just can foster people's trust in Him (see the note at the end of this chapter).
68. See *True to the Faith*, s.v. "justice."
69. 1 Ne. 10:21; see also *True to the Faith*, s.v. "justice."
70. Mosiah 15:9.
71. 2 Ne. 2:7.
72. *True to the Faith*, s.v. "justice."
73. See Alma 34:15–16.
74. Alma 42:15; see also Alma 34:15–16.
75. Alma 11:40–41; see also D&C 19:15–19.

those who have washed their garments in my blood, because of their faith, and the repentance of all their sins, and their faithfulness unto the end."[76] Regarding those who do not repent, Christ said that "they must suffer even as I; which suffering caused myself, even God, the greatest of all, to tremble because of pain, and to bleed at every pore, and to suffer both body and spirit—and would that I might not drink the bitter cup, and shrink."[77] King Benjamin said of the unrepentant, "The demands of divine justice do awaken his immortal soul to a lively sense of his own guilt, which doth cause him to shrink from the presence of the Lord, and doth fill his breast with guilt, and pain, and anguish, which is like an unquenchable fire, whose flame ascendeth up forever and ever."[78]

The Atonement covers sins of every type and degree. Unless a person has denied the Holy Ghost, he or she can be forgiven, regardless of how serious the sin committed. It is important to remember that Christ "descended below all things."[79] In addition, Christ will forgive people as many times as they repent.[80]

One of the most fundamental aspects of the Atonement is its ability to purify and sanctify people when they repent.[81] Isaiah wrote that after repenting, "though your sins be as scarlet, they shall be as white as snow; though they be red like crimson, they shall be as wool."[82] Moroni taught, "Turn ye unto the Lord; cry mightily unto the Father in the name of Jesus, that perhaps ye may be found spotless, pure, fair, and white, having been cleansed by the blood of the Lamb, at that great and last day."[83] Further, Moroni explained: "If ye by the grace of God are perfect in Christ, and deny not his power, then are ye sanctified in Christ by the grace of God, through the shedding of the blood of Christ, which is in the covenant of the Father unto the remission of your sins, that ye become holy, without spot."[84]

---

76. 3 Ne. 27:19.
77. D&C 19:17–18.
78. Mosiah 2:38.
79. D&C 88:6.
80. Mosiah 26:29.
81. See, for example, 3 Ne. 19:25–29.
82. Isa. 1:18.
83. Morm. 9:6.
84. Moro. 10:33.

When a person repents, Christ serves as an advocate between the person and Heavenly Father. Doctrine and Covenants 45:3–5 states, "Listen to him who is the advocate with the Father, who is pleading your cause before him—saying: Father, behold the sufferings and death of him who did no sin, in whom thou wast well pleased; behold the blood of thy Son which was shed, the blood of him whom thou gavest that thyself might be glorified; wherefore, Father, spare these my brethren that believe on my name, that they may come unto me and have everlasting life."[85] As these verses indicate, those who are made pure through the Atonement qualify to receive celestial glory and to be in God's presence.[86] Individuals who do not learn about the gospel, come unto Jesus, and repent during mortality will have the opportunity to do so in the postmortal world and thereby qualify for the celestial kingdom.[87]

Repentance requires not only forsaking sin but also forgiving others, for the Lord has said that "ye ought to forgive one another; for he that forgiveth not his brother his trespasses standeth condemned before the Lord; for there remaineth in him the greater sin."[88] Christ set an example of forgiving others, including when He said on the cross, "Father, forgive them; for they know not what they do."[89] Just as Christ repeatedly forgives individuals, there is no limit to the number of times other people should forgive those who cause offense.[90] People also need to forgive themselves,[91] which is often a difficult task. Additionally, when a person pleads with God to be forgiven of wronging others, the person might also pray that the Atonement will heal and bring peace to those who have been wronged.

Knowledge of the Atonement Can Increase Faith to Repent

The Atonement of Christ can give people hope that they can be forgiven of their sins, and this hope can help people have faith to repent. As Amulek taught, "This being the intent of this last sacrifice, to bring about the bowels

---

85. See also D&C 29:5; John 5:22, 27; 2 Ne. 9:41.
86. See 1 Ne. 10:21; Moses 6:57; D&C 76:69.
87. See D&C 138.
88. D&C 64:9.
89. Luke 23:34.
90. See Matt. 18:22.
91. See, for example, Alma 42:29.

of mercy, which overpowereth justice, and bringeth about means unto men that they may have faith unto repentance."[92] The Spirit of Christ and the Holy Ghost can testify of the Atonement and awaken people to a sense of what is right, to a feeling of hope, and to a desire to change and repent.[93]

Those Who Repent Will Feel Peace

Christ's atoning sacrifice brings peace to those who repent. This peace came to King Benjamin's people after they repented: "The Spirit of the Lord came upon them, and they were filled with joy, having received a remission of their sins, and having peace of conscience, because of the exceeding faith which they had in Jesus Christ who should come."[94] One reason for this peace is that the sins of those who repent will not be mentioned[95] or even remembered.[96] Additionally, the repentant may be "born of the Spirit."[97] Because of the Atonement, the repentant who are filled with charity, faith, and virtue will have confidence in the presence of God.[98]

The Atonement Redeems Little Children

Through the Atonement, young children are redeemed. Mormon taught, "And their little children need no repentance, neither baptism. Behold, baptism is unto repentance to the fulfilling the commandments unto the remission of sins. But little children are alive in Christ, even from the foundation of the world; if not so, God is a partial God, and also a changeable God, and a respecter to persons; for how many little children have died without baptism!"[99] This truth means that those who die at a young age or who are not sufficiently competent to know right from wrong cannot sin in the eyes of God and are redeemed through the Atonement of Christ. This truth can bring peace to parents and others. Unfortunately, this aspect of the Atonement is not understood by much of the world.

---

92. Alma 34:15; see also v. 17.
93. See Moro 7:16; Ezek. 36:27; Romans 15:13; Moro. 8:26; D&C 11:12.
94. Mosiah 4:3.
95. See Ezek. 18:22–23.
96. See D&C 58:42–43; Heb. 8:12.
97. Mosiah 27:24; see also v. 25.
98. See D&C 121:45.
99. Moro. 8:11–12.

The Atonement Covers Those Who Sin in Ignorance

Throughout the world's history, the gospel has not been available to vast populations of the earth. For example, many people today have never heard of Christ, let alone the gospel. It would be unjust of God to condemn people to eternal damnation for breaking commandments that these people had no knowledge of. Christ's Atonement makes up for sins committed in ignorance. As Jacob taught, "The atonement satisfieth the demands of his justice upon all those who have not the law given to them, that they are delivered from that awful monster, death and hell, and the devil, and the lake of fire and brimstone, which is endless torment; and they are restored to that God who gave them breath, which is the Holy One of Israel."[100] Similarly, Mormon taught: "For the power of redemption cometh on all them that have no law."[101] Those who do not learn of the gospel in mortality will have ample opportunity in the postmortal world to learn of and accept or reject the gospel. Those who accept the gospel and the ordinances that have been vicariously performed for these people will qualify for exaltation.[102]

The Grace That Is Available through the Atonement Helps People Turn Weaknesses into Strengths

Moroni taught that if people come unto the Christ, He will show them their weaknesses. Then, through Christ's grace, which is available because of the Atonement, Christ will help people turn their weaknesses into strengths.[103] In other words, the Atonement will help people in their efforts to become more like Christ—that is, to be perfect. This aspect of the Atonement highlights the fact that people should continually draw on the Atonement and the opportunity to repent; drawing on the Atonement and repenting should not be a one-time event. Further, Christ understands that because all people have weaknesses, all people will falter at times. Nevertheless, "he sendeth an invitation unto all [people], for the arms of

---

100. 2 Ne. 9:26.
101. Moro. 8:22.
102. See D&C 138.
103. See Ether 12:27.

mercy are extended towards them,"[104] and He will help those who seek His assistance in overcoming their weaknesses.

The Atonement Makes Up for Injustices in Life

Life is hard and is filled with a multitude of injustices. Examples of injustices include physical infirmities, mental disorders, the unexpected loss of a loved one, a lack of opportunities for marriage, and unwanted divorce. Other examples of injustices are related to a person's geographic location and lack of educational opportunities. Injustices are a part of Heavenly Father's plan to test and refine His children.

Though Christ did not personally experience every injustice in the world, He understands what it feels like to experience injustice. Even though He did not experience a broken and hurtful marriage, He understands the pain of those who go through that difficult and traumatic period in their lives, for He too was rejected. Presumably, He experienced the loss of His mortal step-father and therefore understands the pain of losing a family member. He did not experience the loss of a child, but He nevertheless has empathy for parents who have lost children.[105] Jesus understands the sorrow of losing a friend, and He wept at the death of His friend Lazarus.[106] He understands unfairness, for He was unjustly arrested,[107] tried,[108] and condemned by the Jews;[109] scourged at the direction of Pilate;[110] mocked by Roman soldiers and Jews;[111] and unjustly crucified.[112]

It is important to always keep in mind the depth and breadth of Jesus's suffering in Gethsemane and on the cross and thereby the depth and breadth of His understanding and empathy. As the prophet Alma taught concerning Jesus, "He will take upon him their infirmities, that his bowels may be filled

---

104. Alma 5:33; see also 3 Ne. 9:14.
105. For example, Jesus restored life to the daughter of Jairus (see Mark 5:35–43) and to the son of the widow of Nain (see Luke 7:11–16).
106. See John 11:35.
107. See Matt. 26:50; Mark 14:46; John 18:12.
108. See Matt. 26:57–68; Mark 14:55—64.
109. See Matt. 27:20–22; Mark 15:11–14; Luke 23:21–22.
110. See John 19:1.
111. See Matt.26:67–68; Mark 14:65; Luke 22:63–65; Luke 23:11.
112. See Matt. 27:31–50; Mark 15:20–32; Luke 23:33–46; John 19:16–30.

with mercy, according to the flesh, that he may know according to the flesh how to succor his people according to their infirmities."[113] When people experience injustices in mortality and then seek healing through Jesus, they can come to understand the mercy that is extended through His Atonement.

Christ "bind[s] up the brokenhearted."[114] The broken hearted include those who have suffered from other people's sins. Jacob in the Book of Mormon taught, "The righteous, the saints of the Holy One of Israel, they who have believed in the Holy One of Israel, they who have endured the crosses of the world, and despised the shame of it, they shall inherit the kingdom of God."[115] In effect, Jacob was teaching that those who suffer injustices should look for the lessons they need to learn from their circumstances and the people they may help rather than looking inward and complaining. All who accept the gospel and repent will eventually be made whole, and the injustices they experienced will be taken into account at the Final Judgment.

During the Last Supper, Jesus reminded His Apostles that "in me ye might have peace, In the world ye shall have tribulation: but be of good cheer; I have overcome the world."[116] No matter who a person is and what he or she has experienced or is experiencing, Jesus understands and can give peace.

The Atonement Makes Agency Meaningful

God has given all of His children agency: the ability to make meaningful choices. Because all mortals except for Jesus are imperfect, they make bad choices at times. Consequently, they would not be able to inherit eternal life if Jesus had not completed the Atonement and made repentance possible. Ultimately, the Atonement is one thing that makes agency meaningful—the Atonement enables people to learn from their choices, repent and become clean, refine their character, progress toward perfection, and ultimately inherit eternal life. Without the Atonement, agency would have little meaning.

---

113. Alma 7:12.
114. Isa. 61:1.
115. 2 Ne. 9:18.
116. John 16:33.

The Atonement Fulfills the Old Testament Law of Sacrifice

Christ's Atonement fulfilled the law of sacrifice that was instituted during Adam's day: "And after many days an angel of the Lord appeared unto Adam, saying: Why dost thou offer sacrifices unto the Lord? And Adam said unto him: I know not, save the Lord commanded me. And then the angel spake, saying: This thing is a similitude of the sacrifice of the Only Begotten of the Father, which is full of grace and truth."[117] The law of sacrifice continued through the centuries and was practiced at the time of Christ. With His Atonement, the law of sacrifice was fulfilled because Christ's sacrifice was the great and last sacrifice.[118]

The Resurrection Is an Extension of the Atonement

In a sense, Christ's Resurrection is part of the Atonement. His Resurrection enabled humankind to overcome the physical death brought into the world through the fall of Adam and Eve. As Paul wrote, "For as in Adam all die, even so in Christ shall all be made alive."[119] The Lord tied redemption—that is, the Atonement—to resurrection when He told Joseph Smith, "Through the redemption which is made for you is brought to pass the resurrection from the dead."[120] Because of Christ's Atonement and Resurrection, people can progress eternally. Therefore, the importance of the resurrection in Heavenly Father's plan of salvation cannot be overstated.[121]

Indirectly, all other aspects of Christ's mortal life are part of the Atonement because His example and teachings help people know how to become unified with Him and Heavenly Father.[122] Christ's entire life was one of lifting people toward God. Christ taught the higher law and the importance of having faith, repenting, and improving. He demonstrated how to overcome the world by resisting Satan and his evils, how to consecrate His life to the gospel, and how to submit His will to His Father's.

---

117. Moses 5:6–7; see also 3 Ne. 9:19–20; 15:5.

118. See Alma 34:13–14.

119. 1 Cor. 15:22.

120. D&C 88:14–16.

121. For more discussion of Christ's Resurrection and the resurrection of all humankind, see chapter 69 in this volume.

122. See John 17:20–23.

The Atonement Makes Essential Ordinances Possible and Eternally Effective

The Atonement makes possible the ordinances that are essential for receiving exaltation. For example, the cleansing power of baptism is possible only because Christ atoned for the sins of all humankind. Further, Church members renew their baptismal covenants when they participate in the ordinance of the sacrament, which reminds them to think of Christ's Atonement, to repent of their sins, and to strive to become more like Christ.[123] By keeping the covenants associated with ordinances, people are better able to make righteous choices and develop Christlike qualities. Without the Atonement, people could not become spiritually clean,[124] and if people are not clean, the covenants they enter into will not be of force in the world to come.

The Atonement also provides the way in which all who are righteous will be welded into a whole and perfect union, for no perfect union could exist without the redeeming power of the Atonement. Joseph Smith wrote, "For we without them [the fathers and the children] cannot be made perfect; neither can they without us be made perfect. Neither can they nor we be made perfect without those who have died in the gospel also; for it is necessary in the ushering in of the dispensation of the fulness of times, which dispensation is now beginning to usher in, that a whole and complete and perfect union, and welding together of dispensations, and keys, and powers, and glories should take place, and be revealed from the days of Adam even to the present time."[125]

Remember Jesus's Goodness, and Tell Others of Him and His Atonement

Christ's atoning sacrifice is the central message of the gospel and should have a profound effect in people's lives because of its ability to cleanse; encourage Christlike behavior; and bring hope, peace, and joy. All people should ponder "how merciful the Lord hath been unto the children of

123. See D&C 20:77, 79.
124. See 1 John 1:7; Alma 5:21.
125. D&C 128:18.

men."[126] Pondering Christ's Atonement can help people come unto Him, be more obedient, have a deeper reverence for Him, and have a greater love for Him and others.

Those with a knowledge of Jesus's Atonement should share this knowledge with others. As Jacob said, "Wherefore, how great the importance to make these things known unto the inhabitants of the earth, that they may know that there is no flesh that can dwell in the presence of God, save it be through the merits, and mercy, and grace of the Holy Messiah, who layeth down his life according to the flesh, and taketh it again by the power of the Spirit, that he may bring to pass the resurrection of the dead, being the first that should rise."[127] By sharing this message with others, more people will be able to feel the happiness that Jesus referred to when He said, "In the world ye shall have tribulation: but be of good cheer; I have overcome the world."[128] Christ's atoning sacrifice is indeed something to rejoice about! Knowledge of it should also motivate people to love Christ and Heavenly Father more deeply, to serve Them more valiantly, and to strive to become more like Them.

The Atonement will eternally bless those who believe in Jesus and repent!

Note to Chapter 64

1. God's attribute of justice. Regarding the justice of God, Joseph Smith taught the following:

> It is also necessary, in order to the exercise of faith in God unto salvation, that men should have the idea of the existence of the attribute justice in him; for without the idea of the existence of the attribute justice in the Deity, men could not have confidence sufficient to place themselves under his guidance and direction; for they would be filled with fear and doubt lest the judge of all the earth would not do right, and thus fear or doubt,

---

126. Moro. 10:3; see also the title page of the Book of Mormon.
127. 2 Ne. 2:8.
128. John 16:33.

existing in the mind, would preclude the possibility of the exercise of faith in him for life and salvation. But when the idea of the existence of the attribute justice in the Deity is fairly planted in the mind, it leaves no room for doubt to get into the heart, and the mind is enabled to cast itself upon the Almighty without fear and without doubt, and with the most unshaken confidence, believing that the Judge of all the earth will do right.[129]

---

129. *Lectures on Faith*, p. 43.

Chapter 65

THE ARREST AND JEWISH TRIALS OF JESUS

(Early Friday Morning)

After Jesus completed His atoning sacrifice in Gethsemane and the Apostles had awoken, He told them: "Behold, he is at hand that doth betray me."[1] Judas and other men then appeared, and soon afterward Jesus was arrested. Thus began the events that resulted in His Crucifixion. This chapter explores Judas's betrayal, Jesus's arrest, Peter's actions, and the two trials that members of the Sanhedrin held to interrogate Jesus.

As with other events recorded in the Gospels, the Gospel records regarding the events that occurred from the time that Jesus was arrested until the time He was crucified are somewhat fragmentary and differ somewhat from Gospel to Gospel. Regarding the inconsistencies in these accounts, Farrar wrote the following:

> Although sceptics have dwelt with disproportioned persistency upon a multitude of 'discrepancies' in the fourfold narrative of Christ's trial, condemnation, death, and resurrection, these are not of a nature to cause the slightest anxiety to a Christian scholar. . . . After repeated study, I declare, quite fearlessly, that though the slight variations are numerous—though the lesser particulars cannot in every instance be minutely accurate—though no one of the narratives taken singly would give us an adequate impression—yet so far from there being, in this part of the Gospel story, any irreconcilable contradiction, we can see how one Evangelist supplements the details

---

1. Matt. 26:46.

furnished by another, and can understand the true sequence of the incidents by combining into one the separate indications which they furnish.[2]

Judas Betrays Jesus (Matt. 26:47–50; Mark 14:43–45; Luke 22:47–48; John 18:2–9)

Immediately after Jesus told the Apostles that the person who would betray Him was near, Judas approached with a group of armed men. The following is John's account:

> **John 18:2–9.** And Judas also, which betrayed him, knew the place [the garden in Gethsemane]: for Jesus offtimes resorted thither with his disciples. Judas then, having received a band of men and officers from the chief priests and Pharisees, cometh thither with lanterns and torches and weapons. Jesus therefore, knowing all things that should come upon him, went forth, and said unto them, Whom seek ye? They answered him, Jesus of Nazareth. Jesus saith unto them, I am he. And Judas also, which betrayed him, stood with them. As soon then as he had said unto them, I am he, they went backward, and fell to the ground. Then asked he them again, Whom seek ye? And they said, Jesus of Nazareth. Jesus answered, I have told you that I am he: if therefore ye seek me, let these go their way: that the saying might be fulfilled, which he spake, Of them which thou gavest me have I lost none.

The Gospels describe the group that accompanied Judas as a "multitude"[3] or a "great multitude,"[4] and the group included Roman soldiers, temple captains and guards, elders, chief priests, and the servant of the high priest.[5]

---

2.   Farrar, *Life of Christ*, p. 565.

3.   See Luke 22:47.

4.   See Matt. 26:47; Mark 14:43.

5.   See Matt. 26:51; Luke 22:50, 52; John 18:3, 10, 12. During the Feast of the Passover, the temple and the city were guarded by four hundred to six hundred Roman soldiers; their purpose was to prevent or quell any tumult among the numerous pilgrims who were in Jerusalem for the feast. They were principally stationed in the fortress of Antonia, which was near the temple. (See Edersheim, *Life and Times of Jesus the Messiah*, p. 847.) The Jewish temple guards served principally as unarmed police (see Josephus, *Wars*, 4.4.6); it was highly unlikely that the Roman government would have permitted armed Jewish police in Jerusalem. See note 1 at the end of this chapter for a discussion of what may have been involved in securing Roman soldiers to be part of the group.

The group had been sent by elders, chief priests, Pharisees, and scribes.[6] The Jewish leaders, likely including Annas and Caiaphas,[7] presumably wanted armed Roman soldiers and temple guards in the group in order to ensure that nothing prevented Jesus's arrest. For example, the leaders might have feared that Apostles would try to protect Jesus or that He would work a powerful miracle to try to free Himself, and the leaders might have believed that the soldiers and guards could have thwarted these attempts. Likely as another way to ensure that Jesus was arrested without incident, the arrest was arranged to occur late at night.

It is reasonable to assume that Judas first led the group to the house where Jesus and the Apostles had eaten the Passover meal, expecting that they would still be there. Of course, they were not. Judas then likely led the group to Gethsemane, for Jesus and His Apostles often went there and it was unlikely that Jesus would have gone to another house on the night of the Passover meal. It is possible that Jesus had earlier mentioned to all of His Apostles that they would be going to the garden after the Passover meal.

As the group entered the garden, they carried lanterns and torches to light their way in the dark night. Likely, Judas walked a short distance in front of the other men as they approached Jesus, for he had previously told them that he would signal who Jesus was by kissing Him.[8] According to Matthew's record, "and forthwith he [Judas] came to Jesus, and said, Hail, master; and kissed him."[9] In this way, Satan, who was influencing Judas, turned something good—a kiss of purported respect and endearment—into something evil. Judas was a hypocrite supposing he could deceive Jesus and the other Apostles, but Jesus knew who Judas really was. Likely while looking Judas directly in his eyes by the light of the torches and lanterns, Jesus said: "Judas, betrayest thou the Son of man with a kiss?"[10] Even though Judas had submitted his will to Satan, these words may have cut deep in Judas's

---

6.   See Matt. 26:47; Mark 14:43; Luke 22:50, 52; John 18:3, 10. See note 2 at the end of this chapter for a summary of the reasons that the chief priests, Pharisees, and elders conspired with Judas to cause Jesus's death.

7.   See notes 3 and 4 at the end of this chapter for information about Annas and Caiaphas.

8.   See Matt. 26:48; Mark 14:44.

9.   Matt. 26:49.

10.   Luke 22:48.

corrupted heart. However, it was too late for Judas. Judas then rejoined the group that had come to arrest Jesus.

"Knowing all things that should come upon him," Jesus approached the group and asked a question He already knew the answer to: "Whom seek ye?" They answered, "Jesus of Nazareth." Jesus simply responded, "I am he." Upon hearing Jesus's words, the members of the group "went backward, and fell to the ground." Perhaps the men recognized Jesus's divine power, His goodness, and His holiness. Perhaps the soldiers had misgivings about their task, having heard of His mighty miracles and perhaps feared He would use His miraculous power against them. However, if they violated their order to arrest Jesus, they would have been severely punished.

Jesus then asked the multitude again, "Whom seek ye?" Once again, they responded: "Jesus of Nazareth." Jesus answered, "I have told you that I am he: if therefore ye seek me, let these go their way." John's account then states that Jesus made this statement "that the saying [in His Intercessory Prayer] might be fulfilled, which he spake, Of them which thou gavest me have I lost none."[11] Jesus loved His eleven Apostles and was focused on protecting them even when He was about to be arrested.

Peter Draws His Sword to Protect Jesus (Matt. 26:51–54; Mark 14:47; Luke 22:49–51; John 18:10–11)

Peter then drew his sword to protect his beloved Master. Peter must have known that his single sword would be to no avail against the swords and staffs of the trained soldiers. Nevertheless, he was willing to try to protect the Lord. Both John's and Matthew's accounts follow:

John 18:10–11. Then Simon Peter having a sword drew it, and smote the high priest's servant, and cut off his right ear. The servant's name was Malchus. Then said Jesus unto Peter, Put up thy sword into the sheath: the cup which my Father hath given me, shall I not drink it?

Matthew 26:51–54. And, behold, one of them which were with Jesus stretched out his hand, and drew his sword, and struck a servant of the

---

11. See John 17:12.

high priest's, and smote off his ear. Then said Jesus unto him, Put up again thy sword into his place: for all they that take the sword shall perish with the sword. Thinkest thou that I cannot now pray to my Father, and he shall presently give me more than twelve legions of angels? But how then shall the scriptures be fulfilled, that thus it must be?

Peter used his sword to cut off the right ear of Caiaphas's servant, Malchus. Jesus then told Peter to put away his sword and counseled him that "all they that take the sword shall perish with the sword." Jesus also told Peter that if He so desired, He could pray and His Father would send more than twelve legions of angels—that is, between 64,800 and 72,000 angels—to protect Jesus.[12] These angels could have easily delivered Jesus from the soldiers, but being delivered was not part of Jesus's mission.

John's record states that Jesus also said to Peter, "The cup which my Father hath given me, shall I not drink it?"[13] Jesus presumably wanted to make it clear to all those present that He was voluntarily giving up His life to do the will of the Father. Hearing Jesus's words and seeing no further resistance, Judas's group presumably gained confidence that their evil plot would succeed.

Jesus then touched Malchus's ear "and healed him."[14] The miracle was visible instantly and could not honestly be denied. One can only wonder what those in the group thought upon seeing this witness of Jesus's divinity. Was Malchus grateful to Jesus? Did he later report the healing to Caiaphas? Did Malchus later believe that Jesus was the Son of God? Whatever the group members' thoughts, the miracle seemingly made no difference in the multitude's resolve to arrest Jesus.[15]

---

12.   See Matt. 26:53. A Roman legion consisted of fifty-four hundred to six thousand men (see *HarperCollins Bible Dictionary*, s.v. "legion").

13.   John 18:11.

14.   Luke 22:51. It is reasonable to assume that Peter's action would be a cause for immediate arrest. According to Chandler, "the healing of the ear explains why no arrest followed; for, if charges had been made, there would have been no evidence of the gravity of the offense. Indeed, witnesses against Peter would have been completely confounded and humiliated by the result of the miracle." (Chandler, *Trial of Jesus*, vol. 1, p. 53.)

15.   Likewise, the high priest, Caiaphas, most certainly heard about Malchus being healed. But Caiaphas's evil intent was not diminished even by hearing of a miracle performed for one of his servants.

Jesus Condemns the Jewish Leaders and Is Arrested (Matt. 26:55–56; Mark 14:46, 48–49; Luke 22:52–53; John 18:12)

After healing Malchus, Jesus addressed the elders, chief priests, and temple captains who were in the multitude, and then He was arrested:

Luke 22:52–53. Then Jesus said unto the chief priests, and captains of the temple, and the elders, which were come to him, Be ye come out, as against a thief, with swords and staves? When I was daily with you in the temple, ye stretched forth no hands against me: but this is your hour, and the power of darkness.

Matthew 26:55–56. In that same hour said Jesus to the multitudes, Are ye come out as against a thief with swords and staves for to take me? I sat daily with you teaching in the temple, and ye laid no hold on me. But all this was done, that the scriptures of the prophets might be fulfilled. Then all the disciples forsook him, and fled.

John 18:12. Then the band and the captain and officers of the Jews took Jesus, and bound[16] him.

As Jesus pointed out, the men came as thieves with swords and staffs at night; being armed while breaking into a home or other building in the nighttime may have justified lethal defense.[17] Jesus then condemned the group by implying that they were under the power of Satan and were, therefore, enemies to God. By stating "this is your hour, and the power of darkness," Jesus was also indicating His willingness to submit to being arrested and ultimately to being crucified, to fulfill His work on the earth.

Jesus's statement to the elders, chief priests, and temple captains, some of whom may have been members of the Sanhedrin, also challenged the legality of His arrest, for Judaic law forbade arrests and other legal proceedings from occurring at night. Of course, the arrest was illegal for other reasons as well. For example, the Mosaic code and rabbinical rule forbade arrests that were facilitated by traitors of those being arrested. Further, the arrest

---

16. Abraham bound his son Isaac in preparation for sacrificing him, according to God's command (see Gen. 22:1–12). This story is a beautiful symbol of God allowing His Only Begotten son to be sacrificed.

17. See Ex. 22:2; *HarperCollins Bible Dictionary*, s.v. "robbery"; Brown, "The Arrest," in *Life and Teachings of Jesus Christ*, vol. 3, ed. Holzapfel and Wayment, p. 195.

was not the result of a legal mandate from the Sanhedrin, contrary to requirements of the law. Moreover, the person who oversaw the arrest was likely Annas, the former high priest, who no longer had legal authority. The elders, chief priests, and temple captains presumably knew about some or all of these illegalities. Jesus's arrest was a sign of the corruption that was pervasive among the members of the Sanhedrin.[18] One can only wonder at the thoughts of those in the multitude as they heard Jesus tell them that they were arresting Him by the "power of darkness."

The eleven Apostles then fled. Joseph Smith's translation of Mark 14 states that the Apostles fled after hearing Jesus say, "The scriptures must be fulfilled."[19] The Apostles may have fled because they understood that Jesus needed to be taken to fulfill the prophecies of His death and that they should flee to avoid arrest so they could continue the work of the gospel.

A Young Man Flees (Mark 14:51–52)

Mark's account notes that a young man was present. Some people think that this young man was the future Gospel writer Mark,[20] and Jesus and the Apostles may have eaten the Passover meal at the house of Mark's family. If these assumptions are correct and Judas and the multitude had first gone to the home where the Passover meal was eaten, Mark may have followed the group after they left his house, so he could see what was occurring. The young man wore only a linen cloth; if he was Mark, perhaps he had been awakened by the multitude when they arrived at his house and

---

18. For a fuller discussion of the illegalities of Jesus's arrest, see Chandler, *Trial of Jesus,* vol. 1, p. 192.

19. JST Mark 14:50.

20. See Edersheim, *Life and Times of Jesus the Messiah,* pp. 849–850; McConkie, *Mortal Messiah,* vol. 4. p. 132. The assumption that the young man is Mark is based in part on the fact that Mark's Gospel is the only Gospel to mention the young man being present (see Edersheim, *Life and Times of Jesus the Messiah,* pp. 849–850; Brown, "The Arrest," in *Life and Teachings of Jesus Christ,* vol. 3, ed. Holzapfel and Wayment, pp. 205–207). If the young man was indeed Mark, in addition to later writing a Gospel, he was Paul's missionary companion for a time. The young man could also have been Lazarus, the owner of the garden in Gethsemane, or someone else (see Farrar, *Life of Christ,* p. 564).

he did not have time to put on more clothes before following the multitude to Gethsemane.

> **Mark 14:51–52.** And there followed him a certain young man, having a linen cloth cast about his naked body; and the young men laid hold on him: and he left the linen cloth, and fled from them naked.

Mark's Gospel notes that "young men laid hold on" the young man and that he fled, presumably to avoid arrest. The young man's risk of arrest suggests that the Apostles had been at an even greater risk of arrest.

Jesus Is Interrogated (John 18:13–14, 19–24)

After Jesus was arrested, He was bound and taken to Annas and then taken to Caiaphas's palace:[21]

> **John 18:13–14, 19–24.** And [the multitude] led him away to Annas first; for he was father in law to Caiaphas, which was the high priest that same year. Now Caiaphas was he, which gave counsel to the Jews, that it was expedient that one man should die for the people. . . . The high priest then asked Jesus of his disciples, and of his doctrine. Jesus answered him, I spake openly to the world; I ever taught in the synagogue, and in the temple, whither the Jews always resort; and in secret have I said nothing. Why askest thou me? ask them which heard me, what I have said unto them: behold, they know what I said. And when he had thus spoken, one of the officers which stood by struck Jesus with the palm of his hand, saying, Answerest thou the high priest so? Jesus answered him, If I have spoken evil, bear witness of the evil: but if well, why smitest thou me? Now Annas had sent him bound unto Caiaphas the high priest.

John's Gospel alone mentions that Jesus was first taken to Annas. The fact that Jesus was taken to Annas suggests that he exercised significant authority in Jerusalem even though he was no longer the high priest and that he may have been overseeing Judas's betrayal and Jesus's arrest. Farrar wrote the following about Annas: "If there were one man who was more

---

21. Jesus and the multitude may have traversed much the same route that Jesus and His Apostles had traveled between Jerusalem and Gethsemane. Likely, no one but Jesus and the multitude were present on the city streets as they made their way to Annas. At this late time of night on a Jewish holiday, presumably most others in the city were sleeping.

guilty than any other of the death of Jesus, that man was Hanan [Annas]. His advanced age, his preponderant dignity, his worldly position and influence, as one who stood on the best terms with the Herods and the Procurators, gave an exceptional weight to his prerogative decision."[22]

It is possible that an additional reason Jesus was first taken to Annas was to give the chief priests, elders, and scribes time to gather at Caiaphas's palace[23] so they could hold Jesus's first trial. The Jewish leaders surely knew that Jesus was going to be arrested that night, but gathering early Friday morning would likely have taken some time and it may have been convenient to keep Jesus under guard at Annas's home.

There is some question as to whether Annas interrogated Jesus before Caiaphas did and whether the interrogation described in John 18:19–23 was conducted by Annas or by Caiaphas.[24] John 18:19 states that the high priest questioned Jesus. Because the New Testament sometimes refers to Annas as the high priest,[25] John's use of the term *high priest* in this verse could refer to Annas instead of Caiaphas. John 18:24 in the King James Version states, "Now Annas had sent him [Jesus] bound unto Caiaphas the high priest." The word *had* in this verse in the King James Version suggests that Jesus had been sent to Caiaphas before the interrogation mentioned in the previous verses had occurred, implying that Caiaphas was the interrogator. However, unlike in the King James Version and some other Bible translations,[26] yet other Bible translations of John 18:24 use *then* instead of *now* and do not include the word *had*.[27] *Then* and the absence of the word *had* suggest that Annas was the one who interrogated Jesus in verses 19–23.

22. Farrar, *Life of Christ*, p. 569.

23. See Mark 14:53.

24. For a more detailed discussion of the divergent views, see Pike, "Before the Jewish Authorities," in *Life and Teachings of Jesus Christ*, vol. 3, ed. Holzapfel and Wayment, pp. 223–224n23.

25. See Luke 3:2; Acts 4:6.

26. See the English Standard Version, New American Standard Bible, American Standard Version, Contemporary English Version, and Duay-Rheims Bible.

27. See the New International Version, New Living Translation, Berean Study Bible, New King James Version, Christian Standard Bible, International Standard Version, New American Bible, and New Revised Standard Version.

McConkie and Farrar believed that Annas was the interrogator referred to in John 18:19–23,[28] and Talmage and Edersheim believed that Caiaphas was the first interrogator.[29] Edersheim posited that "if Peter's denial, as recorded by St. John [John 18:17], is the same as that described by the Synoptists, and took place in the house of Caiaphas, then the account of the examination by the High-Priest [John 18:19–23], which follows the notice about Peter, must also refer to that by Caiaphas, not Annas."[30] Even if Caiaphas was the interrogator in John 18:19–23, it is reasonable to assume that when Jesus was with Annas, some discussion occurred between them.

In the first recorded interrogation, whether by Annas or Caiaphas, Jesus was asked "of his disciples,[31] and of his doctrine." The exact questions put to Jesus are not known. It is doubtful that Jesus disclosed the names of His disciples, their whereabouts, or what they would likely do next. He would not have wanted to potentially put them in danger.

Regarding Jesus's doctrine, He said that He had spoken openly, including in the temple, and not in secret. He then stated that those who had listened to Him teach could testify regarding what He had taught. In this way, He implicitly called on Jewish law, which required that a charge brought against a person must be brought by at least two witnesses agreeing in all essential details.[32] Both Annas and Caiaphas certainly knew of this requirement. Moreover, the interrogator knew that he had no legal right to attempt to elicit a confession or to trap Jesus when the intent was to find a justification to condemn Jesus. Moreover, the interrogator was totally disregarding the sixth commandment: "Thou shalt not kill."[33] The death penalty, which the interrogator and other Jewish leaders sought to impose on Jesus, should have been their own penalty.

---

28.   See McConkie, *Mortal Messiah*, vol. 4, p. 147; Farrar, *Life of Christ*, p. 571.

29.   See Talmage, *Jesus the Christ*, pp. 596–597; Edersheim, *Life and Times of Jesus the Messiah*, pp. 852–853.

30.   Edersheim, *Life and Times of Jesus the Messiah*, p. 852.

31.   It is unknown whether this use of *disciples* refers to only the Apostles or to all of Jesus's followers.

32.   See Chandler, *Trial of Jesus*, vol. 1, p. 172.

33.   Ex. 20:13.

In response to Jesus's statement, one of the officers present struck Jesus and said, "Answerest thou the high priest so?"[34] Jesus responded to the blow by stating that if he had "spoken evil, bear witness of the evil"—that is, be a witness against Him—"but if well, why smitest thou me?" The officer, not Jesus, was the one who should have been condemned. Imagine what this officer must have felt upon realizing in this life or the next that he had struck the face of the Son of God, the Savior of the world.[35]

Jesus Is Tried by Caiaphas and Other Members of the Sanhedrin (Matt. 26:59–66; Mark 14:55–64)

Jesus was then tried[36] before Caiaphas and other members of the Sanhedrin, which was also referred to as "the council":

Mark 14:55–64. And the chief priests and all the council sought for witness against Jesus to put him to death; and found none. For many bare false witness against him, but their witness agreed not together. And there arose certain, and bare false witness against him, saying, We heard him say, I will destroy this temple that is made with hands, and within three days I will build another made without hands. But neither so did their witness agree together. And the high priest stood up in the midst, and asked Jesus, saying, Answerest thou nothing? what is it which these witness against thee? But he held his peace, and answered nothing. Again the high priest asked him, and said unto him, Art thou the Christ, the Son of the Blessed? And Jesus said, I am: and ye shall see the Son of man sitting on the right hand of power, and coming in the clouds of heaven. Then the high priest rent his clothes, and saith, What need we any further witnesses? Ye have heard the blasphemy: what think ye? And they all condemned him to be guilty of death.

Whereas the members of the Sanhedrin usually met in the temple, on this occasion they met in Caiaphas's palace. Additionally, they met early in the morning, contrary to Jewish law.[37] Matthew's and Mark's records refer to

---

34. This mention of Jesus being struck is the first record of Him being physically assaulted, other than when He was bound before being escorted to Annas and then to Caiaphas.
35. It is reasonable to assume that Jesus later told the Apostles what transpired in this interrogation. However, perhaps this officer or one of the others present was spiritually touched by what Jesus later said and related this experience to John.
36. See note 5 at the end of this chapter for information on Jewish trials.
37. See Edersheim, *Life and Times of Jesus the Messiah*, p. 858.

"all the council" seeking witnesses who would speak against Jesus. *All* may refer to all those who were present at the meeting; Jost asserted that "the most prominent men who represented the Law, such as Gamaliel, Jochanan b. Zakkai, and others, were not present."[38] Likewise, it is doubtful that Joseph of Arimathea and Nicodemus were present, for later they tenderly sought to bury Jesus and anoint His body with expensive ointment and oils.

Caiaphas and others in the council had looked for people who would testify that Jesus had committed a crime that the Jewish law indicated was punishable by death. The witnesses were presumably found beforehand, for it would have been difficult to find them very early in the morning. It is possible that they were promised payment for coming to this early morning meeting, especially since it was the night of the Passover. Matthew's and Mark's records state that many witnesses were brought forward.[39] However, as Matthew noted, they were "false witnesses."[40] For this reason, they "agreed not together," according to Mark. According to Jewish law, a person could not be condemned unless multiple people provided the same evidence against a person.[41]

After many false witnesses had testified, two testified of hearing Jesus say, "I will destroy this temple that is made with hands, and within three days I will build another made without hands." These witnesses were referring to a statement that Jesus had made three years earlier, when He cleansed the temple for the first time. According to John's record (the only Gospel to record Jesus's statement), Jesus said: "Destroy this temple, and in three days I will raise it up. Then said the Jews, Forty and six years was this temple in building, and wilt thou rear it up in three days? But he spake of the temple of his body."[42] Jesus was not stating that He would destroy the temple. It is unclear whether the witnesses simply misremembered Jesus's words or were intentionally misstating them. However, though two witnesses did refer to Jesus's statement, Mark's record indicates that "neither so did their witness agree together." Apparently, these witnesses' testimonies conflicted in some material regards, meaning that they could not be used to condemn Jesus.

38.   As qtd. in Edersheim, *Life and Times of Jesus the Messiah*, p. 856n11.
39.   See Matt. 26:60; Mark 14:56.
40.   Matt. 26:60.
41.   See Deut. 17:6.
42.   John 2:19–21.

Even if the testimonies had agreed, it would have been difficult if not impossible to construe a capital crime from these testimonies. It seems that Caiaphas' purpose was to manipulate the testimonies in order to demonstrate to Pilate[43] that Jesus was dangerous, for the Jewish leaders could claim that Jesus or those who followed Him might attempt to destroy the temple. Thus, they could accuse Jesus of sedition. Caiaphas and the others had seen how vicious Rome could be in putting to death those who were guilty of sedition.[44] However, just days before, Pilate may have either seen or heard of Jesus entering the city unarmed and riding on a donkey, and Pilate likely thought that Jesus was not a threat even though a multitude followed him, for they waved palm branches, not swords. According to Edersheim, a second charge that the Jewish leaders might have derived from these testimonies was that of "divine or magical pretensions" based on the claim that Jesus could rebuild the temple in three days.[45]

After the witnesses gave their testimonies, Caiaphas arose and asked Jesus, "Answerest thou nothing? what is it which these witness against thee?" Jesus remained silent. Caiaphas then asked Jesus a question that he presumably thought would trap Jesus no matter how He responded: "Art thou the Christ, the Son of the Blessed?" If Jesus told Caiaphas that He was the Son of God, the Sanhedrin would charge Him with blasphemy without investigating the accuracy of Jesus's claim. If Jesus said He was not, He would be discrediting Himself and would lose His influence among the general population. If Jesus remained silent, His refusal to answer may have been taken as a slight of the high priest.

Caiaphas's question was somewhat similar to the taunting statements that Satan had confronted Jesus with after He had fasted for forty days in the wilderness: "If thou be the Son of God . . ."[46] Now, Satan was tempting Jesus, through Caiaphas, with His own life, since if He confirmed that He was the Son of God, the Sanhedrin would condemn Him for blasphemy. Satan likely assumed that Jesus was emotionally and physically spent, having suffered the agony of the Atonement in Gethsemane, which caused Him to

---

43.   See note 6 at the end of this chapter for information about Pilate.
44.   See Edersheim, *Life and Times of Jesus the Messiah*, p. 860n25.
45.   Edersheim, *Life and Times of Jesus the Messiah*, p. 859.
46.   Matt. 4:3, 6; Luke 4:3, 9.

bleed from every pore. Now, Satan must have hoped that Jesus would falter. But He did not! Rather, in response to Caiaphas's question, Jesus confirmed that He was the Son of God.[47] Jesus fully comprehended the consequences of His answer and that they were necessary in order for Him to fulfill His role in Heavenly Father's plan.

Jesus then told those present that they would one day "see the Son of man sitting on the right hand of power, and coming in the clouds of heaven." Jesus was presumably referencing Daniel's prophecy concerning the Messiah, a prophecy that the members of the Sanhedrin would have likely been familiar with: "I saw in the night visions, and, behold, one like the Son of man came with the clouds of heaven, and came to the Ancient of days, and they brought him near before him. And there was given him dominion, and glory, and a kingdom, that all people, nations, and languages, should serve him: his dominion is an everlasting dominion, which shall not pass away, and his kingdom that which shall not be destroyed."[48]

Through Jesus's statement, He testified that one day in the future, those present would have a certain witness of His divinity. He might have also been indirectly warning them that at that day, they would have to account for their actions. Though they were currently acting as judges, on a future day Jesus would be their judge!

Upon hearing Jesus's declaration of His Messiahship, Caiaphas rent, or tore, his clothes.[49] The law of Moses prohibited the high priest from doing so,[50] but the rabbinical law that had developed over the years specified that "they that judge a blasphemer first ask the witness, and bid him speak out plainly what he hath heard; and then he speaks it, the judges, standing on their feet, rend their garments and do not sew them up again."[51] However, only Caiaphas rent his garments.

---

47.   See Matt. 26:64; Mark 14:62.

48.   Dan. 7:13–14.

49.   *The Jewish Encyclopedia* (s.v. "blasphemy") explains that rending clothes and not repairing them signifies a "profound degree of mourning."

50.   See Lev. 21:10.

51.   Dummelow, Bible Commentary, p. 714; see also Josephus, *Wars*, 2.15.2, 4; 1 Maccabees, 11:71; Tarbell, *Tarbell's Teacher's Guide to the International Sunday-School Lessons for 1912, 1914*, p. 392.

All had heard Jesus's declaration that He was the Messiah, so Caiaphas asked two questions to the members of the Sanhedrin who were present: "What need we any further witnesses? Ye have heard the blasphemy: what think ye?" All present then "condemned [Jesus] to be guilty of death." Of this condemnation, McConkie explained: "We do not say this was a sentence of death, for the Sanhedrin had no such power in that day. Rather, it was their heartfelt, devil-inspired pronouncement: 'He is worthy of death; he ought to die, according to our law, for he is a blasphemer.'"[52]

Some scholars have asserted that this death sentence was illegally and unjustly imposed for the following reasons, at a minimum: (1) a public interrogation was required to ensure that the accused did not inadvertently make incriminating statements, but Jesus was privately interrogated by Annas or Caiaphas; (2) all the council members present were biased against Jesus, as evidenced by their having previously sought His death and by their bringing in false witnesses; (3) the sentence was based on Jesus's confession only and not on corroborating testimonies, to protect against judicial homicide, among other things; (4) the council did not take any steps to determine whether Jesus's declaration was true; (5) the council did not invite anyone to speak on Jesus's behalf; (6) the vote was unanimous, meaning there were no defenders of Jesus and the judges may have conspired against Him; (7) votes were not taken in an orderly manner, as prescribed; and (8) Jewish law stipulated that a guilty verdict in a capital case could not be given on the same day as the trial, to ensure fairness.[53]

Jesus was not brought before the Sanhedrin because of a crime He had committed. The stated concern of Caiaphas, Annas, and Pharisees was that Jesus was disrupting the Jewish state's somewhat privileged religious status and limited political freedom under Roman rule and that if Jesus continued to amass followers, the Jewish nation's privileges would be at

---

52. McConkie, *Mortal Messiah*, vol. 4, p. 155.

53. For a detailed discussion of each of these points and others, see Chandler, *Trial of Jesus*, vol. 1, pp. 191–290; see also Dummelow, *Life of Christ*, p. 714; Pike, "Before the Jewish Authorities," in *Life and Teachings of Jesus Christ*, vol. 3, ed. Holzapfel and Wayment, pp. 253–258; Howick, *Life of Jesus the Messiah*, pp. 615–619; Talmage, *Jesus the Christ*, pp. 582, 598–601. Scholars disagree regarding whether all of the items listed here were considered illegal at the time. See also note 7 at the end of this chapter.

risk.[54] However, Caiaphas's real motives included pride, greed, the desire to stop Jesus from further disrupting commerce at the temple, and fear that his Roman-appointed position as high priest would be put in jeopardy if Jesus continued preaching and the number of His disciples increased.

Jesus Is Mocked (Matt. 26:67–68; Mark 14:65; Luke 22:63–65)

Perhaps during a brief adjournment in the trial proceedings, Jesus was hit, spit on, blindfolded, and taunted.[55] The following is Luke's account:

> **Luke 22:63–65.** And the men that held Jesus mocked him, and smote him. And when they had blindfolded him, they struck him on the face, and asked him, saying, Prophesy, who is it that smote thee? And many other things blasphemously spake they against him.

Other than Christ's imprisonment, scourging, and Crucifixion, it is difficult to conceive of greater injustice and humiliation than what these men inflicted on Him. Edersheim eloquently wrote, "These insults, taunts, and blows which fell upon that lonely Sufferer, not defenseless, but undefending, not vanquished, but uncontending, not helpless, but majestic in voluntary self-submission for the highest purpose of love—have not only exhibited the curse of humanity, but also removed it by letting it descend on Him, the Perfect Man, the Christ, the Son of God."[56] Although Christ could easily have retaliated, He did not. He presumably bore the abuse with dignity and humility. Forever after, all who are ridiculed for Christ's and the gospel's sake can gain courage and strength from Christ's example.

Unless those who hurled insults, taunts, and blows repent, they will one day be condemned for their behavior, for as the prophet Alma taught, "Our words will condemn us, yea, all our works will condemn us; we shall not be found spotless; . . . and in this awful state we shall not dare to look up to our God; and we would fain be glad if we could command the rocks and the mountains to fall upon us to hide us from his presence."[57]

---

54. See John 11:47–53.
55. See Matt. 26:67–68; Mark 14:65; Luke 22:63–65.
56. Edersheim, *Life of Jesus the Messiah*, p. 862.
57. Alma 12:14.

Peter and John Follow Jesus, and Peter Denies Three Times Knowing Jesus (Matt. 26:58, 69–75; Mark 14:54, 66–72; Luke 22:54–62; John 18:15–18, 25–27)

At some point after the Apostles fled from the garden of Gethsemane, Peter and another Apostle followed Jesus and the multitude back into the city and to Caiaphas's palace. While there, Peter three times denied knowing Jesus.[58] John's and Mark's accounts follow:

> **John 18:15–18.** And Simon Peter followed Jesus, and so did another disciple: that disciple was known unto the high priest, and went in with Jesus into the palace of the high priest. But Peter stood at the door without. Then went out that other disciple, which was known unto the high priest, and spake unto her that kept the door, and brought in Peter. Then saith the damsel that kept the door unto Peter, Art not thou also one of this man's disciples? He saith, I am not. And the servants and officers stood there, who had made a fire of coals; for it was cold: and they warmed themselves: and Peter stood with them, and warmed himself.

> **Mark 14:66–72.** And as Peter was beneath in the palace, there cometh one of the maids of the high priest: and when she saw Peter warming himself, she looked upon him, and said, And thou also wast with Jesus of Nazareth. But he denied, saying, I know not, neither understand I what thou sayest. And he went out into the porch; and the cock crew. And a maid saw him again, and began to say to them that stood by, This is one of them. And he denied it again. And a little after, they that stood by said again to Peter, Surely thou art one of them: for thou art a Galilean, and thy speech agreeth thereto. But he began to curse and to swear, saying, I know not this man of whom ye speak. And the second time the cock crew. And Peter called to mind the word that Jesus said unto him, Before the cock crow twice, thou shalt deny me thrice. And when he thought thereon, he wept.

In referring to "another disciple," John was presumably referring to himself; in his Gospel, he did not refer to himself by name but by terms such as "the disciple whom Jesus loved" and "the other disciple."[59] Caiaphas's

---

58. It is important to note that Peter did not deny that Jesus was the Messiah; rather, Peter denied that he knew Jesus and associated with Him.

59. See John 13:23; 19:26; 20:2; 21:7, 20; Bible Dictionary, s.v. "John"; Edersheim, *Life and Times of Jesus the Messiah*, pp. 853–854.

palace apparently included an inner court, and people waiting there had made a fire to keep warm. John asked the woman who stood by the door to allow Peter to enter into the inner courts. This woman permitted Peter to enter, and as she looked at him, she thought she recognized him as one of Jesus's disciples. She then said, "And thou also wast with Jesus of Nazareth." All four Gospel writers stated that she used the word *also*, implying that she was aware that John was also one of Jesus's disciples. Peter responded to the woman by saying, "I know not, neither understand I what thou sayest."

Peter then left the warmth of the fire and went "beneath in the palace"—perhaps to a porch that opened into the outer court[60]—and the "cock crew," which Peter undoubtedly heard. At some point afterward, another woman[61] saw Peter and said to those who were there, "This fellow was also with Jesus of Nazareth."[62] Peter then "denied with an oath"[63] that he knew Jesus.

A little while after Peter's second denial, he might have seen members of the Sanhedrin depart after the council meeting had ended, and he may have even faintly heard some of the insults and taunts of those who ridiculed Jesus. Then, a man who was a servant of Caiaphas and a relative of Malchus questioned Peter, "Did not I see thee in the garden with him?"[64] In response, Peter began "to curse and to swear, saying, I know not the man."[65] While Peter was speaking, the cock crew for the second time.

Apparently, at this time Jesus was led from Caiaphas's palace.[66] Luke's account states that "the Lord turned, and looked upon Peter."[67] Jesus's and Peter's eyes might have met, and Peter remembered that Jesus had told him, "Before the cock crow twice, thou shalt deny me thrice." Peter might have denied knowing Jesus for a variety of reasons. For example, when Jesus had told Peter he would deny Jesus three times before the cock crowed twice, He might have not only been giving a prophecy but also been giving

---

60.   See Edersheim, *Life and Times of Jesus the Messiah*, p. 855.
61.   Whereas Matthew 26:71 and Mark 14:69 indicate that the person was female, Luke 22:58 indicates that the person was male.
62.   Matt. 26:71.
63.   Matt. 26:72.
64.   John 18:26.
65.   Matt. 26:74; see also Mark 14:72.
66.   See Farrar, *Life of Christ*, p. 582.
67.   Luke 22:61.

Peter direction. Jesus had previously told Peter that he would receive the keys of the kingdom of heaven,[68] and he received those keys on the Mount of Transfiguration. Therefore, perhaps Peter denied knowing Jesus so that he would remain safe and therefore be able to oversee Jesus's Church, its members, and missionary work. More likely, Peter's denials of knowing Jesus resulted from personal weakness and the influence of Satan and his followers, who exploit people's weaknesses. Satan may even have influenced others to question Peter about knowing Jesus. Satan may have thought that if he caused Peter to fall, then Satan could stop the progression of the gospel, for even if another took Peter's place, the stain of Peter's fall might have caused others to falter too. Perhaps Peter did not tell the truth because he was afraid. In addition, he may have reasoned that there was no need to incriminate himself when Jesus had already given Himself up to be arrested and tried. Perhaps Peter thought that he need not respond honestly to someone who had neither the legal nor the moral right to ask for a confession.

Peter then "went out"—presumably meaning he left Caiaphas's palace—"and wept bitterly." Joseph Smith's translation of Mark 14:72 states that Peter "went out, and fell upon his face, and wept bitterly." He likely prayed from the depths of his heart for forgiveness. He may have also prayed for strength—strength to overcome his weaknesses and Satan's influence and to carry on and stand tall with the other Apostles—and to once again feel worthy to stand with confidence in the presence of the Lord.

Peter's denials of knowing Christ and Peter's bitter tears afterward can give all people hope, for through Christ's atoning sacrifice, Peter was forgiven. In fact, the resurrected Christ appeared to Peter before appearing to any of the other Apostles.[69] Likewise, all other people who repent will become clean through Christ's Atonement and will receive the blessing of being in Christ's presence.[70]

---

68. See Matt. 16:19.
69. See 1 Cor. 15:5.
70. See D&C 76:62, 69.

Jesus Is Perhaps Tried and Condemned Again by the Sanhedrin (Matt. 27:1; Mark 15:1; Luke 22:66–71)

Jesus may have been tried again by the Sanhedrin. The uncertainty regarding whether a second trial was held is the result of differences in the order of events in the accounts of Matthew, Mark, and Luke. (John's account does not mention Jesus being tried by the Sanhedrin.)

All three synoptic Gospels record that Jesus was hit, spit on, blindfolded, and taunted to prophesy. Matthew's and Mark's Gospels indicate that this event occurred after Jesus was tried.[71] Luke's Gospel indicates that this event occurred before Jesus was tried.[72] In addition, Matthew's and Mark's Gospels indicate that after Jesus was hit, spit on, blindfolded, and taunted, a morning meeting was held. Matthew's account states, "When the morning was come, all the chief priests and elders of the people took counsel to put him to death,"[73] and Mark's account states, "And straightway in the morning the chief priests held a consultation with the elders and scribes."[74] Similarly, Luke's trial account begins with "and as soon as it was day, the elders of the people and the chief priests and the scribes came together."[75] Taken together, these facts suggest that a second trial occurred after Jesus was hit, spit on, blindfolded, and taunted. Jesus presumably would not have been mocked in the manner Luke described until after an initial trial, and Luke presumably would not have erroneously ordered these events.

Regarding a second trial, Talmage wrote: "It is probable, that at this early daylight session, the irregular proceedings of the dark hours were approved, and the details of further procedure decided upon. They 'took counsel against Jesus to put him to death'; nevertheless, they went through the form of a second trial."[76] Farrar[77] and McConkie[78] likewise supported the perspective that two trials were held.

---

71. See Matt. 26:59–68; Mark 14:55–65.
72. See Luke 22:63–71.
73. Matt. 27:1.
74. Mark 15:1.
75. Luke 22:66.
76. Talmage, *Jesus the Christ*, p. 583.
77. See Farrar, *Life of Christ*, p. 582.
78. See McConkie, *Mortal Messiah*, vol. 4, pp. 155–166.

On the other hand, Matthew's and Mark's accounts do not mention Jesus being asked questions at the morning meeting and do not even clearly state that He was present. In addition, Luke's account of a trial contains details that are similar to the ones that Matthew and Mark included in recounting the trial that occurred before Jesus was hit, spit on, blindfolded, and taunted. Therefore, the three accounts might be about the same trial, not two separate trials; Luke simply might not have presented the chronology correctly, and the meeting that Matthew and Mark referred to as occurring in the morning might not have been a trial. According to Pike, "Mark's and Matthew's hints of morning proceedings represent the conclusion of the night hearing, and Luke's depiction of just a morning 'trial' is best seen as reflecting his literary arrangement of the data, not as a chronologically separate event."[79] Edersheim likewise believed that only one trial was held.[80]

Although the scriptural accounts are not clear as to whether two trials were held, all the accounts do agree regarding the central point: the Jewish leaders condemned Jesus to die, based on the charge of blasphemy—a charge that was not investigated and could not honestly be sustained against the Son of God.

Assuming there were two trials, the second one was likely held as a token effort to adhere to the requirement that in a capital case, two trials must be held.[81] The following is Luke's account:

> **Luke 22:66–71.** And as soon as it was day, the elders of the people and the chief priests and the scribes came together, and led him into their council, saying, Art thou the Christ? tell us. And he said unto them, If I tell you, ye will not believe: and if I also ask you, ye will not answer me, nor let me go. Hereafter shall the Son of man sit on the right hand of the power of God. Then said they all, Art thou then the Son of God? And he said unto them, Ye say that I am. And they said, What need we any further witness? for we ourselves have heard of his own mouth.

---

79. Pike, "Before the Jewish Authorities," in *Life and Teachings of Jesus Christ*, vol. 3, ed. Holzapfel and Wayment, pp. 225–226.

80. See Edersheim, *Life and Times of Jesus the Messiah*, p. 860.

81. Because of the press of time to take Jesus before Pilate early Friday morning, it seems reasonable to assume that if two trials were held, the second trial was of a somewhat short duration.

Presumably, this second trial was held in the temple's Chamber of Hewn Stone, which was the location where the Sanhedrin typically met.[82] The purposes of this trial were to determine (1) whether to confirm the decision made in the first trial that Jesus's crimes were worthy of death, and, if the decision was confirmed, (2) how to present the matter to Pilate since they did not have authority from the Roman government to take someone's life.

During the trial, one of the council members asked Jesus, "Art thou the Christ?" Jesus replied, "If I tell you, ye will not believe: and if I also ask you [whether I am Christ], ye will not answer me, nor let me go." Jesus was challenging the decision they had made without considering the merits of His defense, which was that He indeed was the Christ. Jesus also told them, "Hereafter shall the Son of man sit on the right hand of the power of God."

According to Luke's record, "then said they all, Art thou then the Son of God?" Jesus responded, "Ye say that I am." Then, as in the first trial, they declared: "What need we any further witness? for we ourselves have heard of his own mouth." The members of the Sanhedrin had again unanimously agreed that Jesus was guilty of blasphemy, again without finding corroborating witnesses and without investigating whether Jesus was truly the Son of God.

Judas Commits Suicide (Matt. 27:3–10)

Upon hearing that Jesus had been condemned to death, Judas began to feel remorse for betraying Jesus:

Matthew 27:3–10. Then Judas, which had betrayed him, when he saw that he was condemned, repented himself, and brought again the thirty pieces of silver to the chief priests and elders, saying, I have sinned in that I have betrayed the innocent blood. And they said, What is that to us? see thou to that. And he cast down the pieces of silver in the temple, and departed, and went and hanged himself. And the chief priests took the silver pieces, and said, It is not lawful for to put them into the treasury, because it is the price of blood. And they took counsel, and bought with them the potter's field, to bury strangers in. Wherefore that field was called, The field of blood, unto this day. Then was fulfilled that which was spoken by Jeremy the prophet, saying, And they took the thirty pieces of silver, the price of him that was

---

82. See Edersheim, *Life and Times of Jesus the Messiah*, p. 864; Farrar, *Life of Christ*, p. 582.

valued, whom they of the children of Israel did value; and gave them for the potter's field, as the Lord appointed me.

It is difficult to imagine the depth of the suffering that Judas experienced as he pondered his betrayal of Christ, which contributed to Him being arrested, tried, and ultimately crucified. Centuries earlier, Joshua had told the Israelites, "And if it seem evil unto you to serve the Lord, choose you this day whom ye will serve; whether the gods which your fathers served that were on the other side of the flood, or the gods of the Amorites, in whose land ye dwell: but as for me and my house, we will serve the Lord."[83] Judas had chosen whose side he was on, and his decision was the direct opposite of Joshua's.

Apparently feeling some remorse, Judas decided to return the "thirty pieces of silver, which, like thirty serpents, coiled round his soul with terrible hissing of death."[84] After approaching the chief priests and elders, he told them that he had sinned because he had "betrayed the innocent blood." Ironically, the person who had betrayed Christ was now bearing witness of Christ's innocence. Perhaps, Judas hoped that his confession would dissuade the chief priests and elders from attempting to cause Christ's death.[85]

That testimony, however, meant nothing to the chief priests and elders. They had accomplished their purpose by trying Jesus and finding Him guilty of blasphemy for claiming to be the Son of God. Therefore, in response to Judas's confession, they stated: "What is that to us? See thou to that." Joseph Smith's translation of Matthew 27 adds to what they said to Judas: "Thy sins be upon thee."[86] Although Judas had conspired with the chief priests and elders, they wanted nothing to do with him. Their reference to Judas's sins implies they recognized that Judas had sinned; if Judas had sinned, so had they. Judas then threw down the thirty pieces of silver and left the temple.

Judas then went outside the city walls and found a vacant potter's field where the Hinnom and Kidron Valleys merge,[87] and hanged himself on a

---

83. Josh. 24:15.
84. Edersheim, *Life and Times of Jesus the Messiah*, p. 870.
85. See Talmage, *Jesus the Christ*, p. 595.
86. JST Matt. 27:4.
87. *HarperCollins Bible Dictionary*, s.v. "potter's field."

tree.[88] Joseph Smith's translation of Matthew 27:6 states, "And straightway he fell down, and his bowels gushed out, and he died." Acts 1:18 similarly states, "Now this man . . . falling headlong, he burst asunder in the midst, and all his bowels gushed out."

Meanwhile, the chief priests had gathered the thirty pieces of silver that Judas had dropped in the temple, and they discussed what to do with the money. They concluded that they could not put it in the general temple treasury because it had been given to Judas as "the price of blood"—that is, to pay for his betrayal of Jesus—and was therefore unclean. After hearing that Judas had hanged himself, the high priests used the thirty pieces of silver to buy "the potter's field"[89] and used it as a place to bury strangers.[90] A potter's field in Jesus's time may have been a field where clay was dug for pottery or perhaps a field in which to discard broken pottery that could not be repaired.[91] Given the latter meaning of a potter's field, it was there that Judas's body was broken and discarded.

This book does not attempt to judge Judas or discuss possibilities regarding his ultimate fate.[92] Instead, it is valuable to point out two simple yet profoundly important principles evident in Judas's life and tragic fall that all

---

88. See JST Matt. 27:6. Perhaps he fell because he hanged himself on a branch and it broke or because the cord around his neck broke or the knot he had tied came undone. Edersheim posited that Judas committed suicide between Pilate's first interrogation of Christ and Christ's appearance before Herod (see Edersheim, *Life and Times of Jesus the Messiah*, pp. 869–871).

89. Acts 1:18 indicates that Judas purchased the field: "Now this man purchased a field with the reward of iniquity." Edersheim explained this seeming discrepancy regarding who purchased the potter's field: "It was not lawful to take into the Temple-treasury, for the purchase of sacred things, money that had been unlawfully gained. In such cases the Jewish Law provided that the money was to be restored to the donor, and, if he insisted on giving it, that he should be induced to spend it for something for the public weal. This explains the apparent discrepancy between the accounts in the Book of Acts and by St. Matthew. By a fiction of law the money was still considered to be Judas', and to have been applied by him in the purchase of the well-known 'potter's field,' for the charitable purpose of burying in it strangers. (Edersheim, *Life and Times of Jesus the Messiah*, p. 871; see also Talmage, *Jesus the Christ*, p. 603n8.)

90. The word *strangers* in Matthew 27:7 presumably refers to foreigners or Gentiles (see *HarperCollins Bible Dictionary*, s.v. "stranger" and "alien").

91. See Jer. 19:11.

92. For an excellent, more detailed discussion of Judas's possible fate, see Talmage, *Jesus the Christ*, pp. 602–604.

people need to understand and always remember. The first principle is that all people are vulnerable to sin, no matter who they are, what positions they hold or have held, and what spiritual experiences they have had. The second principle is that Satan never will support those who choose to follow him.

Good Will Triumph over Evil

The events covered in this chapter demonstrate that there is evil in the world and that evil often occurs in the darkness of night. It is evident from the illegal trials of Jesus that Satan has the power to plant evil in people's hearts, including those with political and ecclesiastical authority. Satan wanted to stop Jesus from completing His earthly mission, but Satan did not know the mind and will of God and that Crucifixion was part of God's plan and would bless all humankind.

Notes to Chapter 65

1. Pilate's consent to send Roman soldiers to assist in arresting Jesus. It is unlikely that the commander of the Roman soldiers would have sent them to accompany Judas without the consent of Pilate, the Roman governor over Judea. Discussing the request with Pilate and then assembling the Roman soldiers likely took several hours. If Pilate did discuss the request with the commander or someone else that night, the discussion may have been the reason that Pilate was ready to sit in judgment of Jesus early the next morning. The discussion may have also been the cause of the dream that Pilate's wife had that night concerning Jesus.[93]

Regarding the Roman soldiers, Edersheim posited the following: "The band was led not by a Centurion, but by a Chiliarch (John 18:12), which, as there were no intermediate grades in the Roman army, must represent one of the six tribunes attached to each legion."[94]

---

93.   See Matt. 27:19; Edersheim, *Life and Times of Jesus the Messiah*, p. 848.
94.   Edersheim, *Life and Times of Jesus the Messiah*, p. 848.

2. Animosity of the chief priest, Pharisees, scribes, and elders. By the time Judas betrayed Jesus, the animosity of the chief priest, Pharisees, scribes, and elders had reached its apex. Many of Jesus's teachings and actions had caused this animosity. For example, on two occasions He had cleansed the temple of money changers, humiliating these Jewish leaders and interrupting their lucrative temple commerce. Jesus had also publicly castigated these Jewish leaders on several occasions, including in the temple courts. In addition, these Jewish leaders were jealous of Jesus's widespread fame and the number of disciples He had attracted through His teaching and His many miracles, which included healing people on the Sabbath and restoring life to the dead. Further, Jesus had declared that He was the Son of God and provided the way to receive eternal life. The Jewish leaders were filled with hatred toward Jesus and therefore conspired to cause His death.

3. Annas. Annas was the son of Seth and was appointed as the high priest by the Roman governor Quirinius (Cyrenius) in AD 6; Annas was removed from his position in AD 15 by Roman governor Valerius Gratus. Annas and his family were influential and gained much of their wealth from the temple. Annas had five sons who became high priests, as did his son-in-law Caiaphas. Though Annas was removed from office before Christ's ministry began, he is referred to as the high priest in Luke 3:2 and Acts 4:6, likely because he continued to have a significant influence among the Jews.[95]

4. Caiaphas. Joseph Caiaphas was the son-in-law of Annas. Caiaphas was appointed as the high priest in AD 18 by the Roman governor Valerius Gratus and was deposed in AD 36–37 by the Roman governor Vitellius. Caiaphas was the high priest at the time the trials were held to convict Jesus.[96] According to John 11:50, Caiaphas said of Jesus that it would be "expedient for us, that one man should die for the people, and that the whole nation perish not." This statement was an ironic prophecy, for the high priest did not understand that Jesus's death would be for the Jewish nation, and well as for people in all other nations of the world.[97]

95.　See *HarperCollins Bible Dictionary*, s.v. "Annas."
96.　See Matt. 26:3, 57; John 18:13, 24.
97.　See John 11:51–52; *HarperCollins Bible Dictionary*, s.v. "Caiaphas."

5. Jewish judicial tribunals. Edersheim stated the following regarding Jewish judicial tribunals:

> The highest tribunal was that of seventy-one, or the Great Sanhedrin, which met first in one of the Temple-Chambers, the so-called *Lishkath haGazith*— or Chamber of Hewn Stones—and at the time of which we write in "the booths of the sons of Annas." The Judges of all these Courts were equally set apart by ordination (Semikkah), originally that of laying on of hands. Ordination was conferred by *three*, of whom one at least must have been himself ordained, and able to trace up his ordination through Joshua to Moses. . . . The appointment to the highest tribunal, or Great Sanhedrin, was made by that tribunal itself, either by promoting a member of the inferior tribunals or one from the foremost of the three rows, in which "the disciples" or student sat facing the Judges. The latter sat in a semicircle, under the presidency of the *Nasi* ("prince") and the vice-presidency of the *Ab-beth-din* ("father of the Court of Law"). At least twenty-three members were required to form a *quorum*. . . . Facing the semicircle of Judges, we are told, there were two shorthand writers, to note down, respectively, the speeches in favour and against the accused. Each of the students knew and sat in his own place. In capital causes the arguments in defense of and afterwards those incriminating the accused, were stated. If one had spoken in favour, he might not again speak against the panel. Students might speak for, not against him. He might be pronounced "not guilty" on the same day on which the case was tried; but a sentence of "guilty" might only be pronounced on the day following that of the trial. It seems, however, at least doubtful, whether in case of profanation of the Divine Name (*Chillul haShem*) was not immediately executed. Lastly, the voting began with the youngest, so that juniors might not be influenced by the seniors; and a bare majority was not sufficient for condemnation.[98]

The Jewish Encyclopedia notes, "The Sanhedrin sat in a semicircle, so that all the members might see one another, while the clerks recorded the reasons which the judges gave either for acquittal or for condemnation (§ 3); three rows of scholars versed in the Law sat in front of the Sanhedrin, one or more of them being called upon at need to fill the bench, in case a quorum

---

98. Edersheim, *Life and Times of Jesus the Messiah*, pp. 856–857.

of judges was not present (§ 4); address to the witnesses in criminal cases, reminding them of the value of a human life."[99]

Since there were no prosecuting or defense attorneys, witnesses brought the charges. Regarding witnesses, Chandler wrote: "Under Hebrew law, both Mosaic and Talmudic, at least two witnesses were required to convict an accused person. The prosecuting witness being included, three were necessary. . . . The witnesses were required to agree in all essential details; else, their testimony was invalid and had to be rejected. The Talmudic provision is: 'If one witness contradicts another, the testimony is not accepted.'"[100]

Chandler also wrote, "The judges were his [the prisoner's] defenders. Now if the verdict was unanimous in favor of condemnation it was evident that the prisoner had had no friend or defender in court. To the Jewish mind this was almost equivalent to mob violence. It argued conspiracy, at least. The element of mercy, which was required to enter into every Hebrew verdict, was absent in such a case. . . . But how did they convict under Hebrew law? By a majority vote of at least two. A majority of one would acquit. A majority of two, or any majority less than unanimity, would convict."[101]

6. Pontius Pilate. Pontius Pilate was the fifth governor of Judea. His term included the years of Jesus's public ministry.[102] Pilate interrogated Jesus about the accusation that He claimed to be the king of the Jews[103] and marveled greatly at Jesus's silence in response to the charges brought against Him.[104] The Gospels present Pilate as somewhat weak when confronted by Jewish leaders and cavalier about administering justice. Pilate knew that the Jewish leaders wanted to kill Jesus because they were jealous of Him.[105] Nevertheless, Pilate capitulated to the will of the people by setting Barabbas free and sending Jesus to be crucified, hoping thereby to satisfy the Jews and prevent a riot.[106] Later, Pilate allowed

99. *Jewish Encyclopedia*, s.v. "Sanhedrin."
100. Chandler, *Trial of Jesus*, vol. 1, pp. 126, 128.
101. Chandler, *Trial of Jesus*, vol. 1, p. 235.
102. See *HarperCollins Bible Dictionary*, s.v. "Pilate, Pontius."
103. See Matt. 27:11; Mark 15:2; Luke 23:3.
104. See Matt. 27:14; Mark 15:5.
105. See Matt. 27:18.
106. See Matt 27:24; Mark 15:14–15; Luke 23:23–24.

Joseph of Arimathea to bury Jesus in Joseph's tomb.[107] At Jewish leaders' request, Pilate permitted a guard to be placed at the tomb.[108]

7. Illegalities of the Jewish trials. Pike wrote the following regarding the illegalities of the Jewish trials:

> Many commentators have claimed that Jesus' "trial" by the Jewish authorities was illegal. For example, James E. Talmage wrote that it was 'truly irregular and illegal, according to Hebrew law.' Elder Talmage[109] relied upon and quoted extensively from earlier non–Latter day Saint authors on this point, especially Alfred Edersheim[110] and Walter Chandler.[111] Decades later, Bruce R. McConkie[112] essentially quoted Talmage in his *Doctrinal New Testament Commentary* when dealing with Jesus' trial. More recent authors have also followed this line of thinking. Although upwards of two dozen infractions of Jewish law in Jesus' trial have been proposed, most commentators have highlighted five to twelve such infractions. . . . Even though a firm determination of all the historical points of this episode is not presently possible, several main points can be summarized: (1) the Gospel authors are united in depicting the Jewish authorities' predetermination to kill Jesus and their arraignment of Jesus prior to delivering Him to Pilate; (2) the focus of the Gospel accounts is on the Jewish leaders' rejection of Jesus, the Messiah, not the legalities of the procedures involved; (3) the Jewish authorities' charge against Jesus was primarily a religious one, emphasizing blasphemy for claiming an exalted relationship with God and prerogatives that only God could grant, and it was further buttressed by concerns or fears about the temple, false prophecy, and Jesus' power over evil spirits and death; (4) their charge against Jesus had a powerful political dimension because of the nature of their messianic conception and the seemingly subversive character of some of Jesus' actions, which allowed them to take Jesus to Pilate for execution; (5) although we are fairly ignorant of Jewish legal practices in Jesus' day, Mark and Matthew indicate that the Jewish authorities were collectively willing to violate their own scripture-based norms to eliminate

---

107. See Matt. 27:58; Mark 15:43–44; Luke 23:51–52.
108. See Matt. 27:62–65.
109. See Talmage, *Jesus the Christ*, pp. 598–601.
110. See Edersheim, *Life and Times of Jesus the Messiah*, pp. 853–861.
111. See Chandler, *Trial of Jesus*, vol. 1, pp. 191–291.
112. See McConkie, *Doctrinal New Testament Commentary*, vol.1. pp. 788–791.

Jesus; (6) Jesus' appearance before Jewish authorities was not a formal trial but an arraignment or hearing; (7) the Mishnah does not provide a valid means of evaluating the legality of Jesus' experience; and (8) the Jewish leaders required Roman authorization and, especially in Jesus' case, had good reason to seek Roman participation in executing Jesus.[113]

---

113. Pike, "Before the Jewish Authorities," in *Life and Teachings of Jesus Christ*, vol. 3, ed. Holzapfel and Wayment, pp. 253, 265–266.

Chapter 66

THE ROMAN TRIALS OF JESUS

(Friday Morning)

This chapter focuses on the events that occurred when Jesus was brought before Pontius Pilate and Herod Antipas to be tried for the crimes that the Jewish leaders accused Jesus of.[1] To understand why Jesus was brought before Roman authorities, it may be helpful to review Rome's governing of the nations and states it had conquered. In these nations and states, Roman law included aspects of the local law that the Roman government saw fit to allow, thereby granting conquered nations a great degree of freedom as long as the local laws were consistent with Roman sovereignty.[2] The question of sovereignty arose whenever the issue of life and death arose; therefore, Rome reserved to itself the final decision of whether to impose the death penalty. Therefore, the Sanhedrin could arrest and try Jesus on the charge of blasphemy because it was a religious offense. The Sanhedrin could also rule that Jesus's crime was worthy of death, but Jesus had to be retried

---

1.   See Chandler, *Trial of Jesus*, vol. 2, p. 29.

2.   During most of Jesus's life and at the time of His death, Tiberius Claudius Caesar Augustus was the emperor of Rome (see *HarperCollins Bible Dictionary*, s.v. "Tiberius"). During this time, the Roman emperor had nearly absolute power. The emperor was the "perpetual Princeps Senatus, or leader of the legislative house and also Pontifex Maximus, or chief of the national religion. He was also the principal Tribune, or guardian of the people, principal Consul, or supreme magistrate over the whole Roman world, with the control of its revenues, the disposal of its armies, and the execution of its laws. And lastly, he was Imperator, or military chief. His empire at the time extended from Gibraltar to the Indus and the Baltic. Whatever Tiberius might have done, Pilate might have done in the provinces he governed." Thus, Pilate had the authority of Rome when Jesus was brought before him early Friday morning. (See Chandler, *Trial of Jesus: The Roman Trial*, vol. 2, p. 34; see also Huntsman, "Before the Romans," in *Life and Teachings of Jesus Christ*, vol. 3, ed. Holzapfel and Wayment, pp. 274–280.)

by Roman authority or the Sanhedrin's proceedings had to be reviewed by Roman authority before the sentence could be carried out.[3] Thus, Jesus was tried before Pilate and Herod.

Though the Jewish leaders surely did not like this requirement, they likely saw some benefits of it when it came to Jesus. If Jesus were crucified by Roman decree, His supporters would be unlikely to rebel, for fear of Roman reprisal. Further, the Sanhedrin may have thought that Jesus's followers would be less likely to blame the Jewish leaders for Jesus's death if it was conducted by Romans rather than by the Jewish leaders. Moreover, the Sanhedrin presumably wanted Jesus to be crucified so that those who believed in Him would see that He could not save Himself and so that they would consequently lose their faith in Him.

As with other events recorded in the Gospels, the Gospel accounts of the events discussed in this chapter are fragmentary and vary somewhat. Therefore, the exact chronology of events and the details of those events are uncertain. The order and details of the events as presented in this chapter are based on careful analysis of the Gospels, various commentaries, and the resulting assumptions regarding the chronology and details of events.[4]

Jewish Leaders Take Jesus to Pilate (Matt. 27:1–2; Mark 15:1; Luke 23:1–2; John 18:28–32)

Early Friday morning, members of the Sanhedrin led Jesus, possibly with His hands bound and a rope tied around His neck,[5] to Pilate's "hall of

---

3.   See Chandler, *Trial of Jesus*, vol. 2, p. 29; Huntsman, "Before the Romans," in *Life and Teachings of Jesus Christ*, vol. 3, ed. Holzapfel and Wayment, pp. 288–289. As Huntsman pointed out, there were some exceptions when it came to religious matters, as indicated by the fact that Jews would have stoned an adulterous woman if Jesus had not intervened (see John 8:2–9) and Jews stoned Stephen (see Acts 7:54–60) and James, the brother of Jesus (see Josephus, *Antiquities*, 20.9.1; *HarperCollins Bible Dictionary*, s.v. "James").

4.   It is assumed that the Apostles were not present during these events and that Jesus recounted these events to the Apostles after His Resurrection. Some people who were present may also have contributed facts regarding the Roman trials of Jesus.

5.   See Matt. 27:2; Mark 15:1; see also Farrar, *Life of Christ*, p. 592.

judgment"[6] so that the Sanhedrin's sentence of death could be authorized
and carried out by Rome.[7]

The following are John's and Luke's accounts:

Luke 23:1–2. And the whole multitude of them arose, and led him unto
Pilate. And they began to accuse him, saying, We found this fellow perverting
the nation, and forbidding to give tribute to Caesar, saying that he himself
is Christ a King.

John 18:28–32. Then led they Jesus from Caiaphas unto the hall of judgment:
and it was early; and they themselves went not into the judgment hall, lest
they should be defiled; but that they might eat the passover. Pilate then went
out unto them, and said, What accusation bring ye against this man? They
answered and said unto him, If he were not a malefactor, we would not
have delivered him up unto thee. Then said Pilate unto them, Take ye him,
and judge him according to your law. The Jews therefore said unto him, It is
not lawful for us to put any man to death: that the saying of Jesus might be
fulfilled, which he spake, signifying what death he should die.

At the time of Jesus's arrest, Pilate[8] and his wife[9] were likely residing
in Herod's palace located in the northwestern corner of Jerusalem.[10] Pilate
was in many ways a merciless and insensitive man who disliked the Jews. For
example, when Pilate first sent Roman troops into Jerusalem from Caesarea,

---

6.   John 18:28. The hall of judgment was apparently a location in Herod's palace.

7.   Since Jesus was crucified at about nine o'clock on Friday morning, the Jewish
leaders likely brought Jesus to Pilate by seven o'clock (see Edersheim, *Life and Times of Jesus
the Messiah*, p. 866; Farrar, *Life of Christ*, p. 592). The Jewish leaders likely picked the early
hour because the Roman trial would need to conclude in time for Jesus to be crucified before
sundown, when the Sabbath began. Pilate had likely been informed ahead of time that Jesus
would be brought to him early that morning (see Huntsman, "Before the Romans," in *Life and
Teachings of Jesus Christ*, vol. 3, ed. Holzapfel and Wayment, p. 291).

8.   Pilate was the fifth Roman prefect, or governor, of Judea (see *HarperCollins Bible
Dictionary*, s.v. "Pilate"; Huntsman, "Before the Romans," in *Life and Teachings of Jesus Christ*,
vol. 3, ed. Holzapfel and Wayment, pp. 276, 280). Talmage wrote, "Pilate maintained his
official residence at Caesarea, on the Mediterranean shore; but it was his custom to be present
in Jerusalem at the times of the great Hebrew feasts, probably in the interest of preserving
order, or of promptly quelling any disturbance amongst the vast and heterogeneous multitudes
by which the city was thronged on these festive occasions" (Talmage, *Jesus the Christ*, p. 586).

9.   Though Pilate's wife is not mentioned by name in the Gospels, tradition indicates
that her name was Procla or Procula (see *HarperCollins Bible Dictionary*, s.v. "Pilate"; Farrar,
Life of Christ, p. 598).

10.   See Edersheim, *Life and Times of Jesus the Messiah*, p. 864.

332 AND THE SON OF GOD

they brought with them military ensigns of the emperor, and the Jews considered these ensigns idolatrous. Jewish leaders petitioned Pilate several times to remove the ensigns, but he would not. When Jews further petitioned Pilate to remove the ensigns, he ordered his troops to kill the Jews.[11] As another example, Pilate likely ordered certain Galileans to be slaughtered during a feast at Jerusalem.[12] Further, Pilate used temple funds to begin building an aqueduct to bring water into Jerusalem. In response, the Jews engaged in a massive protest. To quell the protest, Pilate directed some of his soldiers to dress in Jewish clothes and join the rebelling multitude. After a signal was given, the soldiers killed many Jews and injured others.[13] This man was the official who would judge Jesus on behalf of Rome and would give the command to have Him crucified.

Outside of the palace was an open area called the Pavement. This area contained Pilate's judgment seat,[14] where he conversed with the Jews and rendered judgment on matters brought before him. John's account suggests that Jesus was kept in the judgment hall while Pilate sat in his judgment seat and spoke with the Jewish leaders concerning Jesus. Ironically, the Jewish leaders were concerned about being defiled during the Passover by entering a heathen's judgment hall, where leaven might have been present,[15] rather than about violating Jewish law by finding people to bear false witness against Jesus and by illegally condemning Jesus to death. There is no scriptural mention of Annas or Caiaphas being among the Jewish leaders who met with Pilate, but either or both of them may have been there.

A Roman trial typically proceeded based on a definite accusation, followed by supporting witnesses and evidence.[16] Therefore, Pilate began by asking the Jewish leaders what they were accusing Jesus of. Pilate's question may have taken the Jewish leaders by surprise—they might have assumed that since he had dispatched Roman guards the night before to facilitate

11. See Josephus, *Antiquities*, 18.3.1.

12. See Luke 13:1–2; Huntsman, "Before the Romans," in *Life and Teachings of Jesus Christ*, vol. 3, ed. Holzapfel and Wayment, p. 282.

13. See Josephus, *Antiquities*, 18.3.2.

14. See Chandler, *Trial of Jesus*, vol. 2, p. 95.

15. See Edersheim, *Life and Times of Jesus the Messiah*, pp. 865–866. John's account suggests that these Jewish leaders had not eaten the Passover meal on Thursday night, as had Jesus.

16. See Edersheim, *Life and Times of Jesus the Messiah*, p. 866.

Jesus's arrest, Pilate would not question the Sanhedrin's decision that Jesus was worthy of death.

In answering, the Jewish leaders did not state a charge but instead said, "If he were not a malefactor, we would not have delivered him up unto thee." In essence, they were asking Pilate to accept their decision without completing a retrial or further inquiry and to proceed with the sentence of death. However, Pilate knew that these leaders had brought Jesus to him because they were jealous of and feared Jesus.[17] Because they did not present a charge, Pilate told them that they should take Jesus and proceed with a less-severe sentence. Perhaps Pilate gave this instruction in part because he wanted to wound the pride of these Jews by forcing them to acknowledge Rome's sovereignty over them and their nation.[18] They did just that when they replied, "It is not lawful for us to put any man to death."

The Gospel of John adds the following after presenting the Jewish leaders' reply: "That the saying of Jesus might be fulfilled, which he spake, signifying what death he should die."[19] Jesus had repeatedly taught not only of His death but also of the manner in which He would die.[20] Crucifixion was a form of death that the Roman government used but did not let the Jews use. Had Pilate allowed the Jews to carry out the death sentence themselves, they would have stoned Jesus because Jewish law specified that stoning was how blasphemers were to be killed.[21]

Seeing that Pilate was unlikely to allow Jesus to be crucified unless the Jewish leaders presented a definitive charge against Him, they then presented three false charges against Jesus: (1) He "pervert[ed] the nation," (2) He forbade people from paying "tribute to Caesar," and (3) He said "that He Himself is Christ a King." They did not present the charge of blasphemy, which they had wrongfully convicted Jesus of during the Jewish trials, for blasphemy was not a crime that the Roman government considered worthy of death.

---

17. See Matt. 27:18; Mark 15:10.
18. See Chandler, *Trial of Jesus*, vol. 2, p. 98.
19. John 18:32.
20. See note 1 at the end of this chapter for examples of Jesus's prophecies of His death.
21. See Lev. 24:14, 16, 23.

Regarding the first charge—that Jesus had perverted the nation—during the Jewish trials of Jesus, the Sanhedrin had not found Him guilty of perverting their nation. It is unclear what the Jewish leaders meant specifically in terms of Jesus perverting the nation. The charge may have stemmed from the Jewish leaders' fear that Jesus's miracles would draw many people to Him and away from the Jewish leaders and thus potentially alter Israel's position with Rome.[22] However, performing miracles and teaching others were not crimes under either Jewish or Roman law. Alternatively, the Jewish leaders may have been referring to Jesus stating that if the temple was destroyed, He could rebuild it in three days. Regarding Jesus's statement that He could rebuild the temple, the false witnesses in the Jewish trials did not agree on essential facts; therefore, these testimonies were dismissed. The Jewish leaders' charge that Jesus had perverted their nation was obliquely related to sedition, and the Jewish leaders apparently assumed that Pilate would not ignore the charge since sedition is a form of treason.[23]

The second charge—that Jesus forbade people from giving tribute to Caesar—was likely a reference to what Jesus had said earlier in His ministry when Pharisees had sent people to ask Him whether it was "lawful to give tribute unto Caesar." He had responded, "Render therefore unto Caesar the things which are Caesar's; and unto God the things that are God's."[24] The Gospel records of the Jewish trials do not mention testimonies or evidence regarding this charge or that the Sanhedrin found Jesus guilty of this charge. The Jewish leaders presented this charge to Pilate because forbidding to pay Roman tribute or taxes was a form of treason and because it constituted defiance of Roman law and denial of Roman sovereignty. The Jewish leaders presumably thought that any answer Jesus gave to this charge would condemn Him: If Jesus admitted paying tribute to Caesar, then Jesus's disciples might stop following Him because they hated paying tribute to Caesar. If He denied that tribute should be paid, He would be admitting He was an enemy of Rome.

Regarding the third charge—that Christ claimed to be a king—the Jewish leaders were presumably implying that Christ claimed to be a king in a

---

22. See John 11:47–50.
23. See Chandler, *Trial of Jesus*, vol. 2, p. 101.
24. Matt. 22:17, 21; see also Luke 20:22, 25.

political sense, and this claim was considered high treason under Roman law and could not be ignored by Pilate, particularly since the Roman government considered Palestine to be a hotbed of sedition and insurrection. Of course, in reality Christ had never sought any political station, let alone that of king. In fact, after He had fed a multitude of five thousand, He had retreated to a mountain because a group a men who had seen the miracle wanted to take Him and make Him a king.[25]

The Jewish leaders who presented the charges to Pilate had violated the ninth commandment: "Thou shalt not bear false witness against thy neighbour."[26] The penalty that God had established for bearing false witness is found in Deuteronomy: "If a false witness rise up against any man to testify against him that which is wrong; then both the men, between whom the controversy is, shall stand before the Lord, before the priests and the judges, which shall be in those days; and the judges shall make diligent inquisition: and, behold, if the witness be a false witness, and hath testified falsely against his brother; then shall ye do unto him, as he had thought to have done unto his brother: so shalt thou put the evil away from among you."[27]

Jesus Is Interrogated by Pilate (Matt. 27:11–14; Mark 15:2–5; Luke 23:3–7; John 18:33–38)

Pilate then likely arose from his judgment seat, left Jesus's accusers, and went to the judgment hall to interrogate Jesus regarding the charges levied against Him. The following is John's record:

John 18:33–38. Then Pilate entered into the judgment hall again, and called Jesus, and said unto him, Art thou the King of the Jews? Jesus answered him, Sayest thou this thing of thyself, or did others tell it thee of me? Pilate answered, Am I a Jew? Thine own nation and the chief priests have delivered thee unto me: what hast thou done? Jesus answered, My kingdom is not of this world: if my kingdom were of this world, then would my servants fight, that I should not be delivered to the Jews: but now is my kingdom not from hence. Pilate therefore said unto him, Art thou a king then? Jesus answered,

---

25. See John 6:10–15.
26. Ex. 20:16; see also Ex. 23:1; Deut. 5:20.
27. Deut. 19:16–19.

Thou sayest that I am a king. To this end was I born, and for this cause came I into the world, that I should bear witness unto the truth. Every one that is of the truth heareth my voice. Pilate saith unto him, What is truth? And when he had said this, he went out again unto the Jews, and saith unto them, I find in him no fault at all.

To be appointed as Judea's governor, Pilate likely had to be an intelligent man with some education and political connections. He surely had knowledge of Roman law and Roman gods. He may also have known somewhat of the Greeks and their gods and philosophies. He certainly was aware of the Jews and their religion and political power. He was also the loyal deputy of the Roman emperor Tiberius Caesar Augustus and was charged with carefully watching for acts of treason. Presumably, Pilate knew that Jesus had not committed treason and was not a threat to Rome. Pilate was likely aware that Jesus had cleansed the temple of greed and corruption. Pilate likely knew of the avarice of Caiaphas, his family, and those in charge of the temple, and Pilate may have even approved of Jesus cleansing the temple, because Pilate presumably recognized that corruption could lead to rebellion. It is hard to imagine that Pilate was not aware that Jesus had taught in the temple, that a multitude had followed Him to hear Him teach, and that no violence or threats to Rome had occurred. Pilate may also have been aware that Jesus castigated the scribes, Pharisees, and chief priests and that He did so without violence.

In speaking with Jesus, Pilate apparently brushed aside the first two charges brought against Jesus and focused on the third: that Jesus claimed to be a king. In focusing on this charge, Pilate asked Jesus whether He was "the King of the Jews." Jesus responded by stating, "Sayest thou this thing of thyself, or did others tell it thee of me?" Jesus may have wanted Pilate to indicate whether he was asking if Jesus claimed to be a king in a political sense, meaning He was a threat to Rome, or if He claimed to be a king in a spiritual sense, meaning that Jesus's punishment would be left up to the Jewish leaders. Jesus may also have wanted Pilate to state whether he wondered of his own accord or whether the claim had come from the untrustworthy and prideful members of the Sanhedrin—that is, Jesus may have wanted Pilate to recognize that he was not a firsthand witness of Jesus claiming that He was a king.

Pilate answered, "Am I a Jew? Thine own nation and the chief priests have delivered thee unto me: what hast thou done?" By referring to Jesus's nation, Pilate made it clear that he was referring to Jesus being a king in a political sense, not in a religious sense. Pilate also made it clear that the accusations came from the chief priests, not from him.

Jesus responded that His kingdom was not of this world. In other words, He was not a political king and was not a threat to Rome. As evidence, Jesus then stated that if His kingdom were political, His servants would have prevented the Jewish leaders from taking Him. By this time, Pilate had likely obtained a report from his soldiers that Jesus had not resisted arrest, that He had told Peter to put away his sword, and that He had healed Malchus's ear. If Pilate had heard of Jesus's restoring Malchus's ear and perhaps even restoring life to Lazarus, Pilate may have deeply wondered about the man who stood before Pilate.

Then, for the second time, Pilate asked Jesus whether He was a king. This time, Jesus responded with a more spiritual answer: "Thou sayest that I am a king." Joseph Smith's translations of the accounts of this event in Matthew, Mark, and Luke make clear that Jesus directly stated He was a king. Joseph Smith revised the wording in Matthew to "thou sayest truly; for thus it is written of me,"[28] in Mark to "I am, even as thou sayest,"[29] and in Luke to "yea, thou sayest it."[30] It must have been clear to Pilate that Jesus did not claim to rule a political kingdom.

After Jesus stated that He was a king, He told Pilate that He came into the world to "bear witness unto the truth. Every one that is of the truth heareth my voice." Even as Jesus stood bound before Pilate, He may have been reaching out to the spirit in Pilate to allow His words to be spiritually heard and understood, if possible.[31] Presumably, Pilate understood that Jesus was referring to spiritual truth and was stating that He was a spiritual king. Clearly, the man who stood before Pilate was no rebel and no criminal.

---

28.   JST Matt. 27:11.

29.   JST Mark 15:2.

30.   JST Luke 23:3.

31.   See Edersheim, *Life and Times of Jesus the Messiah*, p. 867. Jesus had taught similar principles during the Feast of Dedication: "My sheep hear my voice, and I know them, and they follow me: and I give unto them eternal life" (John 10:27–28).

Farrar opined that Pilate's "judicial mind and familiarity with human nature told him that Jesus was not only wholly innocent, but infinitely nobler than his raving, sanctimonious accusers."[32] Nevertheless, Pilate did not spiritually understand Jesus's words about who He was and what His purpose was. Therefore, in response to Jesus's statement, Pilate asked, likely rhetorically, "What is truth?"

The truth that Pilate knew about was that the Roman government had an iron hand and that he was in a position of power. He knew about the existence of water, the sky, the sun, the moon, and the stars. He knew that he regularly became hungry and sometimes became ill. He knew of death. He also knew that the Jewish leaders had falsely accused Christ.

In contrast, Pilate did not know about spiritual truth. Perhaps Pilate thought that spiritual truth was not absolute but rather based on one's own perspective or circumstances. He did not recognize that the man standing before him was the Son of the only true God, the Father of all people. Pilate did not recognize that this humble yet confident man was the way to absolute truth and the means to eternal life and that "no man cometh unto the Father, but by [Him]."[33] Pilate did not recognize that Jesus was "full of grace and truth."[34] Pilate did not recognize that Jesus and His Father know all truth and thus are the embodiment of truth.

Jewish Leaders Further Accuse Jesus (Matt. 27:12–14; Mark 15:3–5; Luke 23:4–7; John 18:38)

Pilate, accompanied by Jesus, then went out to the Jewish leaders and rendered his decision of acquittal. Perhaps while pointing at Jesus, Pilate said: "I find in him no fault at all."[35] As far as Pilate was concerned, the trumped-up charges had no merit. Following Pilate's declaration, the chief priests and elders accused Jesus again:

Matthew 27:12–14. And when he was accused of the chief priests and elders, he answered nothing. Then said Pilate unto him, Hearest thou not

---

32. Farrar, *Life of Christ*, p. 595.
33. John 14:6.
34. John 1:14.
35. John 18:38.

how many things they witness against thee? And he answered him to never a word; insomuch that the governor marvelled greatly.

Luke 23:5–7. And they were the more fierce, saying, He stirreth up the people, teaching throughout all Jewry, beginning from Galilee to this place. When Pilate heard of Galilee, he asked whether the man were a Galilaean. And as soon as he knew that he belonged unto Herod's jurisdiction, he sent him to Herod, who himself also was at Jerusalem at that time.

The Jewish leaders would not accept Pilate's verdict. They were now even "more fierce" in the condemnation of Jesus, declaring that He stirred up the people by "teaching throughout all Jewry." However, Jesus's supposed "stirr[ing] up the people" by teaching them was not a crime under Roman law or Hebrew law. Pilate knew this fact well, and so did the condemning Jewish leaders.

Perhaps turning to Jesus, Pilate asked Him whether He wished to respond to the accusations made against Him. Jesus remained silent, choosing not to defend Himself. He presumably stood calmly before Pilate and the Jewish leaders, evidencing a lack of fear of Rome, the Jewish leaders, and even death.[36] Jesus knew that He needed to die in order to fulfill His purpose on the earth. His silence caused Pilate to greatly marvel. Jesus's very being may have pricked Pilate's conscience and caused him to desire to be a just man for that moment.

The Jewish leaders also referred to the fact that Jesus had preached in Galilee. They likely referred to Galilee in hopes that it would change Pilate's mind about condemning Jesus, since the Galilean Jews generally opposed Roman rule more than the Judean Jews did.[37] When the Jewish leaders stated that Jesus was Galilean, Pilate saw an opening to turn the matter of Jesus over to Herod, who governed Galilee, was a Jew, and was in Jerusalem for the Passover.[38] By doing so, Pilate would rid himself of the political problem of Jesus. It is evident that Pilate feared the accusing Jewish leaders: He could

---

36.   Edersheim opined that at this time, Jesus "stood in the calm silence of Majesty, [and] Pilate greatly wondered. Did this Man not even fear death; was He so conscious of innocence, so infinitely superior to those around and against Him, or had He so far conquered Death, that He would not condescend to their words? And why then had He spoken to him of His Kingdom and of that truth?" (Edersheim, *Life and Times of Jesus the Messiah*, p. 868.)

37.   See Chandler, *Trial of Jesus*, vol. 2, p. 108.

38.   See Farrar, *Life of Christ*, p. 596.

have released Jesus because Pilate had acquitted Jesus. Pilate could have commanded the Roman soldiers in Jerusalem to protect Jesus, but Pilate did not. Pilate did not want further trouble from the Sanhedrin and the people the Sanhedrin influenced. Presumably, Pilate thought that Herod was the answer. Perhaps Pilate also thought that turning the matter over to Herod would help mend the relationship between these two Roman appointees. By recognizing Herod's jurisdiction, Pilate would in effect be complimenting Herod. Perhaps Pilate also thought that additional facts might result from Herod's questioning.

Herod Interrogates Jesus (Luke 23:8–12)

Luke was the only Gospel writer to record what transpired when Herod interrogated Jesus:

> **Luke 23:8–12.** And when Herod saw Jesus, he was exceeding glad: for he was desirous to see him of a long season, because he had heard many things of him; and he hoped to have seen some miracle done by him. Then he questioned with him in many words; but he answered him nothing. And the chief priests and scribes stood and vehemently accused him. And Herod with his men of war set him at nought, and mocked him, and arrayed him in a gorgeous robe, and sent him again to Pilate. And the same day Pilate and Herod were made friends together: for before they were at enmity between themselves.

Edersheim posited that Herod was residing in a palace that had previously been owned by the Maccabees and that was close to the palace that Pilate was staying in.[39] Herod was pleased that Jesus was sent to him, because he had heard much of Jesus and consequently wanted to meet Jesus and see Him perform a miracle.

It should be remembered that John the Baptist had condemned Herod for divorcing his first wife and marrying his brother's wife without her first getting divorced. Consequently, Herod imprisoned John and then beheaded him at the request of his step-daughter.[40] Herod is the only person that

---

39. See Edersheim, *Life and Times of Jesus the Messiah*, p. 869.
40. See Matt. 14:3–10.

the Gospels record Jesus calling a fox,[41] and Jesus probably used this term because of Herod's penchant for perpetrating violence indiscriminately.[42]

After Jesus was taken to Herod, he asked Jesus questions "in many words." Jesus did not reply. The chief priests and scribes who were present accused Jesus, and their accusations may have prompted many of Herod's questions. Once again, Jesus remained silent before His interrogator and accusers.[43] Herod was likely angered and could not believe that this man from Nazareth would not answer the one who called himself the king of Galilee. Additionally, Herod might have been upset that Jesus did not perform a miracle for Herod, even though doing so might have motivated Herod to liberate Jesus.

Herod then determined to send Jesus back to Pilate, presumably because the Jewish leaders' accusations had no merit and Jesus appeared to be harmless. For the second time, a Roman leader had acquitted Jesus, and this leader was a Jew, no less. Though Herod did not view Jesus as a criminal, Herod may have thought that Jesus was a fraud, perhaps because Jesus did not perform a miracle for Herod. Likely to demonstrate his resentment that Jesus had remained silent and had not performed a miracle—and perhaps to placate the Jewish leaders—Herod allowed his soldiers to mock Jesus, including by putting a robe on Him to symbolize the assertion that Jesus claimed to be the king of the Jews.

Herod's interrogation of Jesus resulted in nothing as far as the Jewish leaders were concerned. It did, however, result in reconciliation between Herod and Pilate.

Pilate Again States That Jesus Is Innocent, but the Jews Want Him to Be Crucified (Matt. 27:15–23; Mark 15:6–14; Luke 23:13–23; John 18:39–40)

After Jesus had been returned to Pilate, he summoned the Jewish leaders and others and then spoke to them:

Luke 23:13–17. And Pilate, when he had called together the chief priests and the rulers and the people, said unto them, Ye have brought this man unto

---

41. Luke 13:32.
42. See *HarperCollins Bible Dictionary*, s.v. "Herod."
43. Apparently, Herod is the only official who spoke to Jesus but never heard Him reply.

me, as one that perverteth the people: and, behold, I, having examined him before you, have found no fault in this man touching those things whereof ye accuse him: no, nor yet Herod: for I sent you to him; and, lo, nothing worthy of death is done unto him. I will therefore chastise him, and release him. (For of necessity he must release one unto them at the feast.)

Matthew 27:15–23. Now at that feast the governor was wont to release unto the people a prisoner, whom they would. And they had then a notable prisoner, called Barabbas. Therefore when they were gathered together, Pilate said unto them, Whom will ye that I release unto you? Barabbas, or Jesus which is called Christ? For he knew that for envy they had delivered him. When he was set down on the judgment seat, his wife sent unto him, saying, Have thou nothing to do with that just man: for I have suffered many things this day in a dream because of him. But the chief priests and elders persuaded the multitude that they should ask Barabbas, and destroy Jesus. The governor answered and said unto them, Whether of the twain will ye that I release unto you? They said, Barabbas. Pilate saith unto them, What shall I do then with Jesus which is called Christ? They all say unto him, Let him be crucified. And the governor said, Why, what evil hath he done? But they cried out the more, saying, Let him be crucified.

Pilate stated that neither he nor Herod had found Jesus guilty of the charges brought against Him. Therefore, Pilate wanted to release Jesus. It was Pilate's custom to release one prisoner, selected by the Jews, on the day of the Passover. Presumably for that reason, a multitude of Jews[44] had gathered before Pilate with the condemning Jewish leaders.[45] Pilate proposed releasing Jesus or Barabbas. Pilate may have brought forth Barabbas to stand with Jesus before the people. Apparently, Barabbas was a well-known prisoner. Mark's account states that Barabbas had committed murder during an insurrection,[46] Luke's account states that Barabbas had been convicted of sedition,[47] and John's account states that Barabbas was a robber.[48] Of course, murder was a grievous sin, but the insurrection and sedition were

---

44. Due in part to the early hour, presumably a somewhat limited number of people were present.
45. See Edersheim, *Life and Times of Jesus the Messiah*, p. 870.
46. See Mark 15:7.
47. Luke 23:19.
48. John 18:40.

likely against Rome, perhaps causing the Jewish population to somewhat sympathize with Barabbas. It is possible that Pilate chose Barabbas as the prisoner to present with Jesus because Barabbas, a convicted robber and murderer, was in stark contrast to Jesus, who had been deemed innocent by two Roman officials.

There are some interesting similarities and contrasts between Barabbas and Jesus. *Bar-Abbas* is a Greek word that means "son of the father"[49] Because Jesus claimed to be—and indeed is—the Son of God the Father, the Sanhedrin charged Him with blasphemy. Barabbas had been convicted of sedition, insurrection, and murder. Jesus was charged with sedition and perversion of the Jewish nation. Whereas Barabbas had committed murder, Jesus had restored life to the dead. Whereas Barabbas was a robber, Jesus had taught people to "give to him that asketh thee, and from him that would borrow of thee turn not thou away."[50]

Pilate asked the multitude whether he should release Barabbas or "Jesus which is called Christ." Of course, the Greek word *Christ* means "anointed one"[51] and is equivalent in meaning to the Hebrew word *Messiah*.[52] Pilate was presumably emphasizing that many Jews considered Jesus to be the Messiah. Joseph Smith's translation of Mark 15:10 states, "And the multitude, crying aloud, began to desire him to deliver Jesus unto them." In response, Pilate asked: "Will ye that I release unto you the King of the Jews?"[53] It seems that Pilate wanted to be certain that the multitude knew full well that the person the Jewish leaders sought to condemn was referred to as the Messiah and the king of the Jews. Pilate may also have hoped that by referring to Jesus as the king of the Jews, the multitude would persuade the Jewish leaders to side with the multitude and ask for the release of Jesus, in whom Pilate had found no fault.

Perhaps at this point, Pilate sat on his judgment seat. While he was sitting there, "his wife sent unto him, saying, Have thou nothing to do with that just

49.   Edersheim, *Life and Times of Jesus the Messiah*, p. 872; Young, *Analytical Concordance*, s.v. "Barabbas."
50.   See Matt. 5:42.
51.   Young, *Analytical Concordance*, s.v. "Christ."
52.   See Young, *Analytical Concordance*, s.v. "Messiah."
53.   Mark 15:9; see also John 18:39.

man: for I have suffered many things this day in a dream because of him."[54] Pilate might have considered his wife's dream an omen that bad things would result if he allowed Jesus to be crucified.

Presumably while Pilate was learning about his wife's dream, the Jewish leaders began to persuade the multitude to seek the release of Barabbas "and destroy Jesus." By this point, all or most of Jesus's followers may have departed, perhaps out of fear for their lives, and those who remained were persuaded by the Jewish leaders to clamor for Barabbas to be released.

Pilate then again asked which of the two prisoners should be released that day as a token of Roman leniency. In response, "they cried out all at once, saying, Away with this man, and release unto us Barabbas."[55] Still wanting to release Jesus, Pilate then asked: "What shall I do then with Jesus which is called Christ?" All the multitude replied, "Let him be crucified." Pilate said, "Why, what evil hath he done? I have found no cause of death in him: I will therefore chastise him, and let him go."[56] Nevertheless, the Jews chose to release the murderer Barabbas instead of the Messiah, who a few hours earlier had atoned in Gethsemane for the sins of all people.

Jesus Is Scourged and Mocked (Matt. 27:27–30; Mark 15:16–19; John 19:1–3)

According to John's account,[57] Pilate then had his soldiers scourge and mock Jesus:

John 19:1–3. Then Pilate therefore took Jesus, and scourged him. And the soldiers platted a crown of thorns, and put it on his head, and they put on

---

54. Matt. 27:19. Joseph Smith's translation of this verse uses the word *vision* instead of dream (see JST Matt. 29:20).

55. Luke 23:18.

56. Luke 23:22.

57. Whereas John's account indicates that the scourging and mocking occurred at this point, Matthew's and Mark's accounts indicate that the scourging and mocking occurred after Pilate relented to the Jewish multitude's demand to crucify Jesus. John's chronology is followed here because John's account indicates that Pilate brought the mocked and scourged Jesus before the people and once again declared that Jesus was not guilty of any crimes (see John 19:4–5). In addition, the accounts in Matthew, Mark, and Luke indicate that the multitude told Pilate that Jesus should be crucified (see Matt. 27:22–23; Mark 15:13–14; Luke 23:21), somewhat indicating that Pilate's final attempt to release Jesus occurred after Jesus was scourged.

him a purple robe. And said, Hail, King of the Jews! And they smote him with their hands.

Matthew 27:27–30. Then the soldiers of the governor took Jesus into the common hall, and gathered unto him the whole band of soldiers. And they stripped him, and put on him a scarlet robe. And when they had plaited a crown of thorns, they put it upon his head, and a reed in his right hand: and they bowed the knee before him, and mocked him, saying, Hail, King of the Jews! And they spit upon him, and took the reed, and smote him on the head.

Pilate's soldiers stripped off Jesus's clothing, at least down to the waist; they likely tied Jesus's hands to a column or post; and then they scourged Him. Scourging, according to Talmage, "was a frightful preliminary to death on the cross. The instrument of punishment was a whip of many thongs, loaded with metal and edged with jagged pieces of bone. Instances are of record in which the condemned died under the lash and so escaped the horrors of living crucifixion."[58]

It is difficult to comprehend the pain that scourging inflicted. This pain was likely added to when the soldiers placed on Jesus's raw and bleeding back a robe that may have been made of flax or wool.[59] The soldiers then placed a crown of thorns on Jesus's head, placed a reed in His hand to serve as a scepter, mockingly bowed before Him, and said: "Hail, King of the Jews!"[60] They then spit on Jesus; took the reed from Him; and hit Him on the head with the reed, perhaps driving the thorns deeper into His skin. Jesus was called upon to endure and overcome all the evil, pain, and humiliation the world could inflict.

Pilate Again Suggests That Jesus Should Be Released, but the Jews Demand That He Be Crucified (John 19:4–15)

After Jesus was scourged and mocked, Pilate brought Jesus back before the people, perhaps hoping that if they saw this scourged, bleeding, and

---

58. Talmage, *Jesus the Christ*, p. 592; see note 2 at the end of this chapter for Book of Mormon prophecies regarding Jesus being scourged.

59. If the robe was of wool, it may have symbolism related to Jesus being the Good Shepherd (see John 10:11, 14). Matthew 27:28 states that the robe was scarlet, but JST Matthew 27:28, Mark 15:17, and John 19:2 state that the robe was purple.

60. John 19:3.

humble man wearing a crown of thorns and a robe, they would be willing to release Him:

> **John 19:4–15.** Pilate therefore went forth again, and saith unto them, Behold, I bring him forth to you, that ye may know that I find no fault in him. Then came Jesus forth, wearing the crown of thorns, and the purple robe. And Pilate saith unto them, Behold the man! When the chief priests therefore and officers saw him, they cried out, saying, Crucify him, crucify him. Pilate saith unto them, Take ye him, and crucify him: for I find no fault in him. The Jews answered him, We have a law, and by our law he ought to die, because he made himself the Son of God. When Pilate therefore heard that saying, he was the more afraid; and went again into the judgment hall, and saith unto Jesus, Whence art thou? But Jesus gave him no answer. Then saith Pilate unto him, Speakest thou not unto me? knowest thou not that I have power to crucify thee, and have power to release thee? Jesus answered, Thou couldest have no power at all against me, except it were given thee from above: therefore he that delivered me unto thee hath the greater sin. And from thenceforth Pilate sought to release him: but the Jews cried out, saying, If thou let this man go, thou art not Caesar's friend: whosoever maketh himself a king speaketh against Caesar. When Pilate therefore heard that saying, he brought Jesus forth, and sat down in the judgment seat in a place that is called the Pavement, but in the Hebrew, Gabbatha. And it was the preparation of the passover, and about the sixth hour:[61] and he saith unto the Jews, Behold your King! But they cried out, Away with him, away with him, crucify him. Pilate saith unto them, Shall I crucify your King? The chief priests answered, We have no king but Caesar.

Pilate once again declared that he had found no fault in Jesus. Then, perhaps pointing to Jesus, who was likely dripping with blood but standing majestically, Pilate said: "Behold the Man!" The Jewish leaders then cried out, "Crucify him, crucify him." Those cruel words continue to be a witness and warning of the absolute evil that Satan can plant in the hearts of those who allow his influence in their lives.

---

61.   Whereas John's record suggests that Jesus was crucified shortly after the sixth hour (i.e., noon), Mark's record states that Jesus was crucified at the third hour (see Mark 15:25). Mark's account is likely correct because Jesus's death on the cross occurred at about the ninth hour (see Matt. 27:46; Mark 15:34) and death by crucifixion would presumably have taken more than three hours. Therefore, it was likely the third hour when Jesus stood before Pilate for the final time.

These Jewish leaders then declared their religious justification for seeking Jesus's death: Jesus had blasphemed by declaring that He was the Son of God. Presumably, Jesus had demonstrated majestic calmness and confidence during the interrogations, mockery, and even scourging, and if so, Pilate likely noticed. Pilate had noticed that Jesus did not fear death. Pilate had heard Jesus say that His kingdom was not of this world and that He came into the world to bear witness of truth. Pilate had heard his wife's caution resulting from her dream regarding Jesus. Pilate had likely heard of Jesus's recent miracles. For all these reasons, He may have been afraid that Jesus was indeed the Son of God. Upon hearing the Jewish leaders say they sought Jesus's life because He claimed to be the Son of God, Pilate became "more afraid."

Pilate then took Jesus into the judgment hall and asked, "Whence art thou?" Jesus did not respond, which perhaps made Pilate even more afraid. Pilate then asked, "Knowest thou not that I have power to crucify thee, and have power to release thee?" Jesus replied by stating that Pilate could "have no power at all" against Him, except as allowed by God. Then Jesus said to Pilate, "He that delivered me unto thee hath the greater sin." Pilate, the judge, now became the one who was judged. Jesus did not diminish or forgive Pilate's sin, which was to use his authority inappropriately, but Jesus made it clear that the Jewish leaders' sin was greater, for they wanted to kill Jesus because of jealousy and avarice. Jesus's response must have deeply impressed and also deeply troubled Pilate, causing him to wonder further whether Jesus was indeed the Son of God.

Pilate returned to the multitude and again tried to convince them to release Jesus. In response, they said: "If thou let this man go, thou art not Caesar's friend: whosoever maketh himself a king speaketh against Caesar." In effect, they were threatening to inform the Roman emperor, Tiberius Caesar Augustus, that Pilate had set free a man who claimed to be a king and was thus a threat to Tiberius. Moreover, they were implying that if Jesus was set free, they would cause a rebellion against Pilate, which would further displease Tiberius.[62] Both the Jews and Pilate would have well remembered the reprimand that Tiberius had given Pilate for placing shields with Tiberius's

---

62. See Farrar, *Life of Christ*, p. 599; McConkie, *Mortal Messiah*, vol. 4, p. 186.

name in Herod's palace and thus causing a rebellion in that region of the empire. Pilate knew that if he did not comply with the multitude's demand to crucify Jesus, Tiberius might take away from Pilate his position as governor and all its perks or might do something even worse to Pilate.

Pilate made one last attempt to secure Jesus's release. Pilate brought forth Jesus and exclaimed, "Behold your King!" The Jews' frenzy to kill Jesus only grew,[63] and they cried out, "Away with him, away with him, crucify him." Pilate then asked, "Shall I crucify your King?" In both instances that Pilate referred to Jesus as a king, he preceded the word with your, perhaps indicating that Pilate knew that Jesus did not claim to be a political king. The chief priests replied, "We have no king but Caesar." The chief priests had violated the first of the Ten Commandments: "Thou shalt have no other gods before me."[64] They had also publicly committed the very sin they had charged Jesus of: blasphemy. As Talmage wrote, "The people who had by covenant accepted Jehovah as their King, now ejected Him in Person, and acknowledged no sovereign but Caesar."[65] Their corruption had reached its apex. The condemnation and death they sought for Jesus should have been their own.

Pilate Washes His Hands, Releases Barabbas, and Sends Jesus to Be Crucified (Matt. 27:24–26; Mark 15:15; Luke 23:24–25; John 19:16)

Even though Pilate knew that Jesus was innocent and that the Jewish leaders sought His life because of jealousy,[66] Pilate capitulated to the multitude's demand that Jesus be crucified. Pilate was not willing to risk the repercussions that would result if he did not satisfy the multitude. Presumably out of frustration and discouragement, Pilate washed his hands to symbolize his innocence:

> **Matthew 27:24–26.** When Pilate saw that he could prevail nothing, but that rather a tumult was made, he took water, and washed his hands before the multitude, saying, I am innocent of the blood of this just person: see ye to

---

63. See Edersheim, *Life and Times of Jesus the Messiah*, p. 872.
64. Ex. 20:3.
65. Talmage, *Jesus the Christ*, p. 594.
66. See Matt. 27:18; Mark 15:10.

it. Then answered all the people, and said, His blood be on us, and on our children. Then released he Barabbas unto them: and when he had scourged Jesus, he delivered him to be crucified.

Jesus must have made a profound impression on Pilate for him to engage in the rite of washing his hands with water. This rite was established when the Lord had told the ancient Israelites that when someone was found slain by an unknown hand, elders were to behead a heifer and then "wash their hands over the heifer . . . and say, Our hands have not shed this blood, neither have our eyes seen it. Be merciful, O Lord, unto thy people Israel, whom thou hast redeemed, and lay not innocent blood unto thy people of Israel's charge. And the blood shall be forgiven them. So shalt thou put away the guilt of innocent blood from among you, when thou shalt do that which is right in the sight of the Lord."[67]

When Pilate washed his hands before the multitude, he was declaring that he was not responsible for what would be done to Jesus. The Jews understood the import of Pilate's action, and they declared that they accepted full responsibility for Jesus's death: "His blood be on us, and on our children." This decision had grave consequences for the Jews. As Edersheim wrote, "Some thirty years later . . . was judgment pronounced against some of the best in Jerusalem; and among the 3,600 victims of the Governor's fury, of whom not a few were scourged and crucified right over against the Praetorium, were many of the noblest of the citizens of Jerusalem. . . . A few years more, and hundreds of crosses bore Jewish mangled bodies within sight of Jerusalem. And still have these wanderers seemed to bear, from century to century, and from land to land, that burden of blood; and still does it seem to weigh 'on us and our children.'"[68]

Centuries before Jesus's mortal ministry, Jacob in the Book of Mormon had prophesied: "Wherefore, as I said unto you, it must needs be expedient that Christ . . . should come among the Jews, among those who are the more wicked part of the world; and they shall crucify him . . . , and there is none other nation on earth that would crucify their God. For should the mighty miracles be wrought among other nations they would repent, and know that

---

67.   Deut. 21:6–9; see also Deut. 21:1–5; Ps. 26:6; Edersheim, *Life and Times of Jesus the Messiah*, pp. 872–873.

68.   Edersheim, *Life and Times of Jesus the Messiah*, p. 873.

he be their God. But because of priestcrafts and iniquities, they at Jerusalem will stiffen their necks against him, that he be crucified."[69] The depravity of these Jews will forever remain in the annals of history.

Even though Pilate repeatedly suggested that Jesus should be released, the multitude demanded that Jesus be crucified. Therefore, Pilate released Barabbas and sentenced Jesus to crucifixion. Pilate caved to the Jews' demands because he was less concerned about justice than he was about what the people might do and how it might affect his political position and wealth. Consequently, his infamy has continued through the centuries.

One may wonder what became of Barabbas. Barabbas was more the beneficiary of Christ's suffering and death than he could possibly realize at the time, for Christ's Atonement releases people from spiritual death and His Resurrection releases people from physical death.

Just hours before Jesus's death, He stood before Pilate and unbelieving Jews. He had humbly borne the rejection of the Jews, the mocking of Herod's and Pilate's soldiers, and the excruciatingly painful scourging of Pilate's soldiers—experiences that would better enable Him to "succor His people."[70] Now, He would be led to the cross, where He would complete His Atonement and triumph over the world!

Notes to Chapter 66

1. Jesus's prophecies of His death. On numerous occasions throughout Jesus's ministry, He prophesied of His death. The following are some of these prophecies:

After Jesus cleansed the temple in Jerusalem for the first time, the Jews asked Jesus for a sign of His authority. He said, "Destroy this temple, and in three days I will raise it up." (John 2:18–22)

Jesus said to Nicodemus, "And as Moses lifted up the serpent in the wilderness, even so must the Son of man be lifted up." (John 3:14)

69.   2 Ne. 10:3–5.
70.   Alma 7:12.

After Peter testified that Jesus was the Christ, followed by Jesus promising to give Peter the keys of the Church, "from that time forth began Jesus to shew unto his disciples, how that he must go unto Jerusalem, and suffer many things of the elders and chief priests and scribes, and be killed, and be raised again the third day." (Matt. 16:21)

On the Mount of Transfiguration, Jesus taught Peter, James, and John "of his decease which he should accomplish at Jerusalem." (Luke 9:31)

In Galilee, Jesus taught His Apostles that "the Son of man shall be betrayed into the hands of men: and they shall kill him, and the third day he shall be raised again." (Matt. 17:22–23)

Prior to triumphantly entering Jerusalem, Jesus taught His Apostles: "Behold, we go up to Jerusalem; and the Son of man shall be betrayed unto the chief priests and unto the scribes, and they shall condemn him to death, and shall deliver him to the Gentiles to mock, and to scourge, and to crucify him: and the third day he shall rise again. . . . The Son of man came not to be ministered unto, but to minister, and to give his life a ransom for many." (Matt. 20:18–19, 28; see also Luke 18:31–33)

After Jesus rode triumphantly into Jerusalem, he said: "The hour is come, that the Son of man should be glorified. Verily, verily, I say unto you, Except a corn of wheat fall into the ground and die, it abideth alone: but if it die, it bringeth forth much fruit. . . . And I, if I be lifted up from the earth, will draw all men unto me. This he said, signifying what death he should die." (John 12:23–24, 32–33)

In giving the parable of the householder, Jesus stated that the servants of the householder said, "This is the heir [i.e., Jesus]; come, let us kill him, and let us seize on his inheritance. And they caught him, and cast him out of the vineyard, and slew him." (Matt. 21:38–39; see also Mark 12:7–8; Luke 20:14–15)

Two days before the Passover, a woman anointed Jesus's head with special ointment. Jesus said of this anointing, "For in that she hath poured this ointment on my body, she did it for my burial." (Matt. 26:12)

2. Book of Mormon prophecies of Jesus's suffering. The Book of Mormon includes the following prophesies of Jesus's suffering:

"And the world, because of their iniquity, shall judge him to be a thing of naught; wherefore they scourge him, and he suffereth it; and they smite him, and he suffereth it. Yea, they spit upon him, and he suffereth it, because of his loving kindness and his long-suffering towards the children of men." (1 Ne. 19:9)

"Nevertheless, the Lord has shown unto me that they should return again. And he also has shown unto me that the Lord God, the Holy One of Israel, should manifest himself unto them in the flesh; and after he should manifest himself they should scourge him and crucify him, according to the words of the angel who spake it unto me." (2 Ne. 6:9)

"And lo, he cometh unto his own, that salvation might come unto the children of men even through faith on his name; and even after all this they shall consider him a man, and say that he hath a devil, and shall scourge him, and shall crucify him." (Mosiah 3:9)

Chapter 67

THE CRUCIFIXION AND BURIAL OF JESUS

(Friday Morning and Afternoon; Saturday Morning)

Not long before Jesus's death, as He and His Apostles were traveling to Jerusalem, He told His Apostles: "The Son of man shall be betrayed unto the chief priests and unto the scribes, and they shall condemn him to death, and shall deliver him to the Gentiles to mock, and to scourge, and to crucify him: and the third day he shall rise again."[1] Jesus had now been betrayed, tried, mocked, and scourged, and He now would voluntarily face a cruel and agonizing death on the cross. This chapter discusses Jesus's Crucifixion and burial. Many of the details of Christ's death had been prophesied of long ago. In the premortal world, Christ had agreed to die so that all humankind could live eternally, and He now fulfilled His covenant by being crucified; no one had the power to kill Him unless He allowed it.[2] Even in the extremities of Jesus's death, He taught—not only by what He did but also by what He did not do.

The Soldiers Prepare for the Crucifixion and Lead Jesus to Golgotha (Matt. 27:31–33; Mark 15:20–21; Luke 23:26–32; John 19:16–17)

Presumably, once Pilate agreed to Jesus's crucifixion, soldiers gathered the materials required to crucify Jesus and two thieves. The soldiers would

---

1.   Matt. 20:18–19.
2.   See John 10:18.

need three crosses or possibly crossbeams,[3] nails, mallets, and ropes. The soldiers likely also needed to obtain food and drink to consume during their watch. Four soldiers were likely assigned to each cross,[4] and a centurion oversaw the group;[5] additional soldiers may have accompanied the group to decrease the likelihood of an insurrection. After the soldiers finished their preparations, they led Jesus and the two thieves to Golgotha.[6] The following is Luke's account:

> **Luke 23:26–32.** And as they led him away, they laid hold upon one Simon, a Cyrenian, coming out of the country, and on him they laid the cross, that he might bear it after Jesus. And there followed him a great company of people, and of women, which also bewailed and lamented him. But Jesus turning unto them said, Daughters of Jerusalem, weep not for me, but weep for yourselves, and for your children. For, behold, the days are coming, in the which they shall say, Blessed are the barren, and the wombs that never bare, and the paps which never gave suck. Then shall they begin to say to the mountains, Fall on us; and to the hills, Cover us. For if they do these things in a green tree, what shall be done in the dry? And there were also two other, malefactors, led with him to be put to death.

Before Jesus was led to Golgotha, the soldiers took the robe off of Him, which may have caused the clotted wounds of the lashes to open and to cause great stinging pain. The soldiers then put His clothes back on Him.[7] These clothes, which were presumably already bloodstained from His suffering in Gethsemane, would have become further bloodied from the wounds on His back.[8] The soldiers then laid a heavy wood cross or one of its beams on

---

3.   See Dummelow, *Bible Commentary*, p. 716; *HarperCollins Bible Dictionary*, s.v. "crucifixion"; see also Farrar, *Life of Christ*, p. 611. Farrar noted, "It is not certain whether the condemned carried their *entire cross* or only a part of it" (Farrar, *Life of Christ*, p. 612n1).

4.   See John 19:23.

5.   See Edersheim, *Life and Times of Jesus the Messiah*, p. 875.

6.   As Isaiah had prophesied centuries earlier, Jesus "was numbered with the transgressors" (see Isa. 53:12).

7.   See Matt. 27:31; Mark 15:20.

8.   Thinking of how much blood He shed can make the sacramental prayer in Doctrine and Covenants 20:79 even more meaningful.

Him[9] and then began to lead Jesus and the two thieves through Jerusalem and to Golgotha. Typically, a crucifixion procession was led by a centurion or someone who proclaimed the nature of the crime that was committed by each person who would be crucified, and each condemned individual or a soldier carried a light-colored wood placard on which the crime was written.[10] In Jesus's case, a centurion likely led the group to Golgotha and may have carried the wood board that bore the threefold inscription written at the direction of Pilate;[11] alternatively, the board may have hung from Jesus's neck.

As the group walked, a "great company of people" followed; the number of people might have started off relatively small and then increased as the group traveled through the city. Some who followed were likely among those who had demanded that Pilate crucify Jesus. Others who followed believed in Jesus or at least had heard Him teach. Yet others likely followed out of morbid curiosity.

As Christ carried the cross or a crossbeam, His body was terribly weak. Within the last twelve hours, He had endured the unfathomable agony of Gethsemane, where great drops of blood came from every pore, after which He had been arrested, interrogated and tried by Jewish leaders, interrogated and tried by Pilate, tried and mocked by Herod, and interrogated again by Pilate and then had endured the horrific pain of scourging. He likely also felt emotional pain and humiliation from being rejected by His own people. Additionally, He presumably had not eaten or drunk anything since the Passover meal. All these factors had taken a toll, and Jesus likely struggled to carry the cross or crossbeam any longer. The soldiers apparently concluded that He no longer had the physical strength to carry the cross or crossbeam, so they commissioned a man named Simon[12] to carry Jesus's cross.[13]

---

9.   See Farrar, *Life of Christ*, p. 611; see also note 1 at the end of this chapter. Although pictures of Jesus on the cross typically depict the cross as being massive, it could not have been so or it would not have been possible for Jesus or Simon to carry it.

10.   See Edersheim, *Life and Times of Jesus the Messiah*, p. 875.

11.   See Matt. 27:37; Mark 15:26; Luke 23:38; John 19:19.

12.   Mark 15:21 states that Simon was "the father of Alexander and Rufus," implying that early Christians "knew Alexandre and Rufus, indicating that Simon (or at least his sons) did retain associations with the Christian community" (*HarperCollins Bible Dictionary*, s.v. "Simon").

13.   Farrar posited that the group had not yet reached the city gate when the soldiers commissioned Simon (see Farrar, *Life of Christ*, p. 612).

Perhaps they selected Simon because some Jews present suggested that he sympathized with Jesus, perhaps Simon was large and appeared strong, or perhaps he was simply nearby when the soldiers looked for someone to carry the cross or crossbeam for Jesus. As the cross or crossbeam was transferred from Jesus to Simon, Jesus may have expressed gratitude to Simon, whether through words or facial expression. If honest in heart, Simon likely felt the divine majesty of the one he was assisting.

Simon was a Cyrenian; Cyrene was a "city in Cyrenaica (modern Libya) that had a thriving Jewish community of settlers from Egypt."[14] The fact that the person who bore the cross or crossbeam for Christ was from another nation may symbolize that Christ's sacrifice is for all people and that all people can come unto Christ. If Simon was not already a disciple of Christ, Simon's experience while carrying Christ's cross may have led to Simon and some of his family becoming Christians following Christ's death.

As Jesus continued to walk, He heard women weeping. Some of these women may have been His followers or have at least seen Jesus perform miracles or heard Him teach. Some may have waved palm branches as He had entered Jerusalem a few days before. Some who wept may not have had a testimony that Jesus was the Son of God but may have simply thought that Jesus was a good man and that He did not deserve to suffer a horrible death. Others may have wept simply because it was customary to weep when someone was about to die.

Turning to the women who wept, Jesus gave His last sermon in mortality. He told them to weep not for Him but for themselves and their children. He prophetically warned that a day so terrible would come that women in Jerusalem would feel grateful to be barren and would even hope to be covered by the mountains. Then He said, "For if they do these things in a green tree, what shall be done in the dry?" Jesus's statement has several possible meanings. One possible meaning is that if the Romans were willing to crucify Christ, an innocent man (the "green tree"), they would be even more likely to cause serious harm and death after Jesus was gone ("the dry" period). Indeed, less than forty years later, the Romans laid siege on and then destroyed Jerusalem, and some of these women and, even more likely,

---

14.   *HarperCollins Bible Dictionary*, s.v. "Cyrene."

their children may have been in Jerusalem at that time. The starvation and
other suffering that the Romans caused would be reason to weep and even
hope to die.[15] This idea is expanded on in Joseph Smith's translation of
Jesus's statement: "This he spake, signifying the scattering of Israel, and the
desolation of the heathen, or in other words, the Gentiles."[16] The Romans'
destruction of Jerusalem caused further scattering of those in the house of
Israel, particularly the Jews.

Another potential meaning is that if the Jews rejected the Savior when
He was present (i.e., when the tree was green), what would they do after He
died (i.e., when the tree was dry)? Would they choose to believe in Him, or
would they again reject Him and therefore face eternal condemnation and
perhaps cause their children to face eternal condemnation for following after
their parents? Eternal condemnation would certainly be a cause for weeping,
as well as for wailing and gnashing their teeth.[17] In a similar vein, the green
tree may refer to the gospel being present during Jesus's life and shortly
afterward, and the dry may refer to the apostasy that followed; this apostasy
would result in people weeping for the lack of the gospel and priesthood.

Jesus Is Nailed to the Cross (Matt. 27:33–34, 38; Mark 15:22–23, 25, 27–28; Luke 23:33; John 19:17–18)

The group arrived at Golgotha[18] at about nine o'clock[19] on Friday morning,
and Jesus was nailed to the cross. The following is Matthew's account:

Matthew 27:33–34, 38. And when they were come unto a place called
Golgotha, that is to say, a place of a skull, They gave him vinegar to drink

---

15. See Talmage, *Jesus the Christ*, pp. 606–607; McConkie, *Mortal Messiah*, vol. 4,
pp. 208–209; Dummelow, *Bible Commentary*, p. 768.

16. JST Luke 23:31.

17. For example, see Mosiah 16:2; Alma 40:13; D&C 19:5; 21:8; 29:15; 101:91; 112:24.

18. Whereas Matthew 27:33, Mark 15:22, and John 19:17 use the Hebrew word
Golgotha, Luke 23:33 uses the Greek equivalent, *Calvary*. Some modern scholars believe that
Jesus was crucified where the Church of the Holy Sepulchre now stands (see Jackson, "The
Crucifixion," *Life and Teachings of Jesus Christ*, vol. 3, ed. Holzapfel and Wayment, p. 324).

19. See Mark 15:25, which states that Jesus was crucified at the third hour, which is the
equivalent of 9:00 a.m. John 19:14 states that Jesus was still with Pilate at "about the sixth
hour" (i.e., noon). It is likely that Jesus was crucified at 9:00 a.m., given the length of time
Jesus was on the cross, the length and timing of the darkness, and when Jesus's body was
taken down from the cross.

mingled with gall: and when he had tasted thereof, he would not drink. . . .
Then were there two thieves crucified with him, one on the right hand, and
another on the left.

Golgotha "may owe its name to a distinctive physical appearance (a hill
that, at that time, resembled a skull), or it may have been called this simply
because of its habitual use as a site for executions."[20] The exact location
of Golgotha is unknown and disputed, but tradition indicates it was likely
outside of Jerusalem and to the northwest of the temple.[21] Commonly,
crucifixions occurred near frequently traveled public roads, to humiliate
those being crucified and to serve as a warning of the punishment the
Roman government inflicted on criminals.[22]

Farrar posited the following regarding Jesus being nailed to the cross:

> The three crosses were laid on the ground—that of Jesus . . . being placed
> in bitter scorn in the midst. Perhaps the cross-beam was now nailed to the
> upright, and certainly the title . . . was now nailed to the summit of His
> cross. Then, stripped naked of all His clothes, He was laid down upon the
> implement of torture. His arms were stretched along the cross-beams; and
> at the centre of the open palms the point of a huge iron nail was placed,
> which by a blow of a mallet, was driven home into the wood. Through either
> foot separately, or possibly through both together as they were placed one
> over the other, another huge nail tore its way through the quivering flesh.
> . . . There was, about the centre of the cross, a wooden projection strong
> enough to support, at least in part, a human body which soon became a mass
> of agony.[23]

Whereas Farrar posited that all of Jesus's clothes were removed,
Edersheim believed that Jesus did not suffer the indignity of total exposure,[24]
implying that clothing around His loins was retained. Dummelow stated that
a loincloth was the "only garment allowed to criminals at their execution."[25]
After the soldiers removed some or all of Jesus's clothes, a soldier took a

---

20.   *HarperCollins Bible Dictionary*, s.v. "Golgotha."
21.   See *HarperCollins Bible Dictionary*, s.v. "Golgotha."
22.   See Jackson, "The Crucifixion," *Life and Teachings of Jesus Christ*, vol. 3, ed.
Holzapfel and Wayment, p. 322.
23.   Farrar, *Life of Christ*, pp. 617–618; see also note 2 and the end of this chapter.
24.   See Edersheim, *Life and Times of Jesus the Messiah*, p. 880.
25.   Dummelow, *Bible Commentary*, p. 811.

large nail or spike, found a spot between bones in one of Jesus's hands, and used a mallet to drive the nail or spike through the hand. That soldier or another soldier would do the same with Jesus's other hand. Nails were also driven through His wrists, to better support the weight of His body on the cross.[26] The nails or spikes likely pierced two of the three branches of the most sensitive nerves extending into the hand, resulting in excruciating pain. Sometimes the feet of the person being crucified were nailed to the cross by placing one foot on top of the other and then driving a spike through each foot; at other times, each heel was nailed to a side of the stake.[27] Presumably, nails were not driven through Jesus's heels, for none of His bones were broken during the Crucifixion[28] and it would have been almost impossible to drive nails through a part of the heels that would support the body but not break the heel bones. With each blow of the awful mallet, Jesus likely quivered with intense pain. Wood projections may not have been used on the crosses for Jesus and the two thieves, because projections often prolonged death for more than one day and according to Jewish law, the men's bodies had to be removed from their crosses before sundown.[29]

It is almost impossible to conceive of the horrific pain that resulted from crucifixion. In addition to excruciating pain resulting from the nails in Jesus's hands, wrists, and feet, He presumably experienced muscle cramps because His feet and legs were likely in an awkward position and because the weight of His body was supported by only the nails in His hands, wrists, and feet. Further, the wood of the cross likely caused His torn back to hurt even more.

Death by crucifixion was meant to be excruciatingly painful. The victim often lived for hours and sometimes even for days before dying. The nails driven through the hands, wrists, and feet penetrated, crushed, or severed sensitive nerves, making the associated muscles quiver. Death finally came from exhaustion; intense and unremitting pain; inflammation where the nails

---

26. See *HarperCollins Bible Dictionary*, s.v. "crucifixion"; see also Isa. 22:23, 25; note 2 at the end of this chapter.

27. See Jackson, "The Crucifixion," *Life and Teachings of Jesus Christ*, vol. 3, ed. Holzapfel and Wayment, p. 326.

28. See John 19:36.

29. See Edersheim, *Life and Times of Jesus the Messiah*, p. 895.

had been driven into the body and where the skin had been torn during scourging; and sometimes from thirst, hunger, and difficulty breathing.[30]

After Jesus was nailed to the cross, the soldiers lifted it, perhaps with the help of ropes, and then slid and dropped the cross into a prepared hole. Lifting the cross upright and then moving it into the hole likely caused Jesus additional pain.[31] Jesus's cross was positioned between the two thieves' crosses. Jesus's feet were likely only one or two feet from the ground,[32] and He may have been a little higher from the ground than the two thieves were.[33] As Isaiah had prophesied centuries earlier, Jesus "was numbered with the transgressors."[34]

Christ's experience was in stark contrast to the experience of individuals who have surgery in modern hospitals. Today's medical providers attempt to reduce or even remove patients' pain. Additionally, medical providers and hospitals adhere to high standards of cleanliness to help prevent patients from developing infections. Unlike today's medical providers, the Roman soldiers were unconcerned about inflicting pain in the person being crucified. In addition, the soldiers surely did not meet today's cleanliness standards; instead, the soldiers likely had dirty hands and matted hair and were otherwise unclean.

Either before or after Jesus was raised on the cross, He was given a mixture of vinegar and gall to drink,[35] perhaps by a sympathetic woman

30. See Talmage, *Jesus the Christ*, p. 608; *HarperCollins Bible Dictionary*, s.v. "crucifixion."

31. Others, such as Edersheim, are of the opinion that the vertical piece was put in place first or was already in place and that the crossbeam that Christ's hands were nailed to was then lifted up by the soldiers through using ropes, ladders, and forked poles (see Edersheim, *Life and Times of Jesus the Messiah*, pp. 879–880; *HarperCollins Bible Dictionary*, s.v. "crucifixion"). However, it would be very difficult if not impossible to nail or lash the crossbeam to the vertical stake if part of Jesus's body was in the way. Further, if the soldiers used ladders, the soldiers had to carry the ladders from the city, along with a mallet, nails, rope, and perhaps food and water.

32. See Edersheim, *Life and Times of Jesus the Messiah*, p. 879.

33. See Farrar, *Life of Christ*, p. 617.

34. See Isa. 53:12.

35. Whereas Matthew 27:34 states that the drink was a mix of vinegar and gall, Mark 15:23 states that drink was a mix of wine and myrrh; Joseph Smith's translation of Mark's account agrees with Matthew's account. The fact that Jesus would be given vinegar and gall to drink during the Crucifixion was known long beforehand, for Psalm 69:21 states the following regarding the Messiah: "They gave me also gall for my meat; and in my thirst they gave me vinegar to drink."

or by a Roman soldier. The vinegar was sour wine, which was a common drink among the poorer classes.[36] It is not known what gall is. Gall may have been an herb, and it may have received its name because it was bitter and therefore was associated with bile from the gall bladder.[37] Gall may have had narcotic properties,[38] dulling the senses to pain. After Jesus tasted the mixture, He would not drink any more of it. Presumably, He wanted to face the excruciating pain of crucifixion without numbing narcotics and wanted to have a clear mind as He perfectly overcame the world.

A Wood Placard States That Jesus Is the King of the Jews (Matt. 27:37; Mark 15:26; Luke 23:38; John 19:19–22)

All four Gospel writers recorded the words contained on the wood placard that was placed above Jesus's head on the cross. The following is John's account:

> **John 19:19–22** And Pilate wrote a title, and put it on the cross. And the writing was, Jesus of Nazareth the King of the Jews. This title then read many of the Jews: for the place where Jesus was crucified was nigh to the city: and it was written in Hebrew, and Greek, and Latin. Then said the chief priests of the Jews to Pilate, Write not, The King of the Jews; but that he said, I am King of the Jews. Pilate answered, What I have written I have written.

The purpose of the placard was to state the crime that the condemned person had committed. In Jesus's case, Pilate had directed that the placard state "Jesus of Nazareth the King of the Jews" and that it be written in Hebrew, Greek, and Latin. Presumably, the cross was visible from a main road leading to Jerusalem and almost all could read what was written because it was presented in three languages.

Pilate's motives for selecting the wording of the placard are not stated, but it is reasonable to assume that two of his motives were "to avenge himself on, and . . . to deride, the Jews."[39]

---

36. See *HarperCollins Bible Dictionary*, s.v. "vinegar."
37. See *HarperCollins Bible Dictionary*, s.v. "gall."
38. See Smith, *Bible Dictionary*, s.v. "gall."
39. Edersheim, *Life and Times of Jesus the Messiah*, p. 881.

When the chief priests became aware of the wording, they asked Pilate to change it to "He said, I am King of the Jews." Pilate refused and responded, "What I have written I have written." Possibly in ignorance, Pilate witnessed of Christ to all who read what he had instructed to be written.

Jesus Asks His Father to Forgive the Soldiers (Luke 23:34)

After Jesus was lifted on the cross, the first recorded words that He uttered were a prayer of mercy for the soldiers:

Luke 23:34. Then said Jesus, Father, forgive them; for they know not what they do.

Jesus recognized that the Roman soldiers who had driven nails into His hands, wrists, and feet did so because they were ordered to. Even in Jesus's extreme agony, He was concerned for their eternal welfare. Jesus was doing something He had taught in His Sermon on the Mount: "Pray for them which despitefully use you, and persecute you."[40] Jesus lived and died what he taught!

The Soldiers Cast Lots for Jesus's Garments (Matt. 27:35–36; Mark 15:24; Luke 23:34; John 19:23–24)

The four soldiers assigned to Jesus's Crucifixion then divided the clothing that they had previously removed from Him. The following is John's account:

John 19:23–24. Then the soldiers, when they had crucified Jesus, took his garments, and made four parts, to every soldier a part; and also his coat: now the coat was without seam, woven from the top throughout. They said therefore among themselves, Let us not rend it, but cast lots for it, whose it shall be: that the scripture might be fulfilled, which saith, They parted my raiment among them, and for my vesture they did cast lots. These things therefore the soldiers did.

Apparently, it was common for executioners to take possession of the clothes of the person being crucified.[41] Edersheim posited that the articles of clothing the soldiers divided up included a head covering, a cloak-like

---

40. Matt. 5:44.
41. See Talmage, *Jesus the Christ*, p. 608.

outer garment, an inner coat (what John and Matthew called a vesture), a girdle, and sandals.[42] Jesus's clothes may have been well-worn, or they may have been relatively new. They were sufficiently valuable for the four soldiers to want to acquire the items. The inner coat was apparently the most valuable, for it was a single piece of cloth woven together.[43] Since the inner coat could not be divided easily, the soldiers cast lots to determine which of them would get the coat. In doing so, the soldiers were fulfilling the prophecy in Psalm 22:18: "They part my garments among them, and cast lots upon my vesture."[44]

Jesus Is Mocked (Matt. 27:39–43; Mark 15:29–32; Luke 23:35–37)

As Jesus hung on the cross, Jewish leaders, soldiers,[45] and some others present mocked Him. The following is Matthew's account:

Matthew 27:39–43. And they that passed by reviled him, wagging their heads, and saying, Thou that destroyest the temple, and buildest it in three days, save thyself. If thou be the Son of God, come down from the cross. Likewise also the chief priests mocking him, with the scribes and elders, said, He saved others; himself he cannot save. If he be the King of Israel, let him now come down from the cross, and we will believe him. He trusted in God; let him deliver him now, if he will have him: for he said, I am the Son of God.

Because Jesus hung on the cross only a little above the ground, those who were mocking Him could have gotten relatively close to Him, and He would have easily heard the jeers. Insults that are made publicly are often the most painful. Nevertheless, Jesus remained silent. His failure to condemn left open the possibility that they could receive mercy.

---

42. See Edersheim, *Life and Times of Jesus the Messiah*, pp. 881–882.

43. Edersheim stated that "according to tradition, during the seven days of consecration, Moses ministered in a seamless white dress, woven throughout" (Edersheim, *Life and Times of Jesus the Messiah*, p. 882n31).

44. The two prior verses state, "For dogs have compassed me: the assembly of the wicked have inclosed me: they pierced my hands and my feet. I may tell all my bones: they look and stare upon me." (Ps. 22:16–17.) Regarding the reference to dogs, Dummelow noted that dogs "haunt Eastern towns in villages in savage and cowardly packs—fit emblems of the Psalmist's [and Christ's] fierce and yet contemptible foes" (Dummelow, *Bible Commentary*, p. 338).

45. See Luke 23:36–37.

The Jewish leaders may have mocked Jesus because they did not want others who were passing by to take the words on the placard as Rome's validation of Jesus's claim that He was the king of the Jews. The Jewish leaders reasoned that if Jesus was the Son of God, He would not allow Himself to be killed. The Jewish leaders were not content with mocking only Jesus; they also mocked God by saying that Jesus "trusted in God; let him deliver him now, if he will have him." They were again demonstrating their wickedness and disconnection from God. Through them, Satan may have been making one last attempt to cause Jesus to stumble. Perhaps motivated by the jeers from the crowd, the soldiers likewise said to Jesus, "If thou be the king of the Jews, save thyself."[46]

The Thieves Being Crucified Speak with Jesus (Matt. 27:44; Mark 15:32; Luke 23:39–43)

Both of the thieves spoke to Jesus while they hung on their crosses. The following is Luke's account:

Luke 23:39–43. And one of the malefactors which were hanged railed on him, saying, If thou be Christ, save thyself and us. But the other answering rebuked him, saying, Dost not thou fear God, seeing thou art in the same condemnation? And we indeed justly; for we receive the due reward of our deeds: but this man hath done nothing amiss. And he said unto Jesus, Lord, remember me when thou comest into thy kingdom. And Jesus said unto him, Verily I say unto thee, To day shalt thou be with me in paradise.

One of the thieves mocked Jesus as had the Jewish leaders, soldiers, and others. This thief said that not only should Jesus save Himself if He was the Christ but also that He should save the thieves. This thief was apparently concerned only with his own hopeless and excruciatingly painful condition.

The other thief reprimanded the first thief by asking whether the first thief feared God, considering the thieves' imminent death.[47] The second thief knew that his and the other thief's death sentences were just and that

46. Luke 23:37.
47. Joseph Smith's translation of Matthew 27:44 states, "But the other rebuked him, saying, Dost thou not fear God, seeing thou art under the same condemnation; and this man is just, and hath not sinned; and he cried unto the Lord that he would save him. And the Lord said unto him, This day thou shalt be with me in paradise."

Christ had done nothing worthy of death. Whether the second thief had heard Jesus teach or had seen or heard of His miracles is unknown. What is evident is that as the thief hung on the cross, he found at least a degree of faith in Christ. Perhaps turning his head toward Christ, the thief asked that he be remembered when Christ went to His kingdom.

With mercy, Jesus said to the second thief that he would be with Jesus in paradise[48] that very day—there would be no delay following death.[49] Light must have burst forth in this second thief as he hung on his cross. There was life after death, there was a heaven, and he would be there! For him, there would be no period of fiery torment, nor any period of blackness or nothingness. Those merciful words must have enlarged his faith. Though his death would be agonizing, he presumably now felt some hope; previously, he might have thought that if there was a heaven, he would stand condemned before God, as the thief had been condemned before Pilate. Presumably, Jesus's Atonement was beginning to be operative in the thief's life, and in the next life he would have the opportunity to grow spiritually and accept all saving ordinances of the gospel. The mercy of God and Jesus are unbounded. Jesus knew this thief and what he ultimately could become as a son of God.

The Gospel records give no indication that Jesus condemned the first thief, just as Jesus had not condemned the soldiers who drove nails into His hands and feet and had not condemned those in the multitude who had mocked Him. As with the second thief, the soldiers and those who mocked Jesus would have the opportunity, whether in this life or the next, to repent of their sins and accept the gospel. If they did so, Jesus's atoning sacrifice would make them clean. If they refused to believe, they would eventually weep, wail, and gnash their teeth because of their wickedness.[50]

---

48.   Paradise is "that part of the spirit world inhabited by righteous spirits who are awaiting the day of their resurrection. . . . It is a 'state of happiness . . . a state of rest, a state of peace, where they shall rest from all their troubles and from all care, and sorrow' [Alma 40:12]." (McConkie, *Mormon Doctrine*, p. 554; see also 4 Ne. 14; Moro. 10:34; D&C 77:2, 5.)

49.   For a discussion of the postmortal spirit world, see the appendix of this volume.

50.   See Alma 40:13–14.

Jesus Speaks to His Mother and John (John 19:25–27)

At some point while Jesus was on the cross, He saw His mother and John the Beloved. Jesus then spoke to both of them:

John 19:25–27. Now there stood by the cross of Jesus his mother, and his mother's sister, Mary the wife of Cleophas, and Mary Magdalene. When Jesus therefore saw his mother, and the disciple standing by, whom he loved, he saith unto his mother, Woman, behold thy son! Then saith he to the disciple, Behold thy mother! And from that hour that disciple took her unto his own home.

Jesus's mother and the Apostle John were accompanied by the sister of Jesus's mother,[51] Mary the wife of Cleophas and presumably the mother of James and Joses,[52] Mary Magdalene, Salome, and others.[53] Tears must have flowed freely from their eyes as they watched Jesus hanging from the cross. In particular, Mary the mother of Jesus must have been pierced with sorrow, as had been prophesied thirty-three years earlier: shortly after Jesus's birth, she and Joseph had taken Jesus to the temple, and a man named Simeon had told Mary, "Yea, a sword shall pierce through thy own soul also."[54] As Mary looked at Jesus on the cross, she may have reflected on Simeon's prophecy and the fact that it was being fulfilled.

Jesus was surely in excruciating physical pain, and seeing His mother's distress may have caused Him emotional pain as well. He called out to Mary and then said, apparently with some indication that He was speaking of John, "Behold thy son!" Then Jesus said to John, "Behold thy mother!" John understood this most sacred charge from Jesus to care for His mother. John now was to be Mary's son, caring for her as would a son. John did so "from that hour." At some point, he took her to his own home, and he presumably made certain she was cared for during the remainder of her life.[55] Jesus was demonstrating the importance of valuing family relationships and keeping

---

51.   This scripture is the only one that refers to Jesus's mother having any siblings (see Dummelow, *Bible Commentary*, p. 807).

52.   See *HarperCollins Bible Dictionary*, s.v. "Mary."

53.   See Mark 15:40.

54.   Luke 2:35.

55.   It is unknown why Jesus did not place His mother in the care of His brothers and sisters. Perhaps they were not close by.

the fifth commandment, even in the most extreme circumstances: "Honour thy father and thy mother."[56]

Darkness Covers the Land from the Sixth Hour to the Ninth Hour (Matt. 27:45; Mark 15:33; Luke 23:44–45)

At about noon, after Jesus had hung on the cross for about three horrific hours, the land was covered in darkness. Matthew's record states that the darkness was "over all the land."[57] Mark's record states that the darkness was "over the whole land."[58] Luke's record states that darkness was "over all the earth" and that "the sun was darkened." The following is Luke's account:

> **Luke 23:44–45.** And it was about the sixth hour, and there was a darkness over all the earth until the ninth hour. And the sun was darkened.

All three Synoptic gospels state that the darkness lasted from about the sixth hour to the ninth hour—that is, from about noon to 3:00 p.m.[59] It seems appropriate that the light of the sun, which Christ, the Light of the World, participated in creating,[60] was withheld from the land as Christ was dying in agony on the cross. Either figuratively or literally, the sun was mourning, as were other of Jesus's creations, as the prophet Enoch had seen in a vision of Christ's death: "The heavens were veiled; and all the creations of God mourned; and the earth groaned; and the rocks were rent."[61] Certainly, spirits in the premortal and postmortal worlds mourned because of Jesus's suffering, as well as because of the great wickedness that had brought about His cruel death. The extent of the mourning over the death of Jesus Christ, the Son of God, is unknown and presumably is unfathomable!

The darkness during the last hours of Jesus's life may have prompted many in the multitude to depart. Many women who were disciples of Jesus

---

56. Ex. 20:12. Jesus honored His Heavenly Parents by coming to the earth; teaching what He taught; living as He did; and completing the Atonement, including through allowing Himself to be crucified.

57. Matt. 27:45.

58. Luke 23:44.

59. In the Americas, a "thick darkness" covered the land for three days (see 3 Ne. 8:20–23). For more on what occurred in the Americas, see volume 5 of this series.

60. See D&C 88:7.

61. Moses 7:55–56.

remained, standing "afar off" from the cross.[62] The soldiers present likely wondered about the cause of the darkness.

Jesus Speaks to His Father (Matt. 27:46; Mark 15:34–35)

Not long before Jesus died, He cried out to His Father:

Mark 15:34–35. And at the ninth hour Jesus cried with a loud voice, saying, Eloi, Eloi, lama sabachthani? which is, being interpreted, My God, my God, why hast thou forsaken me? And some of them that stood by, when they heard it, said, Behold, he calleth Elias.

Jesus sensed the departure of the presence and loving support of His Father, and Jesus asked why His Father had withdrawn. Heavenly Father knew that for Jesus to overcome the world, including all that Satan and his angels could thrust at Him, Jesus needed to endure part of the Atonement alone. Jesus would then be able to "deliver up the kingdom, and present it unto the Father, spotless, saying: I have overcome and have trodden the wine-press alone, even the wine-press of the fierceness of the wrath of Almighty God."[63]

Some who were present misunderstood Jesus's words to His Father and thought He cried for Elias to come save Him. Farrar explained, "Elijah, the great prophet of the Old Covenant, was inextricably mingled with all the Jewish expectations of a Messiah, and these expectations were full of wrath."[64] But Elijah would not come until almost two thousand years later.[65]

Jesus Says He Thirsts (Matt. 27:48; Mark 15:36; John 19:28–29)

Shortly after Jesus had prayed to His Father, Jesus knew that He had accomplished all that His Father had asked Him to do in mortality. Jesus had overcome the world and had completed the great and sacred Atonement. The following is John's record:

John 19:28–29. After this, Jesus knowing that all things were now accomplished, that the scripture might be fulfilled, saith, I thirst. Now there

---

62. Matt. 27:55; Mark 15:40; Luke 23:49.
63. D&C 76:107.
64. Farrar, *Life of Christ*, p. 628.
65. See D&C 110:13–16.

was set a vessel full of vinegar: and they filled a sponge with vinegar, and put it upon hyssop, and put it to his mouth.

Christ's thirst must have been very great, for He likely had not drunk anything except for a small amount of vinegar and gall since the Passover meal the day before. Between that meal and now, He had bled from every pore in Gethsemane, been tried multiple times, been scourged, and hung on the cross for many hours. Talmage stated that thirst "constituted one of the worst of the crucifixion agonies."[66]

Someone near the cross, presumably a soldier, opened a container of vinegar, poured some on a sponge, put the sponge on a hyssop reed, and put the sponge next to Jesus's parched lips. If this person was a soldier, during his time at the cross he may have begun to learn of Christ and feel of His divinity. Perhaps he even subsequently believed. Some who were present told the person to leave Jesus alone, explaining that they wanted to see whether Elias would save Jesus.[67] Both good and evil were evident throughout Jesus's life and even in the last moments of His mortality.

Jesus Releases His Spirit and Says His Work Is Finished (Matt. 27:50; Mark 15:37; Luke 23:46; John 19:30)

Jesus prayed to His Father one more time and then died. The following is Luke's account:

Luke 23:46. And when Jesus had cried with a loud voice, he said, Father, into thy hands I commend my spirit: and having said thus, he gave up the ghost.

John's account states that Jesus said, "It is finished," after which He "bowed his head" and died.[68] The Joseph Smith translation of Matthew's account states, "Jesus, when he had cried again with a loud voice, saying Father it is finished, thy will is done, yielded up the ghost."[69] Jesus's last cry from the cross may have ruptured blood vessels in His heart,[70] He may have suffocated, His body may have shut down, or He may simply have released

---

66. Talmage, *Jesus the Christ*, p. 613.
67. See Matt. 27:49; Mark 14:36.
68. John 19:30.
69. JST Matt. 27:53.
70. See Farrar, *Life of Christ*, p. 630; Ps. 69:20; Talmage, *Jesus the Christ*, pp. 619–620.

His spirit from His body since He had power over death.[71] Jesus Christ, the Son of God, was dead.

Jesus's Crucifixion was the greatest tragedy in all human history. Nevertheless, His death was one of the greatest blessings for all humankind and was essential to Heavenly Father's plan. As the risen Lord explained to Joseph Smith, "The Lord your Redeemer suffered death in the flesh; wherefore he suffered the pain of all men, that all men might repent and come unto him."[72] Additionally, Jesus died so that He could be resurrected and so that all other people could too. As Paul wrote, "For since by man came death, by man came also the resurrection of the dead. For as in Adam all die, even so in Christ shall all be made alive."[73] Without Christ's Atonement, death, and Resurrection, people could not be cleansed from their sins through repentance and could not live again after mortality and receive a kingdom of glory.

The Veil of the Temple Is Torn, and the Earth Shakes (Matt. 27:51; Mark 15:38; Luke 23:45)

At Jesus's death, the veil of the temple was torn into two pieces and the earth shook. The following is Matthew's account:

Matthew 27:51. And, behold, the veil of the temple was rent in twain from the top to the bottom; and the earth did quake, and the rocks rent.

The veil of the temple was most sacred to the Jews. The veil covered the entrance to the holy of holies, symbolically separating humans from God. On only one day of the year—the Day of Atonement—the high priest parted the veil and entered the Holy of Holies to sprinkle blood on the mercy seat and to make an atonement for Israel.[74]

The fact that the veil was torn in two is rich in symbolism, which can add dimension to this miraculous occurrence. Edersheim postulated that the rending of the veil symbolized the "rending of evil"[75] and that all Jews "must

---

71. See John 10:17–18.
72. D&C 18:11.
73. 1 Cor. 15:21–22.
74. See Lev. 16. See note 3 at the end of this chapter for Josephus's description of the veil.
75. Edersheim, *Life and Times of Jesus the Messiah*, p. 893.

have understood, that . . . God's Own Hand had rent the Veil, and forever deserted and thrown open that Most holy Place."[76] Along these lines, the rent veil may symbolize that God no longer accepted the Jews who had crucified the Holy Messiah, that they could no longer enter into His presence, and perhaps that God would allow the Romans to destroy Jerusalem in coming decades. Regarding the tearing of the veil, Dummelow wrote: "Some see in it a sign that the old covenant was at an end, the sacrifices abolished, and the divine presence withdrawn from the Temple, even the Holy of Holies being now made common ground, open to the feet of all. Others who regard the Holy of Holies as a type of heaven, and the rest of the Temple as a type of earth, see in the rending of the veil the removing of the barrier between heaven and earth . . . through the death of Christ."[77] McConkie wrote that rending the veil of the temple signified that the temple's "ordinances of atonement and forgiveness were done away in him. Thus, did he, making his own body a new temple, as it were, signify that his atonement, and the forgiveness of sins made possible thereby, shall admit all true believers into his eternal Holy of Holies."[78] Jackson stated that exposing "the temple's most sacred place represents the fulfillment of the law of Moses as Israel's religion."[79] Similarly, Talmage wrote, "It was the rending of Judaism, the consummation of the Mosaic dispensation, and the inauguration of Christianity under apostolic administration."[80] The rent veil may also symbolize that Jesus had passed through the veil of death and would return to God and that, consequently, all people would likewise be able to do so.[81]

Finding the veil rent must have struck fear in the hearts of the chief priests, scribes, elders, temple priests, and temple captains. Some may have wondered whether they had indeed crucified the Son of God.

---

76. Edersheim, *Life and Times of Jesus the Messiah*, p. 895; see also McConkie, *Mortal Messiah*, vol. 4, pp. 229–230.

77. Dummelow, *Bible Commentary*, p. 718.

78. McConkie, *Mortal Messiah*, vol. 4, p. 230.

79. Jackson, "The Crucifixion," *Life and Teachings of Jesus Christ*, vol. 3, ed. Holzapfel and Wayment, p. 334.

80. Talmage, *Jesus the Christ*, p. 614.

81. See The Church of Jesus Christ of Latter-day Saints, *New Testament Seminary Teacher Manual*, lesson 33, https://www.churchofjesuschrist.org/study/manual/new-testament-seminary-teacher-manual/matthew/lesson-33-matthew-27-51-28-20.

The veil of the temple being rent was accompanied by a great earthquake[82] that broke apart rocks and may even have moved stones covering the entrances to some sepulchres.[83] The earthquake may also have broken the lintel that hung over the entrance to the Most Holy Place in the temple.[84]

A Centurion Testifies That Jesus Is the Son of God (Matt. 27:54–56; Mark 15:39–41; Luke 23:47–49)

Upon feeling and seeing the results of the earthquake, a centurion and others with him, likely soldiers, "feared greatly."[85] The following is Matthew's account:

> **Matthew 27:54–56.** Now when the centurion, and they that were with him, watching Jesus, saw the earthquake, and those things that were done, they feared greatly, saying, Truly this was the Son of God. And many women were there beholding afar off, which followed Jesus from Galilee, ministering unto him: among which was Mary Magdalene, and Mary the mother of James and Joses, and the mother of Zebedee's children.

From the accounts in the three synoptic Gospels, it is evident that the centurion was deeply touched by what he had witnessed—not only the earthquake but also the darkness and Jesus telling His Father, "It is finished"[86] and then "Father, into thy hands I commend my spirit."[87] The centurion had likely also heard Jesus's hope-filled reply to one of the thieves being crucified.[88] The centurion was presumably a hardened soldier and a Gentile, but a spark of testimony was born in him. According to Luke's account, the centurion "glorified God, saying, Certainly this was a righteous man,"[89] and Matthew's and Mark's accounts indicate that the centurion said that Jesus was truly the Son of God.

---

82. An earthquake also occurred in the Americas; for a discussion of this earthquake, see volume 5 of this series.
83. See Matt. 27:52; Farrar, *Life of Christ*, p. 630.
84. See Edersheim, *Life and Times of Jesus the Messiah*, p. 894; Farrar, *Life of Christ*, p. 60n6.
85. Matt. 27:54.
86. John 19:30.
87. Luke 23:46.
88. See Luke 23:39–43.
89. Luke 23:47.

The centurion's declaration was heard by at least some of Jesus's disciples, including women who had provided service to Jesus during His ministry.[90] Though comparatively few people were present, all people can read of the centurion's testimony. Further, as with the centurion, all people can come to know of Jesus's divinity, including through reading accounts of His Crucifixion.

A Soldier Pierces Jesus's Side (John 19:31–37)

At about the time of Jesus's death, the sun was setting in the western sky, meaning the Jewish Sabbath was fast approaching. To the Jews, it was unlawful for a body to remain on the cross overnight, and they needed to take care of the crucified bodies before the Sabbath began.[91] Therefore, some Jews asked Pilate to direct the soldiers to break the legs of those being crucified, so that they would die sooner and their bodies could be properly taken care of before the Sabbath began. The following is John's account:

> **John 19:31–37.** The Jews therefore, because it was the preparation, that the bodies should not remain upon the cross on the sabbath day, (for that sabbath day was an high day,) besought Pilate that their legs might be broken, and that they might be taken away. Then came the soldiers, and brake the legs of the first, and of the other which was crucified with him. But when they came to Jesus, and saw that he was dead already, they brake not his legs: but one of the soldiers with a spear pierced his side, and forthwith came there out blood and water. And he that saw it bare record, and his record is true: and he knoweth that he saith true, that ye might believe. For these things were done, that the scripture should be fulfilled, A bone of him shall not be broken. And again another scripture saith, They shall look on him whom they pierced.

Pilate granted the Jews' petition, and the soldiers began by breaking the legs of the two thieves. When the soldiers came to Jesus, they saw that He

---

90. See Matt. 27:54–57; Mark 15:39–41; Luke 23:47–49.

91. See Edersheim, *Life and Times of Jesus the Messiah*, p. 895. Jehovah instructed the ancient Israelites, "And if a man have committed a sin worthy of death, and he be to be put to death, and thou hang him on a tree: his body shall not remain all night upon the tree, but thou shalt in any wise bury him that day; (for he that is hanged is accursed of God;) that thy land be not defiled, which the Lord thy God giveth thee for an inheritance" (Deut. 21:22–23).

was already dead, so they did not break His legs. Rather, one of the soldiers thrust his spear into Jesus's side, as soldiers typically did to ensure a quick death after breaking a crucified person's legs.[92]

After the soldier pierced Jesus's side, blood and water came out. The reason that water or a water-like liquid came out may be that as Jesus hung on the cross, he may have experienced a degree of congestive heart failure, causing fluid to collect around His heart and lungs.[93] The spear may have pierced Jesus's heart or lungs and released the fluid.

By not breaking Jesus's legs and instead piercing Him, the soldiers were fulfilling prophecy. For example, as prophesied in Psalm 34:20, "He keepeth all his bones: not one of them is broken."[94] Zechariah prophesied, "They shall look upon me whom they have pierced."[95] In stating that these prophesies had been fulfilled, John gave His own witness, stating that "he that saw it bare record, and his record is true: and he knoweth that he saith true, that ye might believe."[96]

Jesus Is Buried (Matt. 27:57–61; Mark 15:42–47; Luke 23:50–56; John 19:38–42)

All four Gospels contain details about Jesus's burial. All four accounts are presented below in order to provide a fuller picture of what occurred:

Matthew 27:57–61. When the even was come, there came a rich man of Arimathaea, named Joseph, who also himself was Jesus' disciple. He went to Pilate, and begged the body of Jesus. Then Pilate commanded the body to be delivered. And when Joseph had taken the body, he wrapped it in a clean linen cloth, and laid it in his own new tomb, which he had hewn out in the rock: and

---

92.   See Edersheim, *Life and Times of Jesus the Messiah*, p. 895. It was important that the soldiers ensured Jesus had died and that individuals saw the soldiers verify Jesus's death, because after Jesus's Resurrection, these individuals were able to testify that Jesus had indeed died and then been resurrected.

93.   See *Encyclopedia Britannica*, s.v. "congestive heart failure," accessed August 10, 2022, https://www.britannica.com/science/congestive-heart-failure.

94.   Similarly, the Passover lamb symbolized Christ's Crucifixion, and the lamb was to be killed without breaking any of its bones (see Ex. 12:46; Num. 9:12).

95.   Zech. 12:10.

96.   As was John's custom, he referred to himself in third person.

he rolled a great stone to the door of the sepulchre, and departed. And there was Mary Magdalene, and the other Mary, sitting over against the sepulchre.

Mark 15:44–47. And Pilate marvelled if he were already dead: and calling unto him the centurion, he asked him whether he had been any while dead. And when he knew it of the centurion, he gave the body to Joseph. And he bought fine linen, and took him down, and wrapped him in the linen, and laid him in a sepulchre which was hewn out of a rock, and rolled a stone unto the door of the sepulchre. And Mary Magdalene and Mary the mother of Joses beheld where he was laid. And they returned, and prepared spices and ointments; and rested the sabbath day according to the commandment.

Luke 23:50–56. And, behold, there was a man named Joseph, a counsellor; and he was a good man, and a just: (the same had not consented to the counsel and deed of them;) he was of Arimathaea, a city of the Jews: who also himself waited for the kingdom of God. This man went unto Pilate, and begged the body of Jesus. And he took it down, and wrapped it in linen, and laid it in a sepulchre that was hewn in stone, wherein never man before was laid. And that day was the preparation, and the sabbath drew on. And the women also, which came with him from Galilee, followed after, and beheld the sepulchre, and how his body was laid.

John 19:38–42. And after this Joseph of Arimathaea, being a disciple of Jesus, but secretly for fear of the Jews, besought Pilate that he might take away the body of Jesus: and Pilate gave him leave. He came therefore, and took the body of Jesus. And there came also Nicodemus, which at the first came to Jesus by night, and brought a mixture of myrrh and aloes, about an hundred pound weight. Then took they the body of Jesus, and wound it in linen clothes with the spices, as the manner of the Jews is to bury. Now in the place where he was crucified there was a garden; and in the garden a new sepulchre, wherein was never man yet laid. There laid they Jesus therefore because of the Jews' preparation day; for the sepulchre was nigh at hand.

Joseph of Arimathea[97] was a wealthy member of the Sanhedrin and was a disciple of Jesus but kept his discipleship a secret for fear of what the other members of the Sanhedrin would do to him if they knew. Joseph asked Pilate for permission to take Jesus's body in order to properly prepare

---

97. The exact location of Arimathea is unknown, but the city may have been in the hill country north of Jerusalem (see *HarperCollins Bible Dictionary*, s.v. "Arimathaea").

it for burial. Pilate may have known Joseph or known of him because of his membership in the Sanhedrin and his wealth. Additionally, Pilate likely knew that Joseph had not been among those of the Sanhedrin who insisted that Jesus be crucified. Upon hearing Joseph's request, Pilate marveled that Jesus was already dead even without His legs being broken and after less than a day on the cross. Pilate called for the centurion and asked how long ago Jesus had died. After hearing the centurion's answer, Pilate agreed to let Joseph take Jesus's body. Pilate may have been pleased to give Jesus's body to Joseph rather than to have His body placed in a common grave, as was customary,[98] because Pilate may have respected Jesus and because Pilate may have thought that letting Joseph have Jesus's body would be an affront to those who condemned Jesus and insisted that Pilate have Jesus crucified.

With Pilate's permission, Joseph took Jesus's body with the assistance of Nicodemus, a fellow member of the Sanhedrin who had spoken with Jesus during the first Passover of Jesus's ministry.[99] The two men wrapped Jesus in linen, which Joseph had brought, and applied myrrh and aloe, which Nicodemus had brought. According to Dummelow, "the myrrh and the aloe wood were reduced to powder, and inserted between the bandages, which were wound fold upon fold round the body. The enormous quantity (about 75 lb. avoirdupois) of spices, though surprising, is credible as the offering of two wealthy men. According to Jewish and general Eastern custom, the neck and face of the corpse were doubtless left bare."[100]

Joseph and Nicodemus then took Jesus's body to Joseph's sepulchre, which had never been used and was in a garden near the place where Jesus was crucified.[101] They may have then wrapped a napkin around Jesus's head

---

98.   Regarding Jewish burial during New Testament times, the *Harper Collins Bible Dictionary* states that "often, Semitic tradition favored the ritual of secondary burial, according to which the bones of the deceased were gathered after the body had decomposed" in a chamber for approximately a year. The gathered bones were stored "in stone boxes called ossuaries. The bones of multiple family members would be placed in a single ossuary, which might be elaborately decorated or inscribed with names and other information." (*HarperCollins Bible Dictionary*, s.v. "burial.")

99.   See John 3:1–21.

100.   Dummelow, *Bible Commentary*, p. 808.

101.   The fact that Joseph had a new sepulchre may suggest that he was of advanced age. That he chose to use it as Jesus's burial spot is further evidence of Joseph's desire to serve Jesus, even after He had died.

before rolling a large stone in front of the opening to the sepulchre.[102] After they completed these tasks, which they would have done as quickly as possible, for the Sabbath fast approached, they left. Mary Magdalene, Mary the mother of James and Joses, and perhaps other women had been at the sepulchre with Joseph and Nicodemus.[103] After the men left, the women departed and prepared additional spices and ointments to apply to Jesus's body following the end of the Sabbath.[104]

Though Joseph and Nicodemus had previously kept their discipleship a secret, their actions at this time revealed their beliefs. It is unknown whether the other members of the Sanhedrin retaliated against the two disciples. It is also unknown whether these two disciples thereafter publicly joined with others who believed in Jesus. What is known is that Joseph of Arimathea and Nicodemus have been remembered through the centuries for the kindness they showed in preparing Jesus's body for burial. These two men demonstrated that not all members of the Sanhedrin were wicked and refused to recognize that Jesus was the Son of God.

The Tomb Is Sealed (Matt. 27:62–66)

Sometime on Saturday, the chief priests and Pharisees came to Pilate and asked him to secure the sepulchre that Jesus had been placed in:

Matthew 27:62–66. Now the next day, that followed the day of the preparation, the chief priests and Pharisees came together unto Pilate, saying, Sir, we remember that that deceiver said, while he was yet alive, After three days I will rise again. Command therefore that the sepulchre be made sure until the third day, lest his disciples come by night, and steal him away, and say unto the people, He is risen from the dead: so the last error shall be worse than the first. Pilate said unto them, Ye have a watch: go your way, make it as sure as ye can. So they went, and made the sepulchre sure, sealing the stone, and setting a watch.

---

102. See Edersheim, *Life and Times of Jesus the Messiah*, p. 899.
103. Considering the amount of detail available, John may also have been present at the sepulchre.
104. See Luke 23:56.

The Jewish leaders assumed that like them, Jesus's disciples had a propensity to lie and would consequently take Jesus's body and say that He had risen from the dead. The Jewish leaders had previously heard, firsthand or secondhand, Jesus's prophecies of His Resurrection. For example, when the Jews asked Jesus for a sign, He said: "Destroy this temple, and in three days I will raise it up."[105] On another occasion, when scribes and Pharisees asked for a sign of His divinity, Jesus had replied that no sign would be given except the sign of the prophet Jonah, for as Jonah had been in the belly of a whale for three days, the Son of God would be in the earth for three days.[106] The Jewish leaders hoped that crucifying Jesus would stamp out belief in Him, and they were afraid that widespread belief in Him would continue if His disciples stole His body and claimed He had been resurrected.

Therefore, the Jewish leaders decided to approach Pilate. They told Pilate that Jesus had falsely said He would rise after three days, and then they asked Pilate to secure the sepulchre in order to prevent Jesus's disciples from perpetuating Jesus's claim.[107] Pilate agreed to station soldiers at the sepulchre[108] and told the Jewish leaders to make the tomb as secure as they could. Pilate may have wanted to make certain himself that Jesus's body would not be stolen and that He would not be resurrected. The Jewish leaders then went to the sepulchre and, perhaps with the assistance of Roman soldiers, in some way sealed the stone in front of the sepulchre. The soldiers then stood watch.

Neither the Jewish leaders nor the soldiers knew that what they were doing would help certify Jesus's glorious and divine resurrection.[109]

---

105. John 2:19.

106. See Matt. 12:38–40.

107. The chief priests and Pharisees may have previously ascertained where Jesus had been buried and who owned the sepulchre, or Pilate may have informed them of the tomb's location and owner.

108. See Matt. 27:65; 28:11–14.

109. One may wonder whether the chief priests and Pharisees were violating the rabbinical rule concerning the distance Jews were permitted to walk on the Sabbath. These leaders may have traveled more than the permissible distance of two thousand cubits (approximately three thousand feet) in walking to Pilate's location, the sepulchre, and then home (see Smith, *Bible Dictionary*, s.v. "Sabbath day's journey").

Jesus Is the Son of God and Died for All People

As Zechariah 13:6 states, when Christ returns to the earth for His Second Coming, some people will ask Him: "What are these wounds in thine hands? Then he shall answer, Those with which I was wounded in the house of my friends."[110] In addition, those in Jerusalem will look upon Christ, "whom they have pierced, and they shall mourn for him."[111] Though Christ's Crucifixion is a reason to mourn, it is also a reason to rejoice, for by atoning and dying for all humanity, He overcame the world. He is the "great and last sacrifice"[112] and has enabled those who repent to become clean and has enabled all people to be resurrected. Some have said that the cross on which Christ was crucified represents the intersection of time as measured by mortals and time as measured by God. It may also be said that the cross represents the intersection of humanity and the glory of eternity with God.

Talmage was of the opinion that Jesus died of a broken heart.[113] If Talmage is correct, there is great symbolism to be considered. Shortly after Jesus's Resurrection, He told the Nephites, "Your sacrifices and your burnt offerings shall be done away. . . . Ye shall offer for a sacrifice unto me a broken heart and a contrite spirt."[114] In the way Jesus lived and died, He showed how to have a broken heart and a contrite spirit.

The poignant words of the well-known hymn "I Stand All Amazed" can lead to additional awe of and gratitude for Jesus's suffering for each person to ever live on the earth:

> I stand all amazed at the love Jesus offers me,
> Confused at the grace that so fully he proffers me.
> I tremble to know that for me he was crucified,
> That for me, a sinner, he suffered, he bled and died.
>
> I marvel that he would descend from his throne divine
> To rescue a soul so rebellious and proud as mine,

---

110. Zech. 13:6.
111. Zech. 12:10.
112. Alma 34:10, 13–14.
113. See Talmage, *Jesus the Christ*, p. 620.
114. See 3 Ne. 9:19–20; see also 2 Ne. 2:7; 3 Ne. 12:19; Ether 4:15; Moro. 6:2; D&C 59:8.

That he should extend his great love unto such as I,
Sufficient to own, to redeem, and to justify.

I think of his hands pierced and bleeding to pay the debt!
Such mercy, such love, and devotion can I forget?
No, no, I will praise and adore at the mercy seat,
Until at the glorified throne I kneel at his feet.

[Chorus]

Oh, it is wonderful that he should care for me
Enough to die for me!
Oh, it is wonderful, wonderful to me![115]

All who believe can likewise be amazed at the love and grace Jesus Christ
so freely offers.

Notes to Chapter 67

1. The cross. The cross was likely made of wood that was common to the
area, such as from olive or sycamore trees. The upright stake and the crossbar
were likely notched to make them easier to attach to each other.[116] Though the
HarperCollins Bible Dictionary states that the condemned person carried only
the crossbar,[117] Matthew 27:32, Mark 15:21, and John 19:17 all refer to Simon or
Jesus bearing "his cross," possibly indicating that the entire cross was carried. It
is this author's opinion that if Christ carried only the crossbar, it was likely nailed
or otherwise affixed to the stake while it was on the ground, the placard was then
nailed in place, Jesus's wrists and hands were nailed to the crossbeam, and then
the entire cross was raised and then placed in a hole of the appropriate size.

The cross upon which Jesus was crucified has taken on a meaning that
transcends the Romans' cruel method of death. The cross has become
almost a universal symbol representing Jesus and His suffering, grace,

---

115. Charles H. Gabriel, "I Stand All Amazed," *Hymns*, no. 193.
116. See Farrar, *Life of Christ*, p. 612.
117. See *HarperCollins Bible Dictionary*, s.v. "crucifixion."

and redemption. During Jesus's mortal ministry He challenged those who followed Him to take up their crosses and follow Him.[118] Jesus also taught, "For a man to take up his cross, is to deny himself all ungodliness, and every worldly lust, and keep my commandments."[119] Paul taught that "preaching of the cross"—that is, about Jesus being crucified and resurrected—is "the power of God."[120] In the Book of Mormon, Nephi saw that Jesus would be "lifted up upon the cross and slain for the sins of the world."[121] Jacob in the Book of Mormon taught, "But, behold, the righteous, the saints of the Holy One of Israel, they who have believed in the Holy One of Israel, they who have endured the crosses of the world, and despised the shame of it, they shall inherit the kingdom of God, which was prepared for them from the foundation of the world, and their joy shall be full forever."[122] Jesus taught the Nephites, "And my Father sent me that I might be lifted up upon the cross; and after that I had been lifted up upon the cross, that I might draw all men unto me, that as I have been lifted up by men even so should men be lifted up by the Father, to stand before me, to be judged of their works, whether they be good or whether they be evil."[123] All people may want to ponder what the cross symbolizes for them.

The placard that Pilate ordered to be placed over Jesus's head would have been difficult to attach to the cross if the crossbar was placed on top of a stake already set in the ground; however, it is possible there may have been room at the top of the stake for the placard to be placed above Jesus's head since Jesus's nailed hands would have allowed Jesus's body to hang down.

2. Crucifixion. The *HarperCollins Bible Dictionary* states the following regarding crucifixion:

> Condemned persons were nailed or tied to the stake or crossbar, sometimes upside down, sometimes with other sadistic touches added at the executioner's whim. Several features became fairly standard. The victim was often flogged and then paraded to the site of execution wearing around the neck a wooden

---

118. See Luke 9:23.
119. JST Matt. 16:26.
120. 1 Cor. 1:18.
121. 1 Ne. 11:33.
122. 2 Ne. 9:18.
123. 3 Ne. 27:14.

placard proclaiming the crime. The condemned person also carried the crossbar (not the whole cross) to the place of execution, where the upright stake was already in place. Because deterrence was the primary objective, the cross was always erected in a public place. The prisoner was stripped and affixed to the crossbar with nails through the forearms or with ropes. The crossbar was then raised and attached to the upright stake and the victim's feet attached to the upright stake and the victim's feet were tied or nailed to the stake. The weight of the hanging body made breathing difficult, and death came from gradual asphyxiation, usually after a few hours. To prolong the death and thus increase the agony, a small wooden block was sometimes attached to the stake beneath the buttocks or feet to provide some support for the body.[124]

The *HarperCollins Bible Dictionary* states that nails were driven through the forearms of the crucified person. Various scriptures indicate that in Jesus's case, nails were driven through His hands, apparently in addition to nails being driven into His wrists. When He appeared to ten of the Apostles soon after His Resurrection, He said: "Behold my hands and my feet,"[125] and He "shewed unto them his hands and his side."[126] When Christ appeared to the Nephites following His Resurrection, He said: "Arise and come forth unto me, . . . that ye may feel the prints of the nails in my hands and in my feet."[127] He revealed to Joseph Smith that at His Second Coming, "Then shall the Jews look upon me and say: What are these wounds in thine hands and in thy feet?"[128]

3. The temple veil. Exodus 26:31–32 describes details regarding the veil that was to be used in the moving tabernacle and then in temples: "And thou shalt make a veil of blue, and purple, and scarlet, and fine twined linen of cunning work: with cherubims shall it be made: and thou shalt hang it upon four pillars of shittim wood overlaid with gold: their hooks shall be of gold, upon the four sockets of silver." Josephus explained that the veil in the temple in Jerusalem was "of equal largeness with the doors [dividing the two parts of the

---

124. *HarperCollins Bible Dictionary*, s.v. "crucifixion."
125. Luke 24:39.
126. John 20:20.
127. 3 Ne. 11:14.
128. D&C 45:51.

temple]. It was a Babylonian curtain embroidered with blue and fine linen, and scarlet, and purple, and of a contexture that was truly wonderful. Nor was this mixture of colours without its mystical interpretation, but was a kind of image of the universe; for by the scarlet, there seemed to be enigmatically signified fire, by the fine flax the earth, by the blue the air, and by the purple the sea; two of them having their colours this foundation of this resemblance; but the fine flax and the purple have their own origin for that foundation, the earth producing the one, and the sea the other. This curtain had also embroidered upon it all that was mystical in the heavens, excepting that the [twelve] signs, representing living creatures."[129]

Whereas the scriptural accounts refer to a single veil, Dummelow suggested that there were "two veils, a cubit apart, hung before the Holy of Holies. They are said to have been 40 cubits (60 ft) long, 20 wide, and of the thickness of the palm of the hand. Both were rent."[130]

129. Josephus, *Wars*, 5.4.4.
130. Dummelow, *Bible Commentary*, p. 718.

Chapter 68

THE FIRST DAY OF THE RESURRECTION

(Easter Sunday)

Early on Sunday morning, after Christ's physical body had lain in a sepulchre since Friday evening, He rose from the dead, becoming the first person to be resurrected and enabling the resurrection of all humanity. The moment when Christ's spirit was once again joined with His mortal body, never again to be separated, must have been glorious. Thus began Easter Sunday.

This chapter discusses Jesus's Resurrection, the rolling away of the stone from the sepulchre, and the actions of the soldiers who guarded the tomb and of the chief priests who heard the soldiers' report. The chapter also discusses Jesus's appearance to certain women, His appearance to Peter, His appearance to Peter and nine of the other Apostles, and His further instruction to the Apostles.

Jesus Has the Keys of Resurrection

The scriptures do not explain how Jesus's Resurrection was brought about or how He made possible the resurrection of all of Heavenly Father's children. However, it is clear that Jesus, and only Jesus, had the keys and authority from Heavenly Father to bring about the resurrection of all humanity, including Jesus Himself. Regarding Jesus's power over death, He explained: "I have power to lay it [His body] down, and I have power to take it again. This commandment have I received of my Father."[1] It seems clear that Heavenly

---

1. John 10:17–18.

Father gave Jesus the knowledge and authority needed to be resurrected and therefore fulfill the commandment that Heavenly Father had given.

Bringing about the resurrection of all people was a central part of Christ's mortal mission and is central to Father in Heaven's plan of salvation, for "the resurrection from the dead is the redemption of the soul."[2] As the resurrected Christ declared, "I am he that liveth, and was dead; and, behold, I am alive for evermore . . . and have the keys of hell and of death."[3] Christ's spirit and body will never again be separated. Neither will the spirits and bodies of all other people after they have been resurrected.[4] Jacob in the Book of Mormon explained that both the wicked and the righteous will be resurrected:

> O how great the goodness of our God, who prepareth a way for our escape from the grasp of this awful monster; yea, that monster, death and hell, which I call the death of the body, and also the death of the spirit. And because of the way of deliverance of our God, the Holy One of Israel, this death, of which I have spoken, which is the temporal, shall deliver up its dead; which death is the grave. And this death of which I have spoken, which is the spiritual death, shall deliver up its dead; which spiritual death is hell; wherefore, death and hell must deliver up their dead, and hell must deliver up its captive spirits, and the grave must deliver up its captive bodies, and the bodies and the spirits of men will be restored one to the other; and it is by the power of the resurrection of the Holy One of Israel. O how great the plan of our God! For on the other hand, the paradise of God must deliver up the spirits of the righteous, and the grave deliver up the body of the righteous; and the spirit and the body is restored to itself again, and all men become incorruptible, and immortal, and they are living souls, having a perfect knowledge like unto us in the flesh, save it be that our knowledge shall be perfect.[5]

As Alma explained, the resurrection is inextricably connected to Jesus's Atonement: "The atonement bringeth to pass the resurrection of the dead; and the resurrection of the dead bringeth back men into the presence of God; and thus they are restored into his presence, to be judged according to

2.   D&C 88:15–16.
3.   Rev. 1:18.
4.   See Alma 11:45.
5.   2 Ne. 9:10–13.

their works, according to the law and justice."[6] In other words, the Atonement makes the resurrection meaningful because without the Atonement, no one would be worthy to return to God's presence and receive a kingdom of glory. All people should ever be grateful for the marvelous blessings that are available through Jesus's atoning sacrifice and through the resurrection, which Jesus made possible for all of humankind.[7]

Jesus Prophesied That He Would Rise on the Third Day

Jesus was crucified on Friday and rose from the grave on Sunday, the third day after His death. On multiple occasions during His mortal life, He had prophesied that He would rise from the grave. Some people may mistakenly believe that He prophesied He would be in the grave for three full days, but He actually stated that He would rise on the third day.[8] For example, after Jesus had fed five thousand people with five loaves of bread and two fish, He taught His Apostles that He would "be raised the third day."[9] While in Galilee, He told Pharisees: "Behold, I cast out devils, and I do cures to day and to morrow, and the third day I shall be perfected."[10] On some other occasions, Jesus taught His Apostles that He would "be killed, and be raised again the third day."[11] Additionally, as Jesus and His Apostles traveled to Jerusalem together for the last time, He told them of His coming death and Resurrection. Speaking of Himself as the Son of Man, He said: "The third day he shall rise again."[12]

---

6.   Alma 42:23.
7.   See note 1 at the end of this chapter for further discussion of the importance of the resurrection of all humankind.
8.   One exception is when Jesus stated, "For as Jonas was three days and three nights in the whale's belly; so shall the Son of man be three days and three nights in the heart of the earth" (Matt. 12:40). Regarding this statement, Dummelow wrote: "The difficulty is that our Lord only lay in the grave *two* nights. The expression resembles the Jewish inclusive way of reckoning ('on the third day,' etc.), but goes beyond it. The most plausible explanation is that of J. Lightfoot. He supposes that Jesus, speaking in Aramaic, said, 'the son of man shall be three *'onahs* in the heart of the earth.' *'Onah* meant a day and a night, and part of an *'onah* was reckoned as a whole, so that the Gk. Translator not quite accurately rendered the expression, 'three days and three nights.'" (Dummelow, *Bible Commentary,* p. 669.)
9.   Luke 9:22.
10.   Luke 13:32. Regarding Jesus being perfected in His resurrected state, compare Matthew 5:48 and 3 Nephi 12:48.
11.   Matt. 16:21.
12.   Matt. 20:19; Luke 18:33.

The Stone Is Rolled Away (Matt. 28:2–4)

Early Sunday morning, two angels came to the sepulchre in which Jesus's body had been laid. The angels then rolled away the stone that was covering the opening to the sepulchre:

Matthew 28:2–4. And, behold, there was a great earthquake: for the angel of the Lord descended from heaven, and came and rolled back the stone from the door, and sat upon it. His countenance was like lightning, and his raiment white as snow: and for fear of him the keepers did shake, and became as dead men.

Although these verses refer to only one angel, Joseph Smith's inspired translation clarifies that two angels were present.[13] Their countenances were brilliant, and their clothes were as "white as snow." Either while the angels descended from heaven, while they rolled away the stone, or while both occurred, the earth shook. Though the chief priests had asked Pilate to ensure that that the tomb remain secure, the stone and the Roman soldiers could not keep the sepulchre secure from heavenly angels. Of course, the resurrected Christ did not need the angels to roll away the stone in order for Him to arise from the tomb, for He had the power to remove the stone Himself. Instead, these angels were sent to testify that Christ had been resurrected.

The soldiers who were stationed at the sepulchre had presumably heard about or seen the sun becoming dark and felt the earth quaking at the time of Jesus's death. Now they saw angels, and the soldiers fell to the ground as if they were dead. Once they revived, they left the tomb in fear, likely not only because of what they had seen but also because they feared the punishment they would receive because the sealed tomb had been opened under their watch.[14]

The angels who moved away the stone in the presence of the soldiers were the first witnesses to the world that Christ had risen from the grave; the soldiers were the second witnesses.

---

13.   See JST Matt. 28:2; see also Luke 24:4.
14.   Farrar opined that the punishment would be "disgrace and execution" (see Farrar, *Life of Christ*, p. 644).

Women Come to the Tomb and See Angels and the Stone Rolled Away
(Matt. 28:1, 5–7; Mark 16:1–7; JST Mark 16:1–7; Luke 24:1–8; John 20:1)

Likely as the angels were rolling away the stone, several women were traveling to the sepulchre so they could further prepare Christ's body for final burial. The following are Luke's account and Joseph Smith's translation of Mark's account:

> **Luke 24:1–8.** Now upon the first day of the week, very early in the morning, they came unto the sepulchre, bringing the spices which they had prepared, and certain others with them. And they found the stone rolled away from the sepulchre. And they entered in, and found not the body of the Lord Jesus. And it came to pass, as they were much perplexed thereabout, behold, two men stood by them in shining garments: and as they were afraid, and bowed down their faces to the earth, they said unto them, Why seek ye the living among the dead? He is not here, but is risen: remember how he spake unto you when he was yet in Galilee, saying, The Son of man must be delivered into the hands of sinful men, and be crucified, and the third day rise again. And they remembered his words.
>
> **JST Mark 16:1–7.** And when the sabbath was past, Mary Magdalene, and Mary, the mother of James, and Salome bought sweet spices, that they might come and anoint him. And very early in the morning, the first day of the week, they came unto the sepulchre at the rising of the sun, and they said among themselves, Who shall roll us away the stone from the door of the sepulchre? But when they looked, they saw that the stone was rolled away (for it was very great) and two angels sitting thereon, clothed in long white garments; and they were affrighted. But the angels said unto them, Be not affrighted; ye seek Jesus of Nazareth, who was crucified. He is risen; he is not here. Behold the place where they laid him, and go your way. Tell his disciples and Peter that he goeth before you into Galilee; there shall you see him as he said unto you. And they, entering into the sepulcher, saw the place where they laid Jesus. And they went out quickly and fled from the sepulcher; for they trembled and were amazed; neither said they anything to any man, for they were afraid.[15]

---

15. Joseph Smith's translation of Mark's account is used here because this translation includes important clarifications, including that two angels, not one young man, appeared to the women.

Mark's record identifies the women as "Mary Magdalene, and Mary, the mother of James, and Salome." Matthew's record refers to Mary Magdalene and "the other Mary."[16] Luke's record refers to Mary Magdalene, "Mary the mother of James," Joanna, and other women.[17] John's account refers only to Mary Magdalene.[18] Presumably, the reason that every account mentions Mary Magdalene is that she became the first person to see the risen Christ.

As the morning dawned,[19] the women approached the sepulchre. They had brought with them spices, which the women planned to anoint Jesus's body with, demonstrating their love for Him. Apparently, they were unaware that the sepulchre had been sealed and that soldiers had been guarding it. At least some of the women had seen Joseph and Nicodemus roll the stone in front of the entrance to the sepulchre,[20] but the women had not arranged for someone to roll away the stone this morning so they could anoint Jesus's body with the spices. Notwithstanding the obstacle, they proceeded with faith.

When the women arrived at the sepulchre, they saw that the large stone had been rolled away. According to Luke's account, they entered the sepulchre and saw that Jesus's body was missing, which caused the women great concern. They then saw two angels,[21] who told the women not to fear and asked why they sought "the living among the dead." Mark's account describes the angels as being "clothed in long white garments,"[22] and Luke's account describes the angels as being clothed "in shining garments."[23]

The women were frightened and perplexed by the presence of the angels and "bowed down their faces to the earth." The angels then declared that Jesus had risen, and they reminded the women of His prophecy that He would be crucified and then rise the third day. The angels had now given another witness of Jesus's Resurrection. The angels then told the

---

16.   Matt. 28:1.

17.   Luke 24:10.

18.   John 20:1.

19.   See Matt 28:1.

20.   See Matt. 27:59–61; Mark 15:45–47.

21.   The gospel accounts differ in terms of whether the angels were inside or outside of the sepulchre and whether they were sitting or standing (see Matt. 28:2; Mark 16:5; JST Mark 16:3; Luke 24:4).

22.   See Mark 16:5.

23.   Luke 24:4.

women to go tell the Apostles that Jesus had risen and that He would see them in Galilee.

The Women Leave to Tell the Apostles That Jesus Is No Longer in the Tomb (Matt. 28:8; Mark 16:8; Luke 24:9–10; John 20:2)

After hearing the angels' instruction, the women quickly departed and went to inform the Apostles that Jesus's body was no longer in the tomb:

Matthew 28:8. And they departed quickly from the sepulchre with fear and great joy; and did run to bring his disciples word.

John 20:2. Then she [Mary Magdalene] runneth, and cometh to Simon Peter, and to the other disciple, whom Jesus loved, and saith unto them, They have taken away the Lord out of the sepulchre, and we know not where they have laid him.

Matthew's account states that as the women left, they felt both fear and joy; Mark's account states that they felt both fear and amazement. Apparently, the women did not fully understand the angels' statement that Jesus had risen. This lack of comprehension is understandable; presumably, none of them had previously seen angels, and no one had previously been resurrected.

John's account suggests that Mary Magdalene alone went to Peter and John. One can imagine Mary Magdalene's emotions when she reached Peter and John. She was likely short of breath from running and tears might have run down her cheeks as she reported that Jesus's body was not in the sepulchre and that she did not know where His body had been taken. Her love for Jesus must have been evident to these two Apostles. Presumably, she then reported with wonderment that two angels had talked to her and the other women. If Mary Magdalene made her report at John's home, Jesus's mother may have heard the report, for presumably she was staying at John's home.[24] If Mary did hear the report, one can only wonder what her thoughts and feelings were. She likely knew better than anyone else on the earth that God the Father's hand was over all that had occurred.

---

24. See John 19:26–27.

The Chief Priests Bribe the Soldiers to Lie (Matt. 28:11–15)

After the two angels had spoken to the women at the sepulchre, the soldiers who had been stationed there went to the chief priests to report what had happened:

> **Matthew 28:11–15.** Now when they [the women at the sepulchre] were going, behold, some of the watch came into the city, and shewed unto the chief priests all the things that were done. And when they were assembled with the elders, and had taken counsel, they gave large money unto the soldiers, saying, Say ye, His disciples came by night, and stole him away while we slept. And if this come to the governor's ears, we will persuade him, and secure you. So they took the money, and did as they were taught: and this saying is commonly reported among the Jews until this day.

The soldiers may have gone to the chief priests instead of to their centurion or to Pilate for multiple reasons. One potential reason is that the chief priests were the ones who had persuaded Pilate to have the tomb guarded. Additionally, the soldiers might have feared that Pilate would sentence them to death because the stone had been moved and Jesus's body was missing,[25] and perhaps they hoped the chief priests would assist the soldiers in avoiding punishment. After the soldiers had reached the chief priests and reported what had occurred, the chief priests knew they must act. Most of the chief priests were Sadducees, who did not believe in resurrection.[26] If the chief priests did not take action, a major tenet of their beliefs would be discredited. In addition, they knew that if they did not take action, belief in Jesus would continue to expand.

Therefore, the chief priests counseled with the elders regarding what to do. The group decided to bribe the soldiers to lie about what had happened. If the soldiers would falsely state that Jesus's disciples had stolen His body while the soldiers slept, then the chief priests and elders would pay the soldiers a large amount of money and would intervene with Pilate on the soldiers' behalf so that they would not be punished. Certainly, Satan was at the heart of this decision, for he is the "father of lies . . . and stirreth up the children of men unto secret combinations of murder and all manner

---

25.   See Farrar, *Life of Christ*, p. 644.
26.   See *HarperCollins Bible Dictionary*, s.v. "Sadducees."

of secret works of darkness."[27] These chief priests and elders were again disregarding the law of Moses, this time by violating the commandment to not bear false witness.[28] Their evil plan worked in part, for the soldiers' lie was commonly reported among the Jews as of the time that Matthew wrote his Gospel.

Peter and John Run to the Sepulchre (John 20:3–10)

Upon hearing Mary Magdalene's report, Peter and John ran to the sepulchre. Presumably because John was younger, he outran Peter and was the first to arrive at the empty tomb. The following is John's account:

> **John 20:3–10.** Peter therefore went forth, and that other disciple, and came to the sepulchre. So they ran both together: and the other disciple did outrun Peter, and came first to the sepulchre. And he stooping down, and looking in, saw the linen clothes lying; yet went he not in. Then cometh Simon Peter following him, and went into the sepulchre, and seeth the linen clothes lie, and the napkin, that was about his head, not lying with the linen clothes, but wrapped together in a place by itself. Then went in also that other disciple, which came first to the sepulchre, and he saw, and believed. For as yet they knew not the scripture, that he must rise again from the dead. Then the disciples went away again unto their own home.

John stooped down and looked far enough inside the sepulchre to see the linen clothes lying where Jesus's body had lain a few days earlier. After Peter arrived, he entered the sepulchre and saw the clothes and head covering. John followed Peter into the tomb, and when John saw the clothes and head covering, he "believed." Presumably, *believed* refers to John now believing Mary's report; the Gospel accounts indicate that the Apostles did not yet believe that Jesus had been resurrected. Even though Jesus had told the Apostles that following His death, He would rise on the third day, they apparently had not fully comprehended Jesus's words. As with the women, the Apostles had no frame of reference regarding resurrection. Peter and John then left the sepulchre. John may have returned to his home; Peter may have gone somewhere else, wishing to be alone.

---

27.   2 Ne. 9:9; see also John 8:44; Moses 4:4; 5:24; 2 Ne. 2:18; Ether 8:25.
28.   See Ex. 20:16.

Jesus Appears to Mary Magdalene (Mark 16:9; John 20:11–18)

Mary returned to the sepulchre, perhaps arriving shortly after Peter and John had left. She stood outside the sepulcher and wept, presumably because she thought someone had desecrated Jesus's grave and stolen His body. The following is John's account, in which Mary becomes the first mortal in the earth's history to behold a resurrected being:

> **John 20:11–18.** But Mary stood without at the sepulchre weeping: and as she wept, she stooped down, and looked into the sepulchre, and seeth two angels in white sitting, the one at the head, and the other at the feet, where the body of Jesus had lain. And they say unto her, Woman, why weepest thou? She saith unto them, Because they have taken away my Lord, and I know not where they have laid him. And when she had thus said, she turned herself back, and saw Jesus standing, and knew not that it was Jesus. Jesus saith unto her, Woman, why weepest thou? whom seekest thou? She, supposing him to be the gardener, saith unto him, Sir, if thou have borne him hence, tell me where thou hast laid him, and I will take him away. Jesus saith unto her, Mary. She turned herself, and saith unto him, Rabboni; which is to say, Master. Jesus saith unto her, Touch me not; for I am not yet ascended to my Father: but go to my brethren, and say unto them, I ascend unto my Father, and your Father; and to my God, and your God. Mary Magdalene came and told the disciples that she had seen the Lord, and that he had spoken these things unto her.

As Mary stooped down and looked into the sepulchre, perhaps wanting to make certain that Jesus's body was not there, she again saw two angels. One sat where Jesus's head would have lain, and the other sat where Jesus's feet would have lain. One of the angels asked Mary why she was crying, and she responded: "Because they have taken away my Lord, and I know not where they have laid him."

Mary then turned away from the sepulchre and saw Jesus standing nearby, but she did not recognize Him. Jesus asked her why she was crying and who she was looking for. She assumed that the person speaking to her was a gardener, and she asked him whether he had taken Jesus's body and, if so, where. Perhaps she thought that Joseph of Arimathea or someone else had instructed the gardener to move Jesus's body elsewhere. Presumably, her love of and devotion to Jesus were evident as she asked the presumed gardener whether he knew where Jesus's body was and as she said that she would be responsible for it.

Then, Jesus said a single word—"Mary"—and she recognized who had said her name. This realization must have turned her deep sorrow into great joy. In recognition, she addressed Jesus as *Rabboni*, which means "master." Mary attempted to embrace Jesus, but He told her, "Touch me not; for I am not yet ascended to my Father." Joseph Smith's translation of this event states that Jesus said, "Hold me not; for I am not yet ascended to my Father."[29] Perhaps Jesus wanted to present His resurrected body to His Father while it was clean from the touch of mortal hands. Jesus then directed Mary to tell His Apostles that He was going to ascend to heaven to see His Father. Perhaps after additional conversation, Mary left the tomb and went to the Apostles to tell them that she had seen Jesus and what He had said to her.

Jesus Appears to the Other Women (Matt. 28:9–10)

After Jesus appeared to Mary Magdalene, He appeared to the other women as they were on their way to tell the Apostles about the stone being rolled away, the tomb being empty, and the two angels speaking to the women. The following is Matthew's account:

> **Matthew 28:9–10.** And as they went to tell his disciples, behold, Jesus met them, saying, All hail. And they came and held him by the feet, and worshipped him. Then said Jesus unto them, Be not afraid: go tell my brethren that they go into Galilee, and there shall they see me.

Jesus greeted the women with "all hail." It is possible that He then spoke additional words so that the women recognized Him and understood that He was resurrected. They approached Jesus, and He allowed the women to hold Him by the feet, which suggests that by this time He had already appeared before His Father.

---

29.   JST John 20:17. Talmage opined, "We may assume that Mary's emotional approach had been prompted more by a feeling of personal yet holy affection than by an impulse of devotional worship such as the other women evinced. . . . There was about Him a divine dignity that forbade close personal familiarity." (Talmage, *Jesus the Christ*, pp. 632–633.)

Apparently recognizing that the women felt some fear, Jesus told them not to be afraid. Indeed, they had reason to rejoice, for they had witnessed something that no mortal except for Mary Magdalene had witnessed. Jesus then instructed these women, as had the two angels, to tell His Apostles that they would see Him in Galilee.

One can only imagine the joy the women felt as they conversed with the resurrected Lord and then, after He had departed, continued on their way to the Apostles to tell them of all that the women had seen and heard.

The Women Tell the Apostles and Others That Jesus Is No Longer in the Tomb (Mark 16:10–11; Luke 24:10–11)

When the women told the Apostles and others what the women had seen and heard, those they told were disbelieving:

> **Luke 24:9–11.** And [the women] returned from the sepulchre, and told all these things unto the eleven, and to all the rest. It was Mary Magdalene, and Joanna, and Mary the mother of James, and other women that were with them, which told these things unto the apostles. And their words seemed to them as idle tales, and they believed them not.

The women must have been filled with joy as they reported seeing the empty tomb, seeing and hearing the angels, and then seeing the resurrected Christ. The Apostles and others who heard the women did not believe them and perhaps thought they had, because of their sorrow, imagined what they had reported. Even though the Apostles and other disciples had heard Jesus say on many occasions that He would rise on the third day, they did not understand. No one had ever been resurrected before, and so the women's report seemed to be "idle tales."

Jesus Appears to Peter and to Two Disciples, and the Disciples Report to the Apostles (Mark 16:12–13; Luke 24:13–35)

At some point after Peter and John had left the sepulchre, Jesus appeared to Peter and to two disciples. Of the four Gospels, only Luke's account refers to Jesus's appearance to Peter, and Luke's record mentions the appearance only in passing when recounting that after Jesus appeared to the two disciples, they went to the Apostles and others, who said that Jesus had appeared to Peter.[30] The following is Luke's account:[31]

Luke 24:13–35. And, behold, two of them went that same day to a village called Emmaus, which was from Jerusalem about threescore furlongs.[32] And they talked together of all these things which had happened. And it came to pass, that, while they communed together and reasoned, Jesus himself drew near, and went with them. But their eyes were holden that they should not know him. And he said unto them, What manner of communications are these that ye have one to another, as ye walk, and are sad? And the one of them, whose name was Cleopas, answering said unto him, Art thou only a stranger in Jerusalem, and hast not known the things which are come to pass there in these days? And he said unto them, What things? And they said unto him, Concerning Jesus of Nazareth, which was a prophet mighty in deed and word before God and all the people: and how the chief priests and our rulers delivered him to be condemned to death, and have crucified him. But we trusted that it had been he which should have redeemed Israel: and beside all this, to day is the third day since these things were done. Yea, and certain women also of our company made us astonished, which were early at the sepulchre; and when they found not his body, they came, saying, that they had also seen a vision of angels, which said that he was alive. And certain of them which were with us went to the sepulchre, and found it even so as the women had said: but him they saw not. Then he said unto them, O fools, and slow of heart to believe all that the prophets have spoken: Ought not Christ to have suffered these things, and to enter into his glory? And beginning at Moses and all the prophets, he expounded unto them in all the scriptures the things concerning himself. And they drew nigh unto the village, whither they went: and he made as though he would have gone further. But they constrained him, saying, Abide with us: for it is toward evening, and the day is far spent. And he went in to tarry with them. And it came to pass, as he sat at meat with them, he took bread, and blessed it, and brake, and gave to them. And their eyes were opened, and they knew him; and he vanished out of their sight. And they said one to another, Did not

---

30. Jesus's appearance to Peter before the two disciples is also mentioned in 1 Corinthians 15:5.

31. Given the detail included in Luke's account, Luke might have personally heard Cleopas give an account of Jesus appearing to him and the other disciple.

32. Threescore furlongs is approximately seven miles.

our heart burn within us, while he talked with us by the way, and while he opened to us the scriptures? And they rose up the same hour, and returned to Jerusalem, and found the eleven gathered together, and them that were with them, saying, The Lord is risen indeed, and hath appeared to Simon. And they told what things were done in the way, and how he was known of them in breaking of bread.

Only a few days before, Peter had thrice denied knowing Christ, and afterward Peter may have thought that he had fallen too far to ever be forgiven, to be respected by other disciples of Jesus, or to be of use in the Church. Though it is unknown what the resurrected Christ said when He appeared to Peter, Christ presumably extended His infinite love and mercy to His chief Apostle. Christ may have also instructed Peter regarding the gospel work the Apostles were to continue. Christ likely also instructed Peter to tell the other Apostles that He had appeared to Peter, just as He had instructed the women He had appeared to that day that they should tell the Apostles that He had been resurrected.

Presumably sometime on Sunday after Jesus appeared to Peter, Jesus appeared to the two men—one of whom was named Cleopas—as they were traveling to Emmaus. These two disciples had been discussing "all these things"—presumably Jesus's Crucifixion, His body being missing from the tomb, and what the angels had told the women at the sepulchre. The disciples may also have been discussing their hope that Jesus was the Messiah who would free the Jews from Roman rule and what would happen now that Jesus had died.

At some point in the disciples' journey, Jesus joined them, but they did not recognize Him, either because they did not expect to see Him or because He did not want them to discern who He was. He asked them about their conversation and why they were sad, and in response Cleopas asked whether Jesus was a foreigner who did not know what had taken place just two days before. Perhaps desiring that the two disciples share their feelings on the matter, Jesus asked, "What things?" They responded that they spoke concerning Jesus, who had been condemned by the chief priests and delivered to Pilate to be crucified. The two disciples then stated that they had hoped that Jesus would redeem Israel. They also told Jesus that the women had found the tomb empty and had seen angels, who told the women that Jesus had risen from the dead.[33] Additionally, the two disciples reported that Peter and John had seen the empty sepulchre.

Jesus then said, "O fools, and slow of heart to believe all that the prophets have spoken: Ought not Christ to have suffered these things, and to enter into his glory?" Perhaps Jesus was chastising the two disciples because they did not remember the many prophecies stating that Jesus would die and would then rise from the dead. Jesus might also have been chastising the two disciples because they did not recognize Him even after hearing of the women's experience with the angels.

Jesus then instructed the two disciples concerning scriptures that were about Him. Jesus may have referred to the direction that Moses received to set a serpent "upon a pole: and it shall come to pass, that every one that is bitten, when he looketh upon it, shall live,"[34] and Jesus may have explained that the serpent on the pole represented His Atonement and triumph over evil. He may have also discussed some of Isaiah's prophesies, including that "a virgin shall conceive, and bear a son, and shall call his name Immanuel"[35] and that "the government shall be upon his shoulder: and his name shall be called Wonderful, Counsellor, The mighty God, The everlasting Father, The Prince of Peace."[36] Jesus may also have referred to the fifty-third chapter of Isaiah:

> Who hath believed our report? and to whom is the arm of the Lord revealed? For he shall grow up before him as a tender plant, and as a root out of a dry ground: he hath no form nor comeliness; and when we shall see him, there is no beauty that we should desire him. He is despised and rejected of men; a man of sorrows, and acquainted with grief: and we hid as it were our faces from him; he was despised, and we esteemed him not. Surely he hath borne our griefs, and carried our sorrows: yet we did esteem him stricken, smitten of God, and afflicted. But he was wounded for our transgressions, he was bruised for our iniquities: the chastisement of our peace was upon him; and with his stripes we are healed. All we like sheep have gone astray; we have turned every one to his own way; and the Lord hath laid on him the iniquity

---

33. Apparently, the two disciples had not heard that the women had seen Jesus at some point after seeing the angels.

34. Num. 21:8.

35. Isa. 7:14.

36. Isa. 9:6.

of us all. He was oppressed, and he was afflicted, yet he opened not his mouth: he is brought as a lamb to the slaughter, and as a sheep before her shearers is dumb, so he openeth not his mouth. He was taken from prison and from judgment: and who shall declare his generation? for he was cut off out of the land of the living: for the transgression of my people was he stricken. And he made his grave with the wicked, and with the rich in his death; because he had done no violence, neither was any deceit in his mouth. Yet it pleased the Lord to bruise him; he hath put him to grief: when thou shalt make his soul an offering for sin, he shall see his seed, he shall prolong his days, and the pleasure of the Lord shall prosper in his hand. He shall see of the travail of his soul, and shall be satisfied: by his knowledge shall my righteous servant justify many; for he shall bear their iniquities. Therefore will I divide him a portion with the great, and he shall divide the spoil with the strong; because he hath poured out his soul unto death: and he was numbered with the transgressors; and he bare the sin of many, and made intercession for the transgressors.

As Jesus explained the scriptures to the two disciples, their hearts burned. They were likely impressed by the scriptural knowledge and understanding of the man who spoke with them, but they still did not recognize that the man was Jesus.

As the three men approached Emmaus, the two disciples invited Jesus to eat with them. Jesus consented. At the start of the meal, Jesus "took bread, and blessed it, and brake, and gave to them," as was customary for a guest to do.[37] The two disciples now recognized Jesus. Perhaps the recognition came because of the way He blessed the bread or because they could see the wounds in His hands and wrists as He broke the bread and passed pieces to them. Or perhaps Jesus now allowed them to recognize Him. After they recognized Him, He vanished, presumably without further word.

In discussing their visit with Jesus, the two disciples said to each other, "Did not our heart burn within us, while he talked with us by the way, and while he opened to us the scriptures?" These two disciples had learned from the Master that knowledge that comes only from seeing, hearing, speaking, or

---

37.   See Talmage, *Jesus the Christ*, p. 636. Edersheim asserted that "no one asked or questioned, as he [Jesus] took the bread and [spoke] the words of blessing" (Edersheim, *Life and Times of Jesus the Messiah*, p. 914).

reasoning is insufficient for sustaining a spiritual witness of spiritual things. These disciples' witness of the resurrected Christ came in part as their hearts burned within them. Even though they had already walked a significant distance that day, shortly after Jesus left they returned to Jerusalem, perhaps running part or all of the way. Reflecting on their interactions with Jesus likely invigorated them on their journey back to Jerusalem, and though they likely traveled in the dark for at least part of the way, the light of Christ and their special witness was likely burning brightly within them.

Upon arriving in Jerusalem that night, the two disciples found where the Apostles had gathered to eat,[38] likely at a location where they could feel safe from the Jews.[39] The two disciples must have been excited as they knocked on the door of the residence, entered, and explained that they had walked with and been taught by the risen Lord. The Apostles now had the witnesses of Peter, the women, and the two disciples that Christ had been resurrected.

Jesus Appears to Ten of the Apostles and Other Disciples (Mark 16:14; Luke 24:36–43; John 20:19–20)

As the two disciples talked with the Apostles (except for Thomas, who was not present) and possibly others who had gathered, Jesus came into the room.[40] The following is Luke's account:

> **Luke 24:36–43.** And as they thus spake, Jesus himself stood in the midst of them, and saith unto them, Peace be unto you. But they were terrified and affrighted, and supposed that they had seen a spirit. And he said unto them, Why are ye troubled? and why do thoughts arise in your hearts? Behold my hands and my feet, that it is I myself: handle me, and see; for a spirit hath not flesh and bones, as ye see me have. And when he had thus spoken, he shewed them his hands and his feet. And while they yet believed not for joy,

---

38. See Mark 16:14.

39. See John 20:19.

40. Luke 24:33 states and Edersheim opined that the two disciples from Emmaus met with all eleven Apostles (see Edersheim, *Life and Times of Jesus the Messiah*, p. 915). John 20:24 states that Thomas was not with the other Apostles when Jesus appeared. It is possible, that Thomas left the room before Jesus appeared. Mark 16:14 gives the impression that all eleven Apostles were present when Jesus appeared; however, Mark's account is very brief, and Mark may have glossed over the fact that Jesus initially appeared to only ten of the Apostles and thereafter appeared to all eleven Apostles (see John 20:26–29).

and wondered, he said unto them, Have ye here any meat? And they gave him a piece of a broiled fish, and of an honeycomb. And he took it, and did eat before them.

When those assembled saw Jesus, they were terrified because they thought Jesus was a spirit, likely because He had a heavenly countenance and He had not entered through a doorway. Jesus recognized their fear and said, "Peace be unto you."[41] He then asked those in the room why they were afraid. Of course, He knew why they were afraid, and to help them understand who He was, He told them to look at His hands and feet and to handle Him to confirm He had a physical body, which a spirit does not have.[42] Presumably, all those in the room then touched Jesus, perhaps feeling the nail prints in His hands, wrists, and feet and the mark in His side where He had been pierced with a spear. Mark's record indicates that Jesus also "upbraided [the Apostles] with their unbelief"[43]—they had not believed the reports of those who had already seen Him, and they would only believe when they saw Him themselves.

Perhaps because Jesus recognized that those present still had some questions about the nature of His resurrected body, He asked whether they had food for Him to eat. They gave Jesus some fish and honeycomb, and He ate both.

Jesus's appearance at this time makes apparent multiple truths about the nature of resurrected beings. First, resurrected beings have bodies of flesh and bones.[44] Therefore, resurrected beings can eat, walk, stand, sit, and do other things that mortals can do. Second, in contrast to mortals, resurrected being are not bounded by the physical world; for example, Jesus vanished from the sight of the two disciples in Emmaus and entered the residence in Jerusalem without coming through a door. Third, resurrected bodies are whole and perfect;[45]

---

41.   The Apostles had heard Jesus speak similar words during the Passover meal three days before: "Peace I leave with you, my peace I give unto you: not as the world giveth, give I unto you. Let not your heart be troubled, neither let it be afraid." (John 14:27.)

42.   Compare 3 Ne. 11:14–17.

43.   See Mark 16:14.

44.   Doctrine and Covenants 130:22 states, "The Father has a body of flesh and bones as tangible as man's; the Son also." Having risen from the grave, Christ's body was now like that of His Father; it was made of flesh and bones and was refined.

45.   See Alma 11:43; Smith, *Gospel Doctrine*, p. 23.

however, a unique aspect of Jesus's resurrected body is that it contains the marks in His hands, wrist, side, and feet, serving as a witness of who He is. Those marks will be present when He returns for His Second Coming, when the Jews will ask: "What are these wounds in thine hands? Then he shall answer, Those with which I was wounded in the house of my friends"[46]

Jesus Explains Scriptures That Refer to Him (Luke 24:44–48)

Jesus then expounded on scriptures that refer to Him:

Luke 24:44–48. And he said unto them, These are the words which I spake unto you, while I was yet with you, that all things must be fulfilled, which were written in the law of Moses, and in the prophets, and in the psalms, concerning me. Then opened he their understanding, that they might understand the scriptures, and said unto them, Thus it is written, and thus it behoved Christ to suffer, and to rise from the dead the third day: and that repentance and remission of sins should be preached in his name among all nations, beginning at Jerusalem. And ye are witnesses of these things.

Presumably, Jesus taught that all prophesies about Him would be fulfilled, and He likely explained that through His Atonement and death, He had fulfilled the law of Moses. Jesus may have also expounded on certain Old Testament prophecies concerning His suffering in Gethsemane, His Crucifixion, and His Resurrection. He then stated that those present—presumably, particularly the Apostles—were witnesses of what He had taught and that repentance and remission of sins through His atoning sacrifice needed to be preached to all nations.

Jesus Gives the Apostles the Holy Ghost and the Authority to Forgive Sins on Behalf of the Church (Luke 24:49; John 20:21–23)

After Jesus expounded the scriptures, He again told those present to be at peace. Then, He gave instruction that presumably was directed only to the Apostles:

John 20:21–23. Then said Jesus to them again, Peace be unto you: as my Father hath sent me, even so send I you. And when he had said this, he

---

46. Zech. 13:6.

breathed on them, and saith unto them, Receive ye the Holy Ghost: whose soever sins ye remit, they are remitted unto them; and whose soever sins ye retain, they are retained.

Those present likely knew that the future would be challenging, but they could find peace in knowing that Jesus lived and that He had visited with them. Jesus taught that just as Heavenly Father had sent Jesus into the world, Jesus was now sending the Apostles to teach the gospel throughout the world. Likewise, just as Jesus had received authority from Heavenly Father, Jesus was giving the Apostles authority—authority to act on behalf of the Church in helping people to work through the repentance process, including through being baptized.[47] Of course, Heavenly Father and Jesus are the only ones who have the authority to forgive people of their sins.

Jesus then "breathed on" the Apostles and told them to receive the Holy Ghost. Presumably, *breathed on* simply means that Jesus spoke to the Apostles and blessed them. At this time, the Apostles may have received the influence of the Holy Ghost; they presumably did not receive the gift of the Holy Ghost until the day of Pentecost.[48] Because of the witness of the Apostles and the Holy Ghost, many people would come to believe in Christ, and the young Church would rapidly grow throughout the land.

Others Who Had Died Arose from Their Graves (Matt. 27:52–53)

When Jesus died, the graves of some deceased individuals opened. Following Jesus's Resurrection, these individuals arose from their graves and appeared to many people in Jerusalem:

Matthew 27:52–53. And the graves were opened; and many bodies of the saints which slept arose, and came out of the graves after his resurrection, and went into the holy city, and appeared unto many.

These individuals likely arose from their graves on the day Christ was resurrected or shortly thereafter. It is reasonable to assume that these individuals were among those "who had been faithful in the testimony of Jesus while they lived in mortality" and had been in the spirit world

---

47. See McConkie, *Mortal Messiah*, vol. 4, pp. 282–283.
48. See Acts 2:1–5; McConkie, *Mortal Messiah*, vol. 4, p. 282.

"awaiting the advent of the Son of God into the spirit world, to declare their redemption from the bands of death."[49] Many in the Americas were also resurrected shortly after Christ's Resurrection, and they had likely also been faithful while in mortality.[50]

Each person who arose from the grave was an additional witness of Jesus's Resurrection, as well as of the person's own resurrection. Presumably, those who arose from their graves bore witness that Jesus is the Son of God.[51] It is reasonable to assume that these individuals appeared to family members and close friends, and many tears of joy were likely shed when those who had risen from their graves appeared. Accounts of these experiences were likely passed down through families for generations, likely increasing the faith of many.

Jesus's Resurrection Testifies That He Is the Son of God

On this first Easter, Jesus appeared to Mary Magdalene, to other women, to Peter, to two disciples, to ten of the eleven Apostles, and to other disciples who were with the Apostles. The order in which Jesus chose to appear to these individuals is significant. Jesus was demonstrating that women are as important to Him and God as are men and that women can receive a personal witness. Likewise, men do not need to hold high positions in the Church in order to receive a personal witness. People today can ponder the Gospel accounts of Jesus's Resurrection and pray to receive a witness from the Holy Spirit. Jesus's Resurrection is an irrefutable, crowning witness that He is the divine Son of God.

The words of the hymn "He Is Risen!" reflect the joy that can come from reading the Gospel accounts of Jesus's Resurrection. The first verse is presented below as a fitting conclusion to this chapter:

> He is risen! He is risen!
> Tell it out with joyful voice.
> He has burst his three days' prison;

---

49. D&C 138:12, 16.

50. See 3 Ne. 23:7–13.

51. Before Christ died, the righteous in paradise were waiting for Christ's Resurrection and for Him to declare their "redemption from the bands of death" (see D&C 138:14–19).

Let the whole wide earth rejoice.
Death is conquered;
Man is free.
Christ has won the victory.[52]

Note to Chapter 69

1. The significance of the resurrection of all people. It may be difficult to comprehend the importance of the gift of the resurrection of all people, which was made possible through Jesus giving His life and then taking it up again. Without the reuniting of the spirit and the physical body, a person would not be able to reach his or her full potential in the eternities.

As Amulek taught, resurrected bodies are perfect: "The spirit and the body shall be reunited again in its perfect form; both limb and joint shall be restored to its proper frame . . . and even there shall not so much as a hair of their heads be lost; but everything shall be restored to its perfect form."[53] Further, resurrected bodies are not subject to physical pain, illness, infirmities, and degeneration.[54] These truths may become more meaningful and provide comfort to people when they or loved ones experience physical and mental challenges in mortality. Perhaps one reason for mortal limitations is so that people will more fully appreciate the blessings of the resurrection.

Although all resurrected bodies will be perfect, they will vary in degree of glory. As Paul wrote, "There are also celestial bodies, and bodies terrestrial, and bodies telestial: but the glory of the celestial, one; and the terrestrial, another; and the telestial, another. There is one glory of the sun, and another glory of the moon, and another glory of the stars; for one star differeth from another star in glory. So also is the resurrection of the dead."[55] The degree of

---

52.　Cecil Frances Alexander, "He Is Risen," *Hymns*, no. 199.

53.　Alma 11:43.

54.　See JST 1 Cor. 15:53–54; D&C 76:70, 78, 98.

55.　1 Cor. 15:40–42; see also D&C 76:70, 78, 98.

glory in a person's resurrected body will depend on the person's faithfulness in mortality and in the postmortal spirit world prior to being resurrected.[56]

Not all people will be resurrected at the same time. Some faithful individuals who died before Christ did were resurrected shortly after Christ was resurrected.[57] Abinadi and Alma referred to a "first resurrection," consisting of the resurrection of all those who died before Christ's Resurrection. Alma was of the opinion that this first resurrection occurred immediately following Christ's Resurrection and before the resurrection of any individuals who died after Christ's Resurrection.[58] This understanding is consistent with order and justice, for why should those who died before Christ have to wait to be resurrected until after He returns to the earth for His Second Coming?

At Christ's Second Coming, righteous individuals who have died and not yet been resurrected will be resurrected at that time.[59] Thus will begin what is often referred to as the morning of the first resurrection.[60] At a later point during the Millennium, those who chose not to accept the gospel during mortality but accepted it in the postmortal spirit world will be resurrected.[61] After the thousand years of Christ's millennial reign, those who chose not to accept the gospel during mortality or in the postmortal spirit world will be resurrected.[62] This resurrection is often referred to as the second resurrection.[63]

Of course, the most important fact is not the timing of when individuals will be resurrected but that all people will be resurrected. People's spirits and bodies will be united eternally! This great blessing is possible because of God's plan of salvation and Jesus's willingness to give up His life so that the plan of salvation could be accomplished.

---

56. See D&C 76:50–83, 98–103.
57. See Matt. 27:52–53.
58. See Mosiah 15:21–25; Alma 40:16–20. Additionally, Doctrine and Covenants 132:37 indicates that Abraham, Isaac, and Jacob have been resurrected.
59. See D&C 29:13; 43:18; 45:44–46; 76:50–70; 88:97–98.
60. See Rev. 20:6; D&C 76:64–65; McConkie, *Mormon Doctrine*, p. 640.
61. See D&C 88:99.
62. See D&C 88:100–102.
63. See McConkie, *Mormon Doctrine*, p. 640; see also D&C 76:85.

Chapter 69

FINAL EVENTS

(From the Sunday after Jesus's Resurrection to His Final Ascension)

For forty days following Christ's Resurrection, He appeared to and taught the eleven Apostles on multiple occasions.[1] For example, He appeared to the Apostles in Jerusalem, at the Sea of Galilee, and on a mountain in Galilee. This chapter discusses these appearances, as well as Christ's appearance to His brother James. The chapter also discusses Christ's Ascension to heaven from the Mount of Olives.

Jesus Appears to Thomas and the Other Apostles (John 20:24–29)

Thomas, one of the Twelve, had not been with the other ten Apostles when Jesus appeared to them on Easter Sunday. The ten Apostles told Thomas of Jesus's appearance, and Thomas had undoubtedly also heard of Jesus's appearances to Mary Magdalene, the other women, Peter, and the two disciples who walked to Emmaus. Nevertheless, Thomas said that he would not believe unless he could see Jesus for himself and touch the prints of the nails in Jesus's hands, wrists, and feet and the place where the spear pierced Jesus's side. The following is John's account:

> **John 20:24–29.** But Thomas, one of the twelve, called Didymus, was not with them when Jesus came. The other disciples therefore said unto him, We have seen the Lord. But he said unto them, Except I shall see in his hands the print of the nails, and put my finger into the print of the nails,

---

1. See Acts 1:3.

and thrust my hand into his side, I will not believe. And after eight days again his disciples were within, and Thomas with them: then came Jesus, the doors being shut, and stood in the midst, and said, Peace be unto you. Then saith he to Thomas, Reach hither thy finger, and behold my hands; and reach hither thy hand, and thrust it into my side: and be not faithless, but believing. And Thomas answered and said unto him, My Lord and my God. Jesus saith unto him, Thomas, because thou hast seen me, thou hast believed: blessed are they that have not seen, and yet have believed.

Thomas had been with Jesus throughout His ministry and had seen Jesus heal the sick and infirm, restore life to the dead, and perform other miracles. Thomas had also demonstrated His faith in Jesus: After Lazarus had died, Jesus had told the Apostles that He was going to Lazarus's grave in Bethany, where Jesus's life might have been in danger. Amid the Apostles' fear, Thomas exclaimed with courage and great faith, "Let us also go, that we may die with him."[2] After Jesus's Resurrection, Thomas desired to receive the same witness that the other Apostles had received on Easter Sunday.

On the Sunday following Jesus's Resurrection, the eleven Apostles had assembled, and as before, the doors were shut and possibly guarded for fear of the Sanhedrin, their representatives, and their informers. Jesus appeared in the room and told the Apostles, "Peace be unto you."[3] Then, He turned to Thomas and invited him to touch His hands and side so that Thomas could have a sure witness of Jesus's Resurrection, as the other Apostles had.

Jesus then told Thomas to not be faithless and, rather, to believe. Thomas now had his own witness, but he would still need to exercise faith in the days, months, and years ahead as he experienced various challenges and trials.[4] Jesus then told Thomas, "Blessed are they that have not seen, and

---

2.   John 11:16.
3.   Jesus had twice said "peace be unto you" when He appeared to ten of the Apostles on the day of His Resurrection (see John 20:19, 21).
4.   Smith noted the following about Thomas: "Early traditions, as believed in the fourth century, represent him as preaching in Parthia or Persia and as finally buried at Edessa. Later traditions carry him farther east. His martyrdom is said to have been occasioned by a lance, and is commemorated by the Latin church on December 21, by the Greek church on October 6, and by the Indians on July 1. The tradition that he preached in India is evidenced by a place near Madras known as St. Thomas' Mount." (Smith, *Bible Dictionary*, s.v. "Thomas.") Additionally, "at least two apocryphal gospels are attributed to him (*Gospel of Thomas, Infancy Gospel of Thomas*)" (*HarperCollins Bible Dictionary*, s.v. "Thomas").

yet have believed." Jesus's instruction to Thomas provides a valuable lesson to all people. Faith in Jesus should not be dependent on seeing, hearing, or touching Him. Faith is borne of the witness of the Holy Spirit, which is available to all.

Jesus Gives the Apostles Additional Signs (John 20:30)

John's account states that Jesus gave the Apostles additional signs:

John 20:30. And many other signs truly did Jesus in the presence of his disciples, which are not written in this book.

The signs that Jesus gave to His Apostles are unknown, but it is possible that the signs were similar to those in certain temple ordinances. Whatever the signs were, they were presumably meant to strengthen the Apostles and prepare them for their continuing ministries, both throughout the world and in the spirit world.

Jesus Appears to His Apostles at the Sea of Galilee (John 21:1–8)

On Easter Sunday, the two angels at Jesus's tomb and then Jesus Himself had directed the women who were witnesses of His Resurrection to tell His Apostles to go to Galilee and that He would visit them there.[5] At some point after Jesus appeared to the Apostles on the Sunday following His Resurrection, the Apostles went to Galilee. One evening while there, Peter, James, John, Thomas, Nathanael, and two other Apostles were together. Peter told the other Apostles that he was going to go fishing in the Sea of Galilee (also called Lake Tiberias), and they said they would go with him. The following is John's account:

John 21:1–8. After these things Jesus shewed himself again to the disciples at the sea of Tiberias; and on this wise shewed he himself. There were together Simon Peter, and Thomas called Didymus, and Nathanael of Cana in Galilee, and the sons of Zebedee, and two other of his disciples. Simon Peter saith unto them, I go a fishing. They say unto him, We also go with thee. They went forth, and entered into a ship immediately; and that night they caught nothing. But when the morning was now come, Jesus stood on

---

5. See Matt. 28:5–7, 10; Mark 16:7.

the shore: but the disciples knew not that it was Jesus. Then Jesus saith unto them, Children, have ye any meat? They answered him, No. And he said unto them, Cast the net on the right side of the ship, and ye shall find. They cast therefore, and now they were not able to draw it for the multitude of fishes. Therefore that disciple whom Jesus loved saith unto Peter, It is the Lord. Now when Simon Peter heard that it was the Lord, he girt his fisher's coat unto him, (for he was naked,) and did cast himself into the sea. And the other disciples came in a little ship; (for they were not far from land, but as it were two hundred cubits,) dragging the net with fishes.

Peter may have decided to go fishing because the Apostles were likely in need of money—Judas had been in charge of the money bag, and he presumably had not given it to another Apostle before He had hung himself. Peter, James, and John were fishermen by trade,[6] and thus fishing would have been a logical method of earning money for the Apostles. Peter may also have reasoned that fishing would provide them with needed food. Moreover, Peter may have decided to go fishing because he loved it and the Sea of Galilee and because fishing was a way to occupy his mind while he waited for Jesus to appear to the Apostles.

The seven Apostles set out in a large boat and a small boat and fished all night. They caught nothing, even though nighttime was often the most productive time to fish, as Peter, James, John, and likely the others well knew. Their unusually unsuccessful fishing at night may have helped them come to understand that people are not converted to the gospel in the darkness; they need the light of Christ and the witness of the Holy Ghost.

In the morning, Jesus appeared on the shore and asked whether the Apostles had "any meat"— that is, had they caught any fish. Interestingly, Jesus referred to the Apostles as children. The Greek word used here is *paidia*, which means "a little or young lad."[7] The Apostles had been with Jesus for about three years and had not yet been on their own in the gospel; therefore, in a sense they were still children.[8] The word *children* can also symbolize that the Apostles were children of God. Further, Jesus had

---

6.   See Mark 1:16, 19–20.

7.   Young, *Analytical Concordance*, s.v. "children."

8.   In John's first epistle, he sometimes also referred to members of the Church as children (see 1 Jn. 2:1, 12, 18, 28; 3:7, 18; 4:4; 5:2).

previously used the word *children* to symbolize who would qualify to enter the kingdom of heaven.[9]

The Apostles did not recognize who had asked them whether they had caught fish, and they answered that they had not. Jesus then told the Apostles that they would catch fish if they cast their net on the right side of the boat. Jesus's voice may have been hard for the Apostles to hear two hundred cubits (approximately one hundred yards) away if the water in the sea was not calm. Similarly, the whisperings of the Holy Ghost are often difficult to hear and understand. Even when the whisperings are heard and understood, they can be difficult to obey. Though the Apostles did not recognize Jesus, they followed His instruction to cast their net on the ship's right side—symbolic of the side of Jesus that people should be on—and caught a "multitude of fishes."

After the Apostles caught the fish, John recognized that the man who was standing on the shore was Jesus. Perhaps John recognized Jesus at this point because John remembered a previous time when Peter and others had fished all night without catching anything but then had caught many fish the next morning, after Jesus had told Peter where to cast his net.[10] Or perhaps John recognized Jesus after remembering the parable He had given about the kingdom of heaven being like a net "that was cast into the sea, and gathered of every kind" until it was full.[11] Or perhaps John was able to recognize Jesus because the sun was rising higher and there was more light. Whatever the reason, John said to Peter, "It is the Lord." Likewise, people today may recognize Jesus due to a variety of reasons; the important thing is that people do recognize Him and follow His directions.

Peter put on his fisher's coat because he was not fully clothed and then jumped into the sea and swam or waded to Jesus on the shore. The other Apostles came to the shore in a little boat that dragged the net full of fish.

Jesus Instructs the Apostles to Bring Him the Fish They Caught (John 21:9–14)

When the Apostles arrived on the shore, they saw that Jesus was cooking fish on a fire and also had bread. Presumably, Jesus had acquired the fish and

9.   See Matt. 18:1–5; see also Matt. 5:9.
10.   See Luke 5:4–10.
11.   Matt. 13:47.

the bread miraculously and possibly had also kindled the fire miraculously. The following is John's account:

> **John 21:9–14.** As soon then as they were come to land, they saw a fire of coals there, and fish laid thereon, and bread. Jesus saith unto them, Bring of the fish which ye have now caught. Simon Peter went up, and drew the net to land full of great fishes, an hundred and fifty and three: and for all there were so many, yet was not the net broken. Jesus saith unto them, Come and dine. And none of the disciples durst ask him, Who art thou? knowing that it was the Lord. Jesus then cometh, and taketh bread, and giveth them, and fish likewise. This is now the third time that Jesus shewed himself to his disciples, after that he was risen from the dead.

Many lessons can be derived from this experience. Christ directed the Apostles to bring the fish to Him. Likewise, the Apostles were to bring people unto Christ by teaching them the gospel—the Apostles were to be fishers of people.

As another example, after the Apostles brought the fish to the shore, they counted the fish. The total was 153 fish—truly an abundant catch. Similarly, by following Jesus's guidance, disciples can bring many other people to Him. Additionally, just as the fish were counted, it is important to be aware of and account for all people who accept the gospel, so they can be watched over and not overlooked or lost. Further, John's account uses the word *great* to describe the fish. Similarly, all of God's children are great in His sight.

Even though the net was filled with many large fish, the net did not break. Likewise, the Church can accommodate all of its members. Its infrastructure expands so the Church can meet the needs of every member, no matter the location.

After the Apostles counted the fish they caught, Jesus invited the Apostles to eat the fish and bread that He had provided. The meal was simple, just as the principles of the gospel are simple. Just as Jesus provided food for the Apostles and also helped them acquire fish, He would provide for the Apostles' physical needs and prepare the way for them as they took the gospel to the world.

The resurrected Son of God had now appeared to His Apostles as a group for the third time, and they all recognized Him and that He had told them how to catch a large number of fish. There could be no question in their minds that Christ had risen from the grave. Going forward, they were to witness of His Resurrection.

Jesus Instructs Peter to Feed Jesus's Lambs and Sheep (John 21:15–17)

The Apostles ate the meal Jesus had provided,[12] and then Jesus asked Peter whether He loved Jesus "more than these," likely a reference to the 153 fish that the Apostles had caught:

> **John 21:15–17.** So when they had dined, Jesus saith to Simon Peter, Simon, son of Jonas, lovest thou me more than these? He saith unto him, Yea, Lord; thou knowest that I love thee. He saith unto him, Feed my lambs. He saith to him again the second time, Simon, son of Jonas, lovest thou me? He saith unto him, Yea, Lord; thou knowest that I love thee. He saith unto him, Feed my sheep. He saith unto him the third time, Simon, son of Jonas, lovest thou me? Peter was grieved because he said unto him the third time, Lovest thou me? And he said unto him, Lord, thou knowest all things; thou knowest that I love thee. Jesus saith unto him, Feed my sheep.

It may be significant that Jesus asked Peter three times whether he loved Jesus, for just a few days before, Peter had denied three times that he knew Jesus.[13] Jesus first asked, "Lovest thou me more than these?" Presumably, Jesus was asking Peter whether he loved Jesus more than food and the work Peter had done prior to becoming one of Jesus's Apostles. In other words, Jesus was asking whether Peter was still willing to forsake all to follow Him.

Peter responded, "Thou knowest that I love thee." Peter recognized that Jesus knew Peter's heart and his desires. In reply, Jesus told Peter to feed His lambs. That is, Peter was to spiritually nourish those who were young in age and also those who were young in the gospel. The Greek word used here for *feed* is *boskō*, which means not only to feed but also to pasture.[14] Therefore, Peter was not only to teach the gospel to the young in age and young in experience but also to provide a place that they could

---

12. There is no record of Jesus eating the food.
13. See Matt. 26:69–75; Mark 14:66–72; Luke 22:56–62; John 18:17–27.
14. See Young, *Analytical Concordance*, s.v. "feed."

regularly go to find spiritual food. The Apostles may have come to more completely understand that one of the Church's purposes is to provide each member such a place.

Then, for the second time, Jesus asked Peter: "Lovest thou me?" Again, Peter responded, "Thou knowest that I love thee." Jesus replied by directing Peter to "feed my sheep." The Greek word used this time for *feed* is *poimainō*, which means "to tend as a shepherd."[15] Jesus was directing Peter that in addition to feeding and providing pasture for Church members, he should watch over them.

Jesus then asked Peter again, "Lovest thou me?" Peter was grieved because Jesus had now asked the question three times. Peter responded, "Lord, thou knowest all things; thou knowest that I love thee." Jesus replied by telling Peter to "feed my sheep." The Greek word used for *feed* here is the same one used in Jesus's first reply: *boskō*. Therefore, Jesus was telling Peter to provide spiritual food and pasture to those who are older in age or more mature in gospel experience and testimony. Thus, through Jesus's three replies, He was telling Peter to spiritually nourish and care for people of all ages and of all levels of experience in and testimonies of the gospel.

When Jesus used the words *lambs* and *sheep*, He preceded the words with *my*. The lambs and sheep are His. Further, since all people are children of Heavenly Father, they are all presumably Jesus's lambs and sheep, even if they do not follow Him. Therefore, though the Apostles had primary responsibility for those who believed in Jesus, His use of *my* implies that all people, regardless of whether they are disciples of Jesus, need to be spiritually nourished and cared for.

Also of note is that when Jesus asked Peter the first and second time whether he loved Jesus, the Greek word used for *love* is *agapaō*, which is the highest form of love: Christlike, self-sacrificing love. The Greek word for *love* used in Peter's response each time is *phileō*, which means to be a friend and does not refer to the highest form of love. The third time Jesus posed His

---

15. Young, *Analytical Concordance*, s.v. "love."

question to Peter, the Greek word used for *love* is *phileō*.[16] One of the great messages of this brief interchange between Jesus and Peter—a message that Peter likely remembered ever afterward—is that Jesus accepts people where they are in their spiritual progression and their love for Him. A further lesson from this interchange is that people need to love Jesus in the highest sense and also view Him as a friend. In turn, for Jesus to consider people His friends, they need to be His disciples and keep His commandments.[17]

Jesus Tells Peter about How He Will Die (John 21:18–19)

Jesus then alluded to how Peter would die:

John 21:18–19. Verily, verily, I say unto thee, When thou wast young, thou girdedst thyself, and walkedst whither thou wouldest: but when thou shalt be old, thou shalt stretch forth thy hands, and another shall gird thee, and carry thee whither thou wouldest not. This spake he, signifying by what death he should glorify God. And when he had spoken this, he saith unto him, Follow me.

Jesus stated that when Peter was young, he had the freedom to wear what he wanted, go where he wanted, and do what he wanted. Jesus then told Peter that when he was old, his hands would be stretched out—that is, Peter's arms would be stretched out on a crucifixion cross. Someone, presumably an executioner, would clothe Peter, likely with a loincloth,[18] and would take Peter to the place of execution.[19] Peter would give his life as his final witness that Jesus is the Son of God.[20]

After Jesus referred to Peter's death, Jesus told Peter to follow Him. Peter was to follow Jesus's teachings and example, including by consecrating

---

16. See Young, *Analytical Concordance*, s.v. "love." According to Young, Greek has words referring to other types of love. For example, *philadelphia* means brotherly love, *philarguriz* means love of silver, *philoteknos* means love of one's children, *philandros* means love of husband (and presumably love of wife), and *philanthrōpia* means love of humankind. (See Young, *Analytical Concordance*, "love.")

17. See Luke 12:24; John 15:14. The Doctrine and Covenants contains several examples of Jesus calling Church members His friends (see D&C 84:77; 88:3, 62, 117; 93:45; 94:1; 98:1).

18. See Dummelow, *Bible Commentary*, p. 811.

19. See Dummelow, *Bible Commentary*, p. 811.

20. According to Christian tradition, Peter was crucified upside down in Rome at the direction of Emperor Nero (see *HarperCollins Bible Dictionary*, s.v. "Peter").

His life to the ministry, leading the Church, being valiant in the face of adversity, healing the sick and infirm, and lifting the downtrodden. Peter was to follow Jesus even in death, sealing his witness with his blood, as Jesus had. Peter was also to follow Jesus by continuing his ministry in the next life and assisting in the Restoration of the gospel in the latter days.

Peter Asks Jesus about John's Future (John 21:20–23)

After Jesus told Peter about his death, Peter turned and saw John. Peter then asked Jesus, "What shall this man do?" Peter may have wished to know whether John too would be crucified or whether John would die in a different way. The following is John's account:

> **John 21:20–23.** Then Peter, turning about, seeth the disciple whom Jesus loved following; which also leaned on his breast at supper, and said, Lord, which is he that betrayeth thee? Peter seeing him saith to Jesus, Lord, and what shall this man do? Jesus saith unto him, If I will that he tarry till I come, what is that to thee? follow thou me. Then went this saying abroad among the brethren, that that disciple should not die: yet Jesus said not unto him, He shall not die; but, If I will that he tarry till I come, what is that to thee?

Jesus responded to Peter, "If I will that he tarry till I come, what is that to thee? Follow thou me." Peter's ministry would be different in some respects from John's. Peter would continue his ministry on the earth for a time and then would die and go to the spirit world, where he would minister among the dead. John had a different calling, which Peter may have sensed.

A revelation that Joseph Smith received makes it clear that Jesus granted Peter and John what they desired:

> And the Lord said unto me: John, my beloved, what desirest thou? For if you shall ask what you will, it shall be granted unto you. And I said unto him: Lord, give unto me power over death, that I may live and bring souls unto thee. And the Lord said unto me: Verily, verily, I say unto thee, because thou desirest this thou shalt tarry until I come in my glory, and shalt prophesy before nations, kindreds, tongues and people. And for this cause the Lord said unto Peter: If I will that he tarry till I come, what is that to thee? For he desired of me that he might bring souls unto me, but thou desiredst that thou mightest speedily come unto me in my kingdom. I say unto thee, Peter,

this was a good desire; but my beloved has desired that he might do more, or a greater work yet among men than what he has before done. Yea, he has undertaken a greater work; therefore I will make him as flaming fire and a ministering angel; he shall minister for those who shall be heirs of salvation who dwell on the earth. And I will make thee to minister for him and for thy brother James; and unto you three I will give this power and the keys of this ministry until I come. Verily I say unto you, ye shall both have according to your desires, for ye both joy in that which ye have desired.[21]

Further information regarding John's desire and ministry[22] is provided in 3 Nephi 28:6–9, in which Jesus talks to the three Nephite disciples who received the same ministerial calling as John did:

Behold, I know your thoughts, and ye have desired the thing which John, my beloved, who was with me in my ministry, before that I was lifted up by the Jews, desired of me. Therefore, more blessed are ye, for ye shall never taste of death; but ye shall live to behold all the doings of the Father unto the children of men, even until all things shall be fulfilled according to the will of the Father, when I shall come in my glory with the powers of heaven. And ye shall never endure the pains of death; but when I shall come in my glory ye shall be changed in the twinkling of an eye from mortality to immortality; and then shall ye be blessed in the kingdom of my Father. And again, ye shall not have pain while ye shall dwell in the flesh, neither sorrow save it be for the sins of the world; and all this will I do because of the thing which ye have desired of me, for ye have desired that ye might bring the souls of men unto me, while the world shall stand.

An important principle can be found in Peter's question and Jesus's response. Just as Peter and John had different desires, responsibilities, and paths, so do all other people in the Church, and all people can contribute in their own way, according to their abilities and circumstances. For example, in most cases a single mother must devote almost all of her time to earning an income and caring for her children. She therefore has limited time for Church service aside from teaching her children the gospel, and for a time perhaps all she is asked to do is fulfill a ministering assignment. Someone else may have a lighter load at home and may be asked to serve in a more

---

21. D&C 7:1–8.

22. For further information about John's mission, see note 1 at the end of this chapter.

time-consuming calling. Regardless of a person's responsibilities, he or she is important to Jesus and can contribute to His Church. In explaining that people with different abilities and circumstances play valuable roles in the Church, the Apostle Paul used the body as an analogy: "For the body is not one member, but many. . . . And the eye cannot say unto the hand, I have no need of thee: nor again the head to the feet, I have no need of you."[23]

Jesus Appears on a Mountain in Galilee (Matt. 28:16–20; Mark 16:15–18)

Apparently, during one of Jesus's visits with the Apostles, He directed them and perhaps other disciples to go to a mountain in Galilee. They did so, and Jesus appeared to them there. The following are Matthew's and Mark's accounts:

> **Matthew 28:16–20.** Then the eleven disciples went away into Galilee, into a mountain where Jesus had appointed them. And when they saw him, they worshipped him: but some doubted. And Jesus came and spake unto them, saying, All power is given unto me in heaven and in earth. Go ye therefore, and teach all nations, baptizing them in the name of the Father, and of the Son, and of the Holy Ghost: Teaching them to observe all things whatsoever I have commanded you: and, lo, I am with you alway, even unto the end of the world. Amen.

> **Mark 16:15–18.** And he said unto them, Go ye into all the world, and preach the gospel to every creature. He that believeth and is baptized shall be saved; but he that believeth not shall be damned. And these signs shall follow them that believe; in my name shall they cast out devils; they shall speak with new tongues; they shall take up serpents; and if they drink any deadly thing, it shall not hurt them; they shall lay hands on the sick, and they shall recover.

Matthew's account indicates that among those present, "some doubted." The eleven Apostles had already seen the resurrected Christ on multiple occasions, so it seems likely that those who doubted were not the Apostles but were other disciples who had not previously seen Christ as a resurrected,

---

23.   1 Cor. 12:14, 21; see also vv. 14–31.

glorified being.[24] One may wonder what the eleven Apostles and any other disciples were thinking and discussing as they ascended the mountain to the appointed place[25] and sat and waited for Christ to appear. The eleven Apostles may have shared their witness of the risen Lord with any others who were present.

After Jesus arrived, He declared that "all power is given unto me in heaven and in earth." Presumably, Jesus wanted those present to know that He, as the resurrected Son of God, had been glorified by His Father and had received all power from His Father. Jesus had received power prior to His mortal ministry, but He may not have received a fullness of power until after His Resurrection, when He had completed His earthly mission and overcome the world.

Jesus's power includes the keys to open the doors of spirit prison and enable all the spirits who are there to receive an opportunity to hear and accept the gospel. His power also extends to other worlds He created under the direction of His Father.[26] Of course, Jesus also has power over this earth. He used this power to commission the Apostles, the Seventy, and other disciples and to bless them in fulfilling their responsibility to teach the gospel. The sure witness that came from seeing Jesus as a resurrected being must have been an anchor to them as they preached the gospel. Likewise, people today can receive the witness of the Holy Spirit that Jesus is the Son of God, and this witness can serve as an anchor throughout life.

Jesus instructed the eleven Apostles and perhaps others present to "teach all nations, baptizing them in the name of the Father, and of the Son, and of the Holy Ghost."[27] Whereas Jesus had previously instructed

---

24. Dummelow stated that Matthew's reference to the eleven Apostles "does not of necessity imply that no others were present, but only that the words of Jesus were mainly addressed to them. . . . That the meeting was by appointment renders it probable that all the disciples who could possibly be brought together were present." (Dummelow, *Bible Commentary*, p. 720.) It is possible that those who were present with the Apostles were the more than five hundred men who Paul stated saw the resurrected Christ on one occasion (see 1 Cor. 15:6; Dummelow, *Bible Commentary*, p. 720; Talmage, *Jesus the Christ*, p. 643).

25. The location may have been where Jesus had delivered the Sermon on the Mount and had ordained the Apostles (see McConkie, *Mortal Messiah*, vol. 4, p. 297).

26. See D&C 76:24.

27. If the group Jesus was speaking to included individuals who were not Apostles, He may have likewise commissioned these individuals to preach the gospel. If the group was large, this event might cause people to look to the time in the latter days when Adam will appear at the sacred place called Adam-ondi-Ahman (see D&C 116).

the Apostles to preach the gospel only to members of the house of Israel,[28] the Apostles were now to preach to all people. In the latter days, that same commission has been given to members of The Church of Jesus Christ of Latter-day Saints. Those Jesus was instructing were to teach everyone to keep the commandments and to covenant to do so by being baptized. Keeping the commandments is not only the way to obtain eternal life but is also the way to achieve peace and happiness.

Additionally, Jesus provided assurance that He would always be with His Apostles; He would never forsake them. This promise can also apply to those who are called to serve missions in the latter days. As missionaries strive to keep the commandments and teach the gospel, Jesus will guide and strengthen them.

Jesus also stated that signs would follow, or accompany, those who believed that He is the Son of God. The signs, which were to occur in Jesus's name, included casting out devils, speaking in tongues, not being harmed by poisonous snakes or drinks, and healing the sick.[29]

The minutes or hours spent with Jesus on the mountain were likely sacred to those present. Afterward, they and perhaps other Church members may have considered this mountain to be a sacred place because of what had transpired there.

Jesus Appears to James (1 Cor. 15:7)

At some point after Jesus appeared to His Apostles for the first time after His Resurrection, He appeared to James. This appearance is mentioned only by Paul in his First Epistle to the Corinthians:

1 Corinthians 15:7. After that [appearing to Peter, the eleven Apostles, and five hundred men], he was seen of James; then of all the apostles.

Various Bible commentators have asserted that the James referred to here is Jesus's brother James.[30] Jesus had four brothers, and Matthew's and

---

28. See Matt. 10:5–6.

29. All of these signs are gifts of the Spirit (see 1 Cor. 12:4–11; Moro. 10:8–18; D&C 46:11–29).

30. See, for example, *HarperCollins Bible Dictionary*, s.v. "James"; Smith, *Bible Dictionary*, s.v. "James, the Epistle of."

Mark's gospels indicate that the brothers' names are James, Joses, Simon, and Judas.[31] Both gospels list James's name first, perhaps implying that James was the eldest brother after Jesus. It is unknown whether as the brothers grew up their parents told them who Jesus's actual father was and who Jesus really was, but presumably their parents did not.[32] There is some indication that during Jesus's ministry, some or all of Jesus's brothers did not believe that He was the Son of God.[33] However, shortly after Jesus's Resurrection, at least some of His brothers gathered with disciples of Jesus, which suggests that these brothers came to believe in Jesus's divinity.[34] When Jesus appeared to James, the two men may have embraced and James may have felt the prints of the nails in Jesus's hands, wrists, and feet and felt the mark in His side. James now had a sure knowledge that his brother was indeed the Son of God.

Perhaps Jesus's appearance to James is mentioned in the scriptural record because James later significantly contributed to building the kingdom of God on the earth. For example, James was chosen by Peter, James, and John to be the first bishop of the Church in Jerusalem because of his outstanding virtue.[35] James was called James the Just, and he helped resolve the dispute among Church leaders regarding whether converted Gentiles needed to be circumcised.[36] Further, in Paul's letter to the Galatian Saints, he implied that James had been called as an Apostle: "But other of the apostles saw I none, save James the Lord's brother."[37]

James is also widely accepted to be the author of an epistle that has been included in the New Testament. James 1:5–7, which encourages people

31. See Matt. 13:55; Mark 6:3.
32. In recounting the events that occurred at Jesus's birth, Luke stated that "Mary kept all these things, and pondered them in her heart" (Luke 2:19).
33. See John 7:3–5.
34. See Acts 1:13–14.
35. See Eusebius, *Church History*, vol. 2, p. 52; see also *HarperCollins Bible Dictionary*, s.v. "James."
36. See Acts 15:13–29.
37. Gal. 1:19. Paul may have felt particularly close to James because Jesus had appeared to James alone, as Jesus had appeared to Paul. Eusebius, citing Clement of Alexandria, wrote that "after the resurrection the Lord imparted the higher knowledge [gnosis] to James the Just, John and Peter. They gave it to the other apostles, and the other apostles to the Seventy." (Eusebius, *Church History*, vol. 2, p. 53.) The accuracy of this account is uncertain, and what that higher knowledge might have been is unknown.

to sincerely pray for knowledge, inspired Joseph Smith to pray to find out which church was true, and this prayer led to Him seeing the Father and the Son and the gospel being restored in the latter days.[38] James's epistle contains additional important principles. For example, he explained that both faith and good works are essential in order to obtain eternal life: "Even so faith, if it hath not works, is dead, being alone. Yea, a man may say, Thou hast faith, and I have works: shew me thy faith without thy works, and I will shew thee my faith by my works."[39]

Regarding James's death, the *HarperCollins Bible Dictionary* states: "Both the Jewish historian Josephus and the Christian Hegesippus (according to the fourth-century church historian Eusebius) report that James was put to death by the priestly authorities in Jerusalem a few years before the destruction of the temple in 70 CE."[40] Eusebius described the manner of James's death: he "was thrown down from the parapet [of the temple] and beaten to death with a fuller's club."[41] As with many others, James gave his life to seal his testimony that Jesus is the Son of God and the promised Messiah.

Jesus Continues His Ministry for Forty Days (Luke 24:44–49; Acts 1:3–5)

In addition to Jesus's appearances already discussed in this chapter, He likely met with His Apostles and perhaps other disciples many other times during the forty days following His Resurrection. The following is one of the few additional records of what Jesus taught:

> **Acts 1:3–5.** To whom [the Apostles] also he shewed himself alive after his passion by many infallible proofs, being seen of them forty days, and speaking of the things pertaining to the kingdom of God: and, being assembled together with them, commanded them that they should not depart from Jerusalem, but wait for the promise of the Father, which, saith he, ye have heard of me. For John truly baptized with water; but ye shall be baptized with the Holy Ghost not many days hence.

---

38. See Joseph Smith—History 1:8–20.
39. James 2:17–18.
40. *HarperCollins Bible Dictionary*, s.v. "James."
41. Eusebius, *Church History*, vol. 2, p. 53.

When Jesus met with His Apostles during this forty-day period, He taught them of "things pertaining to the kingdom of God." These things may have included instruction on where the Apostles should travel, insight regarding the doctrine they were to teach; the nature and mission of the Holy Ghost; and the significance of the Holy Ghost in bearing witness of the truth, of Jesus's divinity, and of Heavenly Father. Jesus may have also taught them how to organize the young Church, including by appointing prophets, apostles, evangelists, pastors, and teachers.[42] He may have taught them that the purpose of the Church was for the "perfecting of the saints, for the work of the ministry, for the edifying of the body of Christ."[43]

Presumably, Jesus also taught the Apostles of the importance of thoroughly understanding the scriptures, their context, and their spiritual significance.[44] The scriptures testify of Jesus, including His Atonement and Resurrection, and the Apostles were also to testify of Jesus and what He did. They needed to bear solemn witness of Christ's Atonement and of its importance to all people. The Apostles also needed to be able to help those they taught to understand the scriptures. They needed to be able to refute false doctrine, especially as they preached the gospel to the gentile world, which was filled with various philosophies and concepts of God. They needed to be able to use the scriptures, accompanied by the Holy Ghost, to lift and inspire people to repent and be baptized.

Jesus may have taught the Apostles more about the premortal world, the plan of salvation, and their future role in teaching the gospel in the postmortal spirit world. Additionally, He may have taught them about future events, including regarding the growth of the early Church, the Apostasy, the Restoration of the gospel in the latter days, His millennial reign on the earth, the Final Judgment, and the sanctification of the earth. He likely also taught the Apostles more completely about the ordinances of baptism, conferral of the gift of the Holy Ghost, and the sacrament. He may have also taught more about the priesthood, including its sealing powers. Jesus may have also taught many other things during this forty-day period.

---

42. See Eph. 4:11.
43. Eph. 4:12.
44. See Luke 24:45.

Jesus also told the Apostles to stay in Jerusalem until they received "the promise of the Father" and were "endued with power from on high."[45] That is, they were to wait to receive the gift of the Holy Ghost.[46] Additionally, in response to a question regarding Jesus's return and restoration of His kingdom, He told the Apostles: "It is not for you to know the times or the seasons, which the Father hath put in his own power. But ye shall receive power, after that the Holy Ghost is come upon you: and ye shall be witnesses unto me both in Jerusalem, and in all Judea, and in Samaria, and unto the uttermost part of the earth."[47]

Jesus Ascends into Heaven (Mark 16:19–20; Luke 24:50–53; Acts 1:9–12)

At the end of Jesus's forty-day ministry, He led the eleven Apostles to Bethany, along the southeastern slope of the Mount of Olives:

Luke 24:50–53. And he led them out as far as to Bethany, and he lifted up his hands, and blessed them. And it came to pass, while he blessed them, he was parted from them, and carried up into heaven. And they worshipped him, and returned to Jerusalem with great joy: and were continually in the temple, praising and blessing God. Amen.

Acts 1:9–12. And when he had spoken these things, while they beheld, he was taken up; and a cloud received him out of their sight. And while they looked steadfastly toward heaven as he went up, behold, two men stood by them in white apparel; which also said, Ye men of Galilee, why stand ye gazing up into heaven? this same Jesus, which is taken up from you into heaven, shall so come in like manner as ye have seen him go into heaven. Then returned they unto Jerusalem from the mount called Olivet, which is from Jerusalem a sabbath day's journey.

Either before or when Jesus met with the Apostles on this last occasion, He likely told them that the time had come for Him to ascend to His Father and for the Apostles to assume responsibility for taking the gospel to the

---

45.   This instruction implies that during at least part of this forty-day period, the Apostles were in Jerusalem, not Galilee.

46.   The Apostles likely received the gift of the Holy Ghost on the Day of Pentecost, about ten days after Jesus ascended into heaven (see Acts 2:1–18).

47.   Acts 1:7–8; see also v. 6.

world. For the Apostles, one era was ending and another era was beginning. One may wonder what the Apostles thought and felt as they met with Jesus for the last time. They loved Him and had been with Him for more than three years. They had seen His miracles, had heard His teachings, had witnessed His mercy toward and love for them and others, and were witnesses of His Resurrection.

Now, Christ "lifted up His hands, and blessed" these eleven men, who were to be His witnesses.[48] Then, He was "carried up into heaven," and "a cloud received him out of their sight." As the Apostles looked heavenward, two angels appeared and testified that at a future time, Christ would descend from heaven in a cloud and return to the earth. Indeed, Christ will return for His glorious Second Coming!

The Apostles returned to Jerusalem and frequently went to the temple, where they praised and blessed God. Likewise, people today can regularly attend the temple and praise God. By serving in the temple and feeling the Spirit there, people will be better prepared for when Christ returns.

Jesus Is the Redeemer of the World

God's plan for His children provides a way for them to progress eternally, and Jesus is central to that plan. Without Jesus, humankind could not inherit eternal life. The Gospel records of Matthew, Mark, Luke, and John are independent witnesses of Jesus, and each unequivocally affirms that He is the divine Son of God, that He came into the world from the realms of glory, that He atoned for the sins of all humankind, and that He is the Redeemer of the world. These Gospels are records of Jesus's teachings and miracles, His goodness and holiness, and His sacrifice. Jesus's life, teachings, and miracles have inspired billions of people to believe in Him and in His Father. Ultimately, all people will bow before Jesus and acknowledge that He is the Son of God.[49] Because of Jesus Christ, peace and joy in this life are possible, as is eternal life.

---

48. See Luke 24:50.
49. See Isa. 45:23; Rom. 14:11; Philip. 2:10; Mosiah 27:31; D&C 76:110; 88:104.

The first verse of the hymn "I Know That My Redeemer Lives,"[50] penned by Samuel Medley, provides a fitting concluding witness of Jesus Christ, the Son of God:

> I know that my Redeemer lives.
> What comfort this sweet sentence gives!
> He lives, he lives, who once was dead.
> He lives my ever-living Head.
> He lives to bless me with his love.
> He lives to plead for me above.
> He lives my hungry soul to feed.
> He lives to bless in time of need.

This author adds his own witness that Jesus Christ is the divine Son of God.

Note to Chapter 69

1. The Apostle John's calling to write the book of Revelation. John received a calling in the premortal world to write the book of Revelation, in which he described a vision he received regarding the last days, Christ's Second Coming, and the Millennium. John's calling to write the book of Revelation was mentioned by an angel who showed Nephi many of the same things that John saw:

> And it came to pass that the angel spake unto me, saying: Look! And I looked and beheld a man, and he was dressed in a white robe. And the angel said unto me: Behold one of the twelve apostles of the Lamb. Behold, he shall see and write the remainder of these things; yea, and also many things which have been. And he shall also write concerning the end of the world. Wherefore, the things which he shall write are just and true. . . . And behold, the things which this apostle of the Lamb shall write are many things which thou hast seen; and behold, the remainder shalt thou see. But the things which thou shalt see hereafter thou shalt not write; for the Lord God hath ordained the apostle of the Lamb of God that he should write them.[51]

50.   Samuel Medley, "I Know That My Redeemer Lives," *Hymns*, no. 136.
51.   1 Ne. 14:18–25.

Appendix

THE SPIRIT WORLD

While on the cross, Jesus said to the penitent thief, "To day shalt thou be with me in paradise."[1] The meaning of Jesus's statement was clarified as follows by Joseph Smith: "This day thou shalt be with me in the world of spirits: then I will teach you all about it and answer your inquiries."[2] This appendix discusses what Jews during Jesus's day believed about the afterlife, truths that have been revealed about the postmortal spirit world, and spirit paradise and prison. This chapter also discusses Jesus's visit to the spirit world following His death, the teaching that occurs in the spirit world, and ministering spirits.

Jewish Beliefs about the Afterlife

Initial insight about Jesus's statement to the penitent thief can come from understanding the Jews' beliefs regarding the afterlife. The Jews believed that after people died, their spirits went to *Sheol*. The *HarperCollins Bible Dictionary* states that Sheol "is a biblical term for the netherworld, in some respects the Hebrew counterpart of Hades. . . . The dead in Sheol are referred to as 'shades,' pale reflections of the men and women they had once been. . . . Existence in Sheol is characterized by forgetfulness and inactivity, but Sheol is not a place of punishment in the Bible. Rescue from Sheol is a recurring theme in biblical poetry."[3]

---

1. Luke 23:43; see also Eccl. 12:7.
2. Smith, *Teachings*, p. 309.
3. *HarperCollins Bible Dictionary*, s.v. "Sheol"; see also *Jewish Encyclopedia*, s.v. "Sheol."

Many Jews believed that Sheol comprised two areas: a place where the righteous spirits resided in a state of happiness[4] and a place where the wicked resided in a state of torment.[5] Some people wonder whether Sheol is the same as hades. Talmage explained, "By many their terms 'hades' and 'sheol' are understood to designate the place of departed spirits, comprising both paradise and the prison realm; by others the terms are applied only to the latter, the place of the wicked, which is apart from paradise, the abode of the just."[6] Additionally, Joseph Smith said: "Hades, the Greek, or Sheol, the Hebrew, these two significations mean a world of spirits. Hades, Sheol, paradise, spirits in prison, are all one: it is a world of spirits."[7]

The Jews of Jesus's time believed that Sheol was not the same place as hell, as the *HarperCollins Bible Dictionary* explains:

> The concept of hell is different from Sheol (in the Hebrew Bible) and from Hades (in most Greek literature) in three ways: (1) only the wicked enter hell, whereas good and bad alike occupy Sheol and Hades; (2) the wicked are sent to hell after a final judgment at the end of time, whereas people were thought to enter Sheol or Hades immediately upon death; and (3) hell involves eternal torment, whereas Sheol and Hades were characterized only by absence of life, not enhanced suffering. . . . "Hell" seems to be a circumlocution for "the devil," much as "heaven" is elsewhere a circumlocution for "God."[8]

Regarding the Jewish view of heaven, the *HarperCollins Bible Dictionary* explains that "in the biblical Hebrew, the word for heaven (shamayim) is always plural. . . . The use of the plural probably does not mean that the ancient Hebrews conceived of more than one heaven (different heavens located in different places). . . . It was common to conceive of heaven as having multiple levels or layers. . . . 'Heaven' sometimes become a circumlocution for 'God,' a way of speaking of God without using the divine name. Thus 'kingdom of heaven' . . . is simply another expression for 'kingdom of God.'"[9]

---

4.   See Farrar, *Life of Christ*, p. 625n2; Smith, *Bible Dictionary*, s.v. "paradise"; Edersheim, *Life and Times of Jesus the Messiah*, p. 669.

5.   See Luke 16:19–31; Dummelow, *Bible Commentary*, p. 761.

6.   Talmage, *Jesus the Christ*, p. 627n 1.

7.   Smith, *Teachings*, p. 310.

8.   *HarperCollins Bible Dictionary*, s.v. "hell.

9.   *HarperCollins Bible Dictionary*, s.v. "heaven."

When Christ told the penitent thief, "To day, shalt thou be with me in paradise,"[10] the thief must have felt immense relief, for he was assured that he would be with Christ in paradise and not be with the wicked.

Revealed Truths about the Spirit World

The Book of Mormon and modern revelation—in particular, Joseph F. Smith's vision of the postmortal spirit world[11]—provide a more-correct understanding of the spirit world, where the spirits of the dead go prior to the Final Judgment and resurrection. Brigham Young taught that the spirit world is on this earth[12] and that "everything there will appear as natural as things now do."[13] Perhaps the reason that mortals typically do not see those in the spirit world is because, as Joseph Smith stated, "spirit is matter, but it is more fine or pure, and can only be discerned by purer eyes; we cannot see it; but when our bodies are purified we shall see that it is all matter."[14] According to Doctrine and Covenants 77:2, "the spirit of man [is] in the likeness of his person."[15] Joseph F. Smith taught that "our children were full-grown and possessed their full stature in the spirit, before they entered mortality" and "will possess [the same stature] after they have passed away from mortality, and as they will also appear after the resurrection."[16] Spirits in the spirit world are free from mortal infirmities, and their spirit bodies are presumably perfect in form, as will be their resurrected bodies.[17]

In the spirit world, people continue to have relationships and interact with each other. Doctrine and Covenants 130:2 states, "That same sociality which exists among us here will exist among us there."[18] Similarly, Brigham Young taught, "Spirits will be familiar with spirits in the spirit world— will converse, behold, and exercise every variety of communication one

---

10. Luke 23:43.
11. See D&C 138.
12. See *Journal of Discourses*, vol. 3, pp. 368–369; vol. 4, p. 134.
13. *Journal of Discourses*, vol. 7, p. 333.
14. D&C 131:7–8.
15. D&C 77:2.
16. Smith, *Gospel Doctrine*, p. 455.
17. See Alma 11:43.
18. D&C 130:2.

with another as familiarly and naturally as while here in tabernacles."[19] Additionally, McConkie wrote that "life and work and activity all continue in the spirit world."[20]

People sometimes say that those who die take nothing with them. Certainly, they do not take material things with them, but they do take with them nonmaterial things, such as their character; their talents; their desires for good or evil; their love for family and friends; and memories, including of mistakes[21] and spiritual experiences. As Doctrine and Covenants 130:18–19 states, "Whatever principle of intelligence we attain unto in this life, it will rise with us in the resurrection. And if a person gains more knowledge and intelligence in this life through his diligence and obedience than another, he will have so much the advantage in the world to come."[22]

McConkie noted that in the spirit world, people "possess the same attitudes, inclinations, and feelings there which they had in this life. They believe the same things, as far as eternal truths are concerned; they continue, in effect, to walk in the same path they were following in this life."[23] Similarly, Alma 34:34 explains, "That same spirit which doth possess your bodies at the time that ye go out of this life, that same spirit will have power to possess your body in that eternal world."[24] People who continually strived during mortality to become better disciples of Christ will continue to do so in the spirit world, "only in a much greater degree—learning, increasing, growing in grace and in the knowledge of the truth."[25] Those who were not interested in spiritual matters during mortality will have this inclination in the spirit world. Nevertheless, they and all others will have the opportunity to learn and spiritually grow. In the spirit world, there is still much to learn, much to do, and much progress to be made.

19.	*Journal of Discourses*, vol. 7, p. 239.
20.	McConkie, *Mormon Doctrine*, p. 762.
21.	Though mistakes will be remembered, it is important to understand that through repentance and Christ's Atonement, sins that are scarlet will be "as white as snow" (Isa. 1:18), "shall not be mentioned" (Ezek. 18:22), and will not be remembered by the Lord (see D&C 58:42–43; Heb. 8:12). Additionally, those who have repented can have peace of conscience (see Mosiah 4:2–3).
22.	D&C 130:18–19.
23.	McConkie, *Mormon Doctrine*, p. 762.
24.	Alma 34:34.
25.	*Journal of Discourses*, vol. 7, p. 333.

People also take with them the ordinances received during mortality. These ordinances include baptism; confirmation of the Holy Ghost; for men, ordination to the priesthood; and temple ordinances.

Paradise and Spirit Prison

Within the spirit world are two divisions: paradise and spirit prison. Regarding paradise and spirit prison, Joseph F. Smith explained that "the spirits of all men, as soon as they depart from this mortal body, whether they are good or evil . . . are taken home to that God who gave them life, where there is a separation, a partial judgment, and the spirits of those who are righteous are received into a state of happiness which is called paradise. . . . The wicked, on the contrary, have no part nor portion in the Spirit of the Lord,"[26] and they enter spirit prison. So do those who did not learn about the gospel in mortality.[27]

Alma described paradise as "a state of happiness, . . . a state of peace, where they [the righteous] shall rest from all their troubles and from all care, and sorrow."[28] Joseph F. Smith stated that paradise is a place where righteous spirits "expand in wisdom, where they have respite from all their troubles, and where care and sorrow do not annoy."[29] Joseph Smith stated, "The spirits of the just are exalted to a greater and more glorious work; hence they are blessed in their departure to the world of spirits. Enveloped in flaming fire, they are not far from us, and know and understand our thoughts, feelings, and motions, and are often pained therewith."[30]

Regarding the unrighteous, Alma taught that in spirit prison "there shall be weeping, and wailing, and gnashing of teeth, and this because of their own iniquity, being led captive by the will of the devil. Now this is the state of the souls of the wicked, yea, in darkness, and a state of awful, fearful looking for the fiery indignation of the wrath of God upon them; thus they remain in this state, as well as the righteous in paradise, until the time

---

26. Smith, *Gospel Doctrine*, p. 448.
27. See D&C 138:31–32.
28. Alma 40:12; see also 4 Ne. 1:14; D&C 77:2, 5.
29. Smith, *Gospel Doctrine*, p. 448.
30. Smith, *Teachings*, p. 326.

of their resurrection."[31] As Joseph Smith explained, "The great misery of departed spirits in the world of spirits, where they go after death, is to know that they come short of the glory that others enjoy and that they might have enjoyed themselves, and they are their own accusers."[32]

Jesus's Work in the Spirit World

When Jesus died, His spirit entered paradise[33] and "declar[ed] liberty to the captives who had been faithful; and there he preached to them the everlasting gospel, the doctrine of the resurrection and the redemption of mankind from the fall, and from individual sins on conditions of repentance."[34] In response, "the saints rejoiced in their redemption, and bowed the knee and acknowledged the Son of God as their Redeemer and Deliverer from death and the chains of hell."[35] Additionally, the spirits' "countenances shone, and the radiance from the presence of the Lord rested upon them, and they sang praises unto his holy name."[36]

Also while Jesus was in paradise, He exercised the keys necessary to bridge the great gulf that divided paradise from spirit prison and to open the prison doors.[37] Opening the prison doors was essential because it enabled spirits in paradise to visit those in spirit prison and teach them the gospel. In fact, another important action that Jesus took while in paradise was to commission and prepare spirits in paradise to preach the gospel to those in spirit prison. Giving all people, whether in the spirit world or in mortality, the opportunity to accept the gospel preserves the justice and mercy of God.

---

31. Alma 40:13–14.
32. Smith, *Teachings*, pp. 310–311.
33. It is clear that when Jesus died, He went to the spirit world, not heaven, for when Jesus appeared to Mary Magdalene, He told her, "I am not yet ascended to my Father" (John 20:17). Regarding this statement, Talmage wrote that Jesus "had gone to paradise but not to the place where God dwells. Paradise, therefore, is not heaven, if by the latter term we understand the abode of the Eternal Father and His celestialized children" (Talmage, *Jesus the Christ*, p. 622).
34. D&C 138:18–20.
35. D&C 138:23.
36. D&C 138:24.
37. For a discussion of the great gulf between paradise and spirit prison, see pages 344–346 in chapter 32 of volume 2 of this series.

Joseph F. Smith explained the following regarding Jesus's commissioning of spirits in paradise and their missionary work in spirit prison:

> From among the righteous, he [Jesus] organized his forces and appointed messengers, clothed with power and authority, and commissioned them to go forth and carry the light of the gospel to them that were in darkness, even to all the spirits of men; and thus was the gospel preached to the dead. And the chosen messengers went forth to declare the acceptable day of the Lord and proclaim liberty to the captives who were bound, even unto all who would repent of their sins and receive the gospel. Thus was the gospel preached to those who had died in their sins, without a knowledge of the truth, or in transgression, having rejected the prophets. These were taught faith in God, repentance from sin, vicarious baptism for the remission of sins, the gift of the Holy Ghost by the laying on of hands, and all other principles of the gospel that were necessary for them to know in order to qualify themselves that they might be judged according to men in the flesh, but live according to God in the spirit. . . . The dead who repent will be redeemed, through obedience to the ordinances of the house of God, and after they have paid the penalty of their transgressions, and are washed clean, shall receive a reward according to their works, for they are heirs of salvation.[38]

Among those whom Joseph F. Smith saw preaching the gospel were Adam, Eve, "many of her faithful daughters who had lived through the ages," Abel, Seth, many Israelite and Nephite prophets, and latter-day prophets.[39] Additionally, Joseph F. Smith "beheld that the faithful elders of this dispensation, when they depart from mortal life, continue their labors in the preaching of the gospel of repentance and redemption, through the sacrifice of the Only Begotten Son of God."[40]

Teaching the gospel to those in spirit prison is one of the greatest works that takes place in the spirit world. The urgency to share the gospel with all people in spirit prison was demonstrated in a vision that Wilford Woodruff received:

> I saw him [Joseph Smith] at the door of the Temple in heaven.[41] He came and spoke to me. He said he could not stop to talk to me because he was in a

---

38. D&C 138:30–34, 58–59.
39. See D&C 138:38–49, 53.
40. D&C 138:57.
41. It should not be surprising that there is at least one temple in the spirit world.

hurry. The next man I met was Father Smith; he couldn't talk to me because he was in a hurry. I met a half dozen brethren who held high positions on earth, and none of them could stop to talk with me because they were in a hurry. I was much astonished.

By and by I saw the Prophet again, and I got the privilege to ask him a question. "Now," said I, "I want to know why you are in a hurry? I have been in a hurry all my life, but I expected my hurry would be over when I got into the Kingdom of Heaven, if I ever did."

Joseph said, "I will tell you, Brother Woodruff, every dispensation that has had the priesthood on earth and has gone into the celestial kingdom has had a certain amount of work to do to prepare to go to the earth with the Savior when he goes to reign on the earth. Each dispensation has had ample time to do this work. We have not. We are the last dispensation, and so much work has to be done and we need to be in a hurry in order to accomplish it."[42]

Those who accept the gospel in the spirit world will have the opportunity to accept the essential gospel ordinances, which mortals complete vicariously for those in the spirit world. Vicarious work for the dead has occurred since at least shortly after Jesus's Resurrection, for Paul wrote: "Else what shall they do which are baptized for the dead, if the dead rise not at all? why are they then baptized for the dead?"[43]

Ministering Spirits

At times, spirits are permitted to minister to mortals.[44] Moroni explained a role of ministering spirits: "For behold, they are subject unto him [Jesus], to minister according to the word of his command, showing themselves unto them of strong faith and a firm mind in every form of godliness. And the office of their ministry is to call men unto repentance, and to fulfil and to do the work of the covenants of the Father, which he hath made unto the children of men, to prepare the way among the children of men, by declaring the word of Christ unto the chosen vessels of the Lord, that they

---

42.   Durham, *Discourses of Wilford Woodruff*, pp. 288–289.
43.   1 Cor. 15:29.
44.   The keys of ministering angels were given to Joseph Smith by the angel Moroni as part of the restoration of the Aaronic Priesthood (see D&C 13:1; 84:26; 107:20).

may bear testimony of him."[45] This ministering is one of the great works performed by righteous spirits.

As Joseph Smith explained, "There are no angels[46] who minister to this earth but those who do belong or have belonged to it."[47] Brigham Young taught, "We have more friends behind the vail than on this side,"[48] and spirits may be sent to minister to family members and friends in particular, as Joseph F. Smith noted: "Our fathers and mothers, brothers, sisters and friends who have passed away from this earth, having been faithful, and worthy to enjoy these rights and privileges, may have a mission given them to visit their friends and relatives upon the earth again, bringing from the divine presence messages of love, of warning, of reproof or instruction, to those whom they had learned to love in the flesh."[49] Some mortals may be more likely than others to be visited by ministering spirits, for as Moroni explained, one of the gifts of the Spirit is "the beholding of angels and ministering spirits."[50]

Sealings Performed in Mortality for Those Who Have Died

On April 3, 1836, in the Kirtland Temple, the prophet Elijah gave Joseph Smith the keys to seal in heaven the ordinances performed on earth by proper priesthood authority.[51] These keys enable "the hearts of the fathers [to turn] to the children, and [the hearts of] the children [to turn] to the fathers, lest the whole earth be smitten with a curse."[52] The turning of the hearts of the

---

45. Moro. 7:30–31.

46. There is a difference between ministering angels and ministering spirits. Joseph Smith explained this difference: "Angels . . . are resurrected personages, having bodies of flesh and bones—for instance, Jesus said: *Handle me and see, for a spirit hath not flesh and bones, as ye see me have.* Secondly: the spirits of just men made perfect . . . are not resurrected, but inherit the same glory." (D&C 129:1–3.) Notwithstanding this distinction, *angels* are referred to numerous times in the Old Testament, New Testament, and Book of Mormon prior to Christ's Resurrection, meaning that the terms *angel* and *ministering spirit* have frequently been used synonymously. They have been considered synonymous for the purpose of this section.

47. D&C 130:5.

48. *Journal of Discourses*, vol. 6, p. 349.

49. Smith, *Gospel Doctrine*, p. 436.

50. Moro. 10:14.

51. See D&C 110:12–16.

52. D&C 110:15; see also vv. 13–14, 16; Mal. 4:5–6.

fathers and their children includes those in the spirit world turning their hearts to family members in the mortal world and those in the mortal world turning their hearts to family members in the spirit world.

Joseph Smith wrote of the importance of the sealing keys he held: "The earth will be smitten with a curse unless there is a welding link of some kind or other between the fathers and the children . . . for we without them cannot be made perfect; neither can they without us be made perfect. . . . It is necessary in the ushering in of the dispensation of the fulness of times . . . that a whole and complete and perfect union, and welding together of dispensations, and keys, and powers, and glories should take place."[53] The sealing ordinances are this welding link. Therefore, it is essential that the sealing ordinances be completed vicariously for those who did not complete them during mortality and that these individuals have the opportunity in the spirit world to accept these ordinances;[54] otherwise, no one can "be made perfect," a "complete and perfect union" cannot be formed, and a "welding together of dispensations" cannot take place.

Conclusion

God loves all of His children with a perfect love. Therefore, He ensures that they all have the opportunity to learn about and accept the gospel, whether in mortality or in the postmortal spirit world. Those who accept the gospel, repent, and complete saving ordinances in mortality or accept the saving ordinances completed vicariously by others will inherit the celestial kingdom.

---

53.   D&C 128:18.

54.   As already discussed, Wilford Woodruff saw in vision a temple in heaven (see Durham, *Discourses of Wilford Woodruff*, pp. 288–289). It is reasonable to assume that this temple, and perhaps others, are used in part for spirits to accept essential sealing ordinances performed by mortals in temples on the earth.

Bibliography

Books of the Maccabees (King James Bible and Douay Rheims versions). Enhanced Ebooks, 2014.

Callister, Tad R. *The Infinite Atonement.* Salt Lake City, UT: Deseret Book, 2000.

Chandler, Walter M. *The Trial of Jesus from a Lawyer's Standpoint.* 2 vols. 1908. Reprint, Leopold Classic Library, 2015.

Clarke, Adam. *Clarke's Commentary.* Vols. 1 & 3. Nashville, TN: Abingdon, 1810, 1824.

Dummelow, John R. *The One Volume Bible Commentary.* New York: MacMillan, 1975.

Durham, G. Homer, comp. *The Discourses of Wilford Woodruff.* Salt Lake City, UT: Bookcraft, 1946.

Edersheim, Alfred. *The Life and Times of Jesus the Messiah.* Peabody, MA: Hendrickson, 1997.

Edersheim, Alfred. *The Temple: Its Ministry and Services.* Updated ed. Peabody, MA: Hendrickson, 1994.

Eusebius. *The Church History.* Vol. 2. Translated by Paul L. Maier. Grand Rapids, MI: Kregel, 1999.

Farrar, Dean. *The Life of Christ.* Quiver ed. London: Cassell and Company, 1896.

Geikie, Cunningham. *The Life and Words of Christ.* 2 vols. New York: Appleton, 1883.

HarperCollins Bible Dictionary. Edited by Mark Allan Powell. New York: HarperCollins, 1989.

Holland, Jeffrey R. *Witness for His Names.* Salt Lake City, UT: Deseret Book, 2019.

Holzapfel, Richard, and Thomas A. Wayment, eds. *The Life and Teachings of Jesus Christ.* 3 vols. Salt Lake City, UT: Deseret Book, 2006.

Howick, E. Keith. *The Life of Jesus the Messiah.* Silverton, ID: WindRiver, 2012.

Hymns of The Church of Jesus Christ of Latter-day Saints. Salt Lake City, UT: The Church of Jesus Christ of Latter-day Saints, 1985.

Jewish Encyclopedia. 1901–1906. http://www.jewishencyclopedia.com.

Josephus. *The Works of Flavius Josephus.* Translated by William Whiston. Grand Rapids, MI: Kregel, 1971.

Journal of Discourses. 26 vols. London: Latter-day Saints' Book Depot, 1854–1886.

LDS Bible Dictionary. In the Holy Bible. Salt Lake City, UT: The Church of Jesus Christ of Latter-day Saints, 1979.

Ludlow, D. H., ed. *The Encyclopedia of Mormonism.* New York: Macmillan, 1992.

Lyon, T. Edgar. *Apostasy to Restoration.* Salt Lake City, UT: Deseret Book, 1960.

Maxwell, Neal A. *Not My Will, but Thine.* Salt Lake City, UT: Bookcraft, 1988.

McConkie, Bruce R. *Mormon Doctrine.* 2nd ed. Salt Lake City, UT: Bookcraft, 1966.

McConkie, Bruce R. *The Mortal Messiah.* 6 vols. Salt Lake City, UT: Deseret Book, 1980.

Merriam-Webster. http://merriam-webster.com.

Sachar, Abram Leon. *A History of the Jews.* 5th ed. New York: McGraw-Hill, 1975.

Smith, Joseph, Jr. *History of the Church.* 7 vols. 1839–1856. Reprint, Salt Lake City, UT: Deseret Book, 1976.

Smith, Joseph F. *Gospel Doctrine.* 5th ed. Salt Lake City, UT: Deseret Book, 1939.

Smith, Joseph Fielding, comp. *Teachings of the Prophet Joseph Smith.* Salt Lake City, UT: Deseret Book, 1964.

Smith, William. *The New Smith's Bible Dictionary.* Edited by Reuel G. Lemmons. Garden City, NY: Doubleday, 1966.

Sperry, Sidney B. *Doctrine and Covenants Compendium.* Salt Lake City, UT: Bookcraft, 1960.

Talmage, James E. *Jesus the Christ.* Salt Lake City, UT: Deseret Book, 1915. Reprint, Covenant Communications, 2006.

Tarbell, Martha. *Tarbell's Teacher's Guide to the International Sunday-School Lessons for 1912, 1914.* New York: Fleming H. Revell, 1913.

The First Presidency and the Quorum of the Twelve Apostles. "The Family: A Proclamation to the World." Salt Lake City, UT: The Church of Jesus Christ of Latter-day Saints, 1995.

Trench, Richard C. *Notes on the Miracles of Our Lord.* New York: Appleton, 1853.

Young, Robert. *Young's Analytical Concordance to the Bible.* 22nd ed. Edited by William B. Stevenson. New York: Funk and Wagnalls, 1970.

Webster, Noah. *An American Dictionary of the English Language.* 1828.

Wikipedia. http://www.wikipedia.org.

Index

About the Author

Steven R. McMurray grew up in Salt Lake City, Utah. He graduated from the University of Utah with a juris doctor degree in 1971 and has practiced law in Salt Lake City ever since. He has a Martindale-Hubble rating of AV (the highest possible) and is listed in Best Lawyers of America.

From 1964 to 1966, Steve served as a full-time missionary for The Church of Jesus Christ of Latter-day Saints in the Scottish Mission. Afterward, he taught early morning seminary for four years. In 1971 (before MTCs were established), he developed a missionary preparation class and then taught it for five years. For this class, he developed extensive outlines of gospel topics, particularly oriented toward teaching those interested in learning about the Church. Upon request, he provided copies of his outlines to the Church. He also taught at an institute for four years and was a host on Temple Square in Salt Lake City for nine years.

He has served as a counselor in a stake presidency, a member of a high council, a bishop, a branch president, a counselor in a bishopric, an elder's quorum president, a counselor in a stake mission presidency, and a stake missionary. He has also taught Gospel Doctrine several times and has served as a priesthood quorum instructor and a young men's advisor. Steve and his wife, Lorna, who are the parents of nine children, served in the Australia Melbourne Mission.

Upon returning from Australia, Steve began writing a four-book series on the Gospel accounts of Jesus Christ. The writing process lasted more than nine years and was one of the spiritual highlights of his life. Three previous volumes in this series have been published.